THE SOCIAL WORLD
OF THE FLORENTINE HUMANISTS
1390-1460

THE OCIAL WORLD

OF THE

FLORENTINE HUMANISTS

1390 · 1460

BY LAURO MARTINES

PRINCETON, NEW JERSEY

PRINCETON UNIVERSITY PRESS

MCMLXIII

❖

Publication of this book has been aided by
the Ford Foundation program
to support publication, through university presses,
of works in the humanities and social sciences

❖

Printed in the United States of America
by Princeton University Press, Princeton, N.J.

to Julia

ACKNOWLEDGMENTS

AN EARLY version of this work was turned in as a dissertation to the History Department of Harvard University in the autumn of 1959. My thanks go first to Professor Myron P. Gilmore, whose criticism and kindness during the crucial phases of the enterprise helped bring it to its present form.

I am grateful for two fellowships granted by the President and Fellows of Harvard College: the Bayard-Cutting Fellowship in History for 1955-1956 and a Frederick Sheldon Travelling Fellowship for 1956-1957. These awards made it possible for me to begin this work and to carry out all research for it in Italy. A grant from the faculty research fund of Reed College went to defray typing and manuscript fees.

Dr. Hans Baron and Professor Paul Oskar Kristeller indulgently read the penultimate draft. I wish to thank them for their immensely helpful suggestions and criticisms.

To two men I am particularly indebted for their constant encouragement: Professor Felix Gilbert, now of the Institute for Advanced Study in Princeton, and Professor Gene Brucker of the University of California at Berkeley. Ten years ago, on an innocent first visit of mine to Florence, Gene Brucker took me in hand and introduced me to the city's archival riches. It is thanks to him that I stayed on in Florence for seven months and learnt to read that arcane script.

Then and since the archivists of the Archivio di Stato have given me their patient cooperation. I am eager to express my appreciation to them and to Dr. Gino Corti, who often helped me, early in the game, to decipher difficult passages.

Via S. Niccolò, Florence
February 1963

ABBREVIATIONS

ASF, Archivio di Stato di Firenze

A. S. I., Archivio storico italiano

ASS, Archivio di Stato di Siena

BLF, Biblioteca Laurenziana di Firenze

BNF, Biblioteca Nazionale di Firenze

BRF, Biblioteca Riccardiana di Firenze

Calimala, Arte di Calimala

Cambio, Arte del Cambio

Capt. Guelforum, Capitani di Parte Guelfa

Carte Ancisa, Carte dell' Ancisa

Carte Strozz., Carte Strozziane

Consulte, Consulte e Pratiche

Lana, Arte della Lana

Leg. Comm., Signori: Legazioni e Commissarie

Lib. Fab., Libri Fabarum

Magl., Magliabechiana

Mariani, Priorista Mariani

Mercanzia, Tribunale di Mercanzia

Monte, Monte Comune

Mss., Manoscritti

Prest., Archivio delle Prestanze

Proconsolo, Arte dei Giudici e Notai

Provv., Registri delle Provvisioni

Seta, Arte della Seta

Statuta, Statuta Populi et Communis Florentiae,
    3 vols., Freiburg, 1778-1783

CONTENTS

Contents

THE SOCIAL WORLD

OF THE FLORENTINE HUMANISTS

1390-1460

CHAPTER ONE

INTRODUCTION: PROGRAM AND PROBLEMS

THIS is a study of the Florentine humanists and their social position during the period 1390 to 1460. The substantive part of the study begins with the account in Chapter II of the factors that determined social position in Florence. That chapter maps out the larger social environment of the humanists—provides them with a world, so to speak—and governs the arrangement or in some cases the content of all the succeeding chapters. This is why the title of the book refers to the "social world" of the humanists, rather than to their "social position."

The title also specifies seventy years very nearly identical with Cosimo de' Medici's lifetime (1389-1464). In this case the coincidence is not accidental. For we shall see that humanism responded to political change, that the Republic's political foundations were eroded—perhaps decisively—during Cosimo's lifetime, and that the way was thereby prepared for the advent of a prince. It is well known that Cosimo was a key figure in this development. Nevertheless, the new consolidation of power under his leadership had not gone so far by the end of his life as to justify our thinking of him as the *signore* of Florence. He does not seem to have thought of himself in these terms, but aside from this, there is the fact that the old legislative councils occasionally put up enough resistance to delay or block aspects of his domestic and foreign policy. Resistance of this sort would not have been tolerated at Milan under Filippo Maria Visconti, nor at Rimini under the Malatesta.

Since the humanists were not impervious to life around them, it was natural for the stresses in their intellectual movement to change in accordance with the changing tenor of political and social life in the city. Humanism emerged as a distinctive current in Florence during the second half of the fourteenth century and swiftly exhibited a vigorous interest in political and civic affairs. This interest drew its timeliness and cultural force from currents already dominant in Florentine society, a society in which the political class manifested an ardent commitment to the lay ideal of devotion and service to the civil community. In the 1360's and 1370's, under the influence of Florence's trouble and subsequent open conflict with the papacy in central Italy, the ideal was combined for the first time with the concept of the relation between the liberty of Florence and the independence of the various Italian states.[1] Thus all the factors that might have evoked the expression of a fully developed view or ideology were already present in Florence by 1375, but its mature articulation is not discernible until the last decade of the century. Then, as Hans Baron has shown in a remarkable series of studies,[2] Florentine opposition to Giangaleazzo Visconti transformed the intellectual atmosphere, and from this changed setting emerged the richer civic humanism of Lionardo Bruni and the new political and historical perceptions of prominent citizens like Cino Rinuccini and Goro Dati.

For nearly four decades after the Visconti crisis of 1402 the civic strain in humanism was favored by the political optimism of the ruling class, by its territorial designs and a certain flexibility in its social composition. Gradually, however, the great political families were reduced in importance, power, and number—by exile, defamation, and confiscatory taxation. By the late 1450's, in line with this relentless contraction of the oligarchy, political reflection among the humanists had been pushed to the margins of intellectual activity. Other topics were far more fashionable now, and not nearly so dangerous or unpleasant. Not surprisingly, therefore, the leading intellectual concerns of the humanists became literary, philological, aesthetic, and aesthetico-

[1] This fusion of ideas is expressed by Coluccio Salutati in the 1370's. See Eugenio Garin, "I cancellieri umanisti della repubblica fiorentina da Coluccio Salutati a Bartolomeo Scala," *Rivista storica italiana*, LXXI, ii (1959), 192ff.

[2] See especially the following works: "The Historical Background of the Florentine Renaissance," *History*, n.s. XXII (March 1938), 315-327; "A Sociological Interpretation of the Early Renaissance in Florence," *The South Atlantic Quarterly*, vol. 38, no. 4 (Oct. 1939), 427-448; "A Struggle for Liberty in the Renaissance: Florence, Venice, and Milan in the Early Quattrocento," *American Historical Review*, LVIII (1953), 265-289, 544-570; *The Crisis of the Early Italian Renaissance*, 2 vols. (Princeton, 1955); *Humanistic and Political Literature in Florence and Venice at the Beginning of the Quattrocento* (Cambridge, Mass., 1955).

moral. With eloquence and a touch of bitterness, Eugenio Garin has commented on the larger meaning of this change. His own words will best serve us here.

"If early humanism was a hymn to the values of civil life, to the free building by men of an earthly city, the end of the Quattrocento is marked by a flight from the world, by a distinct turning towards contemplation."[3] This change was connected with the "ever growing power of princes," and if *signori* like Lorenzo the Magnificent "often protected the literati, it is no less true that they turned them into courtiers, in whom thought as an occupation pervaded by political concerns is no longer even conceivable." But the cultural impact of the prince did not end here. We sometimes imagine that the establishment of a signory meant no more than "the elimination of the privileged groups of rich merchants and noblemen." The truth is that a signory "extinguished the ardor of political struggle, destroyed the intense palpitation of the life of the city-state. In place of the ideal *respublica* as a cooperative community, as a true society, even if a restricted one, we get Caesar, who banishes everyone from political life and transforms the existing culture—the expression, instrument, and program of a class arrived to riches and power— into an elegant ornament of court, or into a desperate flight from the world."[4]

In 1954, 1957, and 1959 Garin returned to some details of this theme in three articles. In one, for example, he observed that Ficino "is the first great figure to become a philosopher-courtier even in his luxuriant and highly-refined style." Lorenzo, moreover, "makes use of him not only to add brilliance to his house, but also doubtless for subtle reasons of political propaganda."[5] Moving to Poliziano next, Garin noted that "he lives and works in a time when the new [humanistic] culture is no longer an operative force in the city, in that very Florence of humanistic merchants and chancellors, now transformed into mere courtiers

---

[3] *L'Umanesimo italiano: filosofia e vita civile nel rinascimento* (Bari, 1952), p. 103.

[4] *Ibid.*, pp. 103-104.

[5] Garin, "Ritratto di Marsilio Ficino," *Il Quattrocento*, published under the auspices of the "Libera cattedra di storia della civiltà fiorentina" (Firenze, 1954), p. 32.

and professors, often courtier-professors."[6] The new type of chancellor, still a humanist, lost his political influence during the middle decades of the fifteenth century and became "a solemnly ornamental figure like [the old] Poggio Bracciolini or a haughty administrator like Bartolomeo Scala."[7]

Collected together in the preceding fashion, Garin's remarks may seem severe or even a trifle extreme, but in context they are both fitting and just. We have only to consider for a moment the nature of the personal animosities that divided the circle of literary men and humanists around Lorenzo de' Medici. Their invectives and rancors are easily traceable to the fact that they all longed to monopolize his favors and friendship. Scala and Poliziano could not stand each other. Luigi Pulci directed satiric sallies against Ficino, Scala, and Matteo Franco. Scala and Franco responded in kind. The latter, a priest, was particularly resented because Lorenzo arranged for him to be heaped with ecclesiastical dignities. Yet Poliziano himself was not far behind, if at all, in the accumulation of prebends and sinecures, "never enough for this insatiable courtier."[8]

On occasion, the humanist group of the early fifteenth century had also been divided by jealousy and animosity. But these passions had been elicited by motives of a sort quite different from those in Lorenzo's circle and were never determined by the moods of one man, nor framed against the brilliance and power of a single family. Salutati, Rossi, Bruni, Benvenuti, Palmieri, Manetti—all had engaged in political speculation, all served as advisors to the republican Signoria, and all found the time and will to observe the humanistic ideal of civic virtue. To most of these men a life apart from the political community was as unthinkable as life without an order of higher reflection. Indeed, as Garin has pointed out, the early Florentine humanists tended to strike a creative balance between the realms of action and contemplation. And if some of them frequented Cosimo de' Medici or Palla Strozzi or another prominent personality, they frequented him in a political and social *ambience* which—until

[6] Garin, "L'Ambiente del Poliziano," *Il Poliziano e suo tempo, atti del IV convegno internazionale di studi sul rinascimento* (Firenze, 1957), p. 24.

[7] Garin, "I cancellieri umanisti," p. 204.

[8] Enrico Barfucci, *Lorenzo de' Medici e la società artistica del suo tempo* (Firenze, 1945), p. 56.

1434, at all events—made them equals in conversation and permitted each the freedom to go his separate way. In short, Ficino, Landino, Poliziano, Pulci, Scala, Franco, Benivieni, and others all orbited around the grand figure of Lorenzo, but in the earlier fifteenth century no Florentine statesman or banker ever disposed of such power or influence: neither Maso degli Albizzi, nor Niccolò da Uzzano, not even Cosimo de' Medici. But all this was changing in the last decade or two of Cosimo's life.

Represented by the Council of One Hundred after 1458 and the Council of Seventy after 1480, the oligarchy became intensely parochial. Aside from the exchange of views in secret or in secure privacy, political discussion was avoided and those who insisted on this right, or on an independent line of political action, were forced into exile or reduced to silence and contemplative melancholy. A case in point—one of the earliest in the humanist circle—is that of the learned career official, Filippo di Ser Ugolino, who stood out as a courageous opponent of arbitrary government. In 1444 he was banished from the city to a town in the Florentine dominion, where he ended his days teaching Latin to the novitiates of a local religious house. Ten years later he was followed by the humanist statesman, Giannozzo Manetti, who was friendly with certain Florentine exiles and seems to have had unfashionable convictions about what Florentine relations with the Venetian Republic ought to be. Having provoked the rage of the ruling clique, Giannozzo attempted to avoid financial ruin by leaving Florence. He spent the last years of his life in Naples, in a decently self-effacing style. It was Alamanno Rinuccini's turn in the next generation. One of the city's most talented humanists, descendant of an old and wealthy family, Alamanno had been reared so as to prepare him for his "natural" place in the chief councils of the Republic; instead of this he was reduced to mediocre offices by the men around the Medici. In his candid dialogue *On Liberty*, he strives to make the best of an unpleasant political situation by arguing that the truly wise man is he who removes himself from public life when tyranny triumphs, and cultivates an inner serenity in a life apart, which alone comprises human happiness.[9]

[9] Ed. by Francesco Adorno: Alamanno Rinuccini, *Dialogus de libertate*,

Introduction

In view of the differences between the humanists of the two halves of the century—there was naturally some overlapping—it seems correct to say that the humanists of the period 1390 to 1460 comprise a relatively homogeneous group, as different from the men of letters who preceded them as from humanists like Ficino and Poliziano who came after. And although Niccolò Niccoli, Carlo Marsuppini, and Ambrogio Traversari were often in the company of Cosimo de' Medici, we must remember that whatever the nature of their companionship they were never his retainers or dependents. Niccoli, though sometimes pressed, always enjoyed private means; the nobleman, Marsuppini, was independently wealthy; and Traversari, a Camaldolese monk and later general of his order, was actually in a position to help Cosimo—in 1433 he was influential in getting the banker's almost certain execution commuted to a sentence of banishment.[10] Apart from all this, however, Cosimo's relation to these men could not be other than that of first among equals. There were several reasons: first, political power still belonged to a social class, was not yet the monopoly of a single family; next, up to about the middle decades of the fifteenth century the ruling families seem to have retained a realistic faith in their capacity to govern the city; finally, Cosimo had very able peers in the councils during most of his life: such men as Agnolo Pandolfini and Lorenzo Ridolfi, and later on Neri di Gino Capponi and Agnolo Acciaiuoli. All these factors combined to make Cosimo more humanly accessible.

Before considering the problems arising from the biographical scope of this study, it may be well to define the term *Humanist*. I follow Professor Paul Oskar Kristeller in holding that this term properly refers to the men of the period who cultivated the study of grammar, rhetoric, poetry, history, and moral philosophy. Furthermore, since their commitment to these studies was naturally infused with a fervent interest in the classical world, it was the humanist who most perfectly expressed "the general tendency of the age to attach the great-

in *Atti e memorie dell' accademia toscana La Colombaria*, XXII, n.s. viii (1957), 265-303.

[10] See Traversari's *Hodoeporicon*, pp. 198-203, in Alessandro Dini-Traversari, *Ambrogio Traversari e i suoi tempi* (Firenze, 1912).

est importance to classical studies, and to consider classical antiquity as the common standard and model by which to guide all cultural activities."[11] Some humanists translated Greek works into Latin. Others wrote biography, history, verse, moralistic dialogues, panegyrics of men and cities, or familiar letters intended for eventual publication. The humanist who did none of these things took delight in humanistic conversation, or perhaps collected classical statuary and had a warm interest in archaeological questions. His library was likely to include a valuable selection of the Latin and Greek classics.

The early Florentine humanists also exhibited another marked characteristic: they brought a civic vision of the world to their intellectual interests. This is why the image of the public figure, of the man who makes an essential contribution to the community, tends to pervade their thinking; whether they are dealing with morality, biography, history, literary change, or even the artist (as in Alberti's reflections), this image recurs.[12] Here then was one of the guiding perceptions of early Florentine humanism: a sense of the enormous importance of public life and so of the active, energetic citizen. The other guiding perception, already indicated above, was expressed in the humanist's lifelong return to classical literary sources, where he was disposed to find his criteria of action and cultural achievement—although there were humanists like Ambrogio Traversari who did not go nearly so far in their devotion to the cultural ideals of the ancient world.

Eleven men occupy the main part of this study: Coluccio Salutati, Roberto de' Rossi, Niccolò Niccoli, Lionardo Bruni, Poggio Bracciolini, Giannozzo Manetti, Carlo Marsuppini, Matteo Palmieri, Cino Rinuccini, Leon Battista Alberti, and Filippo di Ser Ugolino Pieruzzi. Although the last three are not extensively treated, the pages devoted to them endeavor to convey a clear idea of their social position. The humanist notary and well-known public official, Filippo di Ser Ugolino, is considered in Chapter II (the chapter on social assumptions in Florence) in order to exemplify a point. There is some question as

[11] P. O. Kristeller, *Studies in Renaissance Thought and Letters* (Rome, 1956), p. 557.
[12] See Ch. vii, 4 for a full discussion of this theme.

9

to whether or not Cino Rinuccini was a humanist. One can show that he pursued the study of grammar, rhetoric, poetry, history, and moral philosophy; but one of the foremost students in the field, Dr. Hans Baron, does not rank him among the humanists. The question in doubt is the extent of Cino's commitment to the literary ideals of the classical world. But whatever our judgment concerning his educational preparation and outlook, I include him in this study because his place in Florentine society and his relation to the humanist intellectuals around 1400 serve to throw some light on their social position.

Two men who might have been discussed in the main body of the text have been treated, instead, in the appendix of summary profiles: Ambrogio Traversari and Jacopo di Agnolo da Scarperia. There are perfectly good reasons for this. Let us take Ambrogio first. It was impossible to analyze his situation according to the procedure laid down in the chapter on social assumptions, for being in holy orders, he could not marry, take public office, nor hold property subject to the ordinary taxation of the laity. But financial status, public office, and marriage —as the next chapter will show—are three of the four factors used in the delineation of any given Florentine's social position. The fourth factor, claim to a Florentine family tradition, was also denied us in Ambrogio's case, as he hailed from Portico in the Romagna. Any one of these factors could have been sacrificed in trying to determine his social status in Florence, but, having none of them, it would have been a procedural mistake to try to compare him with the principal humanists of this inquiry. The requisites for such a comparison were missing, and this is why I dealt with Ambrogio in the freer, less structured form of the profiles in Appendix I.

The difficulty in Jacopo da Scarperia's case resulted from a paucity of appropriate documents. So little which the present inquiry would emphasize is known about the details of his life that here again no valid comparison was possible with the other humanists examined in detail. Consequently Jacopo is also treated in a concise profile at the end. But I have reason to believe that there is considerable information about him still to be found, most of it in Florence.

Introduction

Regarding the generality of the conclusions reached in this book, it seems correct to say, first of all, that the men who figure in the main body of the text dominate the picture given by nearly all scholarly work on the humanist movement in Florence during the first half of the fifteenth century. Ambrogio Traversari is the one humanist who deserved a place with the major figures here, for Jacopo da Scarperia is not even referred to in the recent work of Hans Baron and Eugenio Garin, while Saitta mentions him only once.[13] In Burckhardt, Voigt, Gaspary, Monnier, Rossi, Sandys, Saitta, Garin, and Baron the following figures are the ones repeatedly adduced in one combination or another in order to characterize the range of humanism in Florence during the earlier Quattrocento: Salutati, Bruni, Rossi, Niccoli, Poggio, Traversari, Manetti, Marsuppini, Alberti, and Palmieri. The labors of these humanists seem to testify to almost everything that humanism was in Florence during our chosen period. With the exception of Traversari, then, these are the men who will figure prominently in the succeeding pages. And if it be objected that only the "stars" have been put at the focus of the inquiry, I can only say that the selection was unavoidable for two reasons: first, as mentioned above, because most scholarship on the subject tends to make these men almost the only Florentine humanists of the period; and second, because our vision of them is determined to a large extent by what we make of them in the fascinating portraits drawn by the great Quattrocento biographer, Vespasiano da Bisticci.[14]

Yet even admitting the anticipated objection—that only the "stars" of humanism have been emphasized—I must point out that the conclusions arrived at in this study are not confined to eleven figures. For the sketches in Appendix I represent the social profiles of forty-five other men associated with the humanist movement in Florence, men who reached their political maturity (the office-holding age) before 1460. These sketches

[13] G. Saitta, *L'Umanesimo, il pensiero italiano nell' umanesimo e nel rinascimento*, 3 vols. (Bologna, 1949-1951), I, 162.

[14] A useful article on him is Giulio Caprin, "Il libraio fiorentino degli umanisti, Vespasiano da Bisticci," *Il Quattrocento* (supra, n. 5), pp. 139-155.

can stand by themselves, but the reader is urged to consider them in relation to the rest of the work. I urge this because the sketches depend on summary phrases and repetitive themes whose exact meanings issue from different stages of the argument developed in the book.

Appendix I was drawn up more than three years after the essential parts of this study had been completed and is therefore the more significant because it gives full support to the main thesis: namely, that by whatever route one approaches the humanists, one finds that they tend to be—like their disciples, friends, associates in office, and relatives by marriage— men of remarkable political and social importance in the city.

Two questions still remain for this introduction. Was there more than one social type in the humanist ranks? What constituted identity as a Florentine?

The place of Giannozzo Manetti and Matteo Palmieri at the center of this study and the appearance in Appendix I of names like Palla Strozzi and Donato Acciaiuoli, all four of them men of independent means, raise the question of whether or not we should distinguish the "professional" from the "amateur" humanist.[15] The professional presumably counted on his humanistic culture for his livelihood, the amateur did not. But if the distinction be made to turn on the earning of money alone, then the line between amateur and professional was often impossible to draw. Manetti, for example, a statesman and merchant of great wealth, received money for his humanistic accomplishments from Alfonso of Naples and Pope Nicholas V. Palmieri undoubtedly owed part of his distinguished career in public life to contacts made as a humanist and possibly to his study of oratory. At the same time, he enjoyed an independent income, the result of a fortune accumulated by his father in the druggist's trade. Hence shall we call Palmieri a professional or an amateur humanist? Donato Acciaiuoli, another Florentine of private means, was paid by the Signoria for his trans-

---

[15] The distinction has sometimes been made with reference to the Venetian humanists. Cf. Philippe Monnier, *Le Quattrocento, essai sur l'histoire littéraire du XVe siècle italien*, 2 vols., (Paris, 1931), i, 168; Roberto Weiss, "Italian Humanism in Western Europe: 1460-1520," *Italian Renaissance Studies*, ed. E. F. Jacob (New York, 1960), p. 72. Professor Kristeller has also raised the question with me in private correspondence.

lation of Lionardo Bruni's *Historiarum florentini populi libri XII.* Carlo Marsuppini, nobleman and heir to a large fortune, drew a substantial salary from the Studio Fiorentino for his professorship in rhetoric, poetry, and moral philosophy. And what of Niccolò Niccoli, another man of independent means? When he chose, he sometimes drew on his humanistic expertise in order to traffic in manuscripts at a profit.

The point in citing these examples is to indicate some of the problems involved in trying to distinguish between amateurs and professionals in Florence. Still, if the distinction could be made in a cut and dried fashion, how would it bear on the present inquiry?

My interest in undertaking this type of inquiry—deliberately conducted along the boundaries that divide intellectual from social history—was governed by the desire to understand the relation between humanism and humanists on the one hand and Florentine society on the other. I had found that the classic works on different aspects of the Italian Renaissance assert or suggest that humanism was extremely influential and in many circles became the prevailing intellectual mode. Yet it was difficult to see how this happened, unless there was a vital relation, as Burckhardt himself suggested,[16] between the enthusiasm for the new culture and the social life of the cities. For this reason, it seemed imperative to undertake a study which would clarify the nature of that relation. But in order to make it a study of men, not merely an account of "conditions" or "climate," I chose to concentrate on the humanists themselves, on their social and political identities, and on the credit they enjoyed in society, particularly at the sources of power—the upper strata of society. The study thus began to take on the form of an inquiry into the connection between the humanists and the dominant social classes.

Perhaps now we begin to see that it would have been an error in procedure to emphasize differences between the humanist who achieved fame and fortune by his scholarly or literary activity and the one who lived off his lands and business invest-

[16] *The Civilization of the Renaissance in Italy,* with an Introduction by B. Nelson and C. Trinkaus, Eng. tr. S. G. C. Middlemore (New York, 1958), pp. 180-182.

ments, but who perhaps bequeathed little in the way of a literary legacy. For one thing, "professionals" like Marsuppini, Jacopo da Scarperia, and Antonio Rossi handed down very little in the way of *opere*, much less than "amateurs" like Giannozzo Manetti and Leon Battista Alberti. But more important than this: stressing the differences between the two would have blurred the very thing we were after—the connection, if one there was, between humanism and the social groups which enjoyed power and prestige. From this viewpoint, accordingly, it is clear that the putative class of amateurs naturally provided the direct ties between humanism and the foci of power in the social order.

A different kind of definition may help to bring out the element of unity in the humanist ranks. Let us distinguish the professional from the amateur (in Florence, at all events) by holding that the first devoted most of his time or energies to humanistic interests and studies, whereas the second pursued these mainly in his spare time. Keeping this definition in mind, once I defined the objectives of the present inquiry and started to look to the possible bond between humanism and the social groups which disposed of power, a number of highly pertinent observations began to emerge. I found that the amateur humanists were recruited from the ruling class in almost every case. They were merchants, lawyers, noblemen, bankers, *rentiers*, statesmen, or their sons. Apart from seeking a humanistic education, these amateurs cultivated the friendship of the professionals and studied under the same masters, men such as Malpaghini, Chrysoloras, Guarino, Filelfo, and Marsuppini. Moreover, both amateurs and professionals served in the same political magistracies, contracted marriage in the same circles, and frequented persons of the same social class. And if some professionals were far from having the wealth of many amateurs, neither could many amateurs match the wealth of some professionals. In short, while an occupational distinction was discernible here, the distinction passed from sight when the humanists as a whole were viewed in terms of a wider context. For amateur and professional alike belonged to the governing class —a class which naturally included differences with regard to role, income, rank, and antiquity of family stock. It seems clear, accordingly, that stress on occupational differences would have diverted attention from interest in the relations between intellectual movement and social class, one of my chief concerns.

Owing both to its social recruitment and its point of view, once humanism became associated with the dominant groups in Florentine society, then—by the force of that association— it quickly began to share in the dignity that went with political and economic power. In Chapter VII I will attempt to show that the social viewpoint in the assumptions of civic human- ism reflected a certain stage in the changing consciousness or history of the Florentine ruling class. Thus the great propriety of Garin's observation that in the large industrial and com- mercial cities of Italy the celebrated teachers of humanistic studies catered almost exclusively to the sons of the great fam- ilies.[17] For it is this combination, this link between power and a given cultural program, which finally assured the success of humanism. Needless to say, a wealthy Florentine statesman with a humanistic education did not derive his social eminence from the study of humanism. But it might well endow him with brilliance in oratory, or clarity and grace of expression, an ease with words, a fund of historical examples, and a certain urbane *contegno*. Probably one would be right to suppose that in the eyes of the multitude prominent figures like Palla Strozzi and Piero de' Pazzi lent some sort of dignity to the *studia hu- maniora*. In the world of their peers, however, this was viewed the other way: Palla and Piero were the ones who stood to gain luster from their contact with humanism.

It remains to explain how the term *Florentine* is used in this study with reference to humanists.

As far as possible, I have tried to restrict the term to men who grew up in Florence, or who were affiliated with the city and its humanist movement in such a way or during so long a period of time that they either thought of themselves as Florentines, or—in scholarship on the subject—came to be per- manently associated with the city. Poggio Bracciolini, for ex-

[17] *L'Educazione in Europa (1400-1600), problemi e programi* (Bari, 1957), p. 119.

ample, was born in a small Tuscan town and lived a very large part of his life away from Florence. Nevertheless, he has a place in the present work for a number of reasons: apart from the justification for this in scholarship, it was in Florence he studied *notaria* and made his first contacts with humanism, there that he paid taxes, had some property, was matriculated in a major guild (the *Guidici e Notai*), and held the office of first chancellor for five years. Furthermore, aside from the fact that his closest friends lived in Florence, that he was in constant communication with them, he married a Florentine and finally settled there. Another case involves Leon Battista Alberti: he was never a permanent resident of the city, but he too is associated with Florence in scholarship. For he was a Florentine by descent, tradition, and grooming, and he was constantly in and out of Florence after 1427. Indeed, despite being in holy orders, his financial interests in the city were such that he needed an agent to represent him there. His work, *Della Famiglia*, provides a picture of the domestic life, assumptions, and habits of the typical Florentine family of great wealth, a family much influenced in its outlook by some of the customs of the old political and landed nobility.

The reader will find a biographical sketch of Giovanni Malpaghini in Appendix I. An expert in the field might question Giovanni's inclusion in this study, for he drifted from Ravenna to Venice, Padua, Rome, and probably to other places before finally settling in Florence. But it seemed best to include doubtful figures, not only for the sake of obtaining a wider cross-section, but also to avoid the charge of having chosen to treat only those men who went to support the main conclusions of this work. Giovanni, moreover, spent the last twenty-five years of his life in Florence, held a professorship in rhetoric and poetry for some years at the Studio Fiorentino, and was one of the teachers of well-known humanists like Niccolò Niccoli, Jacopo da Scarperia, and Lionardo Bruni.

These observations seem to take care of the problems that may arise from my use of the term *Florentine*. We need not forget that, like Giovanni Malpaghini, Guarino and Filelfo also lectured at the Studio Fiorentino. But their residence in Florence was relatively brief, several years in each case, and they did not put roots down. The two are in fact more correctly associated with other parts of Italy and with the fortunes of humanism there: Guarino with Venice, Verona, and especially Ferrara; Filelfo with Milan.

CHAPTER TWO

SOCIAL PLACE IN FLORENCE:
ASSUMPTIONS AND REALITIES

1. WEALTH

FLORENTINE sources of the fifteenth century —chronicles, diaries, letters, domestic handbooks, and public documents—exhibit a striking degree of harmony in their assumptions about the factors that determined elevated social place. Broadly speaking, four factors were commonly taken to be important: honorably-acquired wealth, a substantial record of service in public office, descent from an old Florentine family, and bonds of marriage with another family of some political and economic consequence. Possessed in full, these were the attributes which best conferred superior social rank, and the more a man lacked them the more humble or lowly was his social position.

An account of the social importance of wealth in Florence seems a useful point of departure. For as wealth and poverty often influenced or determined the other factors associated with social place, the economic factor appears to merit a certain priority. Let us consider this factor in its relation first to marriage.[1]

Promises of marriage were sealed by a financial arrangement:[1] the father of the bride-to-be drew up a promise to pay a dowry, specifying its terms and sum. Other considerations also affected decisions about marriage, such as political reputation and antiquity of lineage, but these lacked the material precision of dowries. If a girl of the upper class wished to marry, she had to have a dowry. The more handsome it was the more likely was she to marry according to her family's ambitions. Normally, dowries involved government securities, cash, property, or a certain combination of these. A girl who could not lay claim

---

[1] Alessandra Strozzi, *Lettere di una gentildonna fiorentina del secolo xv ai figliuoli esuli*, ed. C. Guasti (Firenze, 1877), pp. 395, 458, 467; Giovanni Morelli, *Ricordi*, ed. V. Branca (Firenze, Felice Le Monnier, 1956), pp. 208, 253, 263-264; and the obvious assumptions in *ASF, Carte Strozz., 3a serie*, 130, f. 12r, a letter from Piero di Filippo Strozzi to his brother, Simone, and dated 6 December 1409.

to a dowry was unlikely to find a husband, unless she came from the poorest sector of the lower classes, and even then she was probably expected to have a marriage portion of some sort, such as linen or a few items of furniture.[2]

A family of the "better sort" faced economic and social ruin if, being burdened with debts, it had also to provide for several unmarried daughters. Their distress exposed the head of the family to temptations: he might be persuaded to sell his vote or influence in the governing councils in return for a loan which covered the dowry of one of his daughters.[3] Similarly, a man in search of a wealthy bride might offer his political influence to an intermediary who helped negotiate a marriage involving a substantial dowry.

Business diaries of the period show that marriages were often listed with the introitus or exitus accounts of the family. It is there that Florentines recorded all moneys received or paid out as dowries.[4] Nevertheless, whatever a testator might choose to do with his estate, his wife's dowry reverted to her on his death. If she died first, it passed to her heirs. Thus, although on the balance sheets dowries were treated like business items, they had an existence or identity independent of the family's ordinary fortunes. Protected in this fashion, a widow was thereby enabled to use her original dowry for a second marriage.

Since the family was the basic social unit,[5] the way in which Florentines treated marriage was surely revealing. The incidence of wealth or poverty was sharply brought out in every marriage contract, and so we may believe that financial matters significantly affected other phases of life also.

In a collection of memoirs, written for his sons at the beginning of the fifteenth century, Giovanni Morelli observed: "Be

[2] One of the Republic's standing commissions sometimes donated money for the dowries of poor girls. *Statuta Populi et Communis Florentiae*, 3 vols. (Freiburg, 1778-83), III, 353.

[3] Giovanni di Bicci de' Medici seems to have been skilled at corruption of this type. See Giovanni Cavalcanti, *Istorie fiorentine*, 2 vols. (Firenze, 1838-39), II, 400.

[4] Examples: ASF, *Carte Strozz.*, *2a serie*, 17 bis (Marco Parenti's *Ricordi*), ff. 67v, 70v; ASF, *Mss.*, 77 (Lapo dei Curiani's *Libro di conti e memorie*, 1326-1429), f. 8r/v; and BNF, *Cod. Panciatichiano*, 368, 1, ff. 1r/v, 5v.

[5] *Vide* esp. L. B. Alberti, *I primi tre libri della famiglia*, ed. F. C. Pellegrini and E. R. Spongano (Firenze, 1946).

sure to have cash on hand at all times. Guard it carefully and use it wisely, for it is your best friend and dearest relative."[6] This advice perfectly accorded with another of his counsels: "try to have at least one friend in your district; do whatever you can for him and don't worry about spending time and money. If you are rich and have no other way of getting friends, be prepared to buy them with your money."[7] An anonymous merchant of the second half of the fourteenth century, interested in laying down rules of conduct for Florentine merchants in distant lands, penned a similar set of directives. The substance of his message is contained in the following remark: "remember that money is all the help you have. It is your defense, honor, profit, and adornment."[8]

These quotations are typical of the sage counsel of the day. The economic struggle in Florence was keen, but its harsh moral effects were not confined to the lower classes. Even the richest merchants sometimes exhibited the marks of a severe early schooling. Thus, late in life Giovanni di Bicci de' Medici still expressed bitterness at the "poverty" and political obscurity of his youth. One of his recorded outbursts came in the mid-1420's, when he spurned the advances of the Uzzano-Albizzi faction, which sought his personal support in an effort to decrease the size of the oligarchy and tighten its control.[9] The faction hoped to introduce two reforms: to change the method of setting up the purses containing the names of those eligible for public office, and to slash the representation of the artisans and *gente nuova* (the upstarts) in the Republic's legislative councils.[10] When Giovanni refused to cooperate and his refusal

[6] *Ricordi*, p. 279, "Ingegnati d'avere de' contanti e sappigli tenere e guardare cautamente, e que' sono i migliori amici si trouvino e i migliori parenti." Cf. Giovanni Rucellai, *G. R. e suo Zibaldone*, ed. A. Perosa (London, 1960), pp. 9-10.

[7] *Ibid.*, p. 253, "ingegnati d'acquistare uno amico o più nel tuo gonfalone e per lui fa ciò che tu puoi di buono, e non ti curare mettervi del tuo. Se se' ricco, sia contento comperare degli amici co' tuoi danari, se non ne puoi avere per altra via."

[8] The anonymous directives were found and published by Gino Corti, "Consigli sulla mercatura di un anonima trecentista," in *A.S.I.*, 398, cx (1952), 114-119.

[9] Niccolò Machiavelli, *Istorie fiorentine*, ed. *Nuova Biblioteca Popolare* (Torino, 1853), pp. 152-153.

[10] Brunetto Dami, *Giovanni Bicci dei Medici* (Firenze, 1899), pp. 64-67.

was made known in the city, some of the men who opposed the faction went to him. They evidently hoped to organize their opposition along tougher lines and they wanted Giovanni to take a leading part. But the shrewd merchant-banker turned them away also, declaring: "I don't want any favors or praise which may put me in a position to help bring about a change in government. I prefer to look after my own business affairs. This is what has raised me above the other citizens. I know that trade is the source and basis of my being honored by the Republic, but I am not fortunate in business for the sake of the Republic. For when I was poor, far from having been honored, not a citizen who knew me pretended that he'd ever seen me."[11] Giovanni says, in effect, that he became an influential political figure after he amassed a large fortune. Only then did those who once avoided him begin to seek out his friendship.

It would be simple-minded to say that Florentines made friendships on the basis of an economic calculation, if only because we should then be unable to explain some of the friends of wealthy men like Niccolò da Uzzano, Agnolo Pandolfini, and Palla di Nofri Strozzi. Their behavior, however, did not change the nature of advice in the manuals of conduct. As a guide to action, the desirability of having friends richer than oneself was an ordinary admonition of the household. A moralist of the third quarter of the fourteenth century urged young men always to cultivate the friendship of men of good breeding, men "richer and with more authority than you."[12] He advised them to get into the habit of giving presents as a way of making friends or of holding on to them. But he made

[11] Cavalcanti, *Istorie,* I, 97, "Io rinunzio ogni favore e ogni laude, dalle quali potessi acquistare alcuna forza di movimento di novità; però che io voglio attendere alle mercanzie, le quali di nonnulla m'hanno fatto eccelso sopra gli altri cittadini. Io conosco che le mercatanzie sono l'origine e il fondamento che la Repubblica mi esalta, e per la Repubblica le mercantanzie non mi glorificano; però che, quando io ero indigente, non che la Repubblica mi alzasse, ma cittadino non ci era che mi conoscesse, e mostrava di non mi avere mai veduto." Giovanni's political caution was matched by his care and intelligence in business affairs, as in his bookkeeping and commercial policy. See Raymond de Roover, "I libri segreti del Banco de' Medici," *A.S.I.,* II (1949), 237-238; also R. de Roover, "Lorenzo il magnifico e il tramonto del Banco dei Medici," *A.S.I.,* II (1949), 176.

[12] Paolo da Certaldo, *Libro di buoni costumi,* ed. A. Schiaffini (Firenze, Felice Le Monnier, 1945), p. 97, "e usa sempre con più ricco di te e con maggiore di te e con uomo di buoni costumi."

a point of stressing the fact that they should give according to their ability only and that they should not overlook strategic friendships, such as those involving highly-placed persons.[13]

The object here is to trace some of the ramifications that grew out of the attitude towards wealth in Florence. It has been indicated that the marriage contract rested on an economic agreement, that political distinction might be a function of great wealth, and that friendship was sometimes viewed according to a "mystique" of money (hence, in Morelli's case, the designating of cash in the imagery of family and friendship). All this, it appears, the Florentines discerned. What probably escaped their attention was the influence of the old nobility on the spending habits of the merchant. For although the merchant class triumphed politically over the old landowning families at the end of the thirteenth century, the ideal of noble blood was not wholly purged from the minds of those who came to form the new ruling sector of society.[14] Intermarriage, commercial association, and residential proximity gradually produced an upper class whose outlook combined the utilitarian and acquisitive psychology of the merchant with the nobleman's emphasis on visible style and the proud notions of honor. In the dominant social circles men had to observe a certain level of conduct, and that level necessitated the capacity and willingness to spend. Far from observing the careful frugality of his thirteenth-century ancestor, the merchant of the fifteenth century fondly indulged in heavy expenditure. Thus Giovanni Rucellai, who spent most of his life amassing a great fortune, declared that "it is much sweeter to spend money than to earn it";[15] and again, "I think I've done myself more honor by having spent money well than by having earned it. Spending gave me a deeper satisfaction, especially the money I spent on my house in Florence."[16] This attitude seems to have reached its grandest

---

[13] *Ibid.*, pp. 98, 228, 231.

[14] Nicola Ottokar, *Il Comune di Firenze alla fine del dugento* (Firenze, 1926), pp. 58, 69ff.; Gino Masi, *La struttura sociale delle fazioni politiche fiorentine ai tempi di Dante* (Firenze, 1930); Salvemini, *La dignità cavalleresca* (Firenze, 1896), pp. 58-59.

[15] Giovanni Rucellai, *Autografo dallo Zibaldone* (Firenze, 1872), p. 5.

[16] G. Marcotti, *Un mercatante fiorentino e la sua famiglia* (Firenze, 1881), p. 46, "E credo che m'abbi fatto più honore l'averli bene spesi

expression with Lorenzo the Magnificent, who in the early 1470's calculated that his family disbursed no less than 663,755 florins between 1434 and 1471, mainly for buildings, charity, and taxes. But he was pleased with this expenditure because, he said, "I think it casts a brilliant light on our condition in the city."[17]

Florentines engaged in a wide range of expenditures. In the upper strata of society, as we said, the "right" kind of marriage was costly:[18] it presupposed having a fortune large enough either to permit the giving of a rich dowry or to merit a woman with one. To attend the festivities of such a marriage, moreover, might entail an additional expense, as shown in the example of an Adimari girl, wife to a Strozzi, unable to attend a wedding party because she had neither enough jewelry nor the necessary brocades.[19] Again, it was customary for some families, not necessarily the richest, to spend a fortune on their wardrobes;[20] cloth of high quality was exceedingly expensive and the swift eye of the merchant missed nothing. Leon Battista Alberti observed that in the city's first families, men dined "in such rooms and at such tables as were fit for the highest prelates."[21] Massive town houses, large country estates, family *loggie*, private chapels, donations for the grounds and buildings of monasteries and churches—these were the marks of a family's wealth, the visible signs of its honor and stature.[22] Nor are the resources of proud

---

ch'averli guadagnati e più contentamento nel mio animo e massimamente delle muraglie ch'io ho fatte della casa mia di Firenze."

[17] See the documents in William Roscoe, *Vita di Lorenzo de' Medici* (Pisa, 1816), I, xliv, where Lorenzo asserts that his father and grandfather spent "663,755 tra muraglie, limosine, e gravezze, senza l'altre spese, di che non voglio dolermi, perchè quantunque molti giudicassero averne una parte in borsa, io giudico essere gran lume allo stato nostro e pajommi ben collocati, e ne sono molto ben contento."

[18] Illustrative of opinions bearing on the "right" kind of marriage are Donato Velluti, *Cronica domestica*, ed. Lungo and Volpi (Firenze, 1914), p. 139; Cavalcanti, *Istorie*, II, 195; and Strozzi, *Lettere*, pp. 4, 395, 458, 467.

[19] Strozzi, *Lettere*, pp. 592-593.

[20] The wardrobe of the Martelli family, for example, was worth the value of several large urban houses. See the accounts in the family's business diary, ASF, Carte Strozz., 5a serie, 1461, ff. 29v, 30r.

[21] *De iciarchia*, in *Opere volgari*, ed. Anicio Bonucci (Firenze, 1842-1849), III, 33, where the author has Niccolò Cerretani say that in the houses of the "cittadini primari della terra nostra . . . la sala, la mensa,—tutto [è] parato a imitazione de' massimi prelati."

[22] Alberti, *Della famiglia*, pp. 330-332; and Lapo Mazzei, *Lettere di un notaro a un mercante*, ed. C. Guasti, 2 vols. (Firenze, 1880), I, 4; II, 91, 121.

expenditure exhausted by these examples. By lending large sums of money to the Republic, Cosimo de' Medici earned great social and political prestige.[23] Others again, leading taxpayers, expected concrete recognition of their contributions to the state's coffers. Gabbriello Panciatichi, the city's third highest taxpayer in 1427,[24] petitioned for and received a tax indulgence, knowing that his appeal would carry more weight if he alluded to the civic duty of paying taxes in order to preserve the constitution and liberties of Florence.[25] The Panciatichi had ranked among the city's first taxpayers for decades, so that Gabbriello's allusion to the idea of civic virtue was in effect a reminder of the singular contributions of his family.

Gabbriello's petition for a tax indulgence, a very common practice in Florence, indicates that something of the nobleman's personal way of managing government had been drawn into the assumptions of the city's political class. In true oligarchical fashion, a limited number of families were closely associated with government office and policy, and the political prominence of an individual usually entailed distinction for his whole family as well.[26] By the same token, when the coercive power of the state was turned against an individual, his relatives also had to be prepared to withstand direct and indirect persecution.

But what had personal government to do with the Florentine attitude towards wealth? The connection is not obscure. Suffice it to note that because a statesman's power to show favor or do injury was very great, his personal wealth tended to appear greater than in reality it was. For money *and* political power invested individuals with a social standing which no amount of money by itself could bestow.

If wealth was essential to the acquisition and maintenance of superior social rank, then rank was lost as a family lost its wealth. The decline might go on for decades, but the end—unless fortune changed—was unavoidable and clear for all to see. In the

[23] Cavalcanti, *Istorie*, I, 502, 541. Needless to say, it also increased animosity against him.

[24] G. Canestrini, *La scienza e l'arte di stato* (Firenze, 1862), p. 153.

[25] *ASF, Provvisioni*, 117, f. 277v. Gabbriello was always taxed "ut est debitum cuiuslibet civis statum et libertatem patrie anelantis pro ipsis statu et libertate conservandis."

[26] This observation will be amplified and illustrated in part 2 of this chapter.

dominant strata of Florentine society, poverty led to social isolation, to humiliation and shame, to political ostracism. There seems no other way to interpret the following passages.

Speaking of Giovanni Corsini, one memorialist of the times asserted that in the 1420's both Giovanni and his father "were so immersed in a brimming expanse of misery and poverty that far from his [Giovanni's] being esteemed by men in government, he was even despised by his own relatives."[27] Leon Battista Alberti observed: "Whoever is favored little by fortune will not find it easy to acquire honor and fame by means of his virtues . . . for although I will not say that poverty is wholly repressive, it often throws virtue into the shadows, subjecting it to a hidden and obscure misery."[28]

He took this view even further in another passage from *Della famiglia*: "And so, let us call happy the large family whose numerous men are rich and honored and loved, and consider that one unfortunate which has but few men, and those both poor and disliked. For while the first family will be feared, the other shall have to suffer scorn and injury; while those will justly attain honors, these will be hated and humbled; and while one family will be invited to great and glorious things, the other will be excluded and disdained."[29] These citations reveal an essential part of the social morality of upper-class Florence: wealth was associated with *virtù* and honor, poverty with dishonor.

To avoid distortion, let it be noted that some of Alberti's writings contain views *prima facie* at variance with the above

---

[27] Cavalcanti, *Istorie*, ii, 195, "e il padre era tanto, col figliuolo, attuffato nello strabochevole profondo di tutte le miserie, che, non che, fusse reputato in tra gli uomini del governo, ma da' suoi medesimi era schifato."

[28] From Book iv of *Della famiglia*, not in the Pellegrini-Spongano edition. See the edition in the series of the *Biblioteca classica economica* (Milan, undated), p. 274, "E a chi la fortuna poco seconda, non a costui sarà facile acquistar buon nome e fama di sue virtù. La povertà quanto chicchesia prova, non affermo io al tutto impedisca, ma ottenebra e sottotiene in miseria ascosa e sconosciuta spesso la virtù."

[29] P. 153 (eds. F. C. Pellegrini and R. Spongano, Firenze, Sansoni, 1946), "Adunque chiameremo felice quella famiglia in quale saranno copia d'uomini ricchi, pregiati e amati, e quella reputeremo infelice quale arà pochi, ma infami, poveri e malvoluti uomini. Imperò che dove que' saranno temuti, questi non potranno non sofferire molte ingiurie e sdegni, et dove a quelli sarà gratificato e renduto onore, questi saranno odiati et aviliti, e dove nelle cose magnifiche et gloriose quelli saranno chiamati e ammessi, questi saranno exclusi et schifati."

passages. For as he grew older, he gave increasing prominence to his mordant criticism of the luxury, indolence, avarice, and corruption of the moneyed.[30] Indeed, on at least one occasion he goes so far as to suggest that virtue is mainly a characteristic of the hard-working poor.[31] Evidently, therefore, this phase of Alberti's work requires clarification, and we may state it thus: his reflections on the corrupting power of wealth are those of a moralist, an indignant commentator on the vices of Italian society. They are not descriptive views, like those contained in the passages quoted above, where Alberti is merely looking at the social forms or civic manifestations of the rich man's *virtù*. There he is *observing* rather than *judging*. For social life in Florence was in fact partly made up of the very practices and forms he sometimes deemed pernicious to the Republic's moral foundations. There was no escaping the fact that the ruling mores of Florentine social life were laid down, in Alberti's words, by "riches and what the multitude calls nobility."[32] But since the object of this chapter is to represent the practical factors or attributes that determined social position in Florence, Alberti's moralizing is less pertinent here than his more detached assertions regarding the world about which he moralized. Hence we need not be detained by apparent differences between his normative and moral statements.

In our account of the social importance of wealth, we must not fail to distinguish between its "honorable" and "dishonorable" forms. Honor in this connection refers to the acquisition of wealth. Clearly, some ways of earning money were more honorable or more socially dignified than others. It will be necessary to consider this theme in some detail.

Although Florence was a city of sharp commercial and finance practices, the "official" attitude of the business community (as expressed, for example, in manuals of conduct) included a severely critical view of disreputable or dishonest commercial activity. The moral assumptions behind this attitude were at

---

[30] See especially his *De iciarchia*, in *Opere volgari*, III, 29-30, 50, 84-85.

[31] *Dialogo de repubblica* (Venice, 1543), p. 11r, "così è che la necessità habiti in casa de poveri, quale dicono fu madre della industria, et insieme con la industria sempre crebbe virtù."

[32] *De iciarchia*, pp. 84-85, "la ricchezza, e quella che il vulgo chiama nobiltà, furono cacciate di cielo, però che come elle fanno qui tra noi questa stima, poter ciò che ella vuole."

once Christian, self-interested (i.e., protective of trade), and possibly even a bit chivalric. The object here, however, will be to bring out, so far as they were present, the *social* elements in the criticism against the amassing of riches in a certain way.

If a merchant proposed to acquire or maintain a place in the governing class, one of his foremost cares involved the question of his personal honor. To understand this, we have only to note the incidence and importance of the word *onore* in Alberti's *Della famiglia*. Or, looking into some of the other writings of the period, time and again we come upon the association of dishonor with sharp business practices, quick gain, or usury. Paolo da Certaldo, for instance, declared that "Usury is certainly destructive . . . just as it ruins the goods and honor of the world, so it corrupts the body and soul."[33] Or again, "Profit made in a disreputable fashion ought rather to be called injury and loss."[34] Giovanni Morelli warned the merchant to enter only into legal contracts, and neither to accept nor lend money at usurious rates, for nothing was more damaging to one's honor and good name.[35] Lionardo Bruni stressed the fact that Palla Strozzi's riches "were well-acquired,"[36] and singled this out as one of the things that made Palla the most fortunate man in Florence. Bruni's implied criticism of "ill-got" wealth was taken much further by Giovanni Cavalcanti, who denied that rapid gain could ever bear investigation. Paraphrasing one of his contemporaries, Cavalcanti remarked that "as no river ever swelled with clear water, so no fortune was ever made from licit and honest gain."[37]

Florentine feeling against usury and swift gain was rooted in a strong medieval tradition,[38] but one may also suppose that it formed part of the natural reaction of a society where trade and finance dominate economic life. Seen in this light, Florentine indignation against immoral business procedure seems to have

---

[33] *Libro di buoni costumi*, p. 185, "Quella cosa che molto guasta . . . questa sì è l'usura; e come guasta l'avere e l'onore del mondo, così guasta l'anima e'l corpo."

[34] *Ibid.*, p. 131, "Lo guadagno che s'acquista con mala fama sì è da essere appellato danno."

[35] *Ricordi*, pp. 225, 249.   [36] Marcotti, pp. 63-64.

[37] *Istorie*, II, 189, "come niùno fiume ingrossò mai d'acqua chiara, così niuno arrichì mai di guadagno lecito né onesto."

[38] Cf. Marvin B. Becker, "Three Cases Concerning the Restitution of Usury in Florence," *Journal of Economic History* (September, 1957), pp. 445-450. The footnotes of this article supply a useful bibliography.

been a form of coercion such as any society may require for its own survival. But the feeling against rapid gain was also inevitably turned into a resentment against new wealth, which in turn was associated with "shady" business practices, greed, and materialistic ruthlessness. And of course, in the mouths of men who represented the old Florentine families, these moral epithets were apt to take on a strong political and social flavor. Several examples will illustrate this.

Filippo Villani, a doctor of law whose family dated back to the mid-thirteenth century, despaired of the idea of trying to educate or refine the city's *nouveaux riches*. Writing at the beginning of the fifteenth century and describing the upstarts whose parents or grandparents had been obscure country types, Filippo said: "the impertinence of rustics, intensified by wealth, has always been contrary to worthy pursuits . . . born humbly, they never praise nor cultivate fine customs, to which, at any rate, they can never adapt themselves. Instead, they heap up lucre, believing that they are ennobled by it."[39]

Sharper and more damning criticism was expressed by Giovanni Cavalcanti, who was descended from one of the city's most distinguished families. He bitterly assailed the practice of giving a greater share of public offices "to the rich men rather than to those who were gifted and good."[40] "These newcomers were too coarse for the great questions of state," he complained. "They were avaricious men who made money on the unpaid salaries of soldiers and who bought up the debts of the Commune."[41] Some of them he accused of being baseborn adventurers and usurers, others of defrauding the Republic or of having been corrupted with gifts. He ended by agreeing with those citizens who accused the upstarts of having "taken our riches in the name of defending the freedom of our native land."[42]

[39] *Liber de civitatis florentiae famosis civibus*, ed. G. C. Galletti (Florentiae, 1847), pp. 31-32, "Sed parum profuerunt boni viri studia, quibus agrestis insolentia, opulentiis fatigata, semper fuit adversa . . . cum obscure nati nunquam laudent colantque mores bonos, cum quibus ullo unquam tempore convenire non possunt; sed auri cumulum, quo se aestimant nobilitari."

[40] *Istorie*, I, 41, "E si davano le degnità più agli uomini dotati di fortuna, che a copiosi di virtù."

[41] *Ibid.*, I, 43, "Questi novelli erano uomini rozzi a' gran fatti; uomini avari; mercatanti de' crediti de' soldati; compratori de' debiti del Comune."

[42] *Ibid.*, I, 66, "Voi ci avete tolto le nostre ricchezze sotto nome di difendere la libertà della patria."

One of the strongest indictments of the link between political power and new or dishonorable wealth appears in Alberti's *Della famiglia*: "O mad, bombastic, arrogant, petty tyrants who excuse your vicious lives—you cannot bear to have as equals (which would be fitting) citizens who are not as rich as you, though they be perhaps of more ancient stock; nor can you live without oppressing those who are weaker than you, and yet you want to control the state. . . ./ He is lowest of all who shall lust after and usurp what belongs to the public. . . ./ That I should enter government (as nearly everyone does) for the sake of money, or take the state to be my shop; that I should use it as a source for my daughters' dowries, or somehow make a private thing out of anything public, transforming what my country grants as an honor into private profit or loot; absolutely not, O my Lionardo."[43]

Like the Cavalcanti citations, this passage all but declares that Florence was governed by grasping merchants who unrelentingly turned public office to private gain. There is also the suggestion that their wealth was by no means the oldest that could be found in Florence. But it may be that the indictment was exaggerated. Alberti was descended from an early thirteenth-century family which had long played a leading part in public affairs, and hence he would have been most reluctant to admit that his family could have political superiors in Florence. As for Cavalcanti's views, it is not unlikely that they concealed some bitterness, for he was cast into debtors' prison at least twice.

But even allowing for exaggeration in the passages adduced, there remains the fact that they contain a sharp element of social criticism. By means of metaphor, association, and direct statement, Alberti's observations draw together economic, social, political, and moral factors—all adding up to an eloquent and in-

[43] Pp. 276-278 (Pellegrini-Spongano edition), "O pazzi, fumosi, superbi, proprii tiranneschi, che date scusa al vitio vostro: non potete sofferire gli altri meno ricchi, ma forse piu antichi cittadini di voi, essere pari a voi quanto si richiede: non potete vivere senza sforzare i minori, pero desiderate lo stato. . . ./ et quello sarà sopra tutti pessimo il quale bramerà et usurperà le cose publiche. . . ./ che io volessi, come quasi fanno tutti, ascrivermi lo stato quasi per mia ricchezza, riputarlo mia bottega, ch'io pregiassi lo stato tra lle dote alle mie fanciulle, ch'io in modo alcuno facessi del publico privato, quello che la patria mi permette a dignità trasferendolo a quadagno, a preda; non punto, Lionardo mio."

teresting result. Given the nature of Florentine social traditions,[44] when a strong political class was insufficiently endowed with the "gentle" virtues, how could it fail to provoke moral protestations from the old ruling families, even—or perhaps especially— when the key issues were economic and social in nature? Evidently, since the new men were a fact in government, it was not enough to charge them with political incompetence (though this too was done); their morals had to be impugned. Therefore, to express indignation over the sources of their wealth was in some ways the most effective campaign against them: it denied their social fitness. Besides, was the oligarchy not held together by more than money? *Mere* wealth was not the way to distinguished rank. For although it is true that social advance was partly predicated on wealth, that wealth, in theory at least, must not have been too rapidly acquired nor too recently, nor could it be too closely associated with usurious contracts or other dishonorable trade procedures.

Moral censure, as we shall see, was not the only mode of social rejection. In some quarters, lowly trades and all forms of bodily labor were assumed to be socially degrading. This view seems to have been a permanent feature of the social code of upper-class Florence. The code was partly based on the city's hierarchy of occupational dignities, in which the grades more or less reflected the constitutional arrangement of the Florentine guild structure.[45] There were seven major and fourteen minor guilds, and the various degrees of social rank which these enjoyed were roughly distributed according to what the twenty-one guilds represented in political, economic, and traditional terms. First in dignity was the custom-honored legal profession. Beside the lawyers were ranked the international bankers and merchants (wool and silk were the chief items of enterprise). Next were the furriers and wealthy merchants who imported spices, drugs, dyes, and specialties. Then came the tradesmen and artisans of the fourteen minor guilds; retailers, butchers, ironmongers, leathermakers, stationers, and so forth. Finally, at the base of the social pyramid stood the wool and silk workers: dyers, weavers, spinners, washers, combers, and beaters. They

[44] Treated in parts 2-5 of this chapter.
[45] Alfred Doren, *Le arti fiorentine*, tr. G. B. Klein, 2 vols. (Firenze, 1940).

had no political representation and were at the juridical mercy of the *Seta* and *Lana* guild consulates.

We will not know precisely how the various economic pursuits, from physical labor to international finance, commanded different degrees of social dignity, until we examine a few texts. A convenient beginning is offered us in Matteo Palmieri's work, *Della vita civile* (1438-1439). Written in the form of a dialogue, it represents the general social outlook of the rich merchant: a conservative man, paternalistic, fond of his landed estates, and one who at times affected the ways of the old Florentine nobility.

According to *Della vita civile*, the unskilled workers and artisans should be dispersed throughout the city. Furthermore, Palmieri continues, "let the working masses and the humblest sector of the middle class struggle for the good of the Republic. Those who are lazy and indolent in a way that does harm to the city, and who can offer no just reason for their condition, should either be forced to work or be expelled from the Commune. The city would thus rid itself of that harmful part of the poorest class."[46] How the toiling masses should live is also clearly implied: if in "the lowest orders of society they earn enough food to keep going from day to day, then they have enough."[47] Next, moving up the social scale, Palmieri declared that those arts are servile which deal in petty merchandise. "Low too are the trades of those who buy from merchants in order to sell immediately at a profit. . . . For trade is certainly paltry and low when it is mean and done on a small scale."[48]

Similar attitudes are struck in Alberti's *Della famiglia*, except that the point of view there reflects, if anything, an even higher position in society: it is the viewpoint of the great merchant-

---

[46] *Della vita civile*, ed. Felice Battaglia (Bologna, 1944), p. 157, "che tutto il vulgo e la meno scelta parte del popolo s'affatichi e faccia pro commune della republica. Chi fusse ozioso et inerte, in modo nocesse e desse danno nella città, se non è da giusta cagione impedito, sia costretto all'opera o veramente mandato fuori, acciòchè la città si purghi della nociva plebe."

[47] *Ibid.*, p. 158, "In nell' ínfima plebe basti solo il vitto necessario che dì per dì con loro esercizii s'acquistano."

[48] *Ibid.*, p. 157, "Vili sono ancora l'arti di coloro che cooperano da mercatanti per subito con guadagno vendere. . . . La mercatanzia, quando è povera e piccola, certo è inliberale e vile." Palmieri is in this passage following Cicero verbatim. See the *De Officiis* (London, 1928), I, xlii, "Sordidi etiam putandi, qui mercantur a mercatoribus, quod statim vendant. . . . Mercatura autem, si tenuis est, sordida putanda est."

nobleman. Alberti observes that parents distinguish themselves by rearing their children graciously and honorably. Some men, however, "are given to greed, and in trying to turn their sons into good household managers, they make them miserly and servile instead. For respecting, as they do, riches more than honor, they have their sons learn ugly trades and socially inferior skills."[49] The condition of the petty retailer or hawker is also sharply rejected: "I certainly would not like to buy and sell now this and now that—a low calling, suitable for wage earners."[50]

But trade on an international scale was something else. Bernardo Castiglionchio, a Florentine nobleman and cleric, said to his father in the early 1370's: "It is true, I know, that some of your brothers and relatives were merchants; but they dealt in noble and honorable merchandise, not in humble goods. Travelling to France and England, they traded in cloth and wool, like all the best and most important men of Florence. This type of trade is considered very comely and grand, and those who practice it are liked and greatly respected in our country. This is why there is no one in our family who can be said to have demeaned himself because of having followed an inferior trade."[51]

A generation or so later, Goro Dati stated a similar view. He was a silk merchant who traveled widely in Italy and Spain; he also served in the Republic's highest offices. The men of Florence, he said, go abroad in their youth and acquire experience, virtues, knowledge, and wealth. "A Florentine who is not a merchant, who has not traveled through the world, seeing foreign nations and peoples and then returned to Florence with some wealth, is a man who enjoys no esteem whatsoever."[52] In Palmieri's *Della vita*

---

[49] *Della famiglia*, p. 29, "et non fare come forse usano molti vechi dati alla avarítia, e quali ove e' cercano e figliuoli fargli massai, ivi gli fanno miseri et servili, dove egli stimano più le richeze che lo onore, insegnano a'figliuoli arti bructe et vili exercitii."

[50] *Ibid.*, p. 298, "Ma io possendo non vorrei avere a vendere et comperare ora questo ora quello, che sono faccende da mercennarii, et vili occupationi."

[51] Lapo di Castiglionchio, *Epistola*, ed. Lorenzo Mehus (Bologna, 1753), p. 148, "Vero è, che so che alcuni de' vostri fratelli, e consorti furono mercatanti, ma di mercatanzie nobili e oneste, non vili, passando in Francia, e in Inghilterra, trafficando panni, e lane, come fanno tutti li maggiori, e migliori uomini della città: il quale esercizio è reputato bello e grande, e chi quello esercita, è accetto nella patria e riverito; sicchè per viltà d'arte nullo di nostra famiglia puo essere reputato ignobile."

[52] Dati, *L'Istoria di Firenze dal 1380 al 1405*, ed. L. Pratesi (Norcia, 1904), p. 60, "chi non è mercatante e che non abbia cerco il mondo e

civile, the wealthy Agnolo Pandolfini states that trade "is certainly praiseworthy when it is rich and great, when it transports large volumes of diversified goods between many places and then sells them without miserliness."[53]

It would have been relatively simple for Leon Battista Alberti to offer a philosophic vindication of the superior virtues of large-scale commercial enterprise. For he might have argued that as the end of business management is profit, it calls—as he himself once observed—for "mind, industry, and other similar virtues of the soul, as in . . . the architect, the physician, and the like."[54] Naturally, the servile trades such as "smithery or hired labor" also aim at making money; but these require "coming and going, working with one's arms, and similar exertions."[55] We may thus imagine Alberti concluding that since these occupations are connected with movements of the body rather than the soul, they belong to a lower and inferior order of being.

Florentines also had other reasons for raising the supposed dignity and importance of international trade above other economic pursuits. One of the common themes of the time was that trade on a large scale gave strength to the Republic—indeed, was the foundation of its greatness. The Republic's official dispatches not infrequently expressed the view that merchants "are the cream of our citizenry, the foundation of our power. Without them the Republic would be nothing."[56] Or more fully: "we take it to be our duty and obligation to favor our merchants," for "trade is necessary and most useful to every city and dominion."[57] But sympathy for the exalted role of the merchant was not restricted to official government circles.

---

veduto l'estranie nazioni delle genti e tornato alla patria con avere, non è reputato da niente."

[53] P. 157, "quando [la mercatanzia] fusse grande e copiosa, mandante e conducente di molti luoghi," etc. Cf. Cicero (supra, n. 48).

[54] *Della famiglia,* p. 216, "In noi sono apte a guadagnare l'industria, lo 'ngegno e simili virtù riposte negli animi nostri come son queste: essere . . . architetto, medico, e simili."

[55] *Ibid.,* p. 216. "Sonci ancora apte a guadagnare le operationi del corpo, come di tutte l'opere fabrili e mercennarie, andare, lavorare con le braccia, et simili exercitii."

[56] *Commissioni di Rinaldo degli Albizzi,* ed. C. Guasti (Firenze, 1867-1873), I, 66, "mercatoribus nostris, qui sunt praecipuum nostrarum virium nostreque potentie fundamentum, et sine quibus hec nostra Respublica nichil esset" (December 1404).

[57] ASF, *Leg. Comm.,* 11, f. 42v, "ci pare nostro officio et debito dar favore a nostri mercatanti . . . essendo la mercatantia arte necessaria et utilissima a ogni cita et regno."

In his polemic against the spreading despotism of the Visconti, written around 1400, Cino Rinuccini praises Ridolfo de' Bardi, a great merchant-banker, on the grounds that "the Republic is enhanced not only by military power, but by commercial enterprise as well."[58] His tribute to Ridolfo in the polemic comes after a section devoted to the laudatory appraisal of various Florentine statesmen and warriors. Alberti's *Della famiglia* also abounds with references to the social utility of commerce on a large scale: for commerce creates employment, abundance, wealth; and wealth, in turn, creates the conditions for great political, military, and artistic resources.[59]

Even the Republic's honor was invoked to highlight the merchant's alleged attachment and service to his community. An excellent example of this appears in a petition favoring Ser Paolo di Ser Lando Fortini, former chancellor of the Republic and one of the city's more authoritative political figures. Aimed at securing a tax reduction for Ser Paolo, the petition states that he had formed a commercial company ("ut notum esse putant fere toti populo florentino") together with several other Florentines. Their intention had been to trade in Rome, Valencia, and other parts of the world. Ser Paolo told the Signoria that he had "hoped to earn some honorable wealth and other profits for himself and native land, while winning honor for your city."[60] Instead, however, he lost more than 12,000 florins. The petitioner's reference to the winning of honor for the Republic was cursory, but it was not an uncommon appeal of the period, nor was it complete humbug.

Judging by the evidence above, it appears that the idea of civic virtue in Florence was not confined to political and administrative matters, nor to the abstractions of humanists; it also pervaded the economic life of the city.

Since most wealthy Florentines owned farms or productive

[58] *Risponsiva alla invettiva di Messer Antonio Lusco*, in Coluccio Salutati, *Invectiva in Antonium Luschum*, ed. D. Moreni (Florentiae, 1826), p. 245, "perchè non solo l'arme, ma la mercanzia amplificano la Repubblica."

[59] Pp. 210, 211, 220, 319.

[60] *ASF, Provv.*, 122, f. 15r, "cum idem Ser Paulus contraxisset societatem cum quibusdam vestris civibus quos fideles et diligentissimos fore putabat in excercitiis mercatoris in urbe rome valentie et aliis mundi partibus exqua honorem civitate vestre et patrie sibique alia emolumenta et lucra honorabilia et honesta consequi sperabat" etc. The petition was enacted on 12 April 1431.

land parcels in the Florentine countryside, it seems necessary to define the social attitude towards farming. Surprisingly enough, no sustained scholarly work has been published as yet on the early agrarian history of Florence. Here and there in the documents and printed material we get vague impressions of what was going on, but very little of this is adaptable to generalization because it lacks a context of previous study.

The reports for the catasto of 1427 make it perfectly clear that some of the city's inhabitants lived entirely or largely on the rents from their lands.[61] A man who had neither trade nor profession and whose landed rents accounted for the bulk of his income was known as a *scioperato*. Four to six medium-sized farms (*poderi*) ranked him among the upper 8 per cent of all taxpayers.[62] The *scioperato*'s place in Florentine society, his station in life, equaled that of the well-to-do merchant. There was constant intermarriage between the two groups;[63] moreover, *scioperati* could be the sons of merchants,[64] so that the difference between the two (apart from the occupational one) was best distinguishable in political terms. For although *scioperati* sat in the legislative councils with the representatives of the seven major guilds,[65] they could not match the power of these merchants, because the Florentine constitution assigned a dominant political role to the major guilds. When a *scioperato* had a name like Ricasoli, Adimari, or Lamberteschi, however, the antiquity of his family might give him enough standing in society to offset his political handicaps.

The merchant's esteem for farming, for absentee farming, was taken over from the old nobility. Earlier, however, there was for a long time considerable resistance even to frequenting the

[61] For some carefully-documented observations on landholding in the fourteenth century see P. J. Jones, "Florentine families and Florentine diaries in the fourteenth century," *Papers of the British School at Rome*, xxiv (1956), 183-205.

[62] This assertion is based on my index of the catasto inventories of 1427. A farm of medium size was worth from 200 to 300 florins. In 1427 about 8.3 percent of all family heads declared net assets of 1000 florins or more.

[63] Cf. the marriages contracted by the Carradori, Belfredelli, Riccalbani, Filicaia, and Raffacani, in *ASF, Carte Ancisa*.

[64] E.g., when Giovanni Rucellai cautioned his sons to abandon trade unless they were prepared to give it their close personal attention, he was suggesting that they live mainly on real-estate income, that is, as *scioperati*. See Marcotti, p. 107.

[65] *Statuta*, ii, 659-661.

country. During most of the fourteenth century, the truly conscientious merchant avoided lengthy rural visits. Thus Paolo da Certaldo, writing in the 1350's or 1360's, declared that " 'The country makes good animals and bad men'; therefore, frequent it little. Stay in the city, attending to your trade or business affairs, and you shall prosper."[66] In the 1380's the story-teller, Franco Sacchetti, observed that " 'The city should produce good men, the country good livestock.' "[67]

This preference for business affairs and city life was a continuing expression of the ambitious and hardworking merchant type, whose frugality (or what was left of it) still conformed to the spirit of the Commune's early sumptuary laws. But the misgivings about country life vanished before the end of the century, giving way to the view that a stay in the country every year was both desirable and salutary.

In the fifteenth century the upper-class families of Florence customarily retreated to their country houses during the months of August and September. The Republic's legislative assemblies were suspended for five or six weeks and the debates on really important bills were delayed even further, save in critical times.[68] The attractions of the country had become truly irresistible. Giovanni Morelli wistfully remembered his youthful and idyllic days in the family villa.[69] Alberti glorified the pleasures of country life, of genteel farming, and at times even appeared to set the life of the landowner above the competitive urban life of the merchant.[70] The rich merchant and great landowner, Agnolo Pandolfini, believed that "Among the arts which bear some sort of fruit or profit, none is more natural, more basic, better than farming."[71] The country estate, he said, is "a perfect good: it is fertile, abun-

---

[66] *Libro di buoni costumi*, pp. 91-92, " 'La villa fa buone bestie e cattivi uomini,' e però usala poco: sta a la città, e favvi o arte o mercatantia, e capiterai bene."

[67] Cited *ibid.*, p. 91, note 3, " 'Che la città buon' uomini de' fare, La villa buone bestie a notricare'."

[68] E.g., there was no legislation between 27 August and 27 September of 1400, nor between 31 August and 10 October of 1401. See *ASF, Lib. Fab.*, 47, ff. 25r-26r, 65r-66r.

[69] *Ricordi*, p. 416.

[70] *Della famiglia*, pp. 309-315; *De republica*, passim.

[71] Said by Agnolo in Palmieri's dialogue, *Della vita civile*, p. 157, "sopra tutte l'arti, delle quali si cava alcuno frutto, niúna n'è più naturale, più necessaria, né migliore che l'agricultura."

dant, delightful, honorable, natural, and worthy of every free man of good class. Many distinguished men have retired to their country estates after a life of great events and glorious deeds."[72]

The last paragraph indicates that the fifteenth century saw a significant growth in esteem for the leisure and cares of country life. This trend was the natural outcome of a social change which we mean to explore in the third section of this chapter: the triumph of the ideals and traditions of the old family. Furthermore, in the second half of the century, the prestigious side of gentlemanly farming increased because of the city's unstable commercial conditions. Landed wealth, in contrast to commercial enterprise, was normally a safer investment risk, even if the return on land was not a match for trade profits over short periods of time.

Two themes have been set forth in this chapter so far: that the Florentine attitude towards wealth and poverty made money or possessions a necessary component of superior social place; and second, that different forms of economic activity, from physical labor to farming and international trade, enjoyed different degrees of social esteem. Before concluding this part we should ask, were there then no changes in these attitudes? We have already seen that farming underwent a gradual social revaluation. What about the Florentine view of wealth?

Although there is no evidence to show that the first half of the fifteenth century saw a rise in basic living costs,[73] the emphasis in Florence on monetary expenditure seems to have increased noticeably. Let us look for a moment at a basic item like the dowry. During the fourteenth century, the *dote* in upper-class families ranged from 400 to 1000 florins.[74] Our evidence indicates that dowries then gradually became larger, and from about the middle of the fifteenth century the practice in ruling families was

[72] *Ibid.*, p. 52, "La villa è tutta buona, fertile, copiosa, dilettevole, onesta, naturale e degna d'ogni uomo da bene e libero. A quella molti uomini degnissimi sono dopo molti egregii fatti e gloriose opere umane rifuggiti."
[73] See the section by Robert S. Lopez, "The Trade of Medieval Europe: the South," in *The Cambridge Economic History of Europe*, ed. M. Postan and E. E. Rich (Cambridge, 1952), II, 257-359. The general price recovery begins only towards the end of the fifteenth century.
[74] E.g., on Medici dowries in the fourteenth century see Gene A. Brucker, "The Medici in the Fourteenth Century," *Speculum*, XXXII (January-1957), 11; cf. also the Curiani dowries of the same period in the family's *Libro di conti e memorie*, ASF, Mss., 77, f. 8r/v.

to give from 1000 to 2000 or more florins.[75] Indeed, a marriage portion of 1000 florins was disdainfully called a "mere artisan's dowry."[76] And as Alessandra Strozzi found, this meant that it was costing more and more "to marry a young lady into higher rank and more gentility."[77]

Conforming with the trend in dowries, Florentine dress became increasingly luxurious. Brocades and taffeta were more widely introduced, together with fussier tailoring and a passion for wearing a good deal of jewelry. Machiavelli sharply observed that Florentine youth of this period "were freer than their forefathers in matters of dress and feasting, as well as in other sensual pleasures. They spent their time and money in idleness, gambling, and women; their leading interest was to appear splendidly dressed and to speak with acuteness and wit, for he who could bite the others most cleverly was more admired and deemed the most wise."[78]

But the new emphasis on heavy spending is best seen in the evolving style of the fifteenth-century Florentine house.[79] It was larger and more "showy" than its fourteenth-century counterpart, the construction of which was simple, functional, and severe (part of it was often used as a warehouse). The Quattrocento house, on the other hand, was more ornate both within and without. It called for elaborate ironwork and carefully-hewn stone. It often had a decorative cornice. Doors, ceilings, and fireplaces were highly finished. And the more prominent families set off their funishings with panel paintings and later with sculptures.[80]

[75] This statement is based on the dowries noted in a sampling of fifteenth-century published and unpublished *ricordanze*.

[76] By Alessandra Strozzi who, ironically enough, was unable to give her own daughter more than 1000 florins; *Lettere*, pp. 4-5, 395.

[77] *Ibid.*, p. 4, "da metterla in maggiore istato e più gentilezza."

[78] *Le istorie fiorentine*, p. 299, "perchè i giovani più sciolti che l'usitato, in vestire, in conviti, in altre simili lascive spendevano sopra modo, ed essendo oziosi, in giuochi ed in femmine il tempo e le sustanze consumavano; e gli studii loro erano apparire con il vestire splendidi, e con il parlare sagaci e astuti, e quello che più destramente mordeva gli altri, era più savio e da più stimato." On the changing style in feminine dress see E. Polidori-Calamandrei, *Le vesti delle donne fiorentine nel Quattrocento* (Firenze, 1924).

[79] Attilio Schiaparelli, *La casa fiorentina e i suoi arredi nei secoli xiv e xv* (Firenze, 1908). This excellent work was originally planned in two volumes. Only the first was finished.

[80] That paintings were expensive in the fifteenth century can be seen in Neri di Bicci, *Ricordanze* (Ms. in Library of the Galleria degli Uffizi),

As one would expect, the drive towards heavier spending and more luxurious living was not apparent in all sectors of society. Evidence of the trend points to the wealthy merchants, land-owners, bankers, and the more prosperous of the tradesmen. But for us this is the critical social sector, since it more or less circumscribes the world of the Florentine humanists.

2. PUBLIC LIFE

Participation in the public life of Florence was, like wealth, one of the essential factors in high social rank. This was true of both the fourteenth and fifteenth centuries, the chief difference being that public life in the fifteenth century was more thoroughly institutionalized and more difficult to enter. Precisely how early the honors of civil office were courted in Florence is a mystery, but the custom must have gone back at least to the twelfth century.[81]

The statesmen of the Commune's consular period were often noblemen whose ancestors had been feudal lords in the environs of Florence.[82] Such, for example, were the Adimari, Buondelmonti, Lamberti, Pazzi, Ricasoli, Uberti, and Ubertini. But with the Ordinances of Justice of 1293, when a determined body of merchants, bankers, and tradesmen took control of the state, the traditional power of the old *magnati* was permanently broken. Nevertheless, certain features of the nobleman's social outlook impressed themselves on the triumphant merchant-bankers,[83] for some of the old ways (such as government by small magistracies) were taken over, and the image of the powerful family remained in the political conscience of the new governing class.

In time, of course, the families that took power at the end of the thirteenth century developed their own traditions, but until

---

passim; cf. also M. Wackernagel, *Der Lebensraum des Künstlers in der Florentinischen Renaissance* (Leipzig, 1938).

[81] So we infer from R. Davidsohn, *Storia di Firenze*, tr. G. B. Klein (Firenze, 1956), I, xii, "Svolgimento della costituzione municipale."

[82] Davidsohn, *ibid.*; *Documenti dell' antica costituzione del Comune di Firenze*, ed. Pietro Santini (Firenze, 1895), pp. 39-41; cf. also the names adduced by Enrico Fiumi, "Fioritura e decadenza dell' economia fiorentina," *A.S.I.*, IV (1957), 401ff.

[83] In general, A. Sapori, *Studi di storia economica medievale* (Firenze, 1946), esp. "La funzione economica della nobiltà," pp. 705-723; and G. Salvemini, *Magnati e popolani a Firenze* (Firenze, 1899).

then they were not strictly speaking patrician, like the families in an older and more stable oligarchy such as Venice. For the Florentine constitution was in a state of revolutionary flux during the whole second half of the thirteenth century and it was still changing in the early fourteenth century. The Priorate, for example, founded in 1282, was the supreme magistracy of Republican Florence and had still to develop a tradition of permanence. During the Priorate's first years there were six priors, later on there were eight. Again, during the early fourteenth century, two other small but very important councils developed the forms they were to keep almost down to the end of the republican period—the Twelve Good Men (hereafter called the *Dodici*) and the Sixteen Standard-bearers of the Militia companies (hereafter called the *Sedici*).[84] They met on an almost daily basis with the Priorate and were designated the *collegi* or colleges. Their counsel and votes were necessary both in the formulation of foreign policy and in the enactment of legislation.[85]

The Priorate, the *Dodici*, and the *Sedici*, acting together in council, made up the larger executive body of Florentine government. And if the associative link between the state and the new ruling families was to be established, this body had of necessity to develop a tradition of enduring stability. But in view of the dates referred to in the last paragraph (see also the dates given in note 84), and because the associative process required at least two generations, the signs of a *traditional* tie between the state and certain families could not appear before the middle decades of the fourteenth century. This affiliation then resulted in a growing demand for public office, because by the mid Trecento the triumphant families of 1293 and later began to look upon their control of the state as a birthright.[86]

[84] The *Dodici*, set up around 1267, were reorganized and attached to the Priorate in 1321. The *Sedici* went back to about 1250, were reorganized in 1305, then attached to the Priorate. See the "Breve Discorso," Preface to *ASF, Mss.,* 265, entitled, *Gli Dodici Buonomini e gli Sedici Gonfalonieri.*

[85] *Statuta,* II, 664-666.

[86] See N. Rodolico, *La democrazia fiorentina nel suo tramonto* (Bologna, 1905). Two recent articles on the third quarter of the century are M. Becker and G. Brucker, "The *Arti Minori* in Florentine Politics, 1342-1378," *Mediaeval Studies,* XVIII (1956), 93-104; and M. Becker, "Florentine Politics and the Diffusion of Heresy in the Trecento: A Socio-Economic Inquiry," *Speculum,* XXXIV (January-1959), 60-75.

The prominent families of the second half of the fourteenth century normally had two attributes: they possessed a good deal of mercantile or finance capital, and they had regularly appeared in the Signoria for two generations or more. No families better accorded with this description than the Alberti, Albizzi, Medici, Ricci, and Strozzi. Because, as we pointed out, civic virtue was often associated with the economic activity of the great merchants, the public side of life came to hold a significant place in their outlook. As a result, the young men of this circle were reared to seek public office for the sake of family honor and social position,[87] as well as to maintain and strengthen their newly-established family traditions.

But just as the Signoria came to be considered the traditional executive body of government, Florence encountered the problem of the tyrant (September 1342) and five years later was stricken by the Black Plague. These events helped the rise of a new group of rich and ambitious families.[88] The older mercantile and financial families (i.e., the parvenus of the 1280's and 1290's) reacted by stepping up their opposition to the new men and by pressing the claims of their developing magisterial traditions. But they were forced to moderate their stand. The new men successfully entered government in the 1340's and after, so that the older houses, until 1382, were compelled to suffer the most democratic system of representation in the history of Florence.[89] In the 1380's and 1390's, as the social conflict moved towards the first stages of a more permanent resolution,[90] the quest for office

[87] What Guicciardini said in the 1520's already applied: "in Florence you are hardly a man unless you have served in the Signoria at least once." *Dialogo e discorsi del reggimento di Firenze*, ed. R. Palmarocchi (Bari, 1932), p. 113.

[88] See esp. Gene A. Brucker, *Political Conflict in the Florentine Commune: 1343-1378* (doctoral thesis, Princeton University, April 1954); also his more recent and fuller treatment, *Florentine Politics and Society, 1343-1378* (Princeton, 1962). For Brucker the basic problem in Florence during this period concerns the struggle between the older ruling families and the *gente nuova*.

[89] Nevertheless, the commercial oligarchy seems to have retained the upper hand. Becker and Brucker, "The *Arti Minori*."

[90] On the revolutions of 1382 and 1393 see Scipione Ammirato, *Istorie fiorentine*, ed. L. Scarabelli (Torino, 1853), IV, 147ff.; and A. Rado, *Maso degli Albizzi e il partito oligarchico in Firenze dal 1382 al 1393* (Firenze, 1927), pp. 180ff.

grew more and more intense, and in the early fifteenth century came to constitute one of the major problems of the age.

The fourteenth century had been instructive: it taught the commercial oligarchy to maintain its control over the leading magistracies at all times. Thus the suitability of Lionardo Bruni's admonition to the patriciate, when, having just described the workers' revolt of 1378, he warned: "Let this be an enduring lesson to the ruling men of the city: never allow the masses to take the political initiative or to have weapons at their disposal. For once they have tasted a little power, they cannot be held back, convinced they are stronger because of their numerical superiority. Furthermore, the patricians should take special pains to keep themselves informed about the seditious activity of leading public figures, who sometimes set off a revolt of the mob. Salvestro de' Medici, a man from a distinguished, noble and wealthy house, provoked the intervention of the lower classes against the unjust and universally-hated law of *ammonizione*. . . . Once aroused, however, there was no end or measure to the unbridled desire of the lawless rabble, who, being armed, lusted after the property of the rich and honored men, and thought of nothing but robbery, slaughter, and oppression."[91]

But the patricians had no need of the humanist's counsel (written in the 1430's). After nullifying the various fourteenth-century efforts to democratize Florentine government, they kept two powerful families under close surveillance, the Medici and the Alberti. They also set out to restrict the size of the oligarchy; and at the beginning of the fifteenth century the dominant po-

[91] *Historiarum florentini populi*, 3 vols. (Florentiae, 1855-1860), III, 8, "Id perpetuum documentum esse potest praestantibus in civitate viris, ne motum et arma in arbitrio multitudinis devenire patiantur: neque enim retineri possunt, cum semel inceperint fraenum arripere, et plus se posse intelligunt quia plures sunt. Cavenda vero maxime videntur principia seditionum inter primarios cives: ex illis enim ad ista devenitur. Monitoriam legem confitentur omnes pernitiosam destestandamque fuisse. Sed dum eam corrigere voluit Silvester Medix, vir ex famila nobili, ampla et locuplete, majorem in republica labem induxit: praeter propositum et enim credulitatem suam, egentes et opifices et infimae sortis homines facti sunt domini civitatis. Ita, dum paucis admonitis succurrere vult, familiam suam et omnes sui similes dignitate spoliavit, et temeritati multitudinis concitatae subjecit: neque enim finis erat effraenatarum voluntatum hominum egentium et facinorosum, qui arma tenentes, locupletum et honestorum hominum fortunis cupidissime inhiabant, nec aliud quam rapinas caedesque et pulsiones civium meditabantur."

litical faction, captained by men like Maso degli Albizzi, Niccolò da Uzzano and Rinaldo Gianfigliazzi, strove to reduce the council representation of the middle classes and to readmit the old noble families or *grandi* to some of the more coveted magistracies.[92]

The prolonged struggle against the parvenus naturally affected the political and social morality of upper-class Florence. Views were intensified and exaggerated, with the result that the older merchant families ended by believing that government, at least at the top, was their exclusive affair. The result in other ways was equally decisive, for surely there was no great difference in the mind between modes of social perception and of political identification. And so, to calculate the stature of an individual, to identify him socially, Florentines developed the habit of looking to his ancestors' political prominence (or obscurity), as well as to his own activity in public affairs. Thus there appears to be no major Florentine biography of the fifteenth century which fails to consider the subject's connections in government. It will help to look at various examples.

In his *Vita di Dante*, Lionardo Bruni quarrels with Boccaccio's biography of the poet because it slurs over the importance of his service to the Commune. Then, noting Dante's election to the Priorate, Bruni carefully observes that his companions in office were the *optimates* Palmieri Altoviti and Neri di Messer Jacopo degli Alberti.[93] Again, in his brief sketch of Petrarch's life, Bruni tells us: "Petrarch's father, Petracolo, lived in Florence and was often in the service of the Republic. On many occasions he was made an ambassador and charged with very serious missions. He also carried out other assignments involving important matters, and at one point he was made the scribe in charge of legislative records."[94]

[92] Dami, *Giovanni Bicci dei Medici*; Morelli, *Ricordi*, pp. 369ff.; Buonaccorso Pitti, *Cronica*, ed. A. B. della Lega (Bologna, 1905), pp. 135, 184ff.; ASF, *Lib. Fab.*, 47, f. 78r, where we find that a measure was introduced, asking "quod magnates restituantur ad certa offitia." The proposal was made in February 1402, at the peak of the Florentine struggle against Giangaleazzo Visconti. It was defeated in the Council of the People.

[93] *Leonardo Bruni Aretino: Humanistisch-Philosophische Schriften*, ed. with an introduction by Hans Baron (Leipzig-Berlin, 1928), pp. 53-54.

[94] *Ibid.*, p. 63, "Petracolo suo padre abitò in Firenze e fu adoperato assai nella Repubblica; perocchè molte volte mandato fu ambasciatore della città in gravissimi casi, molte volte con altre commissioni adoperato a gran fatti; ed in palagio un tempo fu scriba sopra le riformagioni diputato."

Antonio Manetti's life of the architect, Filippo di Ser Brunellesco, begins with an observation about Filippo's birth and ancestry and goes on at once to a statement about the family's civic dignities. The architect's father, for example, "looked after the affairs of soldiers and dealt with all the captains and condottieri of his time, but particularly with the main ones. Being their procurator, he requested and drew their allotments and salaries. . . . The Ten of War frequently employed him."[95] The biographer then notes that Filippo was related to the Spini and Aldobrandini families through his mother, whose brothers "customarily appeared in the chief dignities of the city. Filippo himself was in the Priorate in 1425. . . . Occasionally he also occupied other offices."[96]

Matteo Palmieri's biography of Niccolà Acciaiuoli starts with an assessment of the family's civic stature. The early chiefs of the Acciaiuoli clan, he says, migrated from Brescia to Florence, where the family, "growing in numbers and power, became so distinguished, owing to their conduct and virtues, that they were great and much honored not only in Florence, but in Sicily as well."[97] Of Niccolà's immediate background, Palmieri noted that his father enjoyed "the supreme honor of the Priorate many times."[98]

The practice of including statements about office and public life in the total assessment of a man's social position is clearly shown in Alessandra Strozzi's first printed letter to her son Filippo in Naples. Filippo's sister, Catherine, had just been engaged to Marco Parenti: "First I want to say that by the grace of God we've promised our Catherine to the son of Parente di Pier Parente, a twenty-five year old youth of good family and an only

[95] *Vita di Filippo di Ser Brunellesco*, ed. E. Toesca (Firenze, 1927), pp. 3-4, "fece fatti di soldati, generalmente di tutti e nostri capitani e condottieri, che furono nel suo tempo e massime de' principali; ed era loro procuratore, e sollecitava e traeva loro stanziamenti e paghe. . . . Fu adoperato molto dallo Ufficio de' Dieci della Balìa."

[96] *Ibid.*, p. 5, "e per ogni lato sono usi avere ed hanno tutte l'onoranze della città. E questo Filippo fu de' Priori nel 1425. . . . E così ebbe degli altri magistrati che occorrevano pe' tempi."

[97] *La vita di Niccolà Acciaioli*, printed in G. B. Ubaldini, *Istoria della casa degli Ubaldini* (Firenze, 1588), p. 143, "Dove crescendo in famiglia e in facultà, vennero a tanto, mediante le virtù, e portamenti loro, che non pure in Firenze erano grandi, e honoratissimi, ma ancora in Cicilia."

[98] *Ibid.*, p. 144, "ebbe il supremo honore del Priorato più volte."

son. Rich, sober, and conscientious, he owns a silk manufactory, and the family plays a certain part in the affairs of state, for the father recently served in the executive council. She is to have a dowry of 1000 florins."[99]

The assumptions here are consistent with certain observations in Poggio's dialogue on the nature of nobility. The characters of the dialogue, Niccolò Niccoli and Lorenzo di Giovanni de' Medici, agree that nobility (i.e., supreme social rank) in Florence is commonly assumed to combine three factors: old wealth, excellence of blood (i.e., distinguished lineage), and a record of service in public office.[100] In the passage quoted, Alessandra was manifestly stressing money, trade, and office. Apparently, however, Marco Parenti's lineage was not all she had desired, for she went on to tell her son that a marriage of greater "gentility" could have been arranged for Catherine; but this had required a dowry of 1400 or 1500 florins, "which would have been my undoing and yours."[101]

We must turn next to another aspect of public life and social rank.

The State Archives of Florence contain numerous business diaries dating from the fourteenth to the sixteenth centuries which in many cases conscientiously record the various offices held by the keeper of the diary or by members of his family.[102] It is a well-known fact that these diaries were primarily intended as a permanent record of commercial and property transactions.[103] Suits at law were so common that frequently, and without much warning, men were summoned before special tribunals or

---

[99] Strozzi, *Lettere*, pp. 3-4, "E'n prima t'avviso come, per grazia di Dio, abbiano allogata la nostra Caterina al figliuolo di Parente di Pier Parenti, ch'è giovane da bene e vertudioso, ed è solo, e ricco, e d'età d'anni venticinque, e fa bottega d'arte di seta; e hanno un poco di stato, ch'è poco tempo che'l padre fu di Collegio. E si gli do di dota fiorini mille."

[100] *De Nobilitate*, in *Opera* (Basilae, 1538), pp. 66-68.

[101] *Lettere*, p. 4, "Essi trovato da metterla in maggiore istato e più gentilezza, ma con mille quattrocento o cinquecento fiorini; ch'era il disfacimento mio e vostro."

[102] Fifteenth-century examples: *ASF, Carte Strozz., 2a serie,* 9, f. 7v; 16, ff. 7r, 9r, 20v, 24v; *Carte Strozz., 4a serie,* 564, ff. 24r-25r; *Carte Strozz., 5a serie,* 146; 1461, f. 73v.

[103] Angelo Fabroni, *Laurentii Medicis Magnifici Vita* (Pisa, 1784), II, 5; Gino Corti, "Consigli," p. 119; Sapori, "La cultura del mercante medievale italiano," *Studi*, p. 289.

courts, where they were expected to produce papers from their private accounts.[104] These accounts were kept with family notarial papers pertaining to wills, sworn testimonies, acts of emancipation, statements of commercial partnership, and marriage contracts. According to Leon Battista Alberti, one member of his clan so valued personal and family papers that he forbade even his wife to go near them. They were kept in his study under lock and key, "almost as if they had been holy or religious."[105]

Just as the record of marriages, births, and deaths in business diaries was a family chronicle, so entries regarding appointments to office were the chronicle of a man's career in public life. This meant that the ruling families (for by and large theirs are the extant diaries) could normally obtain an account of their administrative traditions and their place in the history of the Commune. They had only to look through the family papers. The same account was also a testament of their position in Florentine society, where political pre-eminence and high social rank, as we shall see, occasionally appeared indistinguishable.

When private papers were inadequate or incomplete, the sketch of a family's political history was sometimes obtainable from other sources. One such source was the historical chronicle, exemplified in the works of Compagni, Villani, Stefani, Cavalcanti, and others. The writings of Giovanni and Matteo Villani, for example, were very widely read, and in fifteenth-century Florence scores of ruling families owned their own copies of the Villani chronicle.[106] Here a great political and bureaucratic family, like the Albizzi or Ricci, might follow the exploits of their forebears.

[104] See e.g., the *Ricordanze* (1412-1436) of Antonio de'Rustichi, *ASF, Carte Strozz.*, *2a serie*, 11, f. 24v, "Richordanze questo di 5 di giugnio 1420 a ore 2 di notte che giovanni mio fratello mi diede petizione nel palagio de nostri signiori per farmi de grandi sanza niuna ragione ma solo affine di volermi rubare" etc. Antonio was a money-changer. The dispute concerned conflicting inheritance claims.

[105] *Della famiglia* (Pellegrini-Spongano ed.) p. 346, "sempri tenni le scritture non per le maniche de' vestiri, ma serrate, et con suo ordine allogate nel mio studio quasi come cosa sacrata et religiosa."

[106] The National Library of Florence has numerous copies. Following are nine examples. Three were in the possession of the Strozzi; the others belonged to the Gaddi, Mazzinghi, Banchi, Buontempi, Tornaquinci, and Albizzi families. See *BNF, Mss.* ii, iii, 78, 79, 80, 81, 82; also *Inventari dei manoscritti delle biblioteche d' Italia* (Firenze, 1898), pp. 79, 80, 81, 86.

But better than the chronicles for precision about political personnel were the *prioristi*, parchment lists of the Priorate, also in the possession of many ruling families.[107] The *prioristi* often contained marginalia, chronicle material, and political commentary. One of the Republic's most authoritative statesmen of the first quarter of the fifteenth century, Niccolò da Uzzano, appears to have kept a *priorista* in his private study.[108] Hence he could make no mistake about who was or was not a political upstart, who did or did not belong to the older group of ruling families: his *priorista* held a perfect record of the families which had appeared in the chief magistrature ever since 1282, the year of its founding. Niccolò was the man who in 1426 attached a series of political verses to the walls of the Palazzo della Signoria, calling for a palace revolution and a reduction in the political power of the *gente nuova*.[109]

The difference between social and political pre-eminence was not always clearly discernible. Whether rich or relatively poor, well-connected political figures were frequently in the public eye. One contemporary noted that their behavior could not be concealed "because there are too many eyes at their shoulders. Anyone who does well wins merit, but whoever does badly is discovered, corrected, and punished."[110] With his customary acrid succinctness, Cosimo de' Medici once remarked that when returning from an office in the Florentine dominion, if a man was asked where he had been, "it was a good sign, for nothing [bad] had been heard about him."[111] A primer of conduct, addressing Florentine merchants abroad, warned: "always speak well of those who rule the Commune: but don't speak badly of the

[107] E.g., ASF, Mss., 222; Carte Strozz., 2a serie, 100, 101, 102, 103, 104, 105. Priorista 100 belonged to the Buonaccorsi and Tornabuoni families; 105 belonged to the Nelli. The others are unidentified. The Riccardiana and National libraries in Florence also have *prioristi*.

[108] Walter Bombe, *Nachlass-Inventare des Angelo da Uzzano und des Lodovico di Gino Capponi* (Leipzig-Berlin, 1928), p. 16.

[109] ASF, Inventario Peruzzi-Medici, 231, ff. 262r-264r.

[110] Dati, *L'Istoria*, p. 170, "e chi fa bene n'acquista il merito, e chi fa male tosto è manifesto, e punito e corretto e gastigato."

[111] Recorded by Poliziano, *Angelo Polizianos Tagebuch: 1477-1479*, ed. A. Wesselski (Jena, 1929), p. 96, "era buon segno; perchè non s'era di lui sentito nulla."

others, as they could rise to power and you would be thought neither a friend of theirs nor of their government."[112]

The above quotations reveal that conversation in Florence was intensely concerned with politics and political personalities. Giovanni Cavalcanti's "histories," for example, are a mélange of commentaries on the events of his time. They faithfully reflect the politicized climate of those years. Alessandra Strozzi's letters are studded with observations about the relative prominence or authority of various Florentine statesmen. A similar interest appears in the letters of the notary, Ser Lapo Mazzei, in the chronicles of Giovanni Morelli and Buonaccorso Pitti, and in the practice of inserting political notes into the private business diaries of the age. Even distance could not put an end to political controversy among Florentines far from home. Thus, in 1406 two Florentine ambassadors were charged with interrogating Florentine merchants in Naples. They were to cross-examine the merchants about the slanderous information which one, Bartolommeo di Lapo Corsi, had sent to his father in Florence about "that noble man, our trusted and very dear citizen, Niccolò da Uzzano."[113] Since politics, therefore, was evidently so passionate a theme in the conversation of Florentines, appointment or election to office in Florence must have carried a distinction and prominence such as was not normally found in other *milieux.*

If participation in public life was essential to rank and high estate in 1390, it was still more essential in 1460. Between these dates, the terminal points of our study, an accelerating tribute was paid to the social import of public office. It will not be easy to account for this acceleration; and the difficulty is in our perspective. From a distance of five centuries the social attitudes of 1390 and 1460 appear more alike than different, whatever form they may have taken in their own time; nevertheless, the direction of change may be indicated.

To meet the needs of an expanding dominion, offices in Flor-

---

[112] Paolo da Certaldo, p. 89, "In ogni terra che vai o che stai, dì sempre bene di que' che reggono il Comune; e degli altri non dire però male, però che potrebboro montare in istato, e non t'avrebboro per amico di loro né di loro stato."

[113] ASF, *Legazioni e Commissarie,* 3. f. 69r, "il nobile huomo e carissimo e fidato nostro cittadino Niccholo da Uzzano." The ambassadors were Messer Bartolommeo Popoleschi and Giovanni di Bicci de' Medici.

ence multiplied and their functions became more complicated during the whole first half of the fifteenth century.[114] Although these changes went hand in hand with the entry of a few new families into the upper levels of government, the absolute size of the oligarchy did not increase. On the contrary, from 1382 onward periodic reforms gradually reduced the number of ruling houses: while new families were occasionally taken into the oligarchy, many more of the older type were expelled from government or banished from Florence.[115] The events of 1434 amply illustrate this. After Cosimo de' Medici's triumphant repatriation, dozens of old families were politically liquidated and numerous individuals were exiled.[116] In 1458 Luca Pitti, with the tacit approval of Cosimo de' Medici, again reduced the number of citizens eligible to hold public office.[117] The same year a vigorous campaign was started to readjust the powers of various offices.[118] In some cases the duties of two or more offices were united; in others the term of office was considerably extended, thereby increasing administrative continuity and stability. These reforms were surpassed by another change of profound importance: a new legislative body was created, the Council of One Hundred. It was given full powers over taxation, the hiring of troops, and the approval of the lists (*squittini*) of all who might be eligible to hold office in Florence.[119] This council came under the swift domination of the Medicean faction and all but com-

[114] Cf. Demetrio Marzi, *La cancelleria della repubblica fiorentina* (Rocca S. Casciano, 1910); but see especially the developing pattern of office in *ASF, Tratte*, 66, 67, 78-80.

[115] Francesco Guicciardini, *Storie fiorentine*, ed. R. Palmarocchi (Bari, 1931), pp. 3-5.

[116] See the lists of exiles in Cavalcanti, *Istorie*, I, 600-603; also A. Gelli, "L'esilio di Cosimo de' Medici," *A.S.I.*, x (1882), 53-96, 149-169.

[117] Domenico Buoninsegni, *Storie della città di Firenze* (Firenze, 1637), p. 21; G. B. Mecatti, *Storia cronologica della città di Firenze*, 2 vols. (Napoli, 1755), II, 433; and Filippo de' Nerli, *Commentari* (—, 1728), pp. 48-49.

[118] *ASF, Tratte*, 81, ff. 9v, 16v, 17v-18v, 42r, 48r, 50r/v. Following are some of the changes. The functions of the *Decem Libertatis* and *Regulatores* were united; the office of the *Camerarii Camerae* was discontinued, and the Six of Arezzo and Pistoia were suspended. The terms of the *Conservatores Legum* and the *Magistri Turris* were increased from six months to a year, that of the *Octo Custodiae* from two to four months and then to six.

[119] Vincenzo Ricchioni, *La costituzione politica di Firenze ai tempi di Lorenzo il Magnifico* (Siena, 1913), pp. 39ff.

pletely undermined the two traditional legislative bodies, the Councils of the People and Commune. Still dissatisfied, the oligarchy in 1480 set up the powerful and highly exclusive Council of Seventy.[120]

It is evident that while these measures may have increased the efficiency of Florentine government, they also transformed the ruling class into a ruling caste. That men of humble birth occasionally entered minor administrative and gubernatorial posts, even the Signoria and the *Dieci di Balìa*, was of no consequence for the distribution of power in Florence. On the whole, the ruling families retained the key offices, and increasingly valued them just because they were increasingly difficult to get. This trend extended the power of some offices (e.g., the *Octo Custodiae*), while others suffered a corresponding loss. The concentration of power in fewer hands enhanced the importance and social brilliance of the leading magistracies, and thus, in the period from 1390 to 1460, these offices became more and more essential to the achievement of high social rank.

3. FAMILY: THE SIGNIFICANCE OF A TRADITION

The family in fifteenth-century Florence stands between the individual and society. It mediates and determines his relations with the world at large, for he confronts the social system conditioned by his family's position in society, and his place in public life is governed by the political place of his family.[121]

This is the underlying theme of this section. On it we shall build our account of the nature and importance of family traditions.

In Florence, the man who distinguished himself reflected honor on his family; behaving disgracefully, he disgraced it. By the same token, he could not be born into an illustrious family without concretely sharing in its distinction. He also shared its dishonors and shame. The great fourteenth-century lawyer, Bartolus, is said to have observed that "In Florence and throughout Tuscany liability for a crime committed by one of their member

---

[120] *Ibid.*, pp. 166ff.

[121] Cf. Alberti, *Della famiglia*; and Nino Tamassia, *La famiglia italiana nei secoli decimoquinto e decimosesto* (Milano, 1910), pp. 111-119.

was imposed upon members of the family group. Furthermore, each individual's party affiliation was presumed to be that of the family group or its head."[122] Finding himself legally embroiled in Rome or Venice, the simple Florentine artisan could make no effective appeal to Florence, owing to his political and social obscurity. But men with names like Soderini, Castellani, Peruzzi, Strozzi, or Guicciardini enjoyed the benefits of a family tradition, and traveled from one side of Italy to the other with the knowledge that their families would, if necessary, come to their aid through the diplomatic channels of the Florentine Republic.[123]

The individual who stood out in public affairs bound his family to the state in a special and close relation. Often, indeed, family affairs and affairs of state were so closely bound that they tended to merge. Before Pisa surrendered to Florence in 1406, the Florentines had to guarantee that they would live up to their promises by turning a group of hostages over to Messer Giovanni Gambacorta. The hostages, twenty youths, were the scions of leading Florentine families, the sons in fact of the architects of Florentine foreign policy.[124]

Although the prominent Florentine family was not unique in deeply committing itself to political affairs,[125] it seems to have had distinctive traits. For one thing, its intense political character was not diminished by the fact that its members often displayed a wide range of interests. Two typical families of the upper class will exemplify this.

The Corbinelli and Martelli families belonged to the inner

[122] Anna T. Sheedy, *Bartolus on Social Conditions in the Fourteenth Century* (New York, 1942), p. 51.

[123] The Signoria's correspondence abounds with evidence of this. Normally, Florentine ambassadors were ordered to exercise pressure on officials or princes in Naples, Rome, Milan, Venice, or elsewhere, in efforts to secure favorable decisions for Florentines involved in litigation abroad. See *ASF, Leg. Comm.*, 1-14, passim.

[124] Gino Capponi, *Commentari dell' acquisto di Pisa*, in *Cronichette antiche*, ed. D. M. Manni (Firenze, 1733), pp. 268-269. Following are ten of the twenty hostages: Meo di Messer Vanni Castellani, Niccolaio di Ugo degli Alessandri, Cosimo de' Medici, Jacopo di Messer Rinaldo Gianfigliazzi, Luca di Maso degli Albizzi, Neri di Gino Capponi, Tommaso di Bartolomeo Corbinelli, Giuliano di Niccolò Davanzati, Palla di Nofri Strozzi, and Gherardo di Messer Filippo Corsini.

[125] A similar situation prevailed, for example, in Venice, Pisa, Genoa, Lucca, Siena, and Perugia.

circle of the oligarchy.[126] In the first quarter of the fifteenth century there were five Corbinelli brothers and nine Martelli. Some of the brothers, cleaving to their traditions, deeply involved themselves in politics. In each case, however, the family's "allotment" of leading offices (e.g., *Gonfaloniere di Giustizia* or a seat in the *Decem Baliae*) tended to go to one of the brothers only.[127] The others went into the cloth trade or banking, and occasionally one resided abroad. Giovanni di Niccolò Martelli, for instance, seems to have spent years in Spain. Antonio Corbinelli, on the other hand, at times invested money in commercial enterprise, but he was mainly interested in the Graeco-Roman literary classics; indeed, in the 1420's he owned one of the greatest collections of classical codices then in existence.[128] Another Martelli, Domenico, was a doctor of jurisprudence. He lectured for a time at the University of Bologna and later became an important Florentine diplomat. But despite the diversity of their interests, each of the brothers was perforce a political individual. There was nothing strange in this: the necessity confronted all men of the upper class. At this social level, as we have said, the political action of the individual tended to implicate his family;[129] for him, or for a brother, son, or nephew, to refuse this responsibility was both dangerous and foolish. The folly lay in the fact that the man who provoked the spite of the oligarchy or of a powerful house exposed his own family to persecution or disfavor; the danger was in being subject to grinding taxation, exclusion from public office, the rejection of private petitions, or a costly vulnerability in the law courts. Clearly it behooved a man to take an

[126] L. Martines, "Addenda to the Life of Antonio Corbinelli," *Rinascimento*, VIII, 1 (June 1957), 3-19; Martines, "La famiglia Martelli e un documento sulla vigilia del ritorno dall' esilio di Cosimo de' Medici (1434)," *A.S.I.*, CXVII, 1 (1959), 29-43; see also Pompeo Litta, *Martelli di Firenze*, in his *Famiglie celebri italiane* (Torino and Milano, 1819-1888). The Corbinelli were a thirteenth-century family; the Martelli entered public life for the first time in the 1340's.

[127] Usually the eldest.

[128] See App. I, no. 11; also Rudolf Blum, *La biblioteca della Badia fiorentina e i codici di Antonio Corbinelli* (Città del Vaticano, 1951).

[129] One of the best examples in print of the way whole families were dragged into grave political and legal difficulties is given by Buonaccorso Pitti, *Cronica*, pp. 165-177. Even the pope was brought into the clash between the Pitti on the one hand and the Ricasoli and Peruzzi on the other.

interest in politics, but even then disaster was sometimes unavoidable. In 1411, when the oligarchy struck out at the Alberti clan for the third time, once more alleging a plot, it is difficult to see what might have been done to save the innocent. Citizen after citizen stood up in the executive councils, calling for the expulsion in perpetuity of the families of the conspirators: "Let all the Alberti be banished from the city." "Exile all their children and descendants." "Forbid even their women to live in the family houses." "No Guelf families related to them should be allowed to buy their houses."[130]

Our theme is that responsibility in the patrician household was collective: all members of the family, whether they wished it or not, were associated with its reputation and political traditions. Yet there were significant departures from this system of "tribal" honor and guilt: the most remarkable fifteenth-century example involves the Albizzi family. When Rinaldo, one of the most impassioned enemies of the Medici, was banished in 1434, his brother Luca was permitted to remain in Florence, where, surprisingly enough, he even continued to enjoy the Republic's leading dignities. He was given numerous diplomatic assignments and in 1442 held the supreme executive office, Standard-bearer of Justice, a post for which Messer Rinaldo himself was never drawn.[131] Luca's case, however, aroused the wonder of his contemporaries.[132]

Since the nature of the upper-class family was such that each of its members gave moral qualities to the whole, and the whole to the individual, no man in this order of society could easily free himself from what was commonly supposed about his family. Consequently, contrary to one of Jacob Burckhardt's themes, the prominent Florentine did not enter society, nor circulate in it, as a "free individual," hurt or elevated purely by his own vices or talents. He was too closely associated with and rooted in his family background. Did it follow, therefore, that

[130] *ASF, Consulte e Pratiche*, 41, ff. 27v-29r, 30r, 47v. Dates: August 1411 to October 1411.

[131] *ASF, Priorista Mariani*, I, f. 50r.

[132] Cf. Messer Giuliano Davanzati's oration in Cavalcanti, *Istorie*, II, 182-183. Giuliano was one of the foremost legists and statesmen of his time. See App. I, no. 20.

the man who came from a family of no importance was freer? Certainly not. For generally he could make no social or political claims: he had no environmental resources. Hence he abided in his obscurity, free to move only in the politically impotent world to which he was born.[133]

The first requirement of the family type which enjoyed distinguished social rank was that it be old and established. Two factors produced this trait: wealth and public office, or better, honorably-acquired wealth and a long record of participation in the political affairs of the city. At the beginning of the fifteenth century, most of the dominant families could lay claim to these qualifications. They had entered the Priorate for the first time during its earliest years—the 1280's, 1290's, and the first years of the fourteenth century;[134] or else they were connected by marriage with houses which had figured in public affairs even before the establishment of the Priorate. Furthermore, the wealth of these families antedated their rise to political distinction and often went back to the middle years of the thirteenth century. Leon Battista Alberti gloried in this aspect of his family history: "I say that the Alberti house is to be praised because for two hundred years and more it has never been so poor that it was not reputed to rank among the richest families of Florence. Both in the memory of our elders and in our family papers you will find that the Alberti were always great and famous merchants with distinguished reputations."[135] But as we have said, the Alberti fell out with the ruling faction at the end of the fourteenth century, and although their civic eminence was partly restored after 1434, they never regained their political power of old.

This is the place to analyze a factor repeatedly mentioned but not yet discussed—tradition.

[133] There were exceptions to this from time to time, as we shall later point out in some detail.

[134] Consider, e.g., the Albizzi, Canigiani, Altoviti, Ardinghelli, Soderini, Peruzzi, Corsini, Corbinelli, Guadagni, Capponi, and Spini. See *ASF, Mariani*, I, 9r, 10r, 15r, 20r, 49r, 88r, 91r, 151r, 172r, 202r, 212r.

[135] *Della famiglia*, p. 212, "Dico si può gloriare la casa Alberta che da dugento et più anni in qua mai fu essa si povera, ch'ella non fusse fra lle famiglie di Firenze riputata ricchissima. Né a memoria de' nostri vecchi, né in nostre domestiche scripture troverete che in casa Alberta non sempre fussono grandissimi e famosissimi, veri, buoni e interi mercatanti."

Neither wealth alone, nor civic eminence alone, normally sufficed to attain high social rank. The two, wealth and office, had to be combined; and being combined across a long enough period of time, they produced an entirely new factor—a family tradition. By dint of long association with the Republic's major offices, and by maintaining a solid position either as great land-owners or in the area of banking and international trade, a family developed its specific reputation and authority in the city. This we call its tradition.

In the early fifteenth century, the Fortini (a branch of the Orlandini) were well-known as notaries, landowners, and merchants.[136] Having a talent for dealing with administrative questions, they developed a powerful bureaucratic tradition. The Medici house, renowned in business circles, enjoyed the special allegiance of the lower classes.[137] The Panciatichi, on the other hand, once scorned as usurers, were respected and feared because they combined vast landed wealth and finance capital with an illustrious feudal past.[138] By contrast with the Medici, the Albizzi and Ricasoli were deemed to be intransigeant oligarchs, along with the Peruzzi and Castellani. A final example: the Pandolfini, a family of prominent spice and silk merchants and landowners, were associated with traditions of political caution, wise counsel, and skill in diplomacy.[139]

But in what did the essential strength or virtue of a family tradition consist? The social standing conferred by a tradition could not be achieved through wealth or public office alone. A tradition signified antiquity and stability; it denoted a certain recognized devotion to the Republic. It was associated with re-liability, an excellent practical virtue both in politics and social life. Let an upstart—merchant or *scioperato*—exercise the authority of a given office with more severity than prudence, and he soon ran up against the resistance or vindictive action of the ruling families. A family tradition, on the other hand, permitted

[136] *ASF, Tratte*, 78-80, passim; Cavalcanti, *Istorie*, II, 400; Marzi, p. 160.
[137] Rado, pp. 188-189; Cavalcanti, *Istorie*, I, 502.
[138] See this chapter, Part 5.
[139] *ASF, Leg. Comm.*, 5, ff. 37r, 42v, 62r-63v, 68r; 6, ff. 36r-v, 68v; Strozzi, *Lettere*, p. 81; Gutkind, *Cosimo de' Medici* (Oxford, 1938), p. 64; Alberti, *Della tranquilità dell' animo*, in *Opere volgari*, I, 7.

the individual to invest his administrative and executive posts with a special or higher authority.

Since the triumphant ideal of the old family produced various attendant fashions, it will pay to consider the one which best reveals the growing importance assigned to the claims of old lineage.

In the later fourteenth century, when Florence gradually came under the regenerate domination of the older merchant families, one concomitant feature was a growing and intense concern with family genealogies. Thus, the opening paragraph of Giovanni Morelli's memoirs announces: "Since this entry book hasn't been used yet, it occurred to me, Giovanni di Pagolo di Bartolomeo di Morello di Giraldo di Ruggieri, or rather Gualtieri, di Calandro di Benamato d'Albertino de' Morelli, to write about our ancient condition and ancestry, so far as I can remember, and also about our current and coming situation. I'll do this in order to pass the time and especially to let my sons and relatives know something about our origins and early condition. *For everyone today pretends a family background of great antiquity,* and I want to establish the truth about ours."[140]

We find a similar theme in Buonaccorso Pitti's diary. He began to record his memoirs in 1412, "in order to leave a lasting account of what I have heard and discovered about our antiquity and about all our relatives both ancient and modern."[141] An early example of this genealogical preoccupation appears in the domestic chronicle of the lawyer, Donato Velluti, who wrote in the late 1360's.[142] Velluti's interest was shared by another lawyer of the period, the prominent Florentine statesman, Lapo di Castiglionchio. In a fascinating letter to one of his sons, written in the early 1370's, Lapo shows that he had leafed through the

[140] *Ricordi*, p. 81, "Perchè in questo libro non è scritto per innanzi alcuna cosa, m'è venuto voglia, cioè a me Giovanni di Pagolo di Bartolomeo di Morello di Giraldo di Ruggieri, ovvéro Gualtieri, di Calandro di Benamato d'Albertino de' Morelli, iscrivere di nostra nazione e condizione antica e che di noi seguiterà insino potrò e mi ricorderò; e ciò per passare tempo e che i nostri alcuna cosa ne sappino, perchè oggi ogni catuno si fonda in grande antichità; e però vo' mostrare la verità della nostra." Italics mine.

[141] Pitti, p. 7, "per fare memoria di quello ch'io o potuto trovare e sentire di nostra antichità progiènia e de' parentadi nostri antichi e moderni."

[142] *Cronica domestica*, pp. 3ff.

domestic papers of the Castiglionchi, clearly in search of the family's origins and early condition.[148]

As we move into the fifteenth century, the self-conscious study of family trees grows at a rapid pace, until it seems to become the major "historical" interest of upper-class Florence.[144] This throws light on the Florentine passion for family tombs, since we may suppose that they served, apart from their obvious function, as the tangible signs of a family's physical continuity. Seen in this light, we can understand why the ancestral crypt often set off angry disputes between different families over questions of burial priority on church sites. In these disputes, recourse to family papers was one of the ordinary procedures in the gathering of proof. The disputants also turned to parish records and early traces of armorial bearings on the site of the crypt.[145]

The fashionable and enduring "obsession" with genealogies in upper-class Florence was a landmark on the way to the aristocratic society of the sixteenth century. Whatever this passion was to become under the principate, in pre-Laurentian Florence the esteem for antiquity of family stock was already a major ingredient in the formation of a new class consciousness.

4. MARRIAGE

In fifteenth-century Florence the man of good family ("famiglia da bene") normally contracted marriage with a woman of his own class. This happened with enough frequency to warrant our viewing marriage as an aid in the social assessment of individual Florentines. Why marriage was class-bound (apart from the obvious reasons) it will not be difficult to see.

It has been shown that in the dominant orders of society young

[143] *Epistola*, pp. 31ff.

[144] Other examples: *BNF, Cod. Panciatichiano*, 368, being the *ricordi* of the Valori family; *BRF, Cod.*, 1885, ff. 1r-6v (deals with the origins and development of the Tornaquinci family); *ASF, Acquisti e doni*, 7 (the *ricordi* of Matteo Palmieri), f. 132r; and *ASF, Carte Strozz., 4a serie*, 564 (the *ricordi* of Niccolò Busini), f. 8v, "Richordanza faro questo di primo d'aghosto anno deto [1408] de miei antinati inchominciando del mio bisavolo" etc.

[145] *ASF, Carte Strozz., 4a serie*, 17 bis (the *ricordi* of Marco and Piero Parenti). Folio 70v contains an account of Marco's dispute with Rinaldo di Piero Ciliago over a crypt in the church of S. Croce. The judgment awarding the case to Marco was passed down on 23 August 1473.

women were expected to have a substantial dowry. As a result, no one from this social sector was likely to give his daughter in marriage to a man who could not equal, complement, or otherwise surpass her own background. Similarly, if a wealthy young man married a girl with a small dowry, he was clearly seeking old family traditions or relatives with a distinguished record in public office. In such marriages, accordingly, although one social attribute had been used to procure another, the participants successfully remained within the dominant social strata.

The decisive factor in marriage, as practised among Florentines of the middle and upper classes, was their supposition that it was a political and social alliance between families, not merely a conjugal union between two persons. This alliance was assumed to bind the fortunes of the two families in such a way that if one suffered a political or economic reversal, the other also might be affected, or in any case called in to lend assistance. A few passages from Giovanni Morelli's memoirs will underline this supposition: "[When you decide to marry] Think of this first of all: don't demean yourself with a social inferior; try, instead, to improve your condition, though not to such an extent that she would want to be the husband and make you the wife. See that you marry into a family of prosperous merchants, a family composed of good citizens who do not abuse their standing by behaving arrogantly. Aside from being of old stock in the city, they should also be Guelfs who are honored by the Commune and who are free of all stains such as those associated with treason, robbery, murder, or illegitimacy. . . . Let them not be dogs about money, but rather people who use a tempered politeness. Be sure that your betrothed is well-born, that her mother comes from a family of substance and has honorable relatives."[146]

The diarist repeatedly returned to this theme: "strive to marry

[146] *Ricordi*, p. 208, "E a questo abbi riguardo primamente: di non ti avvilire, ma piúttosto t'ingegna d'innalzarti, non però per modo che ella volesse essere il marito e tu la moglie; ma guarda d'imparentarti con buoni cittadini, i quai non sieno bisognosi e sieno mercatanti e non usino maggiorie. Sieno antichi nella città tua, sieno onorati dal Comune e sieno Guelfi, e non abbino alcuna macula, come di traditore o di ladro o di micidio o di bastardo discesi, o d'altri cose che sono di rimprovero e di vergogna . . . e che non sieno cani del danaio ma usino cortesia temperatamente. . . . Apresso, abbi riguardo ch'ella sia bene nata, di madre di gente da bene e di parentado onorevole."

into a family of well-liked, honorable, powerful citizens; and if there be someone in your district who can help you get ahead, lean on him." Or, "see to it that your father-in-law is a rich merchant, a Guelf of old Florentine stock with a certain share in public life, and a man who is both likable and dear to all." And again, "in marriage connect yourself with a Guelf family in government; it ought to be a powerful and trusted family, free of all scandal."[147]

Morelli returned again and again to these views about marriage because he himself had suffered from not having fully lived up to them. In 1395 he married into a distinguished banking family, the Alberti, who however had recently been expelled from political affairs. They were soon stigmatized with the charge of treason and were long to be subjected to the persecution of the oligarchy. According to Morelli's testimony, this marriage hurt his career in public life, undermined his contacts, and left him exposed, during a period of twenty years, to tax rates aimed at his ruin.

Apart from being an approximate index of social rank, marriage also served, as the Morelli citations show, as a means of social advancement and the consolidation of this advancement. At the beginning of the fifteenth century the Medici family had more than a century of experience in government, but they were not really old stock compared to the Adimari, Buondelmonti, Lamberti, Ricasoli, or other feudal families whose origins went back to the eleventh century and before. In addition, although Giovanni di Bicci de' Medici became an important figure in Florentine political life, he did not inherit his great wealth; it was mainly the product of his own industry in banking and commerce,[148] and so bore an appropriate relation to the accelerating

---

[147] *Ibid.*, "ingegnati d'imparentarti con buoni cittadini e amati e potenti; e se è nel tuo gonfalone chi ti possa atare e metterti innanzi, accostati a esso" (p. 253); "fa che'l parente tuo sia mercatante, sia ricco, sia antico a Firenze, sia guelfo, sia nello istato, sia amato da tutti, sia amorevole" (p. 264); "cioè fa che principalmente ne tuoi parentadi, come altrove s'è detto, tu t'appoggi a chi è nel reggimento e guelfo e potente e bene creduto e sanza macula" (p. 274).

[148] He seems to have got his training in the banking firm of a distant cousin, Vieri di Cambio de' Medici. For a time he "managed its Rome branch, until he established his own firm, at first with headquarters in

tempo of his political preferment. Apparently, therefore, with an eye to these factors and with a perfect sense of what was deemed important in Florence, the elder Medici arranged to have Cosimo married to a daughter of Giovanni de' Bardi, Count of Vernia, and Cosimo's brother, Lorenzo, to one of the Cavalcanti-Malespini girls, whose family also ranked among the distinguished nobility.[149] These alliances with very old Florentine stock strengthened the noble connections of the Medici, who were magnificently endowed with economic and political resources.

During the mid-fifteenth century, marriages in the family of Alessandra Strozzi were concluded only after extensive and meticulous inquiry into the social and political stature of the eligible families.[150] Since the men from this branch of the Strozzi were in exile at the time, they made the political question a major consideration in their marriage alliances. Several letters from Marco Parenti to his brother-in-law, Filippo Strozzi, indicate something about the kind of "research" that went into a marriage. Discussing a possible alliance between the Strozzi and either the Adimari or Tanagli families, Marco informed Filippo (then in exile in Naples) that the Adimari were older and more noble than the Tanagli, though the Tanagli compared favorably with the Canigiani. It was worth considering, however, that if the Adimari were nobler, the Tanagli were currently more prominent in public affairs. The Tanagli also had various relatives among the city's leading statesmen, members of the Alessandri, Guidetti, Ridolfi, and Vettori families. Finally, if civic prominence was a factor to be balanced against the appeal of more ancient and noble stock, money also continued to be a fundamental consideration. Consequently, Marco informed his brother-in-law that the Adimari offered a dowry of 1500 florins, the Tanagli offered a mere 1000 florins, while a third family,

---

Rome, which were transferred to Florence in 1397." Raymond de Roover, "New Interpretations of the History of Banking," in *Cahiers d'Histoire Mondiale*, II (1954), 46.

149 The Cavalcanti were a late twelfth-century family; the Bardi rose to prominence in the early thirteenth century. The Malespini, on the other hand, were old feudal nobility. See Giovanni Filippi, *L'Arte dei mercanti di calimala in Firenze* (Torino, 1889), pp. 187-188; also the *Historia antica di Ricordano Malespini* (Fiorenza, 1568), p. 75.

150 *Lettere*, pp. 4-5, 115, 120, 313, 447-451.

the Della Luna, unsuitable because they had powerful political enemies, promised 4500 florins.[151]

The practice of arranging a marriage between feuding families was not uncommon. In 1466, for example, when various well-known Florentines were exiled for plotting against Piero de' Medici's life, Luca Pitti formed "an alliance with Giovanni Torna-buoni, giving him his daughter as wife, and in consequence he was reprieved from exile."[152] More often, however, leading families contracted marriage alliances chiefly with an eye to increasing the extent and strength of their influence. Hence it is not surprising that upper-class marriages, above all the important ones, were a major topic of conversation in Florence. For they were truly an integral part of the subject of politics, than which nothing was more fervently discussed.

We must believe, then, that the oligarchy regarded ties of marriage with the greatest earnestness. In 1409, for example, three years after the Florentine conquest of Pisa, the Republic enacted a law which in practice, though not in principle, prevented marriages between Florentines and citizens of Pisa. The method used was direct and simple: a tax of 1000 florins was levied on any such marriage contract.[153] The intent of this tax was to help preserve a uniform Florentine treatment of all Pisans, who after all were a subject people. But to maintain a true uniformity of rule would have been impossible if the ruling families of Florence had been allowed to form marriage alliances with the Pisans at will.

Although the fifteenth century experienced, as we have said, some changes in the Florentine attitude towards the main components of social place, assumptions about marriage did not change. Throughout the century, with members of the upper classes at least, the type of marriage which prevailed was that

[151] *Ibid.*, pp. 395, 458.
[152] Luca Landucci, *A Florentine Diary*, tr. A. Jervis (London, 1927), p. 8. The Tornabuoni were closely related to the Medici by marriage.
[153] ASF, *Provv.*, 98; ff. 32v-33r. This law was rescinded a few years later, but I do not have the exact citation. To locate the subsequent *provvisione*, consult one of the eighteenth-century *spoglie* or the *Libri Fabarum* in the State Archives of Florence. 1000 florins was the value of four or five farms of medium size, or an investment large enough to keep five persons on its annual income. Cf. Ch. III.

aimed at greater social distinction or the consolidation of gains in rank.

5. IDEAL AND REALITY

We have seen that rank or place in Florentine society depended on four attributes: honorable wealth, public office, a family tradition, and a well-connected marriage. The more a family was endowed with these the loftier was its place in society.

Yet we must not let ourselves be entirely deceived by the attractions of the ideal type. It is true that when a house had the four attributes it realized a social ideal, but while some families could lay claim to the four parts of our ideal,[154] others—also prominent—could not. In the period from 1390 to 1460, dozens of important families could not meet the four qualifications. In many cases they attained their eminence by means of a special talent, or at any rate without being of old Florentine stock, wealthy, or even prominent in political affairs. Departures from the ideal sometimes involved the possession of critical skills, for example in law or in public speaking, and the omission of one or more of the basic attributes. We will therefore conclude this chapter with an account of certain families and individuals whose specific situations bring out the divergences between ideal and reality.

If we consider the Alberti family for a moment,[155] we find that although the different branches of this house suffered sharp political and economic setbacks in the early fifteenth century, thereby losing favor with their peers, they naturally did not lose their place in the upper class. Excluded from public office between 1393 and 1435, they were subjected to heavy taxation, forced to do without the diplomatic influence of Florence in distant commercial litigation, and exposed to discrimination in the Florentine courts such as the *Tribunale di Mercanzia*. These reversals limited their social mobility, most of all in matters of marriage and family alliances, where political ostracism was a

---

[154] E.g., in the early fifteenth century by some branches of the Acciaiuoli, Albizzi, Barbadori, Baroncelli, Corbinelli, Guicciardini, Peruzzi, Rucellai, Spini, Strozzi, and Tornabuoni.

[155] Luigi Passerini, *Gli Alberti di Firenze*, 2 vols. (Firenze, 1869).

major social handicap. Nevertheless, even the Alberti who lived in exile kept up their Florentine connections, and when the oligarchy was regrouped in 1434, the family returned to the political and social foreground. The old traditions of the Alberti served, after nearly half a century, to hold a place for them, but the members of the house never regained the key position which had been theirs during much of the fourteenth century. In addition, their political influence was greatly surpassed by families whose traditions were neither as old nor as brilliant: such, for example, were the Davanzati, Martelli, Niccolini, Pandolfini, Pitti, and Ridolfi. But if the Alberti traditions protected part of their political legacy, there were other families whose strong traditions and wealth were the very source of their political (and so in a sense social) handicaps. Two examples will suffice.

In the early eleventh century the Panciatichi were already a powerful feudal family with a fortress in the hills around Pistoia.[156] One branch of the family obtained Florentine citizenship in 1329. The branch which interests us was granted citizenship in 1376 and very soon became one of Florence's richest families.[157] The Florentine Panciatichi were great landowners, but they distinguished themselves in money-lending, banking, and international trade. According to their citizenship act of 1376, they were not to hold public office until after 1396. When the time came, however, they were not entered in the lists of eligibility for office. Later, they occasionally secured appointments to lesser posts, but they were systematically excluded from the chief magistracies during most of the fifteenth century.[158]

It would appear that the Panciatichi had no political power in in the city, but the appearance is misleading. Although discriminated against in the distribution of public offices, they exercised a certain influence in the legislative councils through

---

[156] Luigi Passerini, *Genealogia e storia della famiglia Panciatichi* (Firenze, 1858), pp. 2-3.

[157] *ASF, Prestanze*, 1999, arranged alphabetically by Christian name. The highest levy, 600 florins, was assigned to Messer Bartolommeo di Bandino Panciatichi. Date: 1403.

[158] *ASF, Tratte*, 80, ff. 132v, 397r, listing two offices held by Piero di Messer Bartolommeo Panciatichi. Two members of the family actually sat in the Priorate in 1483 and 1494.

relatives and friends. This is attested by the numerous private bills which the Republic enacted in their favor.[159] Indeed, the legislation favoring their petitions seems to be more impressive than that for any other family in the first half of the fifteenth century. In general, their petitions involved requests for tax indulgences or for the right to alienate large quantities of government securities. But appointing the Panciatichi to one of the city's key offices was another matter. Even their strategic marriages failed to overcome the opposition to their political ambitions.[160] They married into the Alberti and Medici families in the later fourteenth century, and in the early fifteenth they contracted marriages with the Albizzi, Capponi, and Peruzzi.[161] The pattern of these marriages rendered their political aspirations obvious to any informed Florentine. Subsequently, one of the Panciatichi, Piero di Giovanni, openly threw in his lot with the faction opposed to the Medici, and when the Medici returned from exile in 1434, Piero was permanently excluded from all participation in the affairs of state.

What kept the Panciatichi out of public office? They were immensely rich; they were great landowners and international bankers; they negotiated clever marriages; and although they could not claim descent from an old Florentine family, their illustrious Tuscan lineage was a matter of celebrity in the city. One explanation of their political failure presents itself: the traditions and antiquity of the Panciatichi house were so distinctive, and the Florentine branch of this clan connected with so many powerful and lawless Pistoian relatives, that had the family been permitted to occupy the chief Florentine offices, their marriage alliances and great wealth, combined with their feudal traditions, might have been such as to make the house a threat to the existing form of the Republic.[162] Perhaps this is why the

[159] *ASF, Lib. Fab.*, 45, f. 13v; 46, f. 139r; 47, ff. 88v, 133v; 48, ff. 23v, 72v, 158v; 49, f. 19r/v; 51, f. 28v.

[160] We can tell by their frequent appearance in the Councils of the People and the Commune that they had political ambitions. See *Tratte*, 147-150, passim under the Drago precinct of the S. Giovanni quarter.

[161] Litta, *Famiglie*, vol. xxviii (Milano, 1868), see tables iv and v. This is simply another edition of the Passerini work.

[162] On the clash in Pistoia between the Panciatichi and the Cancellieri see e.g. the Signoria's letter to the governors of Pistoia, *ASF, Leg. Comn.*, 3, f. 38v (19 November 1401).

oligarchy refused to let the family enjoy any of the city's leading dignities. Besides, it must have been public knowledge that the Panciatichi had good reason to be bitter:[163] successful as they were in obtaining favorable legislation, their exclusion from office must still have hampered their vast economic potential.[164] The political fame of families like the Uzzano, Strozzi, and Peruzzi was a tremendous advantage to the commercial and banking companies of the same names; we can imagine the confidence inspired by names associated with the might and policy of the Florentine state.

If the Panciatichi did not have all the attributes that ideally conferred illustrious social place,[165] there were other houses or their branches that did: for example, the Acciaiuoli, Alessandri, Corbinelli, Guicciardini, Guidetti, Medici, Soderini, Strozzi, Rucellai, and Tornabuoni. All were international merchants and great landowners. Continually found in the key offices, they were part of the hard core of the oligarchy. Allied by marriage with one another or with other principal families, they also claimed traditions of wealth and statesmanship that went back to the late thirteenth century. Yet upper-class Florence included scores of other families, many of which did not enjoy these distinctions. The designated families often exemplified the ideal. The reality, however, was sometimes different.

No single social attribute, such as riches or a well-connected marriage, could guarantee an entrée into public life. The political fortunes of the Panciatichi and Alberti illustrate this, and an even better example is afforded by the Rinuccini, one of the city's richest houses, bound by ties of marriages to some of the first families.[166]

---

[163] See *ASF, Catasto*, 715, f. 315r, where Antonio Panciatichi stated: "io rifutai laredita di mio padre perche tutto se n'era ito in chomune e truovomi senza alchuno traficho"; or *Catasto*, 624, f. 290v, where Bartolommeo di Gabbriello said: "o paghato dal 1430 in qua che mori ghabriello mio padre circha fior. 24,000 e pero non m'e rimaso piu danari di monte e truovomi povero e in famiglia."

[164] For the fullest reports of their enormous wealth: *Catasto*, 79, ff. 134v-147r. See the index of the same register for the folios containing the report of Giovanni di Messer Bartolommeo.

[165] Though one would be at a loss as to where they should be ranked, if not with the distinguished families of the upper class.

[166] Filippo di Cino Rinuccini, *Ricordi storici*, ed. G. Aiazzi (Firenze,

During the third quarter of the fourteenth century, Messer Francesco Rinuccini was one of the Commune's most active and authoritative statesmen. The family thus seems to have had an excellent start in politics. At the beginning of the 1380's Messer Francesco's sons began to appear in office, when suddenly they vanished from the political scene,[167] and the family did not reappear in public life until after 1434. Throughout the half century of their administrative and political eclipse, the Rinuccini were a large and wealthy house.[168] Bred to politics like their social equals, they produced their share of young men who asked nothing better than the right to enter public life. Cino di Messer Francesco, for example, who was prominent in the ruling body of one of the trade guilds, exhibited very strong political interests, but to no avail. Renowned though he was as an orator, he appeared in office only several times, on each occasion in the undistinguished Council of the People.[169]

The reasons for the political difficulties of the Rinuccini are obscure. Evidently they became the victims of political discrimination when they lost the favor of the oligarchy. In 1378 the Guelf faction, or ultra-conservative wing of the governing class, warned the Rinuccini not to accept any public offices. The same year Cino's eldest brother, Giovanni, was knighted by an act of "the People of Florence."[170] This action may have identified the family with a "democratic" current, or perhaps they had already made themselves odious to the "ultras" on other grounds, for in 1387 the Rinuccini were excluded from nearly all offices. Save for a brief interval (1391-1393), the ban remained in effect more than forty years, during which time neither money nor marriage, neither tradition nor ability, could win back or buy their former political position. Yet with only three of the four

---

1840). Aiazzi's introduction is a genealogy and history of the Rinuccini family.

[167] Their last fourteenth-century appearance in the Priorate was in 1381. They returned in 1437. See *ASF, Mariani*, III, f. 714r.

[168] See *ASF, Carte Pucci*, X, 4, genealogical charts of the Rinuccini family.

[169] Cavalcanti, *Istorie*, II, 464; also *ASF, Tratte*, 151, f. 128r; 152, ff. 8r, 26r.

[170] Rinuccini, *Ricordi storici*, pp. xxxiv-xxxv.

components of high social place, the Rinuccini continued to enjoy an exalted position in society.

If items such as wealth or a strategic marriage did not guarantee political preferment, neither did their absence necessarily denote political obscurity. Again, though having a family tradition was important for a career in public life, it was not absolutely essential. In such a case other virtues were necessary, as we shall see by examining the careers of a few other men.

Messer Tommaso Salvetti provides a good beginning. His father, a Pistoian by birth, seems to have received his notarial education in Florence, where he was probably active in minor administrative posts. Tommaso himself was born in 1390.[171] He took a doctorate in law at the University of Bologna, joined its faculty in 1415 and after a few years went on to practice in Florence. In 1420 he was sent to Siena on a diplomatic mission. For the next ten years he moved around in some of the lesser offices of the Republic, and in 1431 served as Florentine ambassador to Forlì.[172] He married in 1426 and again in 1435.[173] His first wife's name is unknown; the second one was Margherita di Antonio Portinari. Resident in the S. Giovanni quarter of the city, the Portinari were an old family and possessors of a proud commercial tradition; but in the early fifteenth century the branch to which Margherita belonged was not well-to-do. The year of his second marriage Tommaso made his début in the Priorate and returned for a second term in 1444.[174] He also served in the Republic's executive advisory councils, sitting either with the *Dodici Buonomini* or the *Sedici Gonfalonieri*, in 1436, 1446, 1450, 1452, and 1465.[175] Unlike his father, therefore, Tommaso rose to some of the state's highest dignities.

Since the Salvetti were not a Florentine family, the basis of Tommaso's political career cannot be sought in his social traditions. That the condition of the family had been modest in Pistoia is intimated by the fact that they there possessed only

[171] *Catasto*, 69, ff. 247v-251v.
[172] *Leg. Comm.*, 6, f. 111r; 9, f. 38r.
[173] ASF, *Carte Ancisa*, ii, f. 797r; NN, f. 427r.
[174] *Mariani*, vi, f. 1356r.
[175] ASF, *Mss.*, 265, f. 115r-v.

a few small properties.[176] Two of Tommaso's brothers, like his father, became practicing notaries, which also suggests something about their modest Pistoian situation; the family may well have inclined towards a specific profession in order to have the assurance of a livelihood. Once in Florence, their material situation seems to have improved. The tax levies of 1427 reveal that the Salvetti reported gross assets of 3773 florins. Subsistence deductions and 723 florins in debts left them with a deficit of 550 florins.[177] But as the catasto commission assigned an impost to them of 4.00 florins per levy, the Salvetti held a place in the lower reaches of the first 10 per cent income group. Apparently, then, they stood in a modest financial position compared with the families of the upper class.

Neither money nor family was behind Messer Tommaso's political distinction and alliance with the Portinari family. Furthermore, since he was active in public affairs by 1420, his marriage to the Portinari girl in 1435 was not the initial cause of his civic prominence. But if the marriage did not directly further his career, neither was he hindered by it, as indicated by the fact that he held his most important offices from 1435 onwards. We can only conclude that a major factor in his rise to eminence was his training in law. In the courts, in the venerable guild of judges and notaries, legislative councils and other public bodies, he came into contact with the chieftains of the city's first families. One of his good friends was the prominent Camaldolese friar and humanist with excellent connections, Ambrogio Traversari, who employed Tommaso's legal services.[178]

Tommaso's profession was a socially strategic one. For in social protocol and public honor the doctor of law was second only to the knight.[179] When a doctor of law was sent on a diplomatic mission together with a knight and merchant-banker, the knight preceded the legist in the conventions, but the legist always came before the merchant-banker, regardless of

---

[176] *Catasto*, 69, ff. 247v-251v.
[177] *Ibid.*
[178] See the monk's letter to Salvetti in Ambrogio Traversari, *Epistolae et orationes*, ed. Lorenzo Mehus (Florentiae, 1759), II, 263.
[179] Cf. Sheedy, pp. 149ff.

the latter's name—Albizzi or Medici, Strozzi or Uzzano. This formality was carefully observed by the Signoria in its correspondence with Florentine ambassadors.[180] And yet despite the dignity of Tommaso's profession, in weighing his career we must not discount the support of friends, the possible influence of the Portinari marriage, his family's notarial connections, and his own skill in extemporaneous oratory.

Less prominent as an office-holder than Messer Tommaso, though equally important in political circles, was Ser Filippo di Ser Ugolino Pieruzzi, a notary.[181] Born in 1388, Ser Filippo was the adopted son of a notary from Vertine (Tuscany) who distinguished himself in those departments of Florentine government requiring some legal skill. In 1427 Filippo's father submitted an inventory to the catasto commission, listing net assets of 2230 florins.[182] This sum put the family in the upper 5 per cent income group. In 1433, however, Filippo himself reported net assets of only 258 florins,[183] which put him in the class of petty shopkeepers. His taxable assets included a small farm, various land parcels, a house, and an unrented cottage. His residence, half of one of the old thirteenth-century towers ("uno mezzo torrione"), was not included among his assets. He also drew an income from his notarial practice and this too went untaxed. All told, therefore, Filippo Pieruzzi was a man of stable means, although the whole of his yearly income from notarial instruments and property was modest indeed, compared with the ordinary revenues of men in his political and social milieu.

Notwithstanding his modest fortune and obscure family background, Filippo's excellent education and skills, like his subsequent career in public life, allowed him to enjoy a good

[180] See e.g., *Leg. Comm.*, 2-4, passim. Letters are always addressed in the following order: to the knight, the legist, and the merchant. When a knight was also a legist, he was always called "miles et judex," even though he had received his doctorate long before being knighted. Finally, the pronoun *voi* was used with knights and *legum doctores*; *tu* was given to merchants.

[181] See the biography in Vespasiano da Bisticci, *Vite di uomini illustri del secolo XV* (Firenze, 1938), pp. 411ff.

[182] *Catasto*, 75, ff. 202v-204v. In lands alone Ser Ugolino had five farms, three vineyards, and various land parcels.

[183] *Catasto*, 494, ff. 159v-160v.

deal of social mobility (he never married). He studied under Chrysoloras, gained a good reading knowledge of classical Greek, collected a valuable library, and was very close to men like Antonio Corbinelli (see App. I, no. 11), Roberto de' Rossi, Niccolò Niccoli, and Ambrogio Traversari (App. I, no. 4). In the second and third decades of the century Filippo was one of the leading participants in the humanistic discussions that took place at Santa Maria degli Angeli, also frequented by Cosimo and Lorenzo de' Medici, Bartolommeo Valori, Franco Sacchetti, Leonardo Dati, Matteo Palmieri, and others. Filippo met other luminaries in the 1420's, when he served in a variety of public posts.[184] From 1429 to 1444 he was the officer in charge of the Republic's legislative records and lists of eligibility for public office. In time, knowledge of his integrity as an administrator spread and he came to be considered one of the city's leading civil servants. His reputation, however, annoyed and finally provoked a clique within the ruling faction. Hampered by his renowned incorruptibility, they decided to remove him from office. They had him cashiered on a series of trumped-up charges and permanently banished from Florence.[185]

The office Filippo lost in 1444, *Notaio delle Riformagioni*, was held before him by Ser Martino di Luca Martini, another notary whose family background betrays no governing traditions. The catasto of 1427 shows that he shared net assets of 3000 florins with two brothers.[186] By our calculations, the Martini family thus stood in the upper 5 per cent of the Florentine populace, although 3000 florins was not an impressive fortune in Ser Martino's political world, where from one-third to one-half this sum made up the ordinary dowry of a young woman. But despite the fact that Ser Martino had neither great wealth nor the support of a family tradition, his command of the chancellery on legislation made him one of the Republic's key political figures.[187]

---

[184] *Tratte*, 134, not paginated. See section on notaries, alphabetically arranged by Christian name. Filippo held at least ten notarial posts between 1412 and 1432.

[185] Cavalcanti, *Istorie*, ii, 194.

[186] *Catasto*, 79, being the *campione* for the Drago precinct of S. Giovanni. See the index in this register for the exact folios.

[187] Since the *Notaio delle Riformagioni* was in charge of the eligibility "purses," he was sometimes in a position to know, months in advance, who

A loyal follower of the Medici house, he waged a long struggle in the guild of judges and notaries against the wealthy and powerful Ser Paolo di Ser Lando Fortini, who was then first secretary of the Republic and one of the foremost opponents of the Medici.

Ser Paolo was "eased out" of his secretarial post by a Medicean Priorate at the end of 1427. The tension between the factions grew. On 17 November 1428 the Sienese ambassador to Florence reported that the city had experienced a night of alarms, owing to an attempt on the part of a fraction of the Signoria to dismiss Ser Martino Martini.[188] He was finally allowed to keep his office until the following year.

Ser Filippo Pieruzzi and Ser Martino Martini were skilled administrators with a thorough working knowledge of Florentine government and the Florentine constitution. Messer Tommaso Salvetti, on the other hand, was trained in argument and oratory, and his preparation in law naturally surpassed that of the notaries. All three were men of moderate to modest material means, and none enjoyed the backing of a Florentine family tradition. Thus their distinction in public life, we repeat, rested on the nature of their skills and educational preparation.

But not all the new men who attained civic prominence, or who founded a noteworthy Florentine family, possessed the special virtues of the two notaries and doctor of law. Quite different were two of the best-known new men of the period, Niccolò di Cocco di Donato and Puccio di Antonio Pucci.

Niccolò di Cocco was the head of a family which came into its own during the second half of the fourteenth century.[189] He and his brothers, and their father before them, were matriculated in the guild of the wool merchants.[190] As a result, their place in the governing councils was with the representatives of the major guilds, although they were widely known as a family of

---

would be drawn for certain offices. This sort of information was often helpful in the program of political factions.

[188] *Archivio di Stato di Siena, Concistoro,* 1915, f. 8r, states that disturbances continued "infine a piu hore di nocte, perche tutti i cittadini erano sollevati, chi pro et chi contra."

[189] There is no scholarly work on this family, now referred to as the Cocchi-Donati.

[190] ASF, *Lana,* 20, f. 47r, containing the matriculations of Niccolò, Zanobi, Antonio, and Giovanni di Cocco. Entered 21 January 1393.

parvenus. According to their tax reports of 1427, they had virtually no fixed assets, such as land or houses. Instead, they listed a gross capital of nearly 12,000 florins, the bulk of which represented investments in the Monte or public debt.[191] The balance sheet also shows more than 6000 florins in liabilities, consisting mainly of what they owed on various parcels of government stock. They must therefore have seemed "low speculators" of the sort condemned by Cavalcanti.

Niccolò di Cocco di Donato had extensive business relations with Cosimo de' Medici, and in the 1420's, when the rivalry within the oligarchy became intense, Niccolò joined the Medici camp. Gonfalonier of Justice in September 1434,[192] he led the palace revolution which terminated the exile of the Medici and regrouped the ruling families. Although Niccolò's family (hereafter called the Cocchi-Donati) had been unremitting office seekers for years, from this time forward they took a more enterprising part in Florentine political life.[193] Appropriately, their post-1434 situation also enabled them to negotiate marriages not hitherto accessible to them.

We have been unable to discover the name of Niccolò's first wife, but he was left a widower and married again in 1436.[194] His second wife was a Serzelli of the main branch, an aggressively bureaucratic family which got its start in the goldsmith's trade about the middle of the fourteenth century.[195] One of Niccolò's sons, Messer Donato, a doctor of law, married into the Spini family in 1438; widowed, he remarried in 1449, his wife this time being a daughter of Piero di Messer Luigi Guicciardini.[196] Another son, Jacopo, was married to Lionarda di Francesco Carducci in 1447. The traditions of the Spini and Guicciardini families accorded with the ideal of social distinction as set forth in the preceding sections of this chapter. In the early years of the fifteenth century, for example, Messer Cristofano Spini was one

---

191 *Catasto*, 69, ff. 279r-281v.   192 Ammirato, v, 219.
193 On their pursuit of office see, e.g., *Lib. Fab.*, 47, ff. 17r, 31r; 48, f. 130v.
194 *Carte Ancisa*, HH, 1, f. 58v.
195 ASF, *Mss.*, 265, f. 108r/v, which lists the *Sedici* and *Dodici*, where the first Serzelli to appear is the "aurifex" Jacopo in 1375.
196 *Carte Ancisa*, HH, 1, f. 58v.

of the foremost advisors in the executive councils.[197] The Guicciardini in the same period ranked among the city's first eighteen or twenty families: they had figured prominently in government for generations, and in their part of Florence, S. Spirito, they consistently appeared among the heaviest taxpayers. The Carducci, on the other hand, were parvenus and therefore no match for the Guicciardini and Spini. None the less, they were well-known merchants of the S. Maria Novella quarter and extremely active in public life during the entire fifteenth century.

In 1400 the Pucci, like the Cocchi-Donati, were still a family without a history in Florence.[198] They were raised to the level of the dynastic families by Puccio di Antonio Pucci, who was a dominant figure in the politics of the minor guilds in the second and third decades of the fifteenth century.[199] The appellation "magister" usually appeared beside his name in the inventories of public-office holders; hence he was probably a smith of some sort. But as he was exceedingly active in public affairs, he cannot have devoted a great deal of time to his trade, if indeed he pursued it at all.

During the first quarter of the fifteenth century, the Pucci fortunes may well have been modest, for the family does not appear on the taxrolls among the upper 10 per cent of names, the bracket which normally included the leading families. In 1414 Puccio married the daughter of a mercer (*merciaio*) and eleven years later contracted a second and more advantageous marriage with Bartolommea di Tommaso Spinelli.[200] According to a contemporary, Giovanni Cavalcanti, the Spinelli family originated in the 1340's, and although he considered them vulgar

[197] *ASF, Consulte*, 40, 42, passim (dates: 1409-1410, 1413-1414).

[198] L. Passerini, *Pucci di Firenze* (Milano, 1869), in the Litta series, *Famiglie celebri italiane.*

[199] Other outstanding members of the minor guilds were Banco di Sandro "coltriciaio," Piero di Lorenzo di Angiolino "pezarius," and Guarente di Giovanni Guarenti "magister." This observation is based on their frequent appearances in important political offices. *Tratte*, 79-80, passim.

[200] *Carte Ancisa*, EE, f. 818v; HH, 2, f. 706v. The *merciaio* was a "merchant who sold a great variety of articles, including arms and armor, hardware, saddles, straps, belts, and other leather goods, dry goods, millinery, notions, jewelry, etc." Florence Edler, *Glossary of Mediaeval Terms of Business, Italian Series 1200-1600* (Cambridge, Mass., 1934), p. 178.

schemers and upstarts,[201] they enjoyed an important place among the political families of the S. Croce quarter.

A brilliant political tactician and a highly effective orator, Puccio associated himself with the Medici during the early phases of the struggle within the governing class. After the Medici triumph, he swiftly became one of the Republic's most influential politicians.[202] In the late 1430's and early 1440's Puccio amassed a large fortune by buying and selling government stock, that is to say, only *after* his new power in government gave him a distinct advantage in such speculation. The Pucci were now in a position to contract more ambitious marriages. Puccio's daughter, Vanna, was married to Giannozzo di Betto Biliotti in 1442.[203] The Biliotti were an old merchant family, resident both in S. Spirito and S. Croce; they were wealthy, well-known in political circles, and very active in the executive councils.[204] In 1447 Puccio's son, Francesco, was married to Bartolommea di Giovanni di Francesco Spini, and later on in the century the Pucci also married into solid families like the Rondinelli, Busini, and Capponi.[205]

The foregoing concerns families and individuals who achieved socio-political prominence, while only partly fulfilling the four requisites of high social place. Barred for a half century from political life and therefore from the occasional advantageous marriage, the Alberti and Rinuccini families depended mainly on wealth and the force of their family traditions in order to retain their high place in society. The Panciatichi, on the other hand, failed to develop a reliable political tradition, despite their wealth, strategic marriages, and Tuscan antiquity. Two other families, the Pucci and Cocchi-Donati, were socially handicapped by their recent origin and new wealth; but they used their political ingenuity to break into the inner circle of the "senatorial" families and to contract socially significant marriages. The Sal-

[201] *Istorie*, II, 571.

[202] *Ibid.*, II, 189-191; see also Poliziano's memoirs, *Angelo Polizianos Tagebuch*, p. 18. In the 1440's there was even a group within the oligarchy known as the "Puccineschi."

[203] *Carte Ancisa*, EE, ff. 821v, 822v.

[204] *Consulte*, 34, 36, passim. The first reference is to the counsels of Giovanni di Bartolo Biliotti, the second to those of Cristofano di Francesco Biliotti.

[205] *Carte Ancisa*, EE, ff. 821v, 822v.

vetti family, newly arrived from Pistoia, won a very respectable place in political society and negotiated well-connected marriages, although they had to rely largely on their legal skills and contacts, and on Messer Tommaso's political genius. Ser Filippo Pieruzzi and Martino Martini, finally, came to be greatly respected and extremely influential in public life, even though they could claim neither material affluence nor Florentine traditions. There were a number of other fifteenth-century families whose importance was not based on the ideal set of factors described in the first four sections of this chapter. It will suffice to mention the Ambrogi, Becchi, and Dello Strinato, who entered the Signoria for the first time between 1437 and 1440.[206]

That there were influential families which departed from the ideal of high social place does not seem to have affected the general Florentine outlook on the question of rank in society. After all, the examples discussed involved a variety of special features. Salvetti, Pieruzzi, and Martini were all in the legal profession;[207] as a result, they presumably worked in government with great ease. Niccolò di Cocco and Puccio Pucci possessed outstanding political talent and great ambition. The Pucci held an influential place among the minor guildsmen, and the Cocchi-Donati (still so "new" that they had no true surname) enjoyed a certain popularity among the middle class. Nevertheless, both families attained their political and social primacy with the backing of Cosimo de' Medici. Thus, remarkable though the Pucci and Cocchi-Donati may have been among the parvenus of the fifteenth century, even they had needed the direct patronage of a family, the Medici, which not only conformed to the ideal of social pre-eminence, but also counted as one of the Republic's most powerful houses.

In short, before the middle of the fifteenth century, and most probably by 1400, the great age of social mobility in Florence was over. Now and then new families entered the inner circle of government and achieved social distinction, but their rise, as we have indicated, required the backing of the legal profession or the patronage of one of the great houses.

[206] ASF, *Mariani*, vi, ff. 1364r, 1375r, 1388r.
[207] The medieval Italian notary performed many tasks which today are only handled by the soliciting attorney.

Two additional questions remain: the practical effect of usurious wealth on social position, and the place of a family tradition in the putative link between wealth and political prominence.

Early in this chapter we noted that usury in Florence was disreputable, if strictly judged according to the code of the upper class. By this standard, a wealthy man who practiced usury could not, presumably, enjoy the respect or company of the patricians. Here again, however, there appeared a cleavage between the ideal and the reality: if usury was not widely practiced by Florentines, it was at all events serenely tolerated. The Panciatichi family offers an excellent example of how harmless, in the end, the "stain" of usury was, particularly when certain other factors were present.

In 1396 the Florentine notary, Lapo Mazzei, in a letter to Francesco Datini, observed with wonder that "Messer Bartolommeo Panciatichi, who at one time scarcely had 200 florins in cash, is now paying a forced loan of 800 florins."[208] Since forced loans or prestanze were sometimes collected six and even twelve times yearly, Bartolommeo's impost was extraordinarily high, in fact the highest in the city.[209] This must have seemed odd in a man reared to be a knight, who fought for Florence against the Pisans, and who won his spurs of knighthood on the field of battle. But about the year 1360, after having settled in Florence, Bartolommeo took up trade and money-lending. There can be no doubt about his business acumen, for he swiftly amassed a huge fortune, much of it by means of usurious transactions. Then, towards the end of his life (d. 1402) he secured a special absolutory decree from Pope Boniface IX.[210] The decree granted Bartolommeo and his heirs remission of the sin of usury. It declared that he had made extensive monetary restitution, and thereby nullified the right of local courts anywhere, lay or ecclesiastical, to proceed against the Panciatichi for usury. The Florentine Republic later enacted a bill recapitulating and acknowledging the

---

[208] *Lettere*, I, 141.

[209] E.g., *ASF, Prestanze*, 1999 or 2000, alphabetically arranged by Christian name. See under Bartolommeo Panciatichi. His basic rate in 1403, the highest in the city, was 600 florins, but it had been, as a cancellation shows, 870 florins. Cf. tables I-IV of App. II.

[210] Passerini, *Panciatichi*, p. 63.

papal action.[211] These proceedings put the sources of Bartolommeo's wealth directly before the public eye, but they did no damage to his family's social position. This is shown by the fact that in the two decades before and after 1400 the Panciatichi contracted marriages with the Alberti, Medici, Albizzi, Capponi, Strozzi, and Peruzzi families. They also had close business dealings with the well-known Serragli, Vettori, and Popoleschi houses.[212] For years, moreover, they included outstanding political personalities among their debtors: Messer Vanni Castellani, Messer Cristofano Spini, as well as others of the Adimari, Albizzi, Biliotti, Cavalcanti, Capponi, Cerretani, Gianfigliazzi, and other families.

There is enough evidence to show that Florentines were involved in litigious entanglements over usury with such frequency as to make it seem a commonplace.[213] Not surprisingly, therefore, the nineteenth-century genealogist, Passerini, observed that nearly all the great merchant families of Florence engaged in usury.[214] But apart from whatever comfort this may have offered, there was also the protective power which issued from a great family name. How could the Panciatichi, direct descendants of great feudal lords, long carry the stain of the usurer, especially when the accused owned vast tracts of land in the Pistoian countryside? There, indeed, they could point to their country houses and stables, to the former sites of their feudal castles and almost surely to the continuing allegiance of certain peasant families.

An allied effect on public opinion, but for quite different reasons, was produced by the Baroncelli, Corbinelli, Peruzzi, and other business families of their class. For while they claimed neither fortresses nor a feudal past, their political and economic leadership, as well as their old urban traditions, served to dispel the suspicion or stigma of usury. Here again, therefore, the Florentine family tradition confronts us as a factor of special value. We will reconsider it with an eye to the connection be-

[211] *ASF, Provv.*, 91, ff. 283r-286v (date: 23 February 1403).
[212] On their business dealings and debtors see *Catasto*, 79, ff. 134r-147v; 498, ff. 334r-344v.
[213] E.g., *ASF, Leg. Comm.*, 5, f. 52r; *Carte Strozz.*, 2a serie, xi, f. 52v; cf. also R. Davidsohn, *Storia di Firenze*, i, 1187-1192.
[214] *Panciatichi*, p. 64.

tween wealth and political pre-eminence, and so conclude our discussion of the differences which set off practical life from the Florentine ideal of elevated social rank.

The great ruling families of Quattrocento Florence originated for the most part during the thirteenth century. The first ingredient in their social rise seems to have been wealth, commercial or landed. Once a family was established, however, wealth did not remain absolutely necessary to its continuing high rank. It was enough if descendants regularly married into the ruling families, or if they continued to take an active part in politics, for political activity and even well-connected marriages maintained the vitality of a family tradition by keeping the family name before the public eye. Large fortunes, after all, were often lost in commercial enterprise or sometimes taxed and squandered away. Political prominence was also subject to the reversals of fortune. But a family tradition endured; it survived generations of financial hardship or even periods of political obscurity, until such time as a change in fortune raised the family to its former position.

Discussing the connection between wealth and tradition, Alberti boasted that his family had continuously ranked with the city's richest families for two hundred years and more. For "it seems that in our country, excepting in our family alone, no great fortune has endured beyond the third generation."[215] It is enough to remember that "Many noble and honorable families of Florence, like the Cerchi, Peruzzi, Scali, Spini, Ricci, and numerous others, who formerly abounded in vast riches, have been reduced to misery and in some cases even to desperate need, owing to the injuries of fortune."[216] To this list the humanist might have added the Mozzi, Franzesi, Tolosini, Panzano, and various branches of the Squarcialupi, Frescobaldi, and Rossi houses. Even the fif-

[215] *Della famiglia*, p. 212, "Anzi pare in la terra nostra, se non solo della nostra famiglia Alberta, gran ricchezza niùna giugnesse mai a' suoi nipoti eredi." I follow the editors here, Pellegrini and Spongano, in taking "nipoti eredi" to mean the third generation.

[216] *Ibid.*, pp. 213-214, "Cerchi, Peruzzi, Scali, Spini, e Ricci, e infinite altre famiglie nella terra nostra amplissime e oggidì ornatissime e nobilissime, le quali già abondavano di grandissime e smisurate ricchezze, si vede quanto subito, ingiuria della fortuna, sieno cadute in infelicità, e parte in grandissime necessità."

teenth century saw the downfall of powerful old families.[217]

But Alberti's observations may be misunderstood. The complete economic ruin of whole houses or clans was uncommon, although the Cerchi, Franzesi, Mozzi, Ricci, Scali, and Tolosini were so ruined.[218] What was common—to such an extent as to constitute a pattern—was the impoverishment within large family groups of individual branches. Now one branch and then another underwent financial crises, but not necessarily at the same time. No two branches of the huge Bardi family, for example, were ever on a perfectly equal footing with regard to wealth. In the early fifteenth century the Bardi included so many households that while some ranked with the richest families in the city, others had very limited resources and paid only the lowest possible tax rates. Again, in 1403 Messer Lotto di Vanni Castellani paid a levy of 30.0 florins per prestanza or forced loan, the nineteenth impost in S. Croce and one of the heavier ones in Florence. Two of his nephews, on the other hand, Michele and Jacopo di Stefano, who made up another Castellani household, were prescribed a prestanza of 1.00 florin and they were unable to pay even that.[219] Yet in an *estimo* of about 1390 their father, Stefano, was assigned a tax rate of 33.0 florins, while his brother, Messer Lotto, was assigned 45.0 florins.[220]

This brings us to an additional point. Since the fortunes of any given household were apt to change from generation to generation, there was a way in which most Florentine wealth was of recent vintage. How it would be judged depended on the perspective of the judge. For instance, in the early fifteenth century the wealth of the Pitti family went back about two hundred

---

[217] The Peruzzi and Spini, mentioned by Alberti, met their ruin in the fifteenth century. Others, like the Castellani and Serragli, followed them. In some cases their destruction was brought about by political vendetta.

[218] E.g., the famous Bardi and Peruzzi bank failures of the 1340's did not end in the complete ruin of the two families. The Peruzzi counted among the city's richest families until their partial exile in 1434. On the wealth of the Bardi consult the inventories of the following men, indexed under Bardi, in *Catasto*, 64: Bardo di Francesco dei Bardi, Lippaccio and Francesco di Benedetto dei Bardi, Larione di Lippaccio dei Bardi, Andrea di Lippaccio, and others. Cf. also table viii of App. ii.

[219] ASF, *Prestanze*, 1995, f. 169r, where their entry of 1.00 florin is followed by a statement (rare in the prestanze registers) that they cannot pay ("Non possono paghare").

[220] ASF, *Estimo*, 183, f. 7r.

years, from the standpoint of the family history as a whole. But Luca Pitti's great fortune in the 1450's was largely the result of his own industry: it did not exist in his father's time.[221] Again, although the original wealth of the Medici family dated back to the middle thirteenth century, the bulk of Cosimo de' Medici's wealth was the product of his father's commercial and banking enterprise; Giovanni di Bicci had begun to build up the capital of this particular branch of the Medici at the end of the fourteenth century.[222] Similar remarks can be made about the Strozzi family, whose traditions were slightly older than those of the Medici. Palla di Nofri Strozzi, possibly Florence's richest man in 1427, inherited his wealth; but his father had made most of it during the second half of the fourteenth century.[223] Were Palla and his father therefore considered upstarts? No, for like all the other Strozzi, they were heirs to the distinguished traditions of the Strozzi house. Their name entitled them to this, so that in some ways a name was more compelling than money.

Once we know that political (and so to some extent social) prominence was not necessarily connected with money, we are not surprised to learn that some Florentine statesmen were men whose economic situation was very modest in relation to the kind of wealth which abounded in their social and political set. On the whole, however, they emerged from backgrounds closely associated with the traditions of the older ruling families.

According to the prestanze of 1403, one of the Republic's most influential statesmen, Messer Rinaldo Gianfigliazzi, ranked just inside the limits of the upper 7 per cent income group in the S. Maria Novella quarter: he paid the 107th levy in a total for the district of 1492 levies.[224] One of his relatives, Tommaso di Messer Roberto Gianfigliazzi, paid the quarter's fifth highest levy. But neither Tommaso nor any other citizen from S. Maria Novella could equal Messer Rinaldo's stature in public life. At different

---

[221] His father's finances reported in Pitti, *Cronica*, pp. 36-37, 60ff., 115, 200.

[222] R. de Roover, "New Interpretations," pp. 45-46; also Brucker, "The Medici in the Fourteenth Century."

[223] Jones, "Florentine Families," pp. 187-190. On Palla's catasto levy in 1427 see Canestrini, *La scienza e l'arte di stato*, p. 153.

[224] See table III of App. II.

times, this man held all the Republic's chief dignities and was Gonfalonier of Justice four times. Among his contemporaries, men like Gino Capponi, Messer Maso degli Albizzi, and Niccolò da Uzzano, it is difficult to find more than one or two who appeared in the executive councils more often than Messer Rinaldo.[225] Moreover, his numerous diplomatic missions suggest that his reputation was recognized abroad, and years later his oratory and political *savoir faire* were still remembered.[226]

It was the force of his family tradition, not money, which served to buttress Messer Rinaldo's political ambitions. For although the Gianfigliazzi were barred from the Signoria during the greater part of the fourteenth century,[227] in the thirteenth century they took a leading part in public affairs and also operated one of the city's largest banking houses, with Southern France as their chief base of operations.[228]

Not unlike Rinaldo Gianfigliazzi's achievement was that of Piero di Lionardo Beccanugi (b. 1377). Piero had the advantage of being a doctor of law, but Rinaldo wore the spurs of knighthood and his economic situation, though moderate, was superior to the legist's, as we shall see. A summary indication of Piero's major offices will highlight his achievement.

He held the Republic's leading dignity, Gonfalonier of Justice, on two occasions, in 1424 and 1437.[229] In 1417 he was a member of the May–June Priorate. Twice he sat among the *Sedici Gon-*

---

[225] *ASF, Consulte*, 34-42, passim (dates: 1399-1414). My tallies indicate that Messer Rinaldo was more prominent in the executive councils than either Gino Capponi, Niccolò da Uzzano, or Giovanni di Bicci de' Medici. Note e.g., the number of Rinaldo's appearances in the debates from 19 July 1399 to 20 May 1401: *Consulte*, 34, ff. 2v, 7r, 9r, 12v, 18v, 20r, 22r, 23r, 25v, 26r/v, 28v, 30v, 32r/v, 33r, 34r, 35r/v, 37v, 38r, 39r, 41r, 45r, 47r, 48r, 49r, 51r/v, 52r, 53v, 55v, 56v, 57v, 62v, 63v, 64r, 67r, 68v, 77r, 82v, 88r, 91v, 102r, 120r/v, 121r, 122v, 123r, 125r/v, 126r, 127v, 128r, 129v, 131v, 133r, 134r, 135r/v, 136v, 137r/v, 138r/v, 139r, 143r, 153v, 156v, 158r, 163v, 165r, 168r, 172v, 173v, 177v, 185r.

[226] Cavalcanti, *Istorie*, II, 462, says that "La sua autentica eloquenza il faceva degnamente essere chiamato il gallo." On some of Messer Rinaldo's missions as an ambassador see e.g., *ASF, Leg. Comm.*, 3, f. 40r/v (sent to Padua); 6, f. 14r (sent to Pisa); also Ammirato, IV, pp. 274, 283, 329, 355, 361.

[227] They entered the Priorate for the first time in 1382, when Messer Rinaldo was made "Vexillifer."*ASF, Mariani*, v, f. 1075r.

[228] Yves Renouard, *Les Hommes d'Affaires Italiens du Moyen Age* (Paris, 1949), p. 128.

[229] *Mariani*, I, f. 104v.

falonieri, in 1419 and 1422; and he was selected for the *Dodici Buonomini* in 1413, 1426, 1435, and 1438.[230] Later he appeared in the two most powerful executive commissions, the Eight on Security and Ten of War, as well as in many other offices of an administrative and judicial nature.[231] Outside Florence proper, Piero was usually given magistracies of the first order: Captain of Pisa, Captain of Cortona, Captain of Arezzo, Governor of Pistoia, and Governor of Arezzo.[232] His full-scale diplomatic activity began not later than November 1409, with a mission to the Pope who was then in Pistoia.[233] Subsequently, he was dispatched as ambassador to Lucca, Siena, the Casentino, and Venice on at least three occasions.[234] In the 1430's and 1440's he also appeared in the executive councils with great frequency and was often requested to address the legislative councils on important measures.[235]

Such was the career of a man who in 1427 had only 530 florins in gross assets, an astonishingly small sum.[236] This figure included the estimated value of his law books—200 florins; another 200 florins were owed to him by one of his cousins, Jacopo Covoni; and the value of three small houses made up most of the remaining 130 florins. In economic terms, therefore, Messer Piero Beccanugi ranked in the class of small to medium shopkeepers.[237] Rinaldo Gianfigliazzi, by comparison, willed a patrimony to his

[230] *ASF, Mss.,* 266, f. 14r/v.

[231] E.g., *Tratte*, 79, ff. 5v, 17r, 19v, 280v; 80, ff. 288v, 392r, 412r, 416v, 425r, 426v.

[232] *Tratte*, 67, ff. 6r, 7v, 10v, 39v, 41v. He was also governor of Pisa for six months, from 18 November 1413.

[233] *Leg. Comm.,* 4, ff. 113r-114r.

[234] *Leg. Comm.,* 5, ff. 71r-90v; 6, f. 87v; 7, f. 71r; 9, f. 50r/v; 10, ff. 43v *et seq.* See also *ASF, Notaio di camera-uscita,* 1, f. 148v, being the notice of one of Piero's missions to Venice in June and July of 1430. The equipment sent along involved ten horses and an allotment of 5.00 florins daily.

[235] *ASF, Lib. Fab.,* 50, ff. 48r, 140r, 141v; 51, ff. 9v, 20v, 186v, 189v; 52, ff. 23v-24r, 35r, 38v, 190r.

[236] *Catasto*, 77. For exact folios see index by surname.

[237] This statement is made on the basis of Piero's goods as reported to the catasto commission. The catasto tax did not include his income as a practicing lawyer, but neither did it include the earnings of shopkeepers. Hence stable property must form the basis of any comparative index. In this connection, it is noteworthy that Piero began to practice law around 1405, for he was made a consul in the lawyers' guild for the first time in January 1407. Twenty years later, as the catasto inventories show, his material situation was still very modest. To doubt the truth of Piero's catasto reports is to imagine that one can somehow prove their falsehood, an impossible task in this case so far as I can tell. Besides, the catasto of

sons, putting them on a level with the smaller international merchants or landowners of medium rank, for in 1427 they reported net assets of 3873 florins.[238]

Wealth obviously did not give Piero Beccanugi his start in public life. What then were the social factors behind his political distinction? Being a doctor of law was undoubtedly valuable, but his importance in politics far surpassed that of the legists whose preferment was founded chiefly or exclusively on their professional qualifications. The *legum doctores* tended to fall into two groups: one group (and Piero belonged to it) was made up of men directly descended from the old Florentine families;[239] the other involved lawyers who were not lineal descendants of the old families and who consequently could not lay claim to Florentine traditions. The second group included "new men" like Messer Nello di Giuliano Martini, Messer Domenico di Ser Mino, Messer Guaspare del Maestro Ludovico, Messer Giovanni di Girolamo da Gubbio, and Messer Tommaso Salvetti.

The decisive social element in Piero's political success was the family tradition of the Beccanugi. They entered the Signoria for the first time in 1284, just two years after its establishment, and during the fourteenth century were regularly appointed to its appended councils, the *Sedici* and *Dodici*. Originally a branch of the Ammanati house, old feudal nobility, the Beccanugi broke from them for political reasons and took a new name. By the 1260's, when it was established that Piero's forebears had suffered exile and that their "tower" had been damaged by the Ghibellines, the Beccanugi were already considered old Guelf nobility.[240] In the fifteenth century, accordingly, neither the

---

1427 was rigorously administered and Piero was too prominent to conceal landed wealth in any amounts worthy of mention. Deposits accredited to his name in banks or business houses would have been reported in their accounts. Finally, as for government securities, no man could give out false information about these because the official Monte accounts were carefully kept, as we can see today from the condition of those records.

[238] *Catasto*, 75. Exact folios there given in the attached index under Gianfigliazzi—Giovanni, Francesco, and Jacopo.

[239] This observation is based on my tabulation of the offices held by Florentine lawyers in the period 1400-1450. Some other lawyers of Piero's group were Filippo Corsini, Giuliano Davanzati, Bartolommeo Popoleschi, Lorenzo Ridolfi, Guglielmo Tanagli.

[240] *Mariani*, I, f. 104r/v; Ammirato, I, 239. Precisely when the break occurred between the Amannati and Beccanugi is unknown.

Strozzi nor the Medici could adduce older or more illustrious origins than the Beccanugi.

The careers of Rinaldo Gianfigliazzi and Piero Beccanugi amply illustrate the fact that wealth was not an absolute or necessary factor in political and social prominence, provided the man in question descended from one of the old ruling families. This condition perfectly describes statesmen like Gino Capponi, Rinaldo Rondinelli, and Messer Bartolommeo Popoleschi, all of whom came of distinguished old stock, although they had relatively little in the way of money or real estate. On occasion, as the tax records show, men of this type enjoyed a moderate economic situation, indicated by their rank just inside the upper 8 per cent income group.[241] The levies assigned to Bartolommeo Popoleschi show, however, that there were those among them whose fortunes were too modest for even this group.[242] In view of the fact that they exercised their offices in an oligarchical situation, were these statesmen apt to be dominated by the wealthy families and groups? Undoubtedly there were cases of this, but there seems to be little evidence that it was common. We must not confuse the statesmen of the old families, however modest their economic situation, with upstart politicians of the Pucci and Cocchi-Donati type, who really needed the sponsorship and protection of one of the powerful old houses.

This account has shown that although men of the upper class were often distinguished by their family traditions, wealth, public prominence, and marriage connections, two of these attributes alone were sometimes enough to confer high place in society. Statesmen like Piero Beccanugi and Rinaldo Gianfigliazzi were fortunate in that they combined the two most effective ones— distinctive family traditions and celebrity in public life; so they too, like the men of the powerful merchant families, disposed of influence and patronage.

[241] E.g., *Prestanze*, 1994 (year: 1403), entries listed alphabetically, Christian name first. See under Cappone and Gino di Neri Capponi, who held the 104th place in a distribution of 2184 *prestanziati*.

[242] *Prestanze*, 1996, listed alphabetically under Bartolommeo di Tommaso Popoleschi and his nephews, who held the 214th place in a distribution of 1492 *prestanziati*.

CHAPTER THREE

THE FORTUNES OF THE FLORENTINE
HUMANISTS

1. THE QUESTION IN SCHOLARSHIP

*S*INCE the chief aim of this inquiry is to define the social position of the men associated with Florentine humanism during the first half and more of the fifteenth century, we may begin—following the order set down in the preceding chapter—by trying to establish their economic situation. The question has a curious history in scholarship: it has attracted much generalization, but no detailed or systematic study. To know where we must begin, therefore, it will be useful to review the generalizations that appear to dominate the field.

In modern historical literature, interest in the economic situation of the Italian humanists goes back to the work of Jacob Burckhardt and Georg Voigt. First published in 1859, Voigt's *Die Wiederbelebung des Classischen Alterthums, oder das erste Jahrhundert des Humanismus* underwent considerable revision later on, and the edition of 1880-1881 incorporated a great deal of new "illustrative material taken from more authentic sources."[1] Burckhardt published his essay on the Italian Renaissance in 1860, but it has been very much more influential than Voigt's work, and therefore we shall consider his views first.

Burckhardt presents a complex picture of the social condition of the humanists.[2] He provides us with examples of men who achieved a European reputation in their own time (e.g., Poggio, Filelfo, Pietro Aretino) and who attained stable, secure positions in society (e.g., Guarino and Vittorino). Some of them, recipients of patronage, he noted, were given large sums of money for translations. And, although offering less detail than Voigt, he discerned in Florence a group of citizen-humanists who enjoyed

[1] Wallace K. Ferguson, *The Renaissance in Historical Thought: Five Centuries of Interpretation* (Cambridge, Mass., 1948), p. 159.

[2] *The Civilization of the Renaissance in Italy*, with an Introduction by B. Nelson and C. Trinkaus, tr. S. G. C. Middlemore, 2 vols. (Harper Torchbooks, New York, 1958), I, 175-278.

solid or even exalted positions in society and who made humanism "an indispensable element in daily life."[3] Niccolò Niccoli, Giannozzo Manetti, Cosimo de' Medici, Piero de' Pazzi, and Donato Acciaiuoli are some of the men he had in mind. Nevertheless, when he came to speak about the *general* condition of the humanists, he drew a picture of men whose interests ultimately put them at the margins of society. For he observed that while their personalities and fame often rendered them impressive to contemporaries, yet they drifted from one city or court to another, were today the favorites and tomorrow the victims of fortune, and on occasion ruined themselves morally and socially by their vast pride, ambition, or restlessness.

Speaking of the fourteenth-century humanists, Burckhardt stated: "They were a crowd of the most miscellaneous sort, wearing one face today and another tomorrow." "The *clerici vagantes* of the twelfth century . . . may perhaps be taken as their forerunners," for they betray "the same unstable existence."[4] Turning to the fifteenth century, he noted that the position of the humanists who went into university teaching, "even where the salary was large, and did not exclude other sources of income, was on the whole uncertain and temporary."[5] But he presented his most comprehensive picture of the general condition of the humanists in the part of his essay entitled, "Fall of the Humanists in the Sixteenth Century." Casting back to the Quattrocento, Burckhardt remarked that as in cultural life they were dominated by a "passion for glory," so "In practical life too their position was one they had continually to fight for."[6] They enjoyed "the overflowing excess of favor and fortune when the luck was on their side," but they had also to face "the uncertainty of the future, in which luxury or misery depended on the caprice of a patron or the malice of an enemy."[7] Hence honor and place, even when attained, were constantly threatened. "But the worst of all was that the position of the humanist was almost incompatible with a fixed home, since it either made frequent changes of dwelling necessary for a livelihood, or so affected the mind of the individual that he could never be happy for long in one place. . . .

[3] *Ibid.*, I, 224.   [4] *Ibid.*, I, 211.   [5] *Ibid.*, I, 219.
[6] *Ibid.*, I, 272.   [7] *Ibid.*, I, 273.

Much as this life reminds us of the Greek sophists of the Empire, as described to us by Philostratus, yet the position of the sophists was more favourable. They often had money, or could more easily do without it than the humanists. . . ."[8] Such was the range of Burckhardt's views concerning the position of the humanists.

Subsequent scholarship was to stress either the *éclat* and success of the humanists, or their economic dependence and social instability. Georg Voigt expressed something of both, but his emphasis depended upon the humanist group he happened to be discussing, whether at Florence, Rome, Padua, or elsewhere. Relying chiefly on Vespasiano da Bisticci and some of the humanist correspondence of the period, he found that among the Florentine literati "professionals" like Niccoli, Bruni, Poggio, and Marsuppini "lived as if in perfect equality with the Florentine nobility."[9] He evidently assumed that this was made possible by their intellectual and literary activity, but that neither their social background nor economic situation would naturally have permitted them such ease of movement among the learned members of the Strozzi, Medici, Corbinelli, Albizzi, and Acciaiuoli families.[10] Be this as it may, the point is that for Voigt the humanist movement in Florence was the work of citizens who enjoyed secure and often prominent positions in Florentine society. This vision, however, has sometimes been lost in twentieth-century scholarship, owing in part perhaps to one of Voigt's general observations towards the end of his great work. He concluded that many humanists taught in universities, but that they did so temporarily, usually for not more than a year or two in any one place, and then only with an eye for money. Yet "their salaries were mostly trifling, especially when compared with those of the jurists and professors of medicine."[11] Like Petrarch, their master, the humanists looked for the highest happiness in the advantages offered by a free and independent life. "But as most of them were poor and not infrequently burdened with a large family, they were compelled to think of situations that might have some guarantee of security." Therefore, except for a few at the courts

[8] *Ibid.*, I, 274.

[9] G. Voigt, *Il risorgimento dell'antichità classica*, Ital. tr. D. Valbusa, 2 vols. (Firenze, 1888-1890), I, 315.

[10] *Ibid.*, I, 289ff.   [11] *Ibid.*, II, 362.

of princes, the majority had to be content "with secondary chancellery posts which, though certainly a nuisance, commanded a great deal of esteem in the public mind."[12]

Thus the question persisted: which side of the general status of the humanists ought rightly to be emphasized? Their brilliant successes or their social instability and economic dependence? Burckhardt and Voigt saw both sides as belonging to one and the same life, but the effect of this perception was to make clear-cut generalization exceedingly difficult and to offer every subsequent student whatever his temperament or the times required. He could either dwell on the darker side of the picture, or in good conscience select from Voigt's larger canvass only the following image of the fifteenth-century humanists: "The high state dignities they enjoyed and the embassies for which they were picked gave them an elevated social position. Courtiers kneeled down before them; princes and cardinals shook their hands amicably; they were the glory of their birthplaces, the ornament of the cities in which they resided. . . . They imagined themselves the masters of public opinion."[13]

Francesco de Sanctis, with his critical moral bent and taste for tersely-expressed judgments, drew a somewhat exaggerated picture of the humanist in his *Storia della letteratura italiana* (1870-1871). Noting that the humanist movement "did not come from the people," he added that the voice of the people "was drowned by the noisy joy of the courts and the literati, exhaled in Latin verses. To the literati fame, honours, and money; to the princes incense."[14] For "The literati were like the soldiers of fortune; they served the persons who paid them best, so that the enemy of today became the patron of tomorrow. They wandered from court to court putting themselves up at auction." De Sanctis immediately followed these assertions with the remark, "This weakness and servility of character . . . had already begun in the time of Petrarch." And finally, "The greater number of the writers were secretaries to princes, and were ready to use their Latin for embroidering the conceptions of other people."[15]

---

[12] *Ibid.*, II, 363.   [13] *Ibid.*, II, 354. Cf. also I, 234.
[14] I quote from the English ed., *History of Italian Literature*, tr. Joan Redfern, 2 vols. (New York, Harcourt, Brace & World, Inc., 1959), I, 372.
[15] *Ibid.*

The Fortunes of the Humanists

The next influential historian to touch on the problem was Adolf Gaspary in his *Geschichte der italienischen Literatur* (1885-1888). His conclusions reveal a well-balanced view. While suggesting that because of tyranny and political agitation the fifteenth century did not provide an ideal context for intellectual activity, he noted, nevertheless, that "enthusiasm overcame the difficulties, and the condition of learned men [i.e., the humanists] . . . was not bad on the whole."[16] Princes gladly took them into their courts, even if only in a decorative capacity, and while Filelfo, Campano, and a few others complained that the literati were not well treated, "They were not without protection. Not since antiquity had writers enjoyed such honors and rewards."[17] Gaspary went on to draw attention to the fact that "Many humanists of that period were distinguished statesmen, like Leonardo Giustiniani and Francesco Barbaro in Venice, and Giannozzo Manetti in Florence."[18]

In 1900 Philippe Monnier brought out his famous essay on the literary history of Italy in the fifteenth century: *Le Quattrocento, essai sur l'histoire littéraire du xve siècle italien.* He drew heavily on Voigt, Burckhardt, De Sanctis, and Gaspary, which was perhaps inevitable; in addition he displayed an intimate knowledge of the humanistic sources of the period. Like Voigt, he dealt with the different schools of humanism according to their geographic location. Unlike him, however, Monnier tended in his generalizations to concentrate on the public success of the humanists and to neglect those who may only have had modest careers. In Florence and Venice, for example, Monnier called attention to a group of literati who were different from "professional" humanists in other parts of Italy, especially from those who sought their fortunes in Rome.[19] The Florentine group, he noticed, consisted of men who enjoyed a secure position in society, while in Venice humanism was in the hands of various members of the patriciate. He specifically mentioned the Zeno, Foscarini, Morosini, Corrèr, Trevisan, Giustiniani, and Barbaro.[20] When the time came for

---

[16] I quote from the Ital. ed., *Storia della letteratura italiana*, tr. V. Rossi, 2 vols. (Torino, 1899-1901), II, i, 102.

[17] *Ibid.*, II, i, 104.   [18] *Ibid.*, II, i, 115-116.

[19] *Le Quattrocento, essai sur l'histoire littéraire du xve siècle italien*, 2 vols. (Paris, Perrin, 1900), I, chs. II-III.

[20] *Ibid.*, I, 168ff.

him to make a more sweeping statement concerning the general condition of the humanist in Italy, he cast his eye over the fifteenth century and concluded: "Rome used him [the humanist] to defend herself against the councils; republics introduced him into their chancelleries; tyrants entrusted their immortality to him. . . . Poet, orator, philosopher, in his own eyes and in those of others, he taught the children [of the great], founded and maintained libraries, composed political letters, drafted love notes, produced diatribes, welcomed distinguished visitors and mourned the illustrious dead. His presence ennobled and graced every function. He formed public opinion, determined the judgment of posterity, was the mold of fashion. He lived in great comfort, provided with prebends and sinecures, had horses and servants, and conversed as an equal with the powerful."[21]

It is instructive to go from this view of the humanist to that presented by Vittorio Rossi in his celebrated reference work, *Il Quattrocento*. First published in 1898, this tome was so greatly revised later that the author himself considered the 1933 edition "a new book."[22] This edition, with subsequent minor corrections and bibliographical addenda, now serves as the standard text.

In Rossi's vision of things, the interests and talents of the humanists tended to put them at the mercy of fortune's vicissitudes. Life for many of them consisted of "painful alternations between prosperous and forbidding events and illusions that faded away at the touch of reality."[23] To be sure, Rossi recognized that some humanists achieved great distinction and enjoyed both social and economic security: e.g., Bruni, Traversari, Guarino, Decembrio, and Vittorino da Feltre. "But the biography of many others adds up to a squalid itinerary." "They pass from one city to another, or from village to village, here lecturers at a university, there tutors in princely or wealthy households, today solemn expositors of the classics, tomorrow intent on getting children to decline *rosa-rosae* and on mollifying humours and tears. To such humble tasks are they sometimes compelled to bend their intellects, normally accustomed to conversing with Livy and Cicero."[24]

---

[21] *Ibid.*, I, 131-132.
[22] V. Rossi, *Il Quattrocento*, ed. A. Vallone (Milano, Fr. Vallardi, 1956), p. vii.
[23] *Ibid.*, p. 44.   [24] *Ibid.*, p. 45.

Rossi then produced the examples of Teodoro Gaza, who moved around from one part of Italy to the other and was often reduced to selling his books; Giovanni Lamola, whose life "was a continuous wandering from city to city"; Giammario Filelfo (Francesco's first son), who also drifted and was constantly abandoning teaching posts or being fired; Tommaso Morroni, a literary adventurer who ended in one of the Sforza prisons (1476); Cosimo Raimondi, an excellent scholar who committed suicide (1435); and Sassolo of Prato, another man of learning—"he threw himself into a river (1449)."[25]

The author of *Il Quattrocento* probably did not mean to suggest that suicides and passionate adventurers were typical of men in the humanist camp. Yet the highly mobile, touchy, ambitious, erratic humanist-type is so prominent in the picture drawn that for Rossi he dominates the field.

Two conceptions are discernible in these summaries: on the one hand, that the humanists generally speaking were poor men of humble origins and that their social situation was plagued by incertitudes; on the other, that most of them enjoyed comfortable means and an enviable or even exalted social position. The two views were already present in the formulations of Burckhardt and Voigt, though sometimes one view prevailed and sometimes the other, depending on the passage. Whether to combine them in some fashion, or to give heavy emphasis to one, became a problem for later historians. De Sanctis and Monnier gave prominence to the figure of the well-to-do humanist who hobnobbed with the mighty and commanded a brilliant reputation. Gaspary took a more sober view: without exaggerating the worldly success of the humanists, he stressed the fact that their economic and social situation was good. Rossi, however, called attention to their relative penury and highlighted the instability and ambiguity of their lives. Scholarship since Rossi's time has gone no further in clarifying the relation between the two rather different conceptions. The views expressed in three recent works attest to this.

In his book, *The Genius of Italy* (1949), Leonardo Olschki maintains that the "throng of learned humanists" came "mostly

[25] *Ibid.*, pp. 45-46.

of low extraction" and that the leaders of the movement—also "mostly of humble origin"—"rapidly rose to positions of influence and power in every section of public life."[26] He seems to have been thinking of humanists at Venice, Florence, Milan, Rome, Naples, and at the despotic courts of Ferrara, Mantua, Rimini, and Urbino.

One of the more interesting works to touch on this question was published in 1940: *Adversity's Noblemen: the Italian Humanists on Happiness*, by Charles Trinkaus. One of its main themes is that the humanist idea of happiness, with the subsidiary notions of nobility and human dignity, was to a large extent a function of the uncertain status, social insecurity, and economic dependence of the humanists.[27] Trinkaus avers that during the Middle Ages it was customary for the writer "to be associated with some definitely limited group," a monastic order, university faculty, guild, or a distinct profession such as law or medicine. Consequently, the medieval writer enjoyed "in most cases a regular and steady income."[28] "Many of the humanists, on the other hand, had no permanent attachments to any associations or institutions. Excepting those who, like Ambrogio Traversari, were drawn into humanism from a secure ecclesiastical position, the humanists tended to be free-lance writers. Their chief visible means of support was the patronage of some affluent lay or ecclesiastical persons."[29] Even their salaried positions are alleged to have been a form of patronage. The author then ventures that it may have been this dependence on sinecures and patronage, and the concomitant sense of economic insecurity, which made the humanists aware "that they lacked a genuine and recognized function within society as it was constituted."[30] Thus, when dwelling on favorite themes such as nobility and human dignity, the emphasis of the humanists on the spiritual side of man was "clearly a desire and hope to overcome or transcend the social and material insecurities and the accompanying emotional stress of this life."[31]

The author of these views was perfectly aware of the fact

26 (Ithaca, ed. 1954), pp. 257, 262.   27 Ch. III.
28 *Ibid.*, p. 39.   29 *Ibid.*, p. 40.   30 *Ibid.*
31 *Ibid.*, p. 70. Also pp. 47, 122, 145.

that some humanists enjoyed worldly success. In this regard, for example, he specifically mentions Poggio and Salutati.[32] But this did not hinder him from associating Poggio's *De Nobilitate* (1440) with the motives of economic and social insecurity, nor from suggesting that Salutati suffered "Insecurity and lack of general recognition."[33] Hence while the poor humanist suffered because he was poor, because he had no social position (thus his tendency to entertain compensatory ideas!), the rich humanist suffered because he was faced by "the question of whether he should go on enjoying the benefits of his wealth now that he was becoming a humanist or whether he should emulate St. Francis and try to practice humanism in rags."[34] In fact, therefore, the humanist could have no social tranquility, regardless of his actual station in life.

By such reasoning, could one not marshal support for almost any thesis? But the most curious feature of the interpretation provided by Trinkaus is that he draws copiously from the works of highly-placed or wealthy men (e.g., Salutati, Poggio, Buonaccorso da Montemagno, Manetti, Pico) in order to illustrate his idea that the moral vision of the humanists was to a large extent influenced by their economic dependence and insecure social place.

More recently the social rootlessness, economic dependence, and psychological instability of the humanist have figured significantly in Arnold Hauser's fascinating work, *The Social History of Art* (1951). Following Edgar Zilsel, he points out that in the fourteenth century Italian writers "still come very largely from the higher classes of society; they were members of the urban aristocracy or sons of the well-to-do bourgeois."[35] The humanists, on the other hand, were presumably not associated with a single class or group, but were recruited from all walks of life. "The representatives of the lower classes come, however, to form an ever-increasing proportion of their total numbers. The most famous, most influential of all of them is the son of a shoemaker."[36] Next we learn that, although the humanists are the first writers

[32] *Ibid.*, pp. 44, 57.   [33] *Ibid.*, p. 61.   [34] *Ibid.*, p. 146.
[35] I quote from the Vintage ed., 3 vols. (Copyright Alfred A. Knopf Inc., New York, 1960), II, 80.
[36] *Ibid.*

in modern times to have "something in the nature of a free market," yet "compared with the modern man of letters, they still led a parasitical life, unless they had private means." But the fact is that "they were usually dependent on the favour of the courts and the patronage of influential citizens, whom they normally served as secretaries or private tutors." The habits of the age were such that "Instead of a court singer or fool, a private historian or professional panegyrist, the gentleman of private means now kept a humanist in the house, but the services he performed, though the forms it [sic] took were somewhat sublimated, were in fact very much the same."[37] At this point, echoing Alfred von Martin's *Soziologie der Renaissance*, Hauser goes on to observe that the humanists were "finally held down" by the upper class because they did "in fact constitute a destructive element on account of their rootlessness."[38] There was thus a "latent conflict between the intellectual and the economic upper class," and "the whole intelligentsia, both literary and artistic, is threatened by the danger of developing either into an uprooted . . . and envious class of bohemians or into a conservative, passive, cringing class of academics." At any rate, the humanist "serves the interests of conservatism" even though his longing for independence really adds up to "an alienation from society."[39]

Previous literature on the subject had already touched this matter of alienation, but scholars had called it social instability or insecurity, or they had talked about the humanist's wandering from city to city, hiring himself out to the highest bidder, committing his basic loyalites to no one, and so forth. Von Martin and Hauser, however, carry the conception so far as to discern signs of an underlying conflict between the humanist and the ruling classes.

The contradictions elicited by our review of the literature on the social situation of the humanists serve to warn us that in the present state of scholarship it is unwise for the historian to advance clear-cut generalizations about the humanists' position. I shall try to say why this is so and then indicate how the present inquiry departs from the tradition of study in this field.

[37] *Ibid.*, II, 81.　　[38] *Ibid.*, II, 82-83.　　[39] *Ibid.*, II, 83.

The Fortunes of the Humanists

It seems clear that the contradictory generalizations in the literature arise from the attempts of historians to work with insufficient evidence. Too much has been based on too little. For one may well ask, where are the specialized studies that ought to have followed the formulations of Burckhardt and Voigt? The present study is the first to make the social position of the humanists the central feature of investigation, and even then it has been necessary to restrict the inquiry to a particular city during some seven decades of its history. The subject is not one which can be settled by holding that many humanists enjoyed high place and were well off, while many others lived in relative obscurity and poverty. We already knew that the two conditions applied to *some* humanists, and it simply will not do to multiply the known cases of both types into *many*, as we should only end by multiplying our lacunae.

What we need, first, is concrete information about the social situation of the humanists in the different parts of Italy. This goes for university cities like Bologna, Padua, and Pisa, for the Venetian and Florentine republics, for a number of the small despotic courts, and especially for humanist circles in Rome, Milan, and Naples. Cities like Genoa and Palermo, and some of the more provincial inland towns such as Perugia and Pavia, undoubtedly raise questions of their own. Furthermore, in studying the circumstances that surrounded intellectual life in these cities, the time element would call for special consideration. For Italian society around 1500 was changing so decisively that it is a mark of innocence to suppose that generalizations about the position of the humanists circa 1400 would hold with equal value for the period after 1500, or even after 1450 or 1460 in some parts of Italy.

In much of the literature examined no attempt was made to distinguish between the situation of the humanists in one type of setting, as in Rome or Naples, from that in another, as in Florence or Venice. The importance of this distinction is not difficult to demonstrate. If, for instance, we decide to study the Italian humanists from the vantage point of the papal curia or Naples, it seems evident that they will look much more like a group of men in search of sinecures and patronage than if we start somewhere else in Italy. For as one pope died and another came on the scene, so their favorites at Rome came and went, humanists among them. Moreover, because some popes expressed far more solicitude for the humanists than others, the incidence of humanists at Rome could well depend on the holder of the papal tiara. The Roman situation thus tended to be a changing one. In Naples, King Alfonso made an effort to attract leading humanists to the city; if one judges the humanists on the basis of those who passed through his court, one would suppose that they were an extremely mobile group and be encouraged to assume that when the king withdrew his favor Naples therewith lost a humanist, who presumably then drifted on to another part of Italy, always in search of his fortune. But perhaps we should stop to ask, how typical are the facts revealed by looking at things from the standpoint of Rome or Naples? How valuable are they for the situation in Florence and for purposes of generalization? A humanist might settle in Naples only after long service somewhere else: such a man was the wealthy statesman, Giannozzo Manetti. Or he might, like Lionardo Bruni, work as a secretary in the papal curia for a few years only, and then return to settle down in his native or adopted city. Or again, like Poggio Bracciolini, he might serve as a papal secretary in Rome for many years, yet always maintain very important social and economic ties elsewhere, including real estate and cash investments.

The point is that the very nature of some courts made various posts and sinecures seem either temporary or entirely dependent on external circumstances, thus giving the condition of the humanists there a somewhat unstable or transient appearance. In such cases the historian would do well to examine the careers of humanists before and after their association with a prince, in order to obtain a more balanced picture of the general status they enjoyed in the larger world of Italian society. If, however, he elected to concentrate purely on the condition of the humanists at the different courts, he might help to close a very large gap in our knowledge by providing us with the first sustained and detailed account of the place and function of the humanist in the aristocratic courts. With a project of this sort, a good beginning might be to classify and study the different types of humanists found at court: the secretary, poet, tutor, librarian, official eulogist, and intellectual companion. Needless to say, a humanist not infrequently served in all these capacities.

The theme of the wandering humanist, of the uprooted scholar or literary man moving from one city or court to another, turned up in almost every study we examined. Certainly the fifteenth century produced dozens of men of this description. But whether or not they were typical is another question. For it can probably be shown that every itinerant humanist like Aurispa, Panormita, or the youthful Valla had his stay-at-home counterpart in humanists like Andrea Giuliano, Francesco Barbaro, and Carlo Marsuppini. Be this as it may, I raise the question because the image of the wandering humanist is often associated with the temporary nature of humanist lectureships in the universities. It is essential to point out here—since it is often said that the jurist enjoyed more social and economic solidity than the humanist—that many noted jurists of the period also moved around from one teaching post to another. The careers of jurists like Paolo di Castro, Giovanni da Imola, Sallustio da Perugia, and Filippo Decio serve to illustrate this.[40]

In studying the views of historians who have commented on the social or economic position of the humanists, we found most of them assuming that the wealthy ones usually acquired their wealth through the generosity of patrons. With one or two exceptions, we shall see that this was not the case in Florence during the first half of the fifteenth century. In Venice the situation was perhaps much the same as in Florence, or very nearly so. We have but to think of the apparent custodians of Venetian humanism during the greater part of the fifteenth century: men like Andrea Giuliano, Francesco and Ermolao Barbaro, Leonardo and Bernardo Giustiniani, Lauro Quirino, Fantino Dandolo, Piero Donato, Piero del Monte, Gregorio Corrèr, Jacopo Zeno, and Francesco Contarini. They were all members of the Venetian patriciate; seven or eight greatly distinguished themselves in

[40] On the least studied of these jurists, Sallustio, see the following: L. Martines, "The Career and Library of a 15th-Century Lawyer," *Annali di storia del diritto: rassegna internazionale*, III-IV (Milano, 1959-1960), 323-332.

public life and most of them inherited wealth. Of the twelve only the patrician from Candia, Lauro Quirino, lived from teaching, though the Serenissima drew on his services too in the realm of public affairs. He ran a school for noblemen in Venice and afterwards taught rhetoric and moral philosophy at the University of Padua.

The nature of the humanist movement at Venice suggests that it may be possible to distinguish professional from amateur humanists. I have already discussed this question in Chapter I, but its importance is such as to justify expansion here on a few details.

Roberto Weiss has observed that "until the last decades of the fifteenth century, Venetian humanism was dominated by amateurs drawn from the ruling class."[41] If for the moment we define a professional as one who lived from his humanistic culture (either as teacher, secretary, or courtier), then it is clear that many of the figures prominently associated with Venetian humanism in the fifteenth century were amateurs, even though accomplished writers or scholars in the humanist vein. Very well, but does this observation provide us with useful insight, or does it rather divide the ranks of the humanists, associating one file with one sector of society and the other, by implication, with a different social sector? Dividing the humanists into two types ought to be in line with our formulation of questions. We should have a particular end in mind, and it is only when the end has been clearly defined that we can know whether or not dividing the humanists in this case is appropriate or necessary. For some arguments concern the genus, others the differentia.

Apart from the reasons already given in the first chapter, the present inquiry does not divide professionals and amateurs—to separate the professional humanists from their pupils, imitators, supporters, and intellectual peers would have been not only to wrench them from the setting in which they lived and functioned as humanists, but also to relegate them to a fictitious isolation, an isolation which did not characterize their condition. Nor could I associate them with the world of artisans and small shopkeepers, still less with the textile proletariat, for neither literary nor

[41] In "Italian Humanism in Western Europe: 1460-1520," p. 72.

archival sources depict the humanists as the intellectual companions of such men. Indeed, amateur or professional, the humanists never exhibit vital contacts with any sector of the lower classes. For whatever the origins of some humanists, their world in Florence reached, as we shall see, from the prosperous ranks of the merchant and professional groups to the top level of political society. Within these limits they worked, married, carried on their conversations, and had their quotidian contacts *as* humanists. It was here too that they vied for honors and political office.

Perhaps enough has already been said to indicate the precise nature of the present inquiry. It departs from the tradition of study in this field by making the question of social position central to the entire investigation. The approach is empirical and the object of study the particular men connected with an intellectual movement in one place and time. A fair sample is achieved by combining the major humanists treated in the main body of the text with the lesser ones treated in Appendix I.

2. SOURCE PROBLEMS

The State Archives of Florence contain thousands of registers of the two principal sources, the *Prestanze* and *Catasto,* from which the material on humanist finances in this study is drawn. A third source, the *Monte* material, also runs to thousands of registers. Kept by the Monte officials, this was a record of all transactions involving government securities during the Monte's history and includes the amounts, dates, and names of all who owned securities. But apart from the fact that the Monte archives provide no information about landed possessions or business investments, this collection, still being collated and catalogued, is officially unavailable for use in research.

Spanning the period from early in the second half of the fourteenth century to 1413, the Prestanze collection is a record of the forced loans—taxes really—levied on Florentine households. Taxation in Florence usually went by household. If five brothers of legal age maintained a single household, they were assigned one levy. The assumption was that their possessions and investments were a collective enterprise. But if they had separate households, or if their patrimony had been legally divided and settled, then each was assigned a separate prestanza or levy. In the period around 1400, as the documents published by Pagnini show (*Della Decima*, I, 201 ff.), the Republic of Florence tended to raise money in parcels of 25,000 florins. This sum was distributed over the sixteen gonfalons according to the supposed resources of each household. Individual prestanze were assigned within each gonfalon by a commission of men drawn from that gonfalon. Since the sum of 25,000 florins might be raised up to a dozen times in one year, the citizen paid a corresponding number of prestanze. Between 1390 and 1403 prestanze varied from a few *soldi* to 250 or 800 or (in one case) 1000 florins per household. The poorest, most miserable members of the populace were declared *miserabili*—there were hundreds of these —and no forced loan was imposed on them. On occasion even beggars failed to qualify for this class. The employed members of the textile proletariat often paid from three to six soldi per prestanza, humble shopkeepers and skilled artisans from twelve soldi to two florins, and small merchants or *scioperati* from two up to five or six florins. Manufacturers, big bankers, and international merchants on a large scale paid a good deal more.

Discussions in the executive councils and complaints in memoirs and chronicles reveal that prestanze were inequitably distributed, probably not always, but apparently much more so after 1394 or 1395. At the working-class level taxation was onerous, for the men from this sector of society were without a voice in government, without their own guilds, and hence without real access to the institutional avenues of political expression. The Church did not interfere in those matters. Taxation also weighed heavily on the men of the *arti minori* or minor guilds, who made up a large part of the lower middle class. For while they were accorded from one-fourth to one-fifth the seats in the legislative councils and leading offices, this number was not only insufficient to secure the passage of legislation or control the decision-making process, it was not even large enough to prevent legislation. Indeed, on questions of political office, public finance, and foreign policy, the representatives in government of the minor guilds often followed the lead of the great mercantile interests.

The Fortunes of the Humanists

Apart from the conclusive evidence of inequitable prestanze contained in the minutes of the executive deliberations—and the evidence on occasion consisted of statements made by the oligarchs themselves[42]—the recorded complaints came from men of the upper classes: chroniclers like Giovanni Morelli and Giovanni Cavalcanti, or members of the Niccoli, Manetti, Panciatichi, and Rinuccini families. Confiscatory prestanze were the cause of many anti-government laments and criticisms which originated in this stratum of society. Hence the extent to which the lower orders were subject to a system of class taxation is by no means the only factor which makes Florentine fiscal records a difficult source for the historian to use. The causes of individual confiscatory taxation were manifold, but so far as we can tell political vendetta was behind most of it, as well as private hatreds between men of different factions. Finally, there were also some wealthy newcomers who, owing to their inadequate contacts in government circles, indirectly carried the partial tax obligations of some of the chief families of the oligarchy.

The catasto was introduced in 1427, after lengthy discussion in the executive councils and with the reluctant, somewhat painful acquiescence of a certain sector of the oligarchy. A new commission was set up to administer the tax and, with one or two exceptions during an eight-year period, prominent oligarchs were significantly absent from it.[43] All household heads in Florence were required to draw up a detailed report of their lands, livestock, houses, business establishments, investments, and government securities. Lawyers were even required to estimate the total value of their law books. Allowing for certain deductions, the government then taxed all net capital at the rate of 0.5 per cent, or ten soldi in gold (one-half florin) per 100 florins. The catasto of 1427, the most rigorous levy collected in fifteenth-century Florence, was very probably as equitable as tax systems ever got in Renaissance Italy. Inventories from each household were collected again in 1430, but a careful study of the appropriate registers, largely by comparing them with those of 1427, indicates

[42] *ASF, Consulte,* 41, ff. 39r-v, 41v, 46v (year: 1411). See also P. Berti, "Nuovi documenti intorno al catasto fiorentino," *Giornale storico degli archivi toscani,* IV (1860), 40-59.
[43] *ASF, Tratte,* 80, f. 409r-v.

101

that there were already some very relaxed features about the census of 1430, especially in the reports of the great families, which were able frequently—as one would have expected—to "adjust" the extent of their holdings with impunity.

It follows, therefore, that the sources should be used with caution, particularly the prestanze. They yield a picture, it is true, an extremely important and helpful picture. But no portrait of an individual man within the whole can ever be entirely accurate; or when one is, we shall only rarely have the means to know it. The reader is urged to consider this, retrospectively of course, in connection with the last part of the preceding chapter, and to keep it in mind when going through the succeeding parts of this one. For I shall often affirm that a given man or family held the tenth, the twentieth, or another place in the prestanze or catasto tax rolls. Financial ratings will thus generally be reported in specific numbers. It should be understood, however, that each rating will denote an approximate rank or place, not a precise or perfectly accurate position.

Having warned against innocent use of the two sources, we must guard next against extremes of skepticism. Just as it is dangerous to take Florentine tax reports or ratings at their face value, so it is foolish to reject their meaning out of hand or to tamper with them by trying to discount the reports or ratings of the families we know to have been either extremely powerful or subject to a strong current of political persecution. For in doing this we would be on our way to making the sources mean anything we desired. This is why I chose to use specific ratings, arrived at on the basis of long and laborious note-taking, counts, and compilations. In the long run the incidence of distortion and error is less grievous this way than if I had followed a procedure which used the documents in a looser, more irregular, or unsystematic fashion. After all, the precise nature or accuracy of important historical documents is often open to question. To what extent, for example, can we trust the chroniclers? Giovanni Cavalcanti, to take one instance, flatly declared that "Niccolò da Uzzano was never assigned a prestanza of more than sixteen florins."[44] Can we rely on such precision? What was the source

[44] *Istorie*, I, 214.

of his information? I suspect it was gossip and rumor, partly based on fact, but certainly erroneous as to exact figures. For while Niccolò's prestanze were for many years almost surely lower than they ought to have been, the fact is that in 1390 his basic levy was 125 florins, while in the mid 1420's it was 224 florins.[45]

What of the men who appeared at the top of the tax lists and whom we also know to have been subject to political vendetta and partisan taxation? Many of the Alberti households were in this situation between about 1394 and 1434. Were they every bit as wealthy as their prestanze suggested? Probably not. But on the other hand, no one has ever doubted that they were wealthy. Hounded though they were by very large prestanze, they were able to go on, year after year, disbursing large sums of money in order to meet their tax obligations. Furthermore, some of the Alberti houses carried on their business affairs both in Florence and elsewhere in Italy, and their catasto inventories of 1427 reveal that at least three branches of the clan continued to figure among the city's richest families. The point of uncertainty, accordingly, is not whether the heavily-taxed Alberti were rich or poor, but what was the extent of their wealth. The parallel case of the Rinuccini family is just as interesting and has been studied elsewhere.[46]

It remains to show that most of the points raised above actually favor the findings of this inquiry. For the financial portraits to be offered of the humanists are based on minimum estimates, and any changes that may hereafter be entertained in scholarship will almost surely have to upgrade the ratings, sums, or properties reported in the succeeding pages. Let us see more precisely why this is so.

Where its enemies were concerned, the oligarchy sometimes engaged in confiscatory taxation; with friends, on the contrary, its tendency was to show indulgence in tax estimates. On this basis, Coluccio Salutati was in an excellent position, since he was

[45] *ASF, Prestanze,* 1262, f. 153v; *Catasto,* 64, f. 65v, which also specifies Niccolò's prestanza during the period leading up to 1427.
[46] L. Martines, "Nuovi documenti su Cino Rinuccini e una nota sulle finanze della famiglia Rinuccini," *A.S.I.,* cxix, 1 (1961), 77-90.

not only a leading political dignitary,[47] as the appropriate sections of this study will show, but also the holder of a tax privilege which exempted his salary as chancellor. Niccolò Niccoli and his brothers seem really to have suffered excessive prestanze rates. The mark of their original wealth, however, is indicated by the complaints of two of the brothers. Bernardo in 1427 bitterly observed: "Too much injustice has been suffered by our small family, as we are all poor now, though we were all born rich." In 1430 Bartolommeo declared: "our family has been ruined by prestanze, for we have paid the Commune more than 40,000 florins."[48] Here therefore, in a questioned source (the catasto), is proof of the family's former wealth and present ruin. Another humanist, Roberto de' Rossi, in 1393 had his name changed by government action to *Dolcini*.[49] Then—though he did not subsequently stand out in public office—he was taken off the *magnati* rosters and given *popolano* status. This could only have been accomplished by powerful backing in high places, an advantage Roberto clearly enjoyed. For the sons of prominent citizens (e.g., Luca di Maso degli Albizzi, Alessandro di Ugo degli Alessandri) were to frequent his house later on, seeking him out as their master of studies. In such circumstances and in view of his *coup* in 1393, might it not be that Roberto would have been the object of any fiscal indulgence practiced by the Albizzi faction?

The city's leading humanist, Lionardo Bruni, enjoyed a highly-prized and rare tax privilege. While I estimate his net capital at about 11,000 florins in 1427, giving him the seventy-second place in the city, two of his contemporaries, Filelfo and Piovano Arlotto, estimated his wealth at from three to more than five times this amount.[50] The information I present concerning Carlo

---

[47] On the most recent statement concerning Salutati's weight in Florentine political affairs see Garin, "I cancellieri umanisti," 187ff.

[48] These statements were made in their catasto reports, cited by G. Zippel in his edition of Lorenzo Benvenuti's *Invettiva contro Niccolò Niccoli*, in *Giornale storico della letteratura italiana*, xxiv (1894), 170-172, n. 2.

[49] ASF, *Registri delle Balie*, 17, ff. 131r-v, 227v. It was only very recently I turned up this hitherto unknown fact about Roberto, which probably will have some bearing on the present form of his profile in Ch. iv, 3 of this work.

[50] Filelfo reported that Bruni's wealth amounted to 60,000 florins: see his *Commentationes florentinae de exilio*, ed. E. Garin, in *Prosatori latini del quattrocento* (Verona, 1952), p. 502. Arlotto reports 30,000 ducats: see his *Motti e Facezie*, ed. G. Folena (Verona, 1953), p. 55.

Marsuppini, Matteo Palmieri, and Giannozzo Manetti will speak for itself. The first was independently wealthy and a great friend of the Medici for about thirty years. Palmieri, a prominent politician, was often in a very strong position to help others; and although the third, Manetti, was undoubtedly subjected to confiscatory taxation, he always had wealth enough to survive the oligarchy's hardest blows. The extent of his patrimony is outlined in his father's catasto report of 1427, but here again we must assume that the reported sum was a minimum figure. For the elder Manetti, who had never bothered very much with politics and was now about to pay a tax on his total net capital, was unlikely to inventory a scrap more than was necessary.

3. COLUCCIO SALUTATI: 1336-1406

Early in this century two Italian scholars, Demetrio Marzi and Francesco Novati, tried to settle the question of Salutati's finances during his occupancy (1375-1406) of the Florentine Republic's chief secretarial post.[51] Taking his official salary, 100 gold florins yearly,[52] as their point of departure, they went on to consider the different lucrative powers to which he had an exclusive right as chancellery head. After careful consideration, they finally fixed his yearly receipts at a minimum of 600 florins,[53] or nearly one-eighth the value (5000 florins) of the Medici Palace in the fifteenth century. Then, copying Marzi, who in his turn had drawn on Villari, Novati changed the designated sum into the *lire* of his own day. He was shocked by the result: the figure seemed much too high. Therefore, he imperturbably cut the *lire* value in half, adducing only the flimsy reason that the gold florin of Salutati's age could not possibly have had the value in *lire* which some scholars had ascribed to it at the beginning of this century.

Marzi and Novati confounded the meaning of Salutati's income by wrenching it from its historical setting. But it will not be difficult to clear away this confusion. The solution depends

[51] Marzi, pp. 139-140; Salutati, *Epistolario*, IV, ii, 570.
[52] Marzi, p. 119.
[53] *Ibid.*, p. 140; Salutati, *loc.cit.*; on the value of the Medici Palace see Raymond de Roover, "New Interpretations," p. 54.

on our use of Florentine economic practice during the early decades of the fifteenth century.

According to the tax introduced in Florence in 1427,[54] property was capitalized on a 7 per cent income basis: that is to say, annual income from land or buildings was taken to equal 7 per cent of capital value. This ratio between income and value was not an innovation; the catasto merely formalized accepted procedure. Next, by evaluating Salutati's earnings on a 7 per cent basis, we may judge his estimated yearly income of 600 florins to have been equivalent, more or less, to the income on property valued at about 8570 florins. To understand the meaning of this sum, its meaning with reference to the distribution of Florentine wealth, we must turn to the catasto again. Legislation on this tax permitted the deduction of debts, house rents, and 200 florins per family member. At one point Salutati's family numbered ten persons,[55] and allowing a deduction for the house, it appears that his annual income approximated the earning power of lands and buildings worth around 6500 florins. In 1427 only about 150 Florentines reported net assets of over 6500 florins.[56] Since there were roughly 9866 family heads who submitted property reports to the catasto commission,[57] Salutati's projected place on the scale of wealth would have been in the upper 2 per cent of the city's population. This place was consistent with the economic level of the era's other first secretaries.[58]

[54] On the catasto cf. the following: Otto Karmin, *La legge del catasto fiorentino del 1427* (Firenze, 1906); Giuseppe Canestrini, *La scienza e l'arte di stato*; G. F. Pagnini, *Della decima e di varie altre gravezze imposte dal comune di Firenze*, 4 vols. (Lisbona-Lucca, 1765-1766). A good recent discussion of the controversy provoked in Florence by the catasto is C. C. Bayley, *War and Society in Renaissance Florence: The* DE MILITIA *of Leonardo Bruni* (Toronto, 1961), pp. 87ff.

[55] Salutati, *Epistolario*, IV, i, 387ff.

[56] See App. II, tables V-VIII.

[57] This total is based on a count of the names of citizens indexed in ASF, *Catasto*, 64-69, 72-81. On 7 June 1428 the catasto commission observed that there were "circa dieci mila" entries "overo partite del catasto," in *Catasto*, 2, f. 16v. A sum of 10,171 family heads was reported by Canestrini, p. 155.

[58] On the mid fourteenth-century chancellor see Marzi, pp. 97-99. Ser Viviano di Neri Viviani, the secretary in charge of laws and statutes ("notaio delle riformagioni") during the years 1378-1414, stood in the upper 2 per cent of his section of the city in 1403, for he was assigned the twenty-seventh levy in a total of 1492 *prestanziati*: see ASF, *Prestanze* 1996, f. 192v. In 1403 Ser Benedetto Fortini, chancellor for a time in 1406,

The cancellation of 2070 florins from his projected assets, re-
ducing them to 6500 florins, might have been larger so as to
cover other potential reductions—debts, for example, or loss in
capital investments. Even then, however, he would have ranked
in the upper 2 per cent level.

The above calculations may be controlled by adducing an important source of the late fourteenth century. About the year
1390 a new estimate was made of the distribution of wealth
among Florentine families. So far only one of the four registers
then kept has turned up in the State Archives of Florence,[59] and
fortunately it is the one containing the entries of the S. Croce
quarter, where Salutati resided. The number of heads entered
in this *estimo* totals about 1509. Only fifty-five of these carried
heavier tax estimates than the humanist, who therefore stood
between the upper 3 and 4 per cent of the populace. But as two
of the city's quarters, S. Giovanni and S. Spirito, were both larger
and wealthier than S. Croce, we may assume that he stood nearer
the upper 4 per cent level in the city-wide estimate. Contrary to
Novati's discomfort over the prospect of Salutati's alarmingly
high income, the 4 per cent estimate does not suggest the full
extent of the humanist's wealth, and possibly our projection based
on catasto material, ranking him among the upper 2 per cent
of all taxpayers, is more accurate. Regardless of our computations,
however, some part of his capital or income is omitted. For while
our projection from catasto data disregards the value of his estates in Stignano and Pescia, as well as the value of his government stock,[60] the *estimo* officials could not lay Salutati's chancellery income under assessment, as it was protected by a special
statute.

---

held a place in the upper 3 per cent of all S. Giovanni taxpayers, being
seventy-fourth in a distribution of some 2499 prestanze: see *Prestanze*, 1999
and 2002, folios alphabetically arranged by Christian name. Ser Paolo
Fortini, chancellor from 1411 to 1427, reported net assets (together with
a brother and nephew) of more than 20,000 florins in 1427: see *Catasto*,
80, folios given in the index there prefixed. On Lionardo Bruni, chancellor
after 1427, see sec. 7 above.

[59] *ASF, Estimo*, 183, f. 9r. The archival catalogue lists this source as
"Framenti vari, pergamencei e cartacei" and as dating from the fourteenth
and fifteenth centuries. Neither the format nor the hand belongs to the
fifteenth century. The date given above, 1390, is my own estimate.

[60] *ASF, Monte Comune*, 493 (date: 1402), f. 31r.

The Fortunes of the Humanists

Thinking in economic terms, we find that men who held office in Florence during the early fifteenth century came mainly from about the first 10 per cent of Florentine families.[61] Within these limits there was a still more restricted governing group, more or less clearly identified by frequencies of appearance in public office. This inner core was made up of men in the upper 3 per cent of the citizenry and entailed roughly 100 families (or about 250 households). Coluccio Salutati's economic position put him at the fringes of this group, but his position in public life enabled him to hold a place at the center.

4. ROBERTO DE' ROSSI: CA. 1355-1417

Although very little is known about Roberto de' Rossi's life,[62] his importance in the early development of Florentine humanism has long been recognized. A brilliant pupil of Chrysoloras and one of the first Florentines to read classical Greek, he was a member of the humanist group which centered around Salutati, Bruni, and Niccoli.

In the thirteenth century the Rossi were a great financial and political house. Before the end of the century, however, they were officially ranked with the *magnati* and held this status down to the fifteenth century. Roberto himself figures as a magnate in the civil records as late as 1393 and until then was automatically excluded from leading public offices.

Roberto owned a house in Florence with some land, most of it under cultivation.[63] He may also have had real estate elsewhere, or an estate in the country, but no documents to prove this have been found as yet. There is no evidence, furthermore, that he was ever matriculated in one of the trade guilds. And since he seems in later life to have devoted himself chiefly to humanistic studies, to the life of the cultivated gentleman,[64] it

[61] This statement is based on my familiarity with the prestanze registers of the years 1390 and 1403, the catasto registers of 1427, and the inventories (*Tratte*) of the holders of public office from 1385 to 1460.

[62] The fullest and most recent study is Aldo Manetti, "Roberto de' Rossi," *Rinascimento*, II (1951), 33-55.

[63] *Prestanze*, 1837, f. 16v; 1968, f. 60v. These folios also recorded the levies imposed on Roberto's "lavoratori" (i.e., his agricultural laborers). Cf. Lionardo Bruni, *Ad Petrum Paulum Histrum Dialogus*, ed. E. Garin, in *Prosatori latini del quattrocento*, p. 76; and Pitti, *Cronica*, p. 207.

[64] Giannozzo Manetti's judgment in a Vatican codex unknown to me (Cod. Vat. Urbin. Lat. 154). Cited by Baron, *The Crisis*, II, 570, n. 55.

The Fortunes of the Humanists

is unlikely that he ever involved himself in commercial activity. He was evidently a *scioperato*. What his landed income may have been is suggested by the comparative level of his forced loans. In the prestanze of 1390 he was levied 1.00 florin per impost,[65] a levy equaling that of the smaller shopkeepers. Ten years later, in keeping with the increased rates for all Florentines, his prestanza was 8.00 florins;[66] but in 1403 it was reduced to 3.00 florins.[67] The general levy of 1403 shows an average of about 0.26 florins per family in the class of solvent cloth workers—e.g., washers, carders, fullers, and even weavers. In the same levy the average shopkeeper and artisan paid a prestanza of just under 1.00 florin. Goro Dati, an international silk merchant on a small scale,[68] was prescribed an impost of 3.00 florins, a sum exactly equaling Roberto de' Rossi's impost. Three of the Pitti brothers, wool merchants whose houses Salutati greatly admired, were assigned prestanze of 2.00, 3.50, and 4.40 florins. The city's most prominent doctor of law, Messer Filippo Corsini, was assessed a tax of 14.65 florins. It is interesting to note, finally, that the "poorest" of the Florentine humanists, Roberto de' Rossi himself, did not compare unfavorably with a group of nine other doctors of law easily picked out in the prestanze registers:[69] for in 1403 they were variously assessed 6.00, 4.00, 3.00, 3.00, 2.50, 2.50, 2.00, 1.50, 0.80 florins.

The aim of these numerical comparisons is to get at Roberto's relative economic position, but the same end may be served by scaling his prestanza of 3.00 florins. The levy of 1403, as administered in his quarter of the city (S. Spirito), numbered 2184 payers of forced loans. About 217 of these were each assigned an impost of more than 3.00 florins. The humanist and forty-three others from S. Spirito were prescribed a forced loan of

[65] *Prestanze*, 1262, f. 221r.   [66] *Prestanze*, 1837, f. 16v.
[67] *Prestanze*, 2000, alphabetically arranged by Christian name.
[68] The extent of his wealth can be found in his business diary, *Il libro segreto di G. D.*, ed. Carlo Gargiolli (Bologna, 1869).
[69] *Prestanze*, 1995, Messer Filippo Villani, Messer Buonaccorso Torelli, Messer Rosso di Andreozzo Orlandi, Messer Lorenzo Fracassini, all resident in S. Croce; *Prestanze*, 1996, Messer Bartolommeo Popoleschi, Messer Marcello Strozzi, Messer Tommaso Marchi, all from S. Maria Novella; *Prestanze*, 1999, Messer Torello Torelli, from S. Giovanni; *Prestanze*, 2000, Messer Jacopo Niccoli and Messer Lorenzo Ridolfi, from S. Spirito. All are entered in these registers alphabetically by Christian name.

exactly 3.00 florins each; so that if he occupied the median or twenty-second place in this group, his was the 239th place in the S. Spirito tax rolls. In other terms, he ranked with Florentines in the first 11 per cent of the taxpaying populace.[70] This rank in 1427 signified a net income from estates valued at between 700 and 900 florins.[71]

Although the preceding computations associate Roberto de' Rossi with the small landowning nobility, they offer only a suggestive, not a precise, delineation of his economic status. The imprecision is due to the fact, already noted, that since the prestanza system of taxation was sensitive to the prejudices of the oligarchy, it might be administered—and often was—either indulgently or with excessive harshness. The result was that some men were forced to pay more than their rightful share of taxes, others less than their share.

5. CINO RINUCCINI: CA. 1355-1417

Cino's place in the history of Florence and his relation to humanism are connected with two aspects of his activity around 1400: he wrote a polemic against the tyranny of the Visconti, and he defended vernacular poetry from the attacks of certain humanists.[72]

Matriculated in the guild of the wool manufacturers in 1386, he was once sententiously called "un lanaiolo fiorentino."[73] He might as well have been called a druggist, a confectioner, or a retailer of notions, for he was matriculated in the guild of physicians and apothecaries and he was not a physician.[74] The point is that while membership in the major guilds denoted a solid social standing, it did not necessarily designate actual participation in a profession or given line of business.[75] That Cino was

[70] Owing to the spread of population in Florence, any percentage of this type has city-wide applicability, the reason for this being that S. Spirito was more densely populated than either S. Croce or S. Maria Novella by about one-third.

[71] This estimate based on the following: *ASF, Catasto*, 64-69, 72-81. My tallies indicate that the first 8.3 per cent of all taxpayers declared net assets of 1000 florins or more.

[72] See Baron, *The Crisis*, I, 79, 260 ff., 285.

[73] By Rossi, *Il Quattrocento*, p. 25.

[74] *ASF, Medici e Speziali*, 21, ff. 59r, 66r.

[75] The one exception being the guild of judges and notaries.

an active merchant, however, is clear from the fact that in 1409 he reported commercial liabilities of 10,000 florins, owing to the loss at sea of three vessels.[76] None the less, he seems to have had ample time to keep abreast of political events, literary quarrels, and the discussions of the humanist circle in Florence.

As early as the mid 1350's Cino's father, a knight and diplomat, had 4500 florins invested in the Monte, the Commune's funded debt.[77] Before the end of the century Cino himself had 28,194 florins in Monte securities,[78] and by 1422 Cino's heirs were collecting the yearly interest on a Monte account of 33,748 florins.[79]

In 1364 "The highest assessment in the entire city was 640 florins, levied against Messer Francesco Rinuccini [Cino's father]."[80] Fourteen years later Messer Francesco "possessed land to the value of 30,000 florins, government securities totaling 14,500 florins, and only 2,500 florins . . . 'tra mercatanzia e danari.' "[81] Again, according to an *estimo* of about 1390 the Rinuccini were the second richest family of the S. Croce quarter.[82] First in this district were the Alberti, a family of bankers with an international reputation. But although some branches of the Alberti were banished from Florence in the 1390's and later, in 1403 the Rinuccini were still S. Croce's second house, another family of enormous wealth, the Serristori, having meanwhile risen to the leading position. It may not be amiss to emphasize the fact that our semi-obscure merchant and polemicist, Cino, so suggestively studied by Hans Baron, was prescribed a prestanza of 120 florins in the same levy in which Giovanni di Bicci de' Medici, for example, paid 37.5 florins per prestanza, Niccolò da Uzzano 20.0 florins, and Messer Maso degli Albizzi 17.5 florins.[83] When we remember that these men had few peers in

---

[76] *ASF, Provvisioni*, 98, ff. 68v-69r.

[77] *ASF, Monte*, 435, entered under 15 January 1355. On Florentine attitudes toward the moral issues raised by the institution of the Monte see Raymond de Roover, "Il trattato di fra Santi Rucellai sul cambio, il monte comune e il monte delle doti," *A.S.I.*, 1 (1953), 3-23.

[78] *Monte*, 358, f. 46r.   [79] *Monte*, 365, f. 41r.

[80] Brucker, "The Medici in the Fourteenth Century," p. 6.

[81] Jones, "Florentine families," p. 197.

[82] *ASF, Estimo*, 183, ff. 15, 38r/v. The first six levies were: Messer Antonio degli Alberti (assessed 413 florins), Ricciardo degli Alberti (202 florins), Messer Giovanni Rinuccini (132 florins), Jacopo Rinuccini (113 florins), Cino Rinuccini (102 florins), and Simone Rinuccini (87.5 florins).

[83] App. II, tables I, no. 2; II, nos. 21, 54; IV, no. 30.

the city, their respective imposts suggest something about the magnitude of Cino's wealth.

A detailed inventory of the Rinuccini fortunes was drafted on the occasion of the tax introduced in 1427, the catasto. This source reveals that Cino's heirs (his sons Jacopo, Francesco, and Filippo) were the three richest citizens in their section, the Bue sixteenth of Florence. But owing to the three-way division of the family fortunes, they held the eighth (no longer the second) place on the S. Croce tax rolls. The first seven places belonged to the leading branches of the Lamberteschi, Serristori, Alberti, Busini, Giugni, Peruzzi, and Baroncelli families.[84]

The actual form of the Rinuccini wealth was conservative. For example, Cino's son, Filippo, reported gross assets of 15,004 florins.[85] He had 3148 florins of this in landed estates (eight farms, two large cottages, and various land parcels), 11,186 florins in government securities, and a mere 670 florins in commercial investments and small loans. The form of Francesco Rinuccini's reported capital was nearly identical with Filippo's. Only Jacopo, who declared gross assets of 17,834 florins,[86] clearly departed from his brothers' conservative pattern of investment: he listed 2827 florins in commercial and finance capital, or almost 16 per cent of all his declared assets.

As the foregoing evidence suggests, far from being a mere "lanaiolo fiorentino," Cino belonged to one of the Republic's richest families. Moreover, despite the fact that they were not prominent in public life, the Rinuccini exhibited the power to obtain political favors by repeatedly securing tax indulgences from the Signoria and legislative councils.[87]

6. NICCOLÒ NICCOLI: 1364-1437

Niccolò Niccoli was an outstanding member of the humanist circle in Florence for about forty years. His prominence was not

---

[84] App. II, table V, nos. 1-7.   [85] *Catasto*, 69, ff. 62r-65r.
[86] *Ibid.*, ff. 65v-72r.
[87] *ASF, Lib. Fab.*, 45, f. 130r/v; 46, ff. 1v, 3r, 8v, 10r; 47, ff. 41r, 42r; 48, ff. 160r, 161r. These sources record the votes on the family's tax indulgences. A tax indulgence was drafted in the form of a petition and presented to the Signoria and colleges, where a favorable vote was required before it could be passed on as a bill to the legislative councils. Cf. L. Martines, "Nuovi documenti su Cino Rinuccini," pp. 77-90.

based on his writings, although he revealed a distinct epistolary bent, but rather on his vigorous promotion of the study of humanistic literature, on his personality, and on his friendships. In Florence he seems to have been almost unrivaled in his passion for classical studies, but this passion was often the source of his troubles. It got him into debt; it turned Coluccio Salutati's sons against him when he refused to return certain manuscripts which the late chancellor had lent him;[88] and because of it, he clashed with three of the age's leading humanists—Lionardo Bruni, Guarino Veronese, and Francesco Filelfo.

Niccolò was fascinated by antique *objets d'art* and owner of one of the best classical libraries in Europe. What was his background and economic situation?[89]

Whatever their place of origin, and Pistoia has been suggested,[90] the Niccoli were already settled in Florence at the beginning of the fourteenth century. By 1350 their name was associated with one of the city's richest houses, for Niccolò's father, Bartolommeo, amassed a large fortune in the manufacture of wool cloth. Like so many Florentines of the period, however, he may also have been involved in money lending, grain futures, or other forms of speculation. For a time the family's good fortune continued. Resident in the very industrial S. Spirito quarter, Niccolò and his five brothers paid the district's sixth highest prestanza (130 florins) as late as 1390.[91] They were therefore deemed to be wealthier than most of the S. Spirito ruling families: for example, the Bardi, Brancacci, Capponi, Corsini, Pitti, Quaratesi, Ridolfi, Serragli, Soderini, and Uzzano.

By 1400 Niccolò and his brothers were assigned separate

[88] In 1427 one of Salutati's sons, Arrigo, declared: "da nicholaio nicholi per quanto mi tocha di libri ch'egl a nelle mani da nostro padre, e quali sono bisongnuoli a miei figluoli per studiar. da quelli libri non o potuto vedere chonto chon detto nicholaio. credo sieno di valuta di fiorini ciento salvo la ragione" [i.e., the interest]. *Catasto*, 74, ff. 120v-127v.

[89] The only monograph on him is Giuseppe Zippel, *Niccolò Niccoli*. See also Vespasiano da Bisticci, *Vite*, pp. 434-444.

[90] See Lionardo Bruni, *Oratio in nebulonem maledicum*, appended to Zippel, *Niccolò Niccoli*.

[91] *Prestanze*, 1262, f. 170r. The first five assessments were: Messer Luigi Guicciardini (380 florins), Antonio and Corso di Niccolò Dietifeci (325 florins), Bartolomeo di Tommaso Corbinelli (180 florins), Filippo di Jacopo Guidetti (175 florins), and Francesco di Domenico Sapiti (140 florins).

prestanze;[92] they evidently broke up their single household in the 1390's. Their individual levies in 1400 varied from 10.0 to 12.0 florins and their economic rank, according to the tax rolls, declined to the upper 3 per cent level of the Florentine population. This decline was partly caused by the breakup of the Niccoli household, but much of it was the result of business mismanagement and discord between the brothers. By 1403 their economic adversity is clearly evident both in the scale of their levies and the distance between them: Piero paid 10.0 florins per prestanza, Bernardo paid 9.00, Giovanni 4.00, Niccolò 3.25, Vettorio 3.00, and Messer Jacopo (a doctor of law) only 2.00 florins.[93] These levies indicate that the brothers now held a place between the upper 3 and 12 per cent of the populace.[94]

The 1390's saw a marked decline in the history of the Niccoli fortunes. Although the exact causes of the decline are still unknown, a few suggestions may be offered.

It is unlikely that the Niccoli wealth was largely made up of conservative investments, such as land or government securities, for the probability of ruin in holdings of this type was remote, especially when such holdings were extensive. This observation is amply supported by the history of the Rinuccini fortune which, despite some grave commercial losses, long survived the Niccoli patrimony because a good deal of it was in the form of landed estates and government securities. The gradual ruin of the Niccoli family was presumably brought about by mismanagement and poor commercial investments.[95] And if, having reached their eco-

---

[92] *Prestanze*, 1837, ff. 44r-46r.

[93] *Prestanze*, 1994, arranged alphabetically by Christian name. On Piero and Bernardo see App. II, table IV, nos. 61, 66. This is the place to note that on 23 December 1401 a bill was enacted in favor of three of the brothers—Bernardo, Piero, and Vettorio. Altogether they owed the city 345 florins in back prestanze. The bill, actually a tax indulgence, allowed them to get away with paying half this sum into the lost fund ("ad perdendum"). They thereby gave up the right to collect any interest on this money and in fact lost the entire prestanza. ASF, *Provvisioni*, 90, ff. 338v-340r.

[94] These percentages were calculated as follows. In 1403 the S. Spirito quarter numbered 2184 *prestanziati*. Of these only fifty-three paid prestanze of more than 10.0 florins. Piero shared the 10.0 florin level with six others; ence his rank was about fifty-seven. Again, only 261 of the 2184 paid vies of 3.00 florins or more.

[95] In 1412—this is a late example—Piero Niccoli was seized by the *con-tiere*, Braccio Fortebracci, who confiscated his horses, money, cargo of ("arnesi"), and other items. ASF, *Leg. Comm.*, 6, f. 21v.

nomic low point, the brothers had an opportunity to improve or restore the condition of the family a decade or two later, they were prevented from doing so by their violent family quarrels.[96] Years later Niccolò was still unmollified: he complained that his house on the Via Maggio and two of the family wool-processing shops had not been rented for nine years, "owing to the wickedness and hatred of some of his vicious brothers."[97]

The inventories for the catasto of 1427 reveal a picture of the family's stricken economic situation.[98] Four of the brothers (not including Niccolò) individually reported gross assets ranging from 500 to 1100 florins. A fraction of this was invested in the wool trade; the balance was the value of a few houses and land parcels. The brothers had neither government securities nor bank deposits. Indeed, they were so weighed down with family obligations and creditors, that they were unable to report even a single florin in net assets. A fifth brother, Messer Jacopo, who died around 1425, left his only child a bequest of 1000 florins (this was to be her dowry), thus fixing her rank among the upper 9 per cent income group.

The best off of the six brothers was the humanist and collector of classical manuscripts, Niccolò. In his accounts for the catasto of 1427 he declared gross assets of 1367 florins.[99] This total omitted his share in the ownership of two houses (unleased); but it included 142 florins in real estate values and the real value of his government securities. The securities had a *nominal* value of more than 2000 florins and they earned an annual interest of not less than 5 per cent. Hence they brought in a yearly income of about 100 florins, although the payments were sometimes suspended in whole or in part. The nominal value of Niccolò's

[96] Their property disputes probably went back to the mid 1390's, but the earliest traces of litigation which I have found date from 1406, when the brothers were completely divided. Chiefly involved were Niccolò, Vettorio, Bernardo, and Giovanni. See *ASF, Notarile antecosimiano*, M 739, ff. 160r, 173v, 175r, 186v-187r, 189r/v, 196v, 204r, 208r-211r; being the notarial acts for the years 1402-1406 of the notary, Ser Domenico Mucini. On another clash between Niccolò and Giovanni in 1421, *Notarile antecosimiano*, P 428, f. 89r, of the acts of Ser Filippo Pieruzzi.

[97] "per la perversita e odio dalcuni suoi scelerati frategli," *Catasto*, 62, f. 325r.

[98] *Catasto*, 65, ff. 120r-121v, 257r-258r, 264r-265r, 474v.

[99] *Catasto*, 81, ff. 489r/503r. Pagination doubled.

securities had exceeded 1000 florins since the beginning of the century,[100] if not earlier, so that despite his abandoning the wool trade, he had long enjoyed a moderate income, even if it was occasionally interrupted. Furthermore, Niccolò also disposed of the dead capital of his valuable library, which had absorbed large sums of money across the years.[101] Part of that library (eventually acquired by Cosimo de' Medici) went to cover Niccolò's debts to Cosimo, incurred during a friendship of more than twenty years. In 1433 those debts amounted to 355 florins which, let it be emphasized, surpassed by one-third the value of Niccolò's well-known house, worth 286 florins.[102]

Niccolò was clearly a man of independent means. He did not exercise a trade and no evidence has been uncovered to show that he involved himself in commercial affairs at any point during the last forty years of his life.[103] From time to time, however, he did buy and sell manuscripts with an eye to profit. He dressed— it was observed—with great elegance; his Florentine apartments were renowned for their beauty; a collection of antique *objets d'art* was one of his prize possessions; celebrities on their way through Florence sought him out; he was frequently seen in the company of Cosimo and Lorenzo de' Medici; and he may even have struck Florentines as something of an aesthete. We are not surprised, therefore, that he failed to convince the catasto officials of his poverty, particularly as he tried to do so while on a pleasure trip to Verona: "Just imagine, O esteemed officials, what sort of tax my poor goods can bear, with all the debts and pressing expenses I have. Which is why, begging your humanity and clemency, I pray that it will please you to treat me in such a way that current taxes will not force me in my old age to die far from my birthplace, where I have spent all I had."[104]

---

[100] *ASF, Monte*, 280 (date: 1404), f. 129v.

[101] Zippel, *Niccolò Niccoli*, pp. 41-45, 109-111.

[102] *Catasto*, 497, f. 561r; 473, ff. 37r-38r, where Niccolò declared: "Egli e debitore a cosmo e a lorenzo di johanni de medici gia piu anni in fiorini trecento cinquanta cinque, i quali anno paghati per mie extremi bisogni in piu tempo e in diversi luoghi come pelor libro del banco manifestamente appare; che se la lor liberalita non m'avesse sovenuto, gia molti anni mi conveneva andar mendicando e stendando per lo mondo."

[103] Indeed, a prolonged search in the State Archives of Florence has failed to show that he was ever even a member of one of the trade guilds.

[104] *Catasto*, 375, ff. 275r-275v (date: 1430), "e pensate honorevoli uficiali

The Fortunes of the Humanists

7. LIONARDO BRUNI: CA. 1370-1444

Lawyer and humanist, landlord and statesman, Lionardo Bruni was one of Florence's richest citizens during the last twenty years or more of his life.

A native of Arezzo, the son of an Aretine grain dealer ("blada-jolus"),[105] he turned up in Florence in the early 1390's, apparently to study law. Why he chose Florence is not entirely clear, for although the Studio Fiorentino was outstanding in the field of notarial science, Bologna was still the greatest European center of legal studies. But as we know that Lionardo's youth was financially difficult—his father and mother died in 1386 and 1388 respectively—it may be that he had relatives or friends in Florence, only forty miles from Arezzo, who were willing to give him some assistance—room and board, for example. Since these costs were relatively dear, such help would not have been unimportant. To convey an idea of the costs, it may be enough to note that servants were paid from 9.00 to 12.0 florins yearly,[106] while the yearly expenses of a young man enrolled in a university away from home averaged about 20.0 florins.[107]

Neither time nor circumstances went against Lionardo. He amassed a large fortune during the early years of the fifteenth century, but his wealth did not escape the notice of contemporaries[108]—no extraordinary matter in Florence, where the system of taxation tended, rather unpleasantly, to get citizens to watch one another. Unfortunately, however, there is a frustrating vagueness in all the extant remarks on the sources of his wealth. His

---

che graveza posso portare in questa misera sustantia avendoci su tanti debiti e tanta expesa d'istrema necessita, e per la qual cosa io pregho la vostra humanita e clementia che vi piaccia trattarmi in modo che nella estrema vechieza la necessita di queste gravezze non mi constringhino a morir fuor della patria nella quale io ho consumato cio ch'io ho."

[105] G. Mancini, "Aggiunte e correzioni alla vita di Leonardo Bruni," in L. Bruni, *Historiarum florentini populi libri xii*, 3 vols. (Florentiae, 1855-1860), I, 29. Overlooked by Franz Beck, *Studien zu Lionardo Bruni* (Berlin-Leipzig, 1912), the biographical section of which is untrustworthy.

[106] Cf. Filippo Manetti's memoirs (1425-1456), BNF, *Magl.*, VII, 1014, f. 33r.

[107] See figures in Gutkind, *Cosimo de' Medici*, p. 230.

[108] E.g., in the 1430's Filelfo had Rinaldo degli Albizzi say that Bruni's wealth amounted to 60,000 florins. See Bk. III of his *Commentationes florentinae de exilio*, ed. Eugenio Garin, *Prosatori latini del quattrocento* (Milano, 1952), p. 502.

good friend, Poggio, suggested that part of it came from legal practice, but he stressed Lionardo's having been much courted by Pope John XXIII, "through whose favor he got a great deal of money."[109] A younger acquaintance and fellow-humanist, Giannozzo Manetti, attributed Lionardo's riches to his "struggles, alertness, and his incredible eloquence."[110] Manetti probably included therewith the gifts of patrons, whose favor may well have rested on the popularity of his literary works.[111] To these sources may be added any fees collected by Lionardo in his capacity as a political observer (i.e., as a sort of "spy") for at least one prince during his secretarial turn at the papal curia.[112] But without probing further into other means at his disposal, let us look next at the extent of his wealth, the outlines of which—probably too modestly—are clearly set forth in his inventory for the catasto of 1427.[113]

According to this report, Lionardo owned five farms in the Aretine *contado* and two near Florence. They were farmed by twenty-three peasants, eleven of whom worked for the humanist on a part-time basis only. He also listed the possession of four family dwellings: two country houses near Arezzo and Fiesole and two family *palazzi* in Florence and Arezzo. His remaining assets, the largest part by far, were broadly divisible into two categories: commercial and finance capital on the one side, government securities on the other. Taken at their nominal value,

---

[109] Poggio, *Oratio funebris in obitu Leonardi Arretini*, in L. Bruni, *Epistolarum libri viii*, ed. Laurentio Mehus (Florentiae, 1741), pp. cxx-cxxi, "Eodemque officio [that of papal secretary], quod semper summa integritate, fide, innocentia admistravit, Gregorii quoque, atque Alexandri, et Johannis tempore, cujus Pontificatus quaestuosissimus fuit, functus est, multasque tum pecunias Johannis indulgentia contraxit."

[110] G. Manetti, *Oratio funebris*, in Bruni, *Epistolarum*, p. xcvi, "ac laboribus denique, et vigiliis, et sua illa incredibili eloquentia amplas divitias comparasset."

[111] Vespasiano, p. 256, says of Lionardo: "there were numerous scribes in Florence who were continually transcribing his works, some intended for Florence, others for foreign export."

[112] In a letter to Francesco, "principi Cortonensium," Bruni rehearsed everything he knew about the papal schism, as well as about other political and military events, all of which he had learned through his papal connections. He ended the letter by saying, "habes acta nostra, quae quoniam ad te liberius scripsi, dolore quodam permotus, occule quaeso has literas ne in aliorum perveniant manus." See L. Bruni, *Epistolarum libri octo* (Basileae, 1535), p. 60.

[113] *Catasto*, 29, ff. 406r/410r-416v/420v. Double pagination.

the securities were worth 3835 florins, on which they drew a yearly interest of from 5 to 8 per cent. A conservative estimate of the real value of these securities is to take them at about 43 per cent of nominal value, leaving an approximate real value of almost 1650 florins.[114]

Lionardo's fascinating report, eleven folio pages in length, includes a column listing the various business and banking houses that carried his investments and cash deposits. Distributed across thirteen accounts, these moneys totaled some 7445 florins. Their soundness as investments is shown by the fact that they were placed with the firms of some of the richest and most powerful men in Florence. Let us note a few of the names and sums: 1309 florins with Vanni di Niccolò di Ser Vanni (in two separate accounts), 1000 florins with Cosimo and Lorenzo de' Medici, 1000 florins with Lorenzo di Messer Palla di Nofri Strozzi, 1000 florins with Niccolà and Cambio di Messer Vieri de' Medici (two separate accounts), 500 florins with Gabbriello di Messer Bartolommeo Panciatichi, 500 florins with Tommaso di Giacomino Tebalducci, 400 florins with Bernardo Portinari, and 400 florins with Francesco di Francesco della Luna.[115]

In order to compare or scale the extent of Lionardo's wealth, the first step is to make an estimate of it. Judging by rents, agricultural produce, and subsequent alienations, his lands in 1427 were worth about 2700 florins. This sum omits the value of his town and country houses because, being used exclusively by the Bruni family, these did not bring in an income. They were therefore not subject to the catasto. All told, accordingly, four items composed Lionardo's taxable capital: farms, securities, and com-

---

[114] See the "Pregi di denari di monte" in *Catasto*, 3, f. 18r, containing the data on which the above estimate is based. The "pregi" given in this source were the officially-recognized real values of government securities.

[115] *Catasto*, 29, f. 416v/420v. To comment here about the wealth and prominence of the Medici and Strozzi families would be superfluous. A summary word about the others will have to suffice. Vanni di Niccolò di Ser Vanni was the sixth highest taxpayer in the Ruote district (his net assets: nearly 5000 florins); Gabbriello Panciatichi was the third richest man in Florence (78,166 florins); Tommaso di Giacomino was third on the tax rolls of the Leon Bianco district (21,366 florins); Bernardo Portinari was fourth in the Vaio district (18,173 florins); and Francesco di Francesco della Luna was the ninth heaviest taxpayer in the city (34,987 florins). The preceding ratings and assets apply only to the period around 1427. Cf. App. II, tables VI-VIII.

mercial and banking investments. In 1427 the net value of these items amounted to about 11,800 florins. But before a tax was prescribed various deductions were permitted. In Lionardo's case, allowing for capital expenditures and the size of his family, the deductions totaled about 735 florins.[116] This left the humanist with a balance sheet of more than 11,000 florins in net assets.

The catasto was calculated on a 0.5 per cent basis, or one-half florin per 100 florins of productive capital. Therefore, discounting his tax privilege so as to permit city-wide comparisons on an equal basis, Lionardo's catasto would have been about 55.0 florins per levy.[117]

If a catasto of 55.0 florins be a rough index of Lionardo's wealth in 1427, some interesting comparisons follow. For one thing, he would have been the fourth highest taxpayer in his district, the *gonfalone* Bue, where only the three Rinuccini brothers preceded him. At the level of his quarter, S. Croce, he would have ranked fifteenth on the tax rolls, and seventy-second for the city as a whole.[118] The Florentines who filed tax returns in 1427 numbered about 10,000; hence the humanist easily ranked in the first per cent of all Florentine taxpayers.

Lionardo's net assets of 11,000 florins are a minimum estimate. These exclude the value of four large houses, as has already been noted, the value of his precious library, and—if he practiced— his earnings as a lawyer. Moreover, at the end of 1427 he was appointed to the Republic's leading secretarial office. Carrying a basic stipend of 100 florins yearly,[119] this office actually entailed powers lucrative enough to quintuple the official salary,

---

[116] A deduction of 200 florins per family member was permitted. To cover property losses, damage, repairs, and the like, a deduction of five per cent the value of real estate was sometimes allowed.

[117] He was in fact assigned a catasto of only 11.0 florins: *Catasto*, 29, f. 417v/421v. But in 1446 his son, Donato, stated that his father's impost in 1427 had been 12.0 florins: *Catasto*, 662, f. 656r. Lionardo's catasto was one-fifth what it ought to have been, owing to a tax privilege bestowed on him by the Republic in 1416. According to the articles of the privilege, he could not be taxed more than a given fixed rate. The appropriate document, a *provvisione*, was published by Emilio Santini, *Leonardo Bruni Aretino*, in *Annali della R. Scuola Normale Superiore di Pisa*, xxii (1910), 133ff.

[118] App. ii, table v, no. 15.

[119] *ASF, Notaio di Camera-uscita*, 1 (date: 1426-1430), f. 82r, which lists the payment of a salary of 100 florins to Ser Paolo di Ser Lando Fortini, the secretary who preceded Lionardo. At the beginning of his term in office the humanist's salary was identical.

The Fortunes of the Humanists

as Marzi noted in Salutati's case. For our purposes this need only
be mentioned, for none of these items substantially affected
Lionardo's economic rank. Cut where one will, his wealth associated him with the income group which included statesmen like
Francesco Soderini, Bartolommeo Valori, Messer Rinaldo degli
Albizzi, and Messer Matteo Castellani;[120] and it greatly exceeded
the declared assets of statesmen like Neri di Gino Capponi, Messer Lorenzo Ridolfi, and the most distinguished members of the
Rucellai and Salviati families.[121]

This account of Lionardo Bruni's wealth refers to the period
around 1427. The following sketch will trace the history of the
family fortunes down to 1458.

By 1433 another house and farm had been added to the
Bruni possessions.[122] Alessandra di Michele Castellani, Lionardo's
daughter-in-law, received the farm as part of her dowry when
she married Donato Bruni. Commercial and banking deposits
were not included in the report of 1433, and perhaps some of
these had been liquidated. The column containing the figures on
government securities disclosed nominal values of 10,012 florins,
irregularly distributed among the various Monte funds.

Since the humanist died in March 1444, the family inventory
for the catasto of 1446 was submitted by Donato.[123] It lists nine
farms and seven houses. The houses were scattered: there were
two in Arezzo, two in Florence (one of them being the former
palace of a ruined old family, the Tolosini), and three in Montevarchi. While one of the Montevarchi houses was a mere cottage,
another was rented out as an hotel or inn ("albergo"). An interest-
paying value of almost 11,000 florins in the Monte was now accredited to the Bruni family; but once again finance and commercial capitals were omitted. Although it seems that in 1446
Donato's estates exceeded any landed aggregate previously re-

[120] They declared the following assets in 1427: Albizzi (11,811 florins),
Castellani (13,234 florins), Valori (9646 florins), and Soderini (10,927
florins).

[121] They declared the following assets: Capponi (4720 florins), Ridolfi
(5249 florins), the sons of Giovanni Rucellai (6164 florins), the sons of
Paolo di Messer Paolo Rucellai (4618 florins), and Bernardo di Messer
Jacopo Salviati (3112 florins).

[122] Catasto, 447, ff. 653r-654r; 491 bis, f. 535r.

[123] Catasto, 661, ff. 686r-689v; 662, ff. 656r-659v.

ported by his father, the high point was actually reached before the death of the humanist, when the family properties included some thirteen or fourteen farms and eight houses. For in the two years after Lionardo's death Donato sold a house in Arezzo, various land parcels, and four farms.[124] These sales brought in more than 2000 florins. Immediately afterwards he also sold the old family seat in Florence for 1200 florins. But before this sale, or at any rate in 1446, Donato's accounts showed assets of more than 9000 florins. His liquidation of various estates in the years just after his father's death suggests that in the period around 1446 he had considerable cash on hand, part of which he apparently aimed to use in real estate speculation, the rest in commercial enterprise, almost certainly in the silk and wool trades.[125]

Donato's inventory for the catasto of 1458 is hardly more than a record of his commercial failure.[126] It shows that all the farms of the earlier reports had been alienated. For example, the great Quarto possession outside Arezzo was sold, a country house included, in July of 1454 for 3000 florins. Four new farms and various land parcels in the Valdarno and Montevarchi areas, acquired after the drafting of the 1446 report, were sold before 1458 for 2140 florins.[127] Gone too were the Tolosini palace, sold for 650 florins, and two Montevarchi houses, sold for more than 200 florins. No mention is made of the family residence in Arezzo. Part of Donato's remaining capital now consisted of two mills, a small river vessel, and several other items, all incompletely valued at about 700 florins.[128] Commercial and miscellaneous assets totaled 4437 florins.[129] He also had 13,165 florins in gov-

---

[124] *Ibid.*; *Catasto*, 801, ff. 1195r-1198v. The second citation contains the report of 1458 and lists all the goods alienated after Lionardo's death.

[125] ASF, *Arte della Seta*, 8, f. 56r, showing that Donato was matriculated as a "setaiolus grossus" in June 1444; ASF, *Arte della Lana*, 21, f. 134r, showing his matriculation in the wool merchants' guild in May 1447.

[126] *Catasto*, 801, ff. 1195r-1198v.

[127] Their buyer was the man whose father commissioned the famous Pazzi Chapel, Jacopo di Messer Andrea dei Pazzi.

[128] The value of one item of wealth was entirely omitted: "ho la quarta parte dalle chiavi d'arezzo della quali non ho ancor tratto alcuno profitto." *Catasto*, 801, f. 1195r.

[129] This included 1600 florins for which he was a creditor of the Republic. He and several others had been singled out to lend money to Florence in the form of a special prestanza.

ernment securities, but their actual value was calculated on a 20 per cent basis, leaving only 2633 florins. Finally, for the first time in all the Bruni inventories, we find a list of thirty-seven creditors. Donato owed them a total of 5600 florins. The group included some of the city's distinguished names: Altoviti, Biliotti, Buondelmonti, Corbinelli, Ginori, Medici, and Ridolfi. When drafting the report, Donato was unable to specify the claims of each of his creditors, "for my [account] book is in the hands of these creditors, and I can't get it back."[130] Evidently his financial situation had not been strong enough to prevent seizure of his accounts. None the less the tax officials, deferring consideration of his credits and liabilities, assigned an estimate of 3338 florins to his non-commercial assets. His final levy, however, was to depend on a subsequent revaluation of the family's fiscal privilege.

Donato Bruni inherited a very large patrimony in 1444, and although fourteen years later he was still a man of some means, he had greatly overreached himself in his commercial affairs. Not only did he lack his father's circumspection, worse still, he could not count on the influence which the elder Bruni had commanded in high government circles.

8. POGGIO BRACCIOLINI: 1380-1459

This sketch of Poggio's fortunes is based chiefly on the primary material appended to Ernst Walser's biographical study.[131] Somewhat thin up to about 1426, the documents collected there then fill out and provide a fascinating picture of the humanist's growing wealth.

His father was a needy, sometimes debt-ridden apothecary; his maternal grandfather had been a notary.[132] Poggio himself, after a brief period of legal study at Bologna, first went to Florence in the late 1390's and entered the city, it seems, with only five *soldi* in his pocket. We do not know for certain how he managed during his three or four years there, but one way or another—

---

[130] *Catasto*, 801, f. 1197r, "Nono tratto fuori partita per partita per non potere perche ilibro mio e nelle mani dessi creditori a nonllo posso riavere." On the term *partita* see Edler, *Glossary*, p. 205.

[131] *Poggius Florentinus, Leben und Werke* (Leipzig, 1914). Still a valuable work is William Shepherd, *The Life of Poggio Bracciolini* (Liverpool, 1837).

[132] Walser, p. 5.

he speaks of having copied codices in his youth—he succeeded in getting an expensive education at the center of European notarial study, the Studio Fiorentino.[133] Matriculated in the guild of judges and notaries in 1402, he took a post as private secretary to the Cardinal of Bari in the autumn of the following year. Before the year's end, however, he passed on to the court of Pope Boniface IX as a writer of apostolic letters. This was the beginning of long years of secretarial work in the papal curia, although later this association was to have various interruptions.

Poggio's income in those years is still a mystery, since no thorough study has as yet been made of the salary structure at the pontifical court in the early fifteenth century.[134] In Florence the prestanze associate Poggio with slender properties. But prestanze were in principle based on an estimate of commercial and landed capital; they were not deemed to be an index of professional earnings. Let us turn, therefore, to the catasto of 1427.

Here we find that Poggio had relatively modest means.[135] To begin with, he owned a house and two cottages in Terranuova. Since these buildings did not bring in an income, they were not computed into his taxable capital. He also listed three land parcels (valued at 211 florins), 45.0 florins in government securities,[136] 261 florins in outstanding loans, and some miscellaneous items. His gross assets finally came to 566 florins. After a subsistence deduction of 200 florins, the remaining capital bound him to a tax of slightly over 2.00 florins per catasto levy.[137]

By adopting some sort of an objective yardstick and restricting ourselves to the S. Giovanni quarter, where Poggio was officially domiciled, we may be able to achieve some precision about his economic position. Ranking him in his own professional class, the

[133] G. Rondini, "Ordinamenti e vicende principali dell' antico studio fiorentino," *A.S.I.* xiv, iv (1884), 41-64. The fees for attending lectures in philosophy, logic, or *notarìa* were identical.

[134] Peter D. Partner, "Camera Papae: Problems of Papal Finance in the later Middle Ages," *The Journal of Ecclesiastical History* iv, i (1953), 55-68. See also the very adequate bibliography in his *The Papal State Under Martin V* (London, 1958).

[135] Walser, pp. 339-341.

[136] This was their real value. Their nominal value was about 100 florins. Walser, p. 140, confuses the two.

[137] The catasto taxed assets at the rate of 0.5 per cent. To this the officials added 6.00 *soldi* for each male member of the family between the ages of eighteen and sixty. *Catasto*, 3, f. 21r.

notaries, we discover that his economic level was relatively high. For of the district's sixty-seven notaries listed as family heads (and S. Giovanni was the most densely-populated quarter), only ten were assigned a heavier tax rate than Ser Poggio,[138] and three of these, who figured among S. Giovanni's leading tax-payers, had extra sources of income.[139] If we then look at com-parative figures elsewhere, the result is similar. In Arezzo, forty miles away, where Florentine tax officials were inclined to be severe in their assessments, only seven of the thirty notaries who filed tax returns were assigned higher catasti than Poggio.[140]

Between 1428 and 1432 Poggio bought two other houses and land parcels in Terranuova for 261 florins.[141] During these years he also tried his hand at making money on the public debt, as indicated by his purchase and sale of Monte securities. In the census of 1433 he reported a gross capital of 1060 florins, but he was permitted a deduction of 800 florins to cover his own sub-sistence and that of his three natural children. Another deduction entirely cancelled his net assets: he owed nearly 715 florins to the Florentine branch of the Medici banking house. The demands on Poggio's assets, therefore, left him with 453 florins in liabili-ties—nevertheless, he was under no serious economic pressure. His estates and securities were intact, and owing to his friend-ship with Cosimo and Lorenzo de' Medici, his debt to the Medici firm was easily deferred in their accounts. Indeed, far from allow-ing the debt to worry him, Poggio soon bought four new pieces of land for 160 florins.[142]

In 1436, when he married into the Buondelmonti family, his bride brought him a dowry of 600 florins. Most of this money seems to have been used to buy a family *palazzo*.[143] Disbursing

[138] *Catasto*, 84, is a summary of the levies assigned in the S. Giovanni quarter in 1427. The notaries are identified by the "Ser" prefixed to their Christian names.

[139] Ser Martino di Luca Martini, Ser Paolo di Lando Fortini, and Ser Giovanni Buonaiuti. The first two were important political figures, the last a prosperous wool merchant. On their net assets see App. II, table VI, nos. 9, 60, 120.

[140] *Catasto*, 273, is a summary of the individual net assets reported by Aretines in 1427.

[141] Walser, pp. 341-343, 346.   [142] *Ibid.*, pp. 351ff.

[143] *Ibid.*, p. 198, note 6, where a reference is made to a house not ac-counted for in Walser's collection of notarial protocols, though a document on its lease is there.

another 615 florins in 1442, he bought two farms and a large strip of land just outside Florence. Before 1446 he spent another 200 florins on some additional land parcels. He had also paid off his Medici debt, for he no longer lists it in his report for the catasto of 1446.[144]

In the ten years from 1433 to 1443 he more than tripled his landed possessions. But the best was still ahead. Between 1449 and 1456 he was involved in at least twenty different transactions, in each of which he was the buyer:[145] he bought two farms, nineteen separate pieces of land, and two houses in Florence. The farms and land parcels cost him 950 florins, the houses 350 and 1200 florins. Most of these purchases were made before July 1451: that is to say, nearly two years before his elevation to the Republic's chief chancellery post, which then carried a yearly stipend of over 400 florins.[146]

We have seen that in the 1420's Poggio already enjoyed a solid economic position according to the standards of his professional class, the notaries. During the succeeding years he gradually acquired a fortune and before he died the Bracciolini family figured among the richest families in the city. The evidence for this is contained in his last catasto report.

Drawn up in 1458, the report lists the possession of estates collectively valued at about 2500 florins,[147] excluding the value of all houses used by the family. Poggio's real holdings in the Monte, together with the outstanding interest, totaled some 970 florins.[148] The bulk of his wealth, however, was in cash deposits with various banking and business houses. These deposits amounted to more than 5000 florins, more than half of which

[144] Docs. 52 and 54 in Walser, pp. 356-357. A farm bought for 490 florins and listed in Poggio's tax returns of 1446 is also not accounted for in Walser's collection of notarial protocols.

[145] *Ibid.*, pp. 374ff.

[146] The official salary was now 600 florins yearly, but 196 went to three assistants. See F. P. Luiso, "Riforma della cancelleria fiorentina nel 1437," *A.S.I.* ser. 5, xxi (1898), 132-147.

[147] Walser, pp. 409-413. Real estate values in this report may be determined by screening all Poggio's previous tax reports and Walser's collection of notarial protocols.

[148] Here again Walser, p. 302, incorrectly added the nominal value of Poggio's securities to the declared net capital. In 1458 the real value of Monte securities was only 20 per cent of their nominal value. Poggio also reported a Monte asset of 320 florins in back interest payments.

(2600 florins) carried in the Medici accounts. Hence Poggio's gross assets came to almost 8500 florins. Allowing him 1500 florins in deductions,[149] his net assets totaled about 7000 florins. And if this figure be scaled according to the most rigorous and comprehensive catasto administered in fifteenth-century Florence, the catasto of 1427, we find only 137 households with larger assets. We may conclude that owing to his lucrative affiliation with the papal curia, owing to his humanistic connections, his commercial acumen, and his Florentine friendships, Ser Poggio (later Messer) managed to raise his family to the economic level of the city's oligarchical households.

9. CARLO MARSUPPINI: 1398-1453

When Lionardo Bruni died in 1444, Carlo Marsuppini, one of the closest friends of the Medici, was chosen to head the Florentine chancellery. The beginning of Carlo's career as a public figure went back to 1431, when he was first appointed lecturer in rhetoric and poetry at the Studio Fiorentino. In time, he became the preceptor of men like Matteo Palmieri, Niccolò della Luna, Donato Acciaiuoli, Alamanno Rinuccini, Pontano, and Landino.

Carlo was born into a distinguished noble family from Arezzo. Messer Gregorio, his father, was a doctor of law who took his degree from the University of Bologna in 1389 and soon after went to France. According to Carlo's biographer,[150] Messer Gregorio then became a secretary to Charles V and thereafter, traveling into Italy with the king, may have served as one of the French crown's judicial representatives in Italy.

In 1418 the elder Marsuppini had already been in Florence for some years. But he retained his Aretine connections and Arezzo remained the home of his major tax obligations. This permitted him to come under the articles of a Florentine statute, enacted in 1418, granting tax exemptions to various Aretines.[151] It seems unlikely that the enjoyment of such a privilege would

---

[149] For example, 1200 florins to cover his and the subsistence of five other family members.

[150] Giuseppe Zippel, *Carlo Marsuppini* (Trento, 1897), p. 7. See also Vespasiano, pp. 315ff.

[151] Zippel, *ibid.*, p. 8.

have signified much, unless Messer Gregorio already possessed a noteworthy fortune. Nothing, however, is actually known about the state of his finances at that time. We suspect that he inherited a modest patrimony, a suspicion prompted by the implications of his professional travel and his marriage to a woman who was not from Arezzo and whom he appears to have met while still a stipendiary of the king of France. So that if he became wealthy by his own industry, he must have used his professional savings for the initial outlay of capital, which he then worked up into a large fortune by means of careful investment and money lending. This, at least, is our inference from the report he submitted to the catasto commission, dated 30 July 1427.[152]

The contents of the report exhibit an investor's turn of mind. To begin with, the Marsuppini did not own a family residence, a surprising thing in so distinguished a family. But the deprivation was deliberate. If they had bought a family *palazzo* in Florence, this would have accorded legal Florentine residence and prevented them from enjoying the special tax indulgence for which certain Aretines qualified. Appropriately enough, therefore, Carlo's father rented town houses both in Florence and Arezzo, and now and then too, as it pleased him, he took a country house.[153] In 1427 less than 4 per cent of all the capital he reported was in real estate: land parcels, half of one farm, and a mill. Ninety-six per cent, or more than 13,000 florins, was in banking and commercial investments.[154] The distribution of these deposits speaks for the skill of the investor's mind, for the money was placed with the firms of leading political and business figures. Some of these were Cosimo and Lorenzo de' Medici, Lorenzo di Messer Palla Strozzi, Tommaso and Alessandro di Giacomino Tebalducci, Antonio Serristori, Francesco di Fran-

---

[152] *Catasto*, 203, ff. 644r-647v. [153] *Ibid.*, f. 647v.

[154] These assets were reported in "fiorini di suggello," "fiorini nuovi," and "lire grossi." I am not sure about the value of "lire grossi." The *suggello* florin is the standard measure used throughout this study. The *fiorino nuovo* in 1427 was worth almost 7 per cent more than the *suggello* florin, a fact established by cross-checking Messer Gregorio's debtors, who list what they owe him in *suggello* florins, thereby setting up a value for *fiorini nuovi*. See e.g., the accounts of Francesco della Luna (*Catasto*, 77, f. 165v), Tommaso di Giacomino di Goggio (*Catasto*, 47, f. 606r), and Ridolfo Peruzzi (*Catasto*, 35, f. 1349v). On the different *fiorini* see Edler, *Glossary*, pp. 124, 317.

cesco della Luna, Ridolfo di Bonifazio Peruzzi, Jacopo Baroncelli, Donato di Ugolino Bonsi, Bartolommeo di Nofri Bischeri, and Parente di Michele Parente.[155]

Carlo's father reported one very large investment of 5500 florins in the silk company of a certain Francesco Borromei. He tried to discount it by adducing Borromei's alleged bankruptcy,[156] but the catasto officials either rejected the view that there had been a bankruptcy or found that Messer Gregorio had comparable assets elsewhere. For the recorded estimates of wealth in Arezzo attribute him with a net taxable capital of more than 13,000 florins.[157] In 1427 this was the largest recorded sum in the Aretine property and business reports, thus attesting that the Marsuppini were deemed the richest family in Arezzo. In Florence proper, where they ranked between the first fifty and sixty families, they held a place in the city's most powerful economic group, made up of the wool manufacturers, great cloth merchants, and bankers.

Since Messer Gregorio retired to Arezzo before the Florentine tax census of 1433, the family's report of that year was drafted by his sons, Carlo and Cristofano.[158] One of the government scribes then entered their statement into one of the *campioni del catasto*, but it was later scratched out because of the family's tax privilege. Still easily legible, the entry records the Monte stock then accredited to the Marsuppini. Distributed among four different funds, the stock was worth 7000 florins in nominal value—the index on which all yearly interest was paid. Its real value, or approximate value on the open market, was 1476 florins. Carlo and Cristofano then suddenly concluded their report by noting that "We have other goods, but they aren't listed because we pay a tax on them in Arezzo together with our father."[159]

The report they submitted was calculated to give as little information as possible about the family finances. Two facts deter-

---

[155] For the assets of these men see App. II, tables V, nos. 2, 6, 7; VI, nos. 1, 18, 19; VII, nos. 1, 3, 5; VIII, no. 11.

[156] *Catasto*, 203, f. 644v. He entered his deposit in the Borromei firm under the column headed: "Questi sono debitori falliti dai quali niente spera mai avere, ma pur gli inporta."

[157] *Catasto*, 273, is a summary of taxable capitals reported in Arezzo. Arranged alphabetically by Christian name.

[158] *Catasto*, 498, ff. 184v-185r.

[159] *Ibid.*, f. 185r. I have found no evidence to show that the brothers paid a catasto in Arezzo in 1433.

mined their reticence: that Florentine taxes were high and that the elder Marsuppini had more than 11,000 florins in commercial and finance investments. He was, for example, one of Messer Palla di Nofri Strozzi's principal creditors—for a sum of 4871 florins—and he also had a deposit of nearly 6000 florins with the Medici firm.[160]

In 1442 the humanist, Carlo, finally submitted an individual inventory of his real estate and Monte assets.[161] He listed one vineyard, two small houses, some pasture land, and half of four farms. The value of these properties was set at nearly 800 florins.[162] His shares in the Monte, bought for 2700 florins, drew a handsome annual interest on their nominal value of 7400 florins. In addition, he received the interest on another group of government securities, nominally valued at 2000 florins but not registered in his name. The report does not allude to it, of course, but Carlo's salary at the Studio is worthy of note: it was 140 florins per year in 1431, and 150 florins after 1435.[163]

In 1444 Carlo was appointed to the leading position in the Florentine chancellery, the office of first secretary. It was one of the most distinguished and highest-paid offices in the Republic. At the time of his death in 1453, the office carried a gross annual salary, apart from "extras," of 600 florins.[164] This salary, the fortune he inherited, his lectureship in the 1430's, all served to give him an income such as was enjoyed by members of the upper class only. Hence it is not surprising that in 1451 he had to be begged to accept a new lectureship at the Studio, despite the fact that he was offered a phenomenal yearly salary of 350 florins and allowed to retain his secretarial post.[165]

The family's money-making talent or interest was clearly evident in Carlo's sons, who became deeply involved in the silk

[160] Strozzi, *Lettere*, p. 43, note i. On the Medici deposit see Cosimo de' Medici's catasto inventory of 1433: *Catasto*, 470, f. 543r.

[161] *Catasto*, 624, f. 383r.　　　　[162] *Ibid.*, f. 383r.

[163] Alessandro Gherardi, *Statuti della Università e Studio fiorentino* (Firenze, 1881), pp. 414, 441.

[164] Though when he entered office his salary was 300 florins per year, out of which he paid an assistant probably not more than 50.0 or 60.0 florins annually. See Marzi, *La cancelleria*, pp. 214 (note 6), 220.

[165] Arnaldo della Torre, *Storia dell'accademia platonica di Firenze* (Firenze, 1902), pp. 351-352. Information taken from letters of Donato Acciaiuoli. The letters, still unpublished, are in the National Library of Florence.

and wool trade.[166] But the talent had been present even in Carlo, who in 1453 was a partner in four different cloth firms:[167] a wholesale silk business and three wool companies, two of which processed and sold wool imported from Spain. Carlo's business associates were members of the Gaetani, Lenzi, Martelli, and Rucellai families. In 1458, five years after his death, the accounts of the liquidated companies still carried outstanding credits of more than 8500 florins. But the task of collecting this money had devolved on Carlo's heirs and others.

10. GIANNOZZO MANETTI: 1396-1459

Giannozzo Manetti once complained to Cosimo de' Medici that he, Giannozzo, had paid some 135,000 florins in taxes to the Republic during the course of his life.[168] Had he truly disbursed so enormous a sum? The figure will seem less impossible if we note that Matteo Palmieri, when reviewing his own accounts, observed that he himself had paid more than 5000 florins in taxes during a period of less than twelve years.[169] Furthermore, the economic resources of the two humanists were very different. For while Matteo was the only surviving son of a moderately wealthy apothecary, Giannozzo came from one of the richest business families in the city. The Manetti wealth, however, as we shall see in a moment, was not of ancient vintage.

Bernardo, Giannozzo's father, had already started his career as a merchant and money-lender when Giannozzo was born, though he was not yet a rich man. That Bernardo was himself the founder of his family's great wealth is indicated by the fact that as late as 1390 (he was already forty-three years old) he was not yet one of the city's leading payers of prestanze, nor was he even listed among the first 20 per cent of all taxpayers in his quarter of the city, S. Spirito.[170] But fourteen years later he was

---

[166] *Catasto,* 826, ff. 608r-611v. This is their catasto report of 1458.
[167] *Ibid.*

[168] The incident is described by a near contemporary, Naldo Naldi, *Vita di Giannozzo Manetti,* in Filippo Villani, *Liber de civitatis florentiae famosis civibus,* pp. 131-136. On Giannozzo see also of course Vespasiano, pp. 259ff.

[169] ASF, *Acquisti e doni,* 7, f. 101v. This manuscript is entitled: *Libro di ricordi di portate ed altre memorie diverse di mess. Matteo di Marco di Antonio Palmieri.*

[170] *Prestanze,* 1262, f. 49r, where he is entered as "Bernardo di Giovan-

assigned a tax high enough to put him very near the upper 3 per cent, for his assessment was the sixty-seventh on a scale of 2184 payers of prestanze in the S. Spirito quarter.[171] This meant that he held a place equal in rank to that of some members of the Corbinelli and Capponi families, and already he stood above the Pitti, Serragli, and most of the Soderini. The records of the Monte show that he was drawing a yearly interest on government securities nominally valued at 2609 florins.[172] But most of his money was tied up in banking and trade enterprises. The outcome shows that his good fortune multiplied.

In 1427 Bernardo Manetti drew up a report for the catasto, and there we find that he was the second richest man in the S. Spirito quarter.[173] For the city as a whole he ranked in the tenth place.[174]

The distribution of Bernardo's assets is both illuminating and interesting. Only 1 per cent (325 florins) was invested in real estate; the real value of his Monte securities accounted for 36 per cent (11,944 florins); and about 63 per cent (20,291 florins) was invested in commercial and finance ventures. This enormous disparity between business capital and real estate (much like the pattern of the first Marsuppini report) was unusual in Florence, where the custom of leading families was to have a large part of their wealth in landed property. But the elder Manetti, who opposed Giannozzo's early devotion to literary studies, may have been the type of merchant-banker who so believed in the accumulation of wealth by means of trade and money lending, that he disdained putting too much capital into land, which after all could not bring in the annual income of a truly sagacious commercial investment.

In 1430 Giannozzo and his brother, Filippo, drew up an inventory of the Manetti assets.[175] The contents show no real departure from the general pattern of their father's 1427 report.

---

nozzo Lambucci." I indexed the first 14 per cent of the levies in this prestanza, 202 names from a total of about 1430. Bernardo's levy was too insignificant to appear anywhere near the level indexed.

[171] App. II, table IV, no. 67.   [172] *ASF, Monte,* 280, f. 158r.
[173] *Catasto,* 23, ff. 311r-312v. See also App. II, table VIII, no. 2.
[174] On the first nine see App. II, tables V-VIII.
[175] *Catasto,* 397, ff. 29r-31v.

The brothers listed a mere 663 florins in lands and houses, 13,000 florins in government securities, and nearly 18,000 florins in commercial and finance capital (e.g., a loan of 2000 florins to Prince Henry the Navigator). Sometime after the drafting of this report, but before 1433, Giannozzo and Filippo established separate households, and from that time on they regularly submitted individual accounts to the tax commissioners.

In May 1433 Filippo reported gross assets of 15,322 florins.[176] Once more landed wealth represented the smallest part of this total, though it was nearly twice that in the report of 1430. He listed two farms valued at 1129 florins, Monte securities having a real value of 9630 florins, and about 4500 florins in commercial and finance capital. Since Filippo's statement accounted for half the family wealth, he had evidently converted some of his business assets (about 3000 florins) into Monte stock. But we should not absolutely reject the suspicion that he may have suppressed some of his commercial accounts.

The two decades following this report were ruinous for Filippo. First of all, he litigated with a Bardi and lost one of his farms to him in 1434.[177] Various pressures, mainly tax obligations, then forced Filippo to sell the other farm.[178] From 1435 onwards he began to sell his government stock, often in large parcels and always at a loss. He sold it for prices ranging from 25 to 31 per cent of its par value.[179] In 1442 Filippo still had a moderate fortune in government securities—4500 florins, though their nominal or par value was 15,595 florins, the sum on which yearly interest was paid. Four years later these securities had been alienated. He reported a credit of 1000 florins in the dowry fund, but it was entered in the name of one of his daughters.[180] Meanwhile, his real estate assets had risen to slightly more than 400 florins, an increase partly accounted for by the fact that his statement listed a house belonging to his wife.

The increase in his real estate values was insignificant com-

[176] *Catasto*, 490, ff. 160v-162v.
[177] *Catasto*, 612, ff. 571r-572r. See also his report of 1458, *Catasto*, 795, f. 396r.
[178] The Badía Fiorentina bought it for 514 florins.
[179] See his business diary, kept between 1425 and 1456, in BNF, *Magl.*, vii, 1014, passim.
[180] *Catasto*, 655, f. 917v.

pared to the patrimony he had gradually seen disappear, and we are not surprised that he felt sick at heart. In his financial statement of 1446 he complained of being ill and of having fallen behind in his tax payments. He frankly declared: "I've been stripped of my wealth by unbearable tax burdens" and "ruined by the effort to pay my taxes and stay in trade."[181]

But Filippo's ruin went further still: in 1451 the only assets he reported were 65.0 florins of Monte and another 57.0 florins for his share in part of a house.[182] He had even been forced to vacate the old family house, having first mortgaged part of it for 300 florins in order to meet the payments due on his personal taxes. Much worse however—he seems to have been made for misfortune—was the loss of his wife and ten children, who died in the late 1440's in one of the periodic plagues.[183] In 1451, accordingly, Filippo and his only remaining son lived with Giannozzo. By 1458 the house mentioned above was his chief means of support, as he had sold it to his brother for 800 florins and was still awaiting payment.[184] But since Giannozzo, bullied by the oligarchy, had found it wise to abandon Florence, his sons supplied their uncle, Filippo, with all or most of his living expenses. These expenses were then deducted from the money owed him on the house.

It is difficult to believe that Filippo's economic prostration was entirely the work of tax commissioners who manipulated the collection of the public moneys. Perhaps gambling, sickness, mismanagement, or even extravagance also served as ingredients in his financial destruction.[185] After all, his brother too was tormented by heavy taxation, yet at the end of his life a large part of his inheritance was still intact. We must not minimize, however, the degree to which men in Florence might be ruined or crippled by the rigging of taxes. The Manetti brothers had fierce

---

[181] *Ibid.*, f. 918r, "La mia sustanzia e chonsumato nella inchomportabile gravezza . . . nono tratto nulla di chomune, e consumatomi per volere pure essere paghante e per non abandonare el comercio."

[182] *Catasto*, 692, f. 492r.

[183] On a single day, 26 December 1449, he lost his wife and two children. See Strozzi, *Lettere*, pp. 57, 65.

[184] *Catasto*, 795, f. 396r.

[185] See Filippo's diary (n. 179), f. 28v, where he entered the following verses without further comment: "Per cinque modi ai roba consumata:/ La gola, el guico, luxuria, e la guerra;/ La quinta sic, fenmina malnata."

political enemies in their district, S. Spirito, and this was a liability with concrete implications for their prescribed tax rates. Two of their chief enemies, Luca Pitti and Niccolò Soderini, captained powerful S. Spirito families.[186] Older, stronger, more distinguished than the Manetti and prouder of their traditions, the Soderini and Pitti may have nourished sharp resentments against the upstart house;[187] and Giannozzo's brilliant reputation as a humanist and statesman was not calculated to mollify them.

Although Filippo's ruin may have been largely the result of political machination, Giannozzo managed to survive, as the following account will show.

Going back to 1433 to consider the other branch of the Manetti fortunes, the first item worthy of interest is that Giannozzo, unlike his father, soon revealed an interest in possessing landed wealth. As early as 1429, for example, he bought a large town house with an adjacent fruit and vegetable garden. He continued making real estate purchases, and by 1433 he had four medium-sized farms (the largest of which with a country house), a fifth smaller farm, a vineyard and cottage, and eighteen other land parcels.[188] Omitting his town and country houses, these estates were valued in all at 1860 florins. His government stock was worth 9621 florins in real values, and the remaining assets, made up of commercial and finance capital, totaled 3089 florins.

The distribution of these items of capital, in contrast to the structure of the elder Manetti's wealth, denotes a conservative spirit. We deduce this from the fact that Giannozzo increased his stable investments by purchasing real estate and converting some of his business capital into government securities. There is reason to think, moreover, that he was being prudent rather than timid. For when the elder Manetti died, leaving his sons one of the largest fortunes in Florence, they had to face a system of taxation which, in the 1430's and 1440's, was administered in an increasingly sectarian and predatory spirit. Worse still, be-

---

[186] Naldi, p. 134. Pitti's power during this period is well known to students of Florentine history. On Soderini see Strozzi, *Lettere*, pp. 125-126.

[187] Besides, although the Soderini were carried as debtors for years in the Manetti accounts, they refused to acknowledge the Manetti as creditors.

[188] *Catasto*, 490, ff. 204v-207r, his tax returns of 1433. The eighteen land parcels were actually acquired by his father in 1416.

cause their father had shunned politics all his life,[189] Giannozzo and Filippo were left without the political connections they ought to have had in view of their wealth and place in society. For this reason, it would have been shortsighted of them to expand their banking and trade interests, or even to try to maintain the old ratio between their business and non-business capital. On the contrary, it was imperative for them to stabilize their assets; and once having done this, the next step was to cast about with an eye to taking an active part in the political life of Florence. The force of these inferences was immediately evident to Giannozzo who, unlike Filippo, chose a career in politics.

Giannozzo's catasto reports of 1442 and 1446 do not list the accounts of his business capital,[190] so that no comparisons can be made between this type of asset, his landed wealth, and his investments in the Monte. Nevertheless, the reports disclose a significant trend. In 1442 his estates and securities brought in yearly receipts of 1472 florins. If then, following Florentine practice on real estate earnings, this income is capitalized on a fourteen-year basis, the principal (20,608 florins) is larger by one-third than all the capital he reported in 1433. Although this estimate takes his government securities at more than their actual market value, it helps to suggest the increase in Giannozzo's "conservative" wealth.

The report he submitted in 1446 also shows a high percentage of non-business capital. It indicates that his landed properties had changed very little; but his government securities had a nominal value of nearly 42,000 florins and a real value of about 10,000 florins.

After 1446 Giannozzo alienated three-fourths of the above-mentioned securities, for at the beginning of 1458 he drew up an inventory listing the possession of securities valued at only 10,666 florins in nominal terms.[191] Part of the money realized on the sale of his securities was absorbed by confiscatory taxation. The rest he used to finance a company in the wool trade. Started in 1450, this company had three partners: Tommaso

---

189 See Ch. IV, 4.
190 *Catasto*, 612, ff. 782r-783r; and *Catasto*, 655, ff. 915r-916r.
191 *Catasto*, 795, ff. 140r-144r, 156r-157v. Cf. also his report in *Catasto*, 796.

and Andrea Tani, and one of Giannozzo's sons, Bernardo.[192] Thousands of florins were invested in the partnership. In 1458 the Manetti accounts still carried some of the firm's debtors for the years 1450-1453: a balance sheet claimed nearly 1000 florins from sixty-eight bad debtors. The company was actually dissolved in 1453. Its assets were then converted into fabrics of various kinds and shipped to Naples, where Giannozzo founded a new wool company. Once again the Tani brothers were brought in as partners. Three years later this partnership was dissolved. In November 1457 Giannozzo founded another wool company in Naples, on this occasion with a certain Giusto Saffrioni. In 1458 the Florentine tax commissioners assigned a value of 4300 florins to the humanist's share in the partnership and in other business enterprises.[193] They based their estimate on a statement received from one of Giannozzo's sons, Bernardo. In the statement, drafted for the catasto of 1458, Bernardo also listed the real value of his father's holdings in the Monte, totaling 2000 florins, and the highest real estate values recorded in any of the Manetti tax returns: 2785 florins in farms, land parcels, and houses.[194]

This statement of finances was the last ever submitted to the tax commission for Giannozzo, who died in 1459. We may hence conclude, having examined his various tax returns, that in the space of one generation the Manetti wealth dwindled (on paper at least) to something less than one-third its maximum amount. But because of the Florentine practice of concealing assets, a different version of the Manetti accounts might well reveal greater wealth. After all, though Florentine officials knew that Giannozzo had important assets in Naples, they had to rely to some extent on his reports. The question is, would a rich Florentine have been disposed to reveal all his business accounts to his political enemies, if he had long been ruthlessly and vindictively taxed? Surely not.

[192] *Catasto*, 795, f. 140r. The company is entered as a "bottega di lana" in his report of 1451, *Catasto*, 693, f. 350r.

[193] *Catasto*, 795, f. 157v, states: "Composto per partito degli ufficiali d'achordo con Bernardo suo figliuolo per lui a di 23 di settembre 1458 pe trafichi e merchantie e contanti computato debitori e creditori del traficho e fuori del traficho in tutto fior 4300."

[194] *Ibid.*, ff. 140r-144r, 156r-157v.

The Fortunes of the Humanists

In 1458 Giannozzo was still one of the Republic's rich citizens, but his family was no longer one of the first ten in Florence, as it had been in the 1427-1433 period.

11. MATTEO PALMIERI: 1406-1475

On his mother's side Matteo Palmieri came from an administrative family, the Sassolini, who resided in the S. Spirito section of Florence.[195] Economically, they belonged to the class of small merchants or wealthy shopkeepers.[196] The Palmieri, his father's side of the family, were druggist-confectioners who held, at the beginning of the fifteenth century, an economic and political place nearly equivalent to that of the Sassolini. Matteo's paternal grandfather was one of the city's more prosperous apothecaries: he ranked as a taxpayer in the upper 13 per cent of the populace.[197] This rank denoted an economic position on a level with small silk and wool merchants, but superior to that of the mass of shopkeepers, notaries, and lesser landowners.

The Palmieri owned a druggist's establishment which brought in an ever-increasing profit during the first third of the fifteenth century. Matteo's father and uncle put their gains into real estate and other forms of capital investment. They divided their households in about 1413, but their trade interests continued to burgeon, so that by 1427 they figured among the first 4 per cent of all Florentine taxpayers. In his financial statement for the catasto officials of 1427,[198] the head of the elder branch of the family, Matteo's uncle, declared net assets of 3523 florins. These assets included farms, houses, government securities, and commercial and finance capital. Matteo's father, head of the other

---

[195] Antonio Messeri, "Matteo Palmieri cittadino di Firenze del secolo xv," A.S.I., ser, 5, xiii, ii (1894), 257-340; G. B. Benvenuti, *Quadri storici fiorentini* (Firenze, 1889); and Vespasiano, pp. 302ff.

[196] Indicated among other things by the fact that his mother received a dowry of 225 florins. See ASF, *Notarile antecosimiano*, P 282, under a protocol of 7 September 1422, not paginated. This *filza* contains some of Ser Ugolino Pieruzzi's protocols for the years 1420-1424.

[197] *Prestanze*, 2002 (date: 1403), arranged alphabetically by Christian name. See "Antonio di Palmieri spetiale." The S. Giovanni quarter numbered 2499 *prestanziati* in 1403. About 296, or 12 per cent, were each assigned levies of 3.00 florins or more. Antonio was levied 2.50 florins; hence he stood just outside this group.

[198] *Catasto*, 80, f. 126r.

branch, reported net assets of 3036 florins.[199] But as always in catasto computations, this figure omitted the value of all dwellings used by the family. In this instance the net assets included three houses, three farms, parts of three other farms, and government securities actually worth about 1064 florins. The store owned by Matteo's father was operated on a capital of 200 florins —the value of its goods and furnishings. His remaining assets consisted chiefly of an investment of 1757 florins, deposited with the banking house of Toso di Albizzo di Fortuna.

Matteo Palmieri came into his inheritance on 21 September 1428. He was then twenty-three years old. Between 1427 and 1433, the year of the third citywide census for the catasto, capital investment in the family store was more than doubled; its total assets fluctuated between 400 and 550 florins.[200] In the same period Matteo acquired additional real estate, entailing an increase of about 200 florins in landed properties. He also rented some land from the Bishop of Florence. And finally, the real value of his shares in the Monte went from 1300 florins in 1430 to nearly 1700 in 1433.

Although Matteo was one of the city's richest apothecaries, he was not (perhaps he never had been) dominated by business exigencies. For one thing, in 1432 he made his first important appearance in public life[201] and in the course of the next ten years acquired a certain prominence in politics. Again, before 1427 his father already had three employees in the family business establishment, so that Matteo's immediate connection with it must have been chiefly managerial, and this on a part-time basis. Finally, the young man's passion for humanistic studies made notable demands on his time, not only because he attended Marsuppini's lectures at the Studio, but also because he was fond of transcribing classical texts.[202] Thus, al-

[199] His gross assets totaled 4635 florins. See *ibid.*, f. 128r/v. Cf. Matteo's *Ricordi* or diary account book, *ASF, Acquisti e doni*, 7, ff. 2v *et seq.* On his rank see App. II, table VI, no. 118.

[200] *Catasto*, 499, ff. 520r-524v; cf. his *Ricordi, loc.cit.*, ff. 12r *et seq.*

[201] Messeri, "Matteo Palmieri," p. 273.

[202] E.g., his *Ricordi* (n. 199), f. 128r, "Richordo di certi libri vendevo a di 13 di maggio [1429]. Vende un Plauto volume picholo. Era di mia mano, choverto di B[ambagia]. Chonessi avanzanti ebbine libr. 32 [about 8.00 florins], e a meza forza il vendo perche nel avea scritto. Chomperollo un chancelliere del Marchese di Ferrara."

though he carefully tended his business accounts (a fact disclosed by his unpublished diary), he was not bound to a vocational routine. Far from hurting him, this detachment may have lent a certain versatility and force to his character, the effect of which did not go unobserved. For in 1433 he married into the Serragli family, whose economic rank and political traditions set it among the city's oligarchic houses. His bride, Niccolosa Serragli, brought him a dowry of 700 florins.[203]

Henceforth Matteo's lot was increasingly connected with Florentine public life. Gradually he withdrew from personal exercise of the apothecary's trade, though two of his nephews remained permanently associated with it. They alone perpetuated the family tradition. In his tax report of 1446, Matteo drily stated, "I have Agnolo, one of my nephews, running a small confectionary and chemist's store."[204] The store's assets were certainly not negligible, but he did not render an account of them: the census of 1446 made no such requirement. At all events, the bulk of his wealth was in lands, buildings, and government stock. These possessions alone brought him a yearly income of about 155 florins (equivalent, roughly, to the yearly rental of fifteen to eighteen medium-sized shops). He could also count on the salaries attached to his numerous public offices.

The economic thread of Matteo's life was now virtually spun. Given though he was to affairs of state, he had in effect become a *rentier*—a status not altered by any events of the next thirty years of his life. In this period, according to the records of the catasto, he increased the value of his landed properties by only 200 florins, from 1250 to 1450 florins.[205] But even the larger of the two sums was probably below the true mark. For as landed properties in the post-1427 inventories were usually given their

[203] The sum was entered in Niccolò di Agnolo Serragli's catasto inventory of 1427. See *Catasto*, 490, f. 315r, where the tax officials stated, "abatesi della sua sustanza fior setecento den 0 per dota ala Cosa suo [sic] figliuola e cancellata di sopra e posto a sustanza di Matteo Palmieri." Although Matteo did not at once receive this money, Messeri, not knowing the size of Niccolosa's dowry, incorrectly stated, "non appare che il Palmieri ne ricevesse una ricca dote" (p. 273).
[204] Entered in his *Ricordi* (n. 199), f. 41r, "Fo fare Agnolo mio nipote un poco di bottega di speziale al canto alle Rondini."
[205] Cf. the real estate values in *Catasto*, 80, ff. 128r *et seq.*; *Catasto*, 499, ff. 520r *et seq.*; and his *Ricordi* (n. 199), ff. 61r *et seq.*

1427 value, contiguous land accretions or rental increments might go unmentioned. Besides, if his mother's lands, separately reported,[206] had been combined with his, the value of his lands would have been greater by a third, another 550 florins. Aside from Matteo's earnings from public office, there remained two other sources of income open to him: the intake from the drug and confectionary stores run by his nephews, and the yearly interest on his government securities. Neither his *Ricordi* nor his tax returns give a picture of the income from the family stores; hence we cannot go into this aspect of his finances. His securities, on the other hand, are clearly accounted for in the documents. In 1433 these were actually worth about 1700 florins, the highest figure assigned to Monte stock in any of his statements to the catasto officials. His securities reached their lowest point in 1458, with a real value of only 944 florins. Eleven years later he reported an additional 550 florins in securities.[207]

But perhaps it is best to limit ourselves to Matteo's actual income from securities. The real value of his securities in 1458 presupposed a nominal share in the Monte of 4500 florins. Viewing annual interest on this share as a type of negotiable instrument, 4500 florins were worth 125 florins per year, or less than two-thirds the ordinary interest on government stock.[208] In 1469, again, Matteo's securities entailed a nominal value of 7000 florins. Taken at three-fifths their normal interest rate, these securities drew a yearly income of not less than 210 florins.

Two stores, managed by Matteo's nephews, belonged to the Palmieri in the 1450's: the one at the "Canto alle Rondini" was operated by Agnolo, the other by the ill-famed Antonio in the "mercato." Although Antonio ran the "mercato" store during most of the 1450's,[209] and probably before and after, we know almost nothing about the assets under his care. In 1458 these assets were computed together with those of Agnolo's establishment (a much larger operation), giving a composite sum of 200 florins. When going over the accounts, however, the catasto

[206] Messeri, "Matteo Palmieri," published her report of 1458.
[207] Palmieri, *Ricordi*, f. 61r.
[208] Messeri, pp. 325-326, published the report of 1458 (1457 Florentine style).
[209] Palmieri, *Ricordi*, ff. 53v, 119v.

officials (indulgently?) entered a value of only 50.0 florins for these assets.[210] Nothing more is heard of the two stores until 1469, when Matteo declared the liquidation of all his commercial assets.

It may be suggestive to conclude this sketch by observing that although Matteo Palmieri became a prominent civic figure, he did not—so we gather from the preceding account—use his offices as a source of personal profit. That this fact was noticed, commented on, and praised by his contemporaries[211] suggests that graft in Florence may have been rampant. At all events, Matteo's exemplary behavior in public office was in some ways consistent with his private life. Typical of him, but not of some other Florentines,[212] was his unwillingness to evict the debt-ridden and unproductive tenants of one of his farms. Their guardian and only means of support had died, leaving a family of fourteen with no means of sustenance. Matteo could not bring himself to evict them. Among the fourteen were nine girls, "barefoot, naked, and struggling desperately to survive, so that it seemed to me [said Matteo] a disgrace to take the bread from their mouth."[213]

12. LEON BATTISTA ALBERTI: 1404-1472

Although Leon Battista Alberti is one of the period's outstanding humanists, he will be considered here in a summary fashion. The reason for this is not only that he was in holy orders, but also that he spent most of his life outside Florence, and hence paid no prestanze, no catasti, nor any other of the city's major levies.[214] Therefore we are unable to do a study of his finances similar to our detailed treatment of the other humanists.

The natural son of an exiled Florentine banker, Battista Alberti was descended from a family illustrious both in politics

---

[210] *Ibid.*, f. 53v.

[211] Vespasiano, pp. 302ff.; see also the funeral oration in Alamanno Rinuccini, *Lettere ed orazioni*, ed. Vito Giustiniani (Firenze, 1953), p. 80.

[212] E.g., Strozzi, *Lettere*, pp. 458, 526.

[213] Palmieri, *Ricordi*, f. 40v, "scalzi e ingnudi e pieni di stento in modo m' e paruto una infamia a torre loro el pane di bocca."

[214] This does not mean he had no investments in Florence. For Marco Parenti was his "procuratore" there during the years 1452-1462. See Parenti's unpublished memoirs, *ASF, Carte Strozz., 2a serie*, 17 bis, ff. 19v, 55v.

and international banking. When his father died, he was intended to inherit a fortune of more than 4000 florins, but two of his uncles fraudulently took possession of the patrimony. The result was that although the young Alberti was sent to the University of Bologna, where he read law for his degree, his student days were marred by considerable poverty.

All of these facts are well known or easily available.[215] Another aspect of his life, however, is somewhat more obscure—the career he turned down. When in about 1428 he completed his legal studies, becoming a *decretorum doctor,* [216] he might have gone to practice canon law in Florence, where his connections were strategic and lucrative. In 1433, for example, the Florentine Signoria wrote to Cardinal Francesco Condulmier, nephew of Pope Eugene IV, strongly favoring "messer Battista degli Alberti . . . di famiglia primaria e nobilissima,"[217] asking that the Cardinal show him preferment in ecclesiastical office and urging him to recommend Battista to the pope and the most influential prelates. With this type of support in Florence, the young humanist could soon have earned up to 500 florins per year as a practicing lawyer.[218] But instead, he solicited and obtained, despite his illegitimate birth, an ecclesiastical benefice. His first living, granted in 1432, involved a church not far from Florence (Gangalandi) and brought him a yearly income of 160 florins.[219] This income was superior to the salaries connected with some of the Florentine Republic's leading administrative posts, such as tax commissioner, government accountant, or the office charged with reviewing the expenses of the Republic's treasury.[220] These com-

[215] Narrated in full by Girolamo Mancini, *Vita di Leon Battista Alberti* (Firenze, 1911).

[216] *Ibid.,* p. 58.

[217] *Ibid.,* p. 91. Letter cited by Mancini.

[218] See on this L. Martines, "The Career and Library of a 15th-Century Lawyer," p. 329.

[219] Mancini, *Alberti,* p. 89. Excluding the first year's annates, his net income would perhaps have been something less than 160 florins, owing to other papal fees.

[220] Each of the ten officials elected to administer the catasto in 1427 was to draw a salary of 8.00 florins per month: ASF, *Provv.,* 117, f. 135r. In 1408 each of four government accountants, elected for four months, was to draw a monthly salary of 6.00 florins: ASF, *Provv.,* 97, f. 80v (in 1431 the term was for six months, the salary 5.00 florins per month). Filippo di Messer Biagio Guasconi and Domenico di Lionardo Buoninsegni were elected "proveditori" of the "Camera del Comune" for one year, be-

parisons may suggest something about the material excellence of Alberti's first benefice.

For the remaining period of his life the best we can do at present is to report the contents of his last will and testament, sworn in 1472. He was by then a canon "and almost certainly a priest."[221]

The major articles of the document are five: (1) the chapel he had started to build in his old church of Gangalandi was to be completed by his heirs; (2) he left 50.0 gold ducats to a certain Luigi Passi of Bologna, for services and aid given to Alberti during his illness; (3) 10.0 gold ducats—about one year's salary— and a cloak to his servant, Claudio; (4) to Bernardo di Antonio degli Alberti and his descendants via the masculine line, Battista willed his palace in Florence, two houses in Bologna, and another outside Bologna with land attached; (5) finally, he left a bequest of 1000 florins to set up in perpetuity a house in Bologna for the use of two needy scholars of the Alberti family. But whenever the family had no need of the foundation, its resources were to be enjoyed by two poor youths already launched in their studies. The historian who discovered Alberti's will found that the last of the five articles was perverted by one of the will's chief executors, Antonio Grassi of Bologna, a legist and high official in the papal curia, who put the scholarship fund under the strict control of the Grassi family.

---

ginning on 1 February 1431, each with a salary of 80.0 florins: *ASF, Camera del Comune, uscita,* 382, f. 24r.

[221] G. Mancini, "Il testamento di L. B. Alberti," *A.S.I.,* LXXII, 2 (1914), 20-52, prints the will in an appendix.

CHAPTER FOUR

PUBLIC OFFICE IN
THE HUMANIST CIRCLE

1. INTRODUCTORY NOTE

*T*HE CRITICAL importance of public office in the history of Florence first appears at the center of political reflection in two sixteenth-century works. One, finished in 1526, was Francesco Guicciardini's dialogue on government in Florence; the other, finished in 1534, was Donato Giannotti's commentaries on the Florentine Republic.[1] But thereafter concentrated interest in the question gradually diminished. It was not reawakened until the end of the nineteenth century, and then only in specialized studies (e.g., Doren's work on the guilds). The most recent large treatment, published in 1913, was Vincenzo Ricchioni's book on the Republic's political structure in the time of Lorenzo the Magnificent.[2] Other works on the system of offices in republican Florence deal with specialized aspects of Florentine government and will often be referred to in the succeeding pages.

Guicciardini's dialogue on the *reggimento fiorentino* is speculative rather than descriptive: its acknowledged aim is to work out an ideal government for Florence, and hence it is a work of deceptive value for the student who merely wants a description of the Republic's political organization. Thus, although Guicciardini assigned the Republic's decline to the abuse of public office, he was not interested in showing how the various magistracies had functioned in the fifteenth century, nor in how they were arranged into an ordered administrative system. Much the same is true of Giannotti's commentaries. Penned in exile, the work of an ardent republican, these commentaries summarily describe (now and then incorrectly) some of the central organs of government under the Medicean Republic,

---

[1] Francesco Guicciardini, *Dialogo e Discorsi del Reggimento di Firenze*; Donato Giannotti, *Della repubblica fiorentina* (Venezia, 1721).

[2] Ricchioni, *La costituzione politica di Firenze*; cf. also A. Anzilotti, *La crisi costituzionale della repubblica fiorentina* (Firenze, 1912), a sketchy but brilliant study.

but they do not distinguish the powers of the various departments, nor give a picture of Florentine administration as a whole. Owing to his personal political situation, Giannotti's turn of mind was necessarily tendentious, interested only in proving that excessive power had been concentrated in the Republic's chief offices and that this was why they fell so easily to the tyrannical subversion of the Medici.

Guicciardini and Giannotti wrote out of their direct experience with Florentine government. Ricchioni's work, on the other hand, written nearly four centuries later, exhibits a detachment naturally not found in them. Yet he too was less interested in the anatomy of the Republic's system of offices, or in how the total system worked, than in showing how its composition at the centers, especially in the Council of Seventy, enabled Lorenzo's followers to take over the political life of the city. Thus he scarcely touched on the powers of the Signoria; he did nothing with the changing character of the potent fiscal commissions; and although he noted that the Eight on Security developed dictatorial powers, he did not explore the office's inner structure. But had he gone into the various departments of Florentine government, he would have found large areas of duplication in authority and jurisdiction, and he might have provided himself with a more searching method of explaining the processes of encroachment through which the Medicean oligarchy extended its power.

The Eight on Security (*Otto di Guardia*), with their enormous powers in the second half of the fifteenth century, are better understood when we take note of the fact that they drew powers from the Ten of War (*Decem Baliae*), who once had the authority to raise armies, dispatch envoys, and deal with foreign states, despite being sometimes at variance with the foreign policy of the Signoria.[3] The Defenders of the Laws (*Conservatores Legum*), set up in 1429,[4] took certain judicial and investigative rights from the *Podestà*, the Captain of the People, the Comptrollers (*Regulatores*), and the Signoria. When the Eight on Security handed out safeguards protecting debtors, they seized rights

[3] E.g., *Commissioni di Rinaldo degli Albizzi*, i, 34.
[4] *ASF, Provv.*, 120, ff. 7v-11r, being the act which established this commission, giving its powers, reasons for its establishment, and method of selecting its personnel.

from the Six on Commerce and the various guild consulates.[5] They also encroached on the Signoria by granting permits to carry arms and to move freely through the city at night.[6] Finally, in the area of fiscal policy and tax administration, there must have been an even greater overlapping of authority, indicated by the fact that a Florentine occasionally had as many as four different government agencies pestering him to pay his taxes.[7]

In short, despite Ricchioni's work and the more specialized work of others (e.g., Marzi, Barbadoro, and Antonelli), the burden of identifying and describing the departments of Florentine government still confronts the student. This section of the present study will touch on the nature and function of some of those departments, but it will not satisfy the needs of the political or constitutional historian. The problem arises here only because of one of our principal assumptions: namely, that the nature and importance of public offices held by the humanists ought to be examined—though hitherto this has not been the practice of scholars in the field[8]—and that this is unavoidable if the social world of the humanists is to be described.

Since one of the aims of this chapter is to bring out the relative social importance of the offices occupied by the humanists, our basic printed source will be the *Statuta Populi et Communis Florentiae* of the year 1415.[9] But whenever this source fails to indicate the social implications of an office, we will look for a solution by noting the type of men commonly found in it.

2. COLUCCIO SALUTATI AND HIS SONS

Salutati was the first of the great humanist chancellors of the Republic. His long term in office (1375-1406) coincided with the rise of civic humanism, and seems to have gone far towards creating the Florentine feeling that the Republic's chancellery should

---

[5] A statute against the Eight's right to do this was enacted in February, 1422: *ASF, Lib. Fab.*, 52, f. 131r/v.

[6] *Ibid.*; also *Provv.*, 92, f. 299v (25 Feb. 1404), a private bill granting a prominent Florentine, Francesco della Luna, the right to bear "omnia et singula arma offendibilia et defendibilia."

[7] Strozzi, *Lettere*, pp. 6-7.

[8] See e.g., Messeri, "Matteo Palmieri," pp. 257-340; E. Santini, *Leonardo Bruni Aretino*, 3ff.

[9] Published in Freiburg, 1778-1783, and hereafter always referred to in the notes as *Statuta*.

be managed by a distinguished man of letters.[10] The post was one of the highest-paid offices in the city. Its holder counted on larger annual earnings than either the treasurer, the cashier, or the municipal accountants.[11] The salary of the priors, which was modest, was largely consumed in office expenses.[12] The legal counsellors of communal officials (the *Sapientes*) drew a monthly salary of only 2.00 florins,[13] while in the same period the chancellor might earn 40.0 to 50.0 florins. And, in the dominion, only leading administrative posts in Arezzo, Pistoia, Pisa, and Livorno, entailed salaries which surpassed that of Florence's first secretary.

The real importance of Salutati's office lay not in its earnings, however, but in the powers attached to it: through these he could influence decisions of state. This is why on one occasion the Signoria, concealing one of its diplomatic moves from the Ten of War, also withheld it from the chancellery head.[14] He was evidently too close to certain members of the Ten or thoroughly shared their outlook. Much of the humanist's influence came from the fact that he handled the paperwork connected with the drawing up of the secret purses naming those eligible for public office. Since appointment to office tended to be made on a rotating basis, months in advance the keeper of the eligibility purses had some idea of how the key offices were to be distributed.[15] The first secretary also dictated the Signoria's correspondence to Florentine ambassadors; he was present (except on very rare occasions) at all the meetings of the executive councils, and the discussions were recorded under his supervision. Consequently, because of his long and intimate association with the Signoria, whose personnel changed six times yearly, his advice on special questions was often solicited.[16]

In view of Coluccio's authoritative position, it is not surprising that in 1400 he and all his descendants, and also his brothers

---

[10] Dati, *L'Istoria*, p. 148.
[11] *Statuta*, III, 212, 215, 217; ASF, *Notaio di Camera-uscita*, 1, f. 137v.
[12] *Statuta*, II, 505.   [13] *Ibid.*, II, 622-623.
[14] *Commissioni di Rinaldo degli Albizzi*, I, 34.
[15] Francesco C. Pellegrini, *Sulla repubblica fiorentina a tempo di Cosimo il Vecchio* (Pisa, 1880), pp. xxxix-xl; or see the method of drawing up the names of those eligible for the *Conservatores Legum*, ASF, *Provv.*, 120, ff. 7v-11r.
[16] Marzi, pp. 118-140. It was also his duty to make out safe-conduct warrants and arms-carrying privileges.

and their descendants, were granted Florentine citizenship in perpetuity. Late of Stignano, the Salutati were thus established in Florence by the period's most eminent humanist. Some idea of his imposing reputation is indicated by the political fortunes of the family for nearly a generation after his death.

The first thing to bear in mind is that in 1400 the Salutati were still "new" in Florence. They were old Stignano stock, associated with a tradition of military service;[17] but in Florence proper they were political upstarts. When Coluccio died in 1406, the political responsibilities of the family passed to his sons. Two of them went into the Church—Messer Lionardo, the *Piovano* of Montecatino, who probably had taken a degree in canon law, and Salutato, who became a cathedral canon in 1409. The Florentine ambassadors in Rome highly recommended them to the Pope in February 1407, and called his attention to the fame of their deceased father.[18] Two other sons, Ser Bonifazio and Ser Antonio, entered the lower rungs of the legal profession; like their father, they became notaries. Arrigo and Simone, finally, went into trade: they were matriculated in the wool guild and the guild of doctors and druggists.[19] The family were thus enrolled in three of the city's seven major guilds, so that their political outlook probably conformed with that of the mercantile upper classes.

For about two decades after Coluccio's death Ser Bonifazio and Ser Antonio frequently appeared in the notarial cadres of the Republic's bureaucracy. They were at different times the notaries attached to the Signoria, the *Sedici,* the State Treasury, the Eight on Security (*Octo Custodiae*), the Approvers of the Guild Statutes, the Six on Arezzo and Pistoia, and other commissions.[20] Their notarial skills thus admitted them into the class of lesser civil servants. But Ser Bonifazio had a more successful career than that of the ordinary notary. In the autumn of 1416, for example, he sat with the Signoria as one of the *Sedici.*[21] The *Sedici,* or Sixteen Gonfaloniers of the Militia Companies, made

[17] Salutati, *Epistolario,* iv, i, 384-386.   [18] *ASF, Leg. Comm.,* 4, f. 11r.
[19] *ASF, Medici e Speziali,* 21, f. 94r/v; *ASF, Lana,* 21, f. 111r/v.
[20] *ASF, Tratte,* 79, ff. 280r, 341r/v, 344r, 357r, 365r, 366v, 367r, 370v, 375r, 379r, *et seq.* (years: 1411-1426).
[21] *ASF, Mss.,* 266, f. 108r/v.

up one of the Republic's major executive bodies. The Priorate did not normally undertake important deliberations without the *Sedici,* and no bill could be passed, or even obtain a hearing in the legislative councils, unless it had previously been voted on by the *Sedici* in a joint meeting with the Signoria.[22] In 1417 Ser Bonifazio appeared among the *Dodici Buonomini,* or Twelve Good Men,[23] the office which together with the Priorate and the *Sedici* composed the Republic's chief executive council. All Florentine legislation began here, and since a bill needed at least twenty-five of this body's thirty-seven votes to pass into the legislative councils, the votes of the *Dodici* were crucial. Ser Bonifazio's terms in the *Sedici* and *Dodici,* however, were not his first appearances in government service. Already in 1412, representing the lawyers' guild, he had sat as one of the Approvers of the Guild Statutes.[24] The task of this body was to examine the legality of the statutes enacted by the guilds in the normal course of their activity. Hence the *Approbatores* were mainly concerned with violations of the Florentine Constitution, and no guild could appeal over their heads.[25]

Bonifazio was appointed to one of the state's charitable societies in March 1419.[26] Although the appointment meant little in political terms, the *Tratte* disclose that such service occurred in the careers of most prominent Florentines. Later in the same year he was made one of the five *Defectuum Officiales.*[27] These commissioners administered the policy on military salaries and on the salaries of the officials attached to the courts of the *Podestà,* the Captain of the People, and the Executor of Justice. They penalized military misconduct; they investigated ordnance shortages; they assigned responsibility for the loss of military equipment and imposed appropriate fines.[28] The following year, 1420, Bonifazio obtained a place in the Ten on Pisa (*Decem*

[22] *Statuta,* ii, 494ff.; also Giannotti, pp. 83ff.
[23] *Mss.,* 266, f. 108r/v. In this period he was a prominent speaker in the executive councils: ASF, *Consulte,* 43, passim.
[24] *Tratte,* 79, f. 280r.
[25] Doren, ii, 220-221.
[26] *Tratte,* 79, f. 219r, the "Capitanei Bigalli." Some prominent holders of this office were Gino Capponi, Niccolò da Uzzano, Rinaldo degli Albizzi, Cosimo de' Medici, Palla di Nofri Strozzi, and others.
[27] *Ibid.,* f. 69r, on 1 August 1419.
[28] *Statuta,* iii, 149-163.

Pisarum).[29] This commission regulated the value and circulation of Pisan currency.[30] It was charged with the defense of Pisa and the Pisan countryside. And the Treasurer of Pisa was forbidden to pay out any money without the written consent of the *Decem Pisarum*. Bonifazio entered his last major office on 23 August 1420, when he began a six-month term as *Podestà* of Borgo S. Lorenzo.[31]

The tradesman, Simone, held no offices in the city equivalent to those of his brother, Ser Bonifazio; but between 1415 and 1424 he held three minor governorships in the Florentine dominion.[32] As governorships were turned to profit without much difficulty, they were eagerly sought after,[33] and hence the power to obtain them indicated a certain strategic influence in administrative circles.

Arrigo was the most politically active of all Coluccio's sons. His civic career, like Simone's, exhibits no single office to match Bonifazio's service in the *Sedici* and *Dodici*. But he held more posts in the dominion and his offices in the city proper were the type normally found in the early careers of important public figures. A rapid look at his dignities outside Florence reveals that between 1411 and 1420 he was honored with six governorships:[34] the important ones took him to Firenzuola, Certaldo, and Arezzo.

Arrigo held the following offices in the city. His first assignment began on 20 September 1405, with an appointment as Treasurer of Arezzo for a period of six months.[35] This was a brilliant first office for one without true Florentine traditions, and very probably he owed it to the solicitation of his powerful father. Two weeks after leaving the post, however, his father died (4 May 1406), and Arrigo was not soon to reappear in an office of equivalent importance. In 1410 and 1414 he was chosen for the commission on the passage of goods through the city gates

[29] *Tratte*, 79, f. 239v.
[30] *Statuta*, III, 113-115, 120ff.
[31] *Tratte*, 67, f. 54r. Borgo S. Lorenzo lies at the foot of the Mugello, northeast of Florence.
[32] *Tratte*, 66, ff. 139r, 144r; 67, f. 134r.
[33] See the words of Ser Filippo di Ser Ugolino in Vespasiano, p. 453.
[34] *Tratte*, 66, ff. 31r, 60r, 90r, 162r; 67, ff. 67r, 41r.
[35] *Tratte*, 78, f. 132v.

(*Portarum Magistri*) and he also served as one of the commissioners connected with the salt tax (*Salis Magistri*).[36] Towards
the end of 1415 he was given a place in the Ten on Liberty
(*Decem Libertatis*). A chronicler of the period observed that this
body was "very important," being a court of appeals which
looked into the validity of contracts and public instruments.[37]
The Ten on Liberty, he said, were a boon to those who could
not pay lawyers' fees in preparing a case. Arrigo was sworn into
this tribunal on the first day of December 1415 and served four
months.[38] In the autumn he was appointed recorder of the Republic's *exitus* accounts for a period of six months.[39] This was a
minor post, one of a type often accepted in order to tide a man
over between rounds of activity in more important offices. Nevertheless, on leaving the treasury he went without another office
for almost nine months.

Early in January 1418, Arrigo returned to government service
as one of the *Conductae Officiales*.[40] Their office was to review,
hire, or discharge the Republic's military personnel. But they
were not makers of policy. Above them stood the Signoria, the
Ten of War, and later the Eight on Security. At the beginning
of 1419 Arrigo sat in the Commission on Decency (*Honestatis
Officiales*),[41] whose task was to prosecute sodomy and to keep
prostitution under rigorous control. The Republic's outstanding
political and social figures did not avoid service in this commission, as a quick review of the relevant rosters discloses: there we
find men like Niccolò da Uzzano (on two occasions), Niccolò
di Ugolino Martelli, Francesco della Luna, Messer Rinaldo degli
Albizzi, Messer Lorenzo Ridolfi, and Neri di Gino Capponi.[42]

The office of *Provisor Turris* was one of those small but lucrative dignities sought after by younger sons, and was normally
given for one year. His task was to review and check the accounts
and voluminous papers of the Officials of the Tower (*Turris
Officiales*). A body of seven men serving for four months, the

---

[36] *Tratte*, 78, f. 213r; 79, f. 108r.
[37] Dati, *L'Istoria*, p. 152.   [38] *Tratte*, 79, f. 47r.
[39] *Ibid.*, f. 310r. The term started on 1 October 1416.
[40] *Ibid.*, f. 61v, from 4 January to the end of May.
[41] *Tratte*, 79, f. 205r. On the nature of the office see *Statuta*, III, 41ff.
[42] *Tratte*, 78, f. 142r/v; 79, ff. 204r/v, 205v, 206r.

Tower Officials managed the Commune's properties—roads, squares, bridges, lands, lucrative rights, and certain rents. They were empowered to assess and tax, and in some cases to sell, the properties of Florence's political "criminals." They also had the right to sell various Florentine gabelles to the highest bidders.[43] Arrigo's tour of duty as *Provisor Turris* began on 10 January 1422.[44] Some ten weeks after having finished his term, he was finally drawn for service in one of the powerful commissions, the Six on Arezzo and Pistoia.[45] They served six months. Their office was to supervise the defenses and military security of the two subject cities. In Arezzo, where the Six maintained an armory, they had the power to dispose of the properties of the city's rebels. In Pistoia they could levy taxes up to any sum required for the setting up and maintenance of the city defenses. Arrigo ended his term in this commission at the end of September 1424. The following February he was back in government service as one of the two *Consignatores Rectorum Forensium*.[46] This office was usually held for a few days, and therefore it was often a suitable post for Florentines who were prominent in political and administrative activities. The duty of the *Consignatores* was to confirm in office the three non-Florentine magistrates: the *Podestà*, the Captain of the People, and the Executor of Justice. His appointment as *Consignator* was to be one of Arrigo's last major assignments. For on 1 April 1425 he took office as one of the Officials of the Tower, and thereafter his name no longer appears in the inventories of the Republic's civil servants.[47]

We have shown that the period's leading humanist, Coluccio Salutati, managed to introduce his sons into the Republic's circuit of offices. Without Florentine political traditions, they attained none the less a certain eminence in public affairs. Coluccio's reputation as a humanist and statesman propelled the family's administrative fortunes for two decades after his death, but the sons were unable to keep the pace set by the father. Two of

---

[43] *Statuta*, II, 3ff., 42ff.   [44] *Tratte*, 79, f. 295r.
[45] *Ibid.*, f. 185v. On the nature of this office see: *Statuta*, III, 70-95.
[46] *Tratte*, 79, f. 376v.
[47] *Ibid.*, f. 148v. His disappearance from public life was not caused by death, as he was still alive in 1427, when he submitted a property report to the catasto commission.

them, Messer Lionardo and Salutato, turned away from civil life when they entered the Church. Ser Bonifazio, the eldest brother, sat in the executive councils; but Arrigo, politically the most ambitious of the brothers, was unable in the end to penetrate the ruling magistracies—the Signoria, the Ten of War, the Eight on Security, and the Six on Commerce. What might the family have done in order to endure as a force in the city? Wealth would have served to open the way to "strategic" marriages, but Coluccio's sons dispersed their patrimony long before the year of the first catasto, and did not recover it.

3. ROBERTO DE' ROSSI AND NICCOLÒ NICCOLI

In his study—by now almost classic—of events and ideas in the Florence of around 1400,[48] Hans Baron noted that the humanists of the period tend to fall into two groups: one, headed by Lionardo Bruni and Coluccio Salutati, fostered the notion of civic virtue and favored an active life in the world; the other, represented by Roberto de' Rossi, Niccolò Niccoli, and Antonio Corbinelli apparently preferred a life of quiet study and sought to avoid participation in public affairs. This view—now the prevailing one—is highly suggestive, and there are elements in the lives both of Roberto and Niccolò which tend to support it. Furthermore, the observations of some contemporaries (e.g., Benvenuti, Manetti) can also be adduced. Nevertheless, let us see how this view accords with rarely-considered evidence of a different sort.

Of the figures mentioned above, it would appear that Lionardo Bruni, the foremost advocate of civic humanism, should have stood first among those who doubted the true value of a life devoted to the political community. It was he who in the first decade of the century came closest to entering the Church: he must have approached taking holy vows in 1407, when he was made a canon of the cathedral of Florence. In 1409, however, he renounced this benefice.[49] Looking at the prevailing scholarly

---

[48] *The Crisis of the Early Italian Renaissance.*
[49] Salvino Salvini, *Catalogo cronologico dei canonici della chiesa metropolitana fiorentina* (Firenze, 1782), pp. 30-32.

view from another standpoint, we have recently shown that one of the three representatives of the apolitical or anti-civic ideal, Antonio Corbinelli, willingly took part in public affairs, and was consequently unlikely to have shared the ideals of a literary set which rejected the assumptions of civic humanism.[50] This leaves only Roberto de' Rossi and Niccolò Niccoli. But the attempt will be made to show that Rossi's special political situation made any stand he may have taken somewhat ambiguous, and that once the conditions of public life in Florence are more fully examined, we may even have to modify our current assumptions about Niccoli.

The aims of this study are such that it would be meaningless to consider Roberto de' Rossi apart from his family, as neither his political ambition, his modest economic situation, nor—so far as we can tell—any individual virtues he revealed as a young man caused him to stand out socially. What counted and what indeed gave him social stature in Florence was the fact that he came of old Florentine stock, the Rossi, who made up one of the city's largest and most venerable clans.[51] Owing to his birth and connections, not because of his personal traits, the state considered Roberto a magnate: a nobleman whose rank distinguished him socially and politically from the *haute bourgeoisie* and which debarred him from election to certain offices in Florentine government. Entire families fell into this category: the Rossi, Adimari, Agli, Bardi, Buondelmonti, Cattani, Cavalcanti, Caviciulli, Frescobaldi, Gherardini, Ricasoli, Squarcialupi, and Tornaquinci.[52] There were other such families, but these were the greatest. They were forbidden to sit in the Republic's chief magistracies— the *Priorate*, the *Sedici*, and the *Dodici*. They could not serve in the powerful Eight on Security. In the *Decem Libertatis*, Florentine law allowed them to have only one of the ten seats.[53] Their quota in the Ten of War was one place out of ten.[54] They were given no representation in the catasto commission, nor in the commission on the passage of goods through the city gates. They

[50] See my "Addenda to the life of Antonio Corbinelli," pp. 3-19.
[51] Note Rinaldo degli Albizzi's attitude towards the Rossi in Cavalcanti, *Istorie*, I, 83-84.
[52] *Statuta*, I, 444-446, for a full list of the *magnati* families.
[53] *Tratte*, 80, f. 34r.
[54] Ammirato, IV, 344, 370; V, 8.

could claim only one of the seven Officials of the Tower and only one of the five major treasury posts.[55] The story was much the same for all other civic dignities: the *magnati* were either wholly excluded from them or given a minimum representation.

Once the political condition of the Florentine magnate is understood, it becomes clear that Roberto de' Rossi's public life was going to be far less full than that of a citizen with the name Capponi, Busini, Rucellai, or Guiccardini—stalwart *popolani* families.

In the early 1380's, when Roberto came of age to hold public office, there were at least twenty-six and probably more members of the Rossi clan in S. Spirito who were eligible to enter government service. In that decade all twenty-six actually appeared in office[56]—another factor which affected Roberto's civic career. For the inventories of the Commune's civil servants, the *Tratte*, disclose that appointments tended to be based on a system of rotation, and any such system necessarily influenced the frequency of Roberto's appearance in office. In this connection, it is noteworthy that not more than four members of the same clan ("de eadem domo, progenie, vel consorteria") could sit contemporaneously in the one legislative council open to the *grandi*, the Council of the Commune.[57] Moreover, this body of 192 citizens was permitted to have only thirty-two *grandi* in all (eight per quarter),[58] and one term must elapse between appointments to it. Since a term lasted four months, a citizen could not appear in the Council of the Commune more than thrice every two years.

---

[55] *Tratte*, 78, f. 58r. On the catasto commission and the treasury posts see: *ibid.*, 80, ff. 1r, 409r.

[56] They appeared in the Council of the Commune: *Tratte*, 142-144, passim, always under "nicchii" in the S. Spirito quarter. The twenty-six Rossi were: Adriano di Messer Fruosino, Andrea di Sandro, Antonio di Tommaso di Messer Rosso, Badino di Sandro, Bernardo di Filippo, Berto di Pino, Boverello di Alberto, Felice di Filippo, Filippo di Messer Bernardo, Gherardo di Dolcino, Giovanni di Ardanno, Giovanni di Francesco, Giovanni di Guerriero, Giovanni di Guidone, Giovanni di Stoldo, Guerriero di Tribaldo, Lorenzo di Ugolino, Lorenzo di Zanobi, Leonardo di Zanobi, Lippo di Stoldo, Nofri di Bonecca, Piero Fornaini, Tommaso di Giovanni, Tommaso di Messer Rosso, Tribaldo di Guerriero, and our own Roberto di Francesco di Dolcino.

[57] *Statuta*, II, 661.

[58] The statutes of 1415 actually state that this council is to have only sixteen magnates, four per quarter: *ibid.*, II, 660. Practice in the 1380's, however, permitted eight per quarter: *Tratte*, 142-144, passim.

But as the Rossi were in competition with the Bardi and Frescobaldi of S. Spirito, they normally entered the Council of the Commune at the rate of only two or three per term.

Roberto de' Rossi's first recorded appearance in public office involved a post in the Florentine dominion—the *podestería* of Chianti, rich vine country in the center of Tuscany. *Podestà* of Chianti,[59] Roberto entered the community on 1 June 1385, with a staff of two notaries and four attendants.[60] His office was to try the district's civil cases for a period of six months, with the notaries as his legal advisors and recorders. The post was not in itself distinguished, though it was one of the minor dominion charges which often served as a training ground for the young men of Florence's ruling families. When Roberto returned from Chianti at the beginning of December, he had already been drawn from the purses for the Ten on Liberty.[61] He participated in the hearings of this judicial body from the time he got back to Florence until the last day of March 1386. We noted above that Florentine law permitted the nobility to hold only one of the ten places in this tribunal. Almost surely, therefore, Rossi was expected to favor litigious claims advanced by the *grandi*. The *Decem Libertatis* dealt especially with property and business claims, disputed contracts, and debt. But they were forbidden to meddle in cases which had already been decided, or which were pending, in any of the guild consulates or the Six on Commerce.[62]

On 1 May 1387 Roberto is found sitting for the first time among the *grandi* in the Council of the Commune.[63] The two-thirds concurrence of this body was necessary for the enactment of all Florentine legislation. Even private petitions came under this heading—requests for citizenship, tax indulgences, legalization of natural children, appointments to certain offices, the right to alienate government securities frozen by inheritance clauses, and so forth. Roberto appeared in the Council of the Commune for a second term on the first day of January 1389.[64] Three years

---

[59] *Tratte*, 65, f. 48r.
[60] *Statuta*, III, 615.
[61] *Tratte*, 78, f. 8r. The term actually began on 1 December.
[62] *Statuta*, III, 23-24.
[63] *Tratte*, 143, not paginated. Arranged by date under S. Spirito.
[64] *Ibid.*, locate by date in the S. Spirito quarter.

later he secured a place among the *Grasciae Officiales*.[65] This commission had six places: five were held by *populares*, one by a magnate, and a term lasted four months. Their job was to supervise the quality and prices of the food staples sold by bakers, grocers, butchers, fishmongers, and poulterers. The commission also kept artisans under surveillance: small tailors, carpenters, masons, shoemakers, and smiths. In some cases the duty of the *Grascia* officials was to fix price and quality levels, in others merely to prosecute fraud or other policy violations. They inflicted fines; and less frequently they had offenders imprisoned, expelled from their crafts, or even sentenced to corporal punishment.[66]

Two weeks after leaving the *Grascia* Commission, Rossi went into the dominion as *Podestà* of Montevarchi.[67] That was on 13 August 1392. The area under the judicial powers of the Montevarchi *podestería*, a rich agricultural region between Florence and Arezzo, was larger than that of Chianti but the staff attached to each of the two posts was identical, two notaries and four attendants. The Montevarchi assignment seems to have been the humanist's last major dignity, though in the autumn of 1393 he joined the nobles in the Council of the Commune for the last time.[68]

Four notable administrative posts and three terms in the Council of the Commune—this was the sum of Roberto de' Rossi's record in office. It was not impressive. It could hardly be compared with the records of prominent public figures like Bartolomeo di Tommaso Corbinelli who, not counting his appearances in the legislative councils, held more than sixty government posts, including terms in *all* the principal magistracies; or Rinaldo degli Albizzi, whose diplomatic career alone numbered fifty-six separate missions;[69] or Niccolò del Buono Busini, who in the twenty-one years from 1392 to 1413 took office on thirty-six different

[65] *Tratte*, 78, f. 55r. The term began on 1 April 1392.
[66] Giulio Rezasco, *Dizionario del linguaggio italiano storico ed amministrativo* (Firenze, 1881), pp. 493ff.
[67] *Tratte*, 65, f. 69r.
[68] *Tratte*, 145, by date under 1 September in the S. Spirito quarter.
[69] *Commissioni di Rinaldo degli Albizzi*, III, 851-860.

occasions, exclusive of his terms in the legislative councils.[70] But all such comparisons are unfair to Rossi. Corbinelli, Albizzi, and Busini were *populares*; they were thus unfettered by the rigorous constitutional restrictions which hampered a nobleman like Roberto. Nevertheless, even after considering Roberto's record in office under the best possible light, it cannot be said that his civic career was extensive enough to refute the notion that he deliberately withdrew from public life. At the same time it must be emphasized that he could have refused the judicial dignities in Chianti and Montevarchi. This was a right accorded by Florentine law.[71] He chose to accept those offices, so he cannot then have actually disdained the idea of civic virtue.[72]

In the 1450's Giannozzo Manetti stated that Rossi deemed the holding of public office an inferior occupation.[73] Yet we saw that he entered office willingly. In fact, although Rossi appeared in only four magistracies during the course of his life (and those merely of medium importance), he somehow managed to develop a political reputation. For in the early years of the fifteenth century he was sometimes summoned by the Signoria to air his views in the executive councils. On these occasions he spoke in a purely private capacity, rather than as a guild or government representative. The minutes of the Signory debates, the *Consulte e Pratiche*, reveal his presence in the executive councils in 1403, 1411, 1412, and 1414.[74] The topics under discussion indicate that in each case he was summoned as an expert on foreign affairs. For this reason, as well as because of his family connections and brilliant humanist reputation, he became a socially influential figure. And in 1412, when the whole Pitti family ran afoul of some of Florence's powerful oligarchs, Buonaccorso Pitti eagerly and thankfully invoked Roberto de' Rossi's help.[75]

---

[70] ASF, *Carte Strozz.*, 4a ser., 564. This is the *ricordanza* of Niccolò del Buono Busini. On his offices see ff. 24r-25r.

[71] *Statuta*, II, 731.

[72] There is no evidence to show that he accepted the dominion posts for reasons of financial need. Besides, if he was willing to "fleece" the *contado* twice, why not four or five times?

[73] In his *Adversus Judaeos et Gentes*, a Vatican codex unknown to me (Cod. Vat. Urbin. Lat. 154). Quoted by Baron, *The Crisis*, II, 570, n. 55.

[74] *Consulte*, 36, f. 123r; 41, f. 11r; 42, f. 124r.

[75] Pitti, *Cronica*, pp. 165-176.

Niccolò Niccoli figures in current scholarship as a man who had a low regard for public office.[76] The source of this impression lies with some of his contemporaries: Poggio Bracciolini, Lorenzo Benvenuti, and Giannozzo Manetti, all of whom observed that Niccolò scorned civic honors.[77] Now although his career in public office was much too undistinguished to invalidate this picture, it does involve a record worth knowing about, especially because it has escaped the notice of his biographers.[78] Moreover, when this record is set beside a sketch of his brothers' careers, it may be possible to regard Niccolò's position on public life in a different light.

We saw in the preceding chapter that the Niccoli were already settled in Florence at the beginning of the fourteenth century and that the origins of their great wealth antedated 1350. Niccolò's father was a wool merchant.[79] The Commune honored him with only a single major dignity: a term of office in the Six on Commerce, a type of supreme court with jurisdiction over important cases of commercial litigation, including those which involved international dispute and the undertaking of reprisals by the state.[80] According to the chronicler, Goro Dati, the Six on Commerce were selected from "the most practical, the most intelligent, and the best-known men of the guilds."[81] The elder Niccoli sat in this tribunal during the summer of 1377.[82] In 1382 he finally entered the Council of the Commune,[83] which suggests that at the end of his life—he died in the 1380's—he may have been afflicted with a sense of the family's obscure political status. But the awareness came too late. He seems to have been unsuccessful in impressing the advantages of a political career on any of his six sons, for none of them—not only the humanist—subsequently

---

[76] Zippel, *Niccolò Niccoli*, p. 40; Baron, *The Crisis*, I, 289ff.

[77] Poggio, *Opera*, pp. 271, 275; L. Benvenuti, *L'invettiva contro Niccolò Niccoli*, pp. 166-186; Manetti in Vatican codex cited by Baron, *The Crisis*, II, 571-572.

[78] Zippel, *Niccolò Niccoli*; Vespasiano, pp. 434ff.; and the sketch by Lorenzo Mehus in Traversari, *Epistolae*, I, xxixff.

[79] ASF, *Lana*, 20, f. 5v, dated 3 Jan. 1363.

[80] Guido Bonolis, *La giurisdizione della Mercanzia in Firenze nel secolo xiv* (Firenze, 1901).

[81] Dati, *L'Istoria*, p. 157.

[82] ASF, *Mercanzia*, 129, by date under 1 July 1377.

[83] *Tratte*, 142, by date under 1 January 1381(2), S. Spirito, "nicchii."

displayed the force of ambition needed to found the political fortunes of a Florentine family.

One of Niccolò's brothers, Jacopo, took a doctorate in law from the University of Bologna in 1398.[84] He then became a prominent figure in the lawyers' guild and sat in the guild consulate on ten different occasions: 1403, 1405, 1407, 1409, 1411, 1415, 1420, 1421, 1423, and 1424.[85] The consulate was the guild's supreme judicial and legislative body, with certain powers of jurisdiction over all the guild members. One side of Messer Jacopo's activity in the guild directory was necessarily political, for the consuls of all the twenty-one guilds were, by right of their consular dignity, voting members of the Council of the People.[86] In 1412 he was appointed one of the Commune's two *Sapientes*, the official part-time legal advisors of municipal officials.[87] At the end of November, 1420, he was finally given an outstanding commission: he and Antonio di Messer Luca Panzano were sent as Florentine ambassadors to the king of Aragon.[88] Among other things, they were to solicit favorable royal intervention in the commercial claims of Florentine merchants with dealings in Sicily.

The subject of our inquiry, Niccolò, eldest of the six brothers, was the first to enter the legislative councils. He entered the Council of the People for the first time at the beginning of February 1392.[89] After that he sat periodically in one of the two legislative councils, although notable spans of time occasionally elapsed between his terms of office. He appeared in the councils, for example, in 1392, 1393, 1398, 1401, 1403, and 1404:[90] that is to say, right through the period when Visconti pressure on the Republic was heaviest. But oddly enough, although he did not reappear in the councils after 1404, he had not yet completely abandoned the notion of an occasional tour of duty in public office. From February to November of 1413 he held one of the

[84] *Il 'Liber secretus iuris caesarei' dell' Università di Bologna*, ed. A. Sorbelli, 2 vols. (Bologna, 1938-1942), I, 124.
[85] *ASF, Proconsolo*, 26, "Libro della coppa," ff. 16v *et seq.*
[86] *Statuta*, II, 661.
[87] *Tratte*, 79, f. 94r. On their functions see *Statuta*, II, 622-623.
[88] *ASF, Leg. Comm.*, 6, ff. 112v-113r.
[89] *Tratte*, 144, by date under "nicchii" in S. Spirito.
[90] *Tratte*, 145 (1 Sept. 1393), 146 (1 Jan. 1398), 147 (1 Oct. 1401; 1 Feb. 1403; 1 May 1404), all under "nicchii" in S. Spirito. The dates here are given according to the modern, not the Florentine, system.

few important offices of his life, a place among the six officials appointed to reduce the city's funded debt.[91] There he replaced a figure of moderate administrative importance, Nozzo di Vanni Manetti, who had died in office. Appointment to this body was by a two-thirds vote of the Priorate and colleges: i.e., by at least twenty-five of thirty-seven votes. The officials over the *diminutio montis* were not a standing commission, but when in office they were authorized, traditionally, to cut down on the public debt by forcing citizens (drawn by lot) to sell their Monte shares to the government at the market price.

In 1414 Niccolò was chosen for the board of trustees of the University of Florence (the Studio Fiorentino), a post normally held for one year.[92] Since the board was empowered to hire lecturers, Niccolò could now exert some influence in the area which governed his interests. But he did not reappear among the trustees for almost twenty years. In November 1434, shortly after the Medici brothers returned from exile, he obtained a second appointment to the Studio directorate.[93] At once the influence of the Albizzi group, supporters of Filelfo, came to an end in the Studio. Niccolò was now about seventy years old, and it seemed unlikely that he would ever hold a post as a civil servant again. Surprisingly enough, however, a year after leaving the Studio trustees, he took office once more: in November of 1436 he was made one of the five *Defectuum* officials.[94] These officials represented one of the major departments of Florentine administration: they supervised the wages and penalized misconduct of the Republic's soldiery (see n. 28 above). During the first decades of the fifteenth century men who appeared in this office were of either considerable or moderate political stature. Some of the prominent individuals who held this office were Maso degli Albizzi in 1405, Francesco della Luna in 1413, Palla Strozzi in 1415, Parigi Corbinelli in 1419, Rinaldo degli Albizzi in 1422, and Buonaccorso Pitti in 1426.[95] Niccolò was one of the five

---

[91] *Tratte*, 79, f. 259r.
[92] Gherardi, *Statuti*, p. 191. Niccolò's Studio posts were noticed by Zippel, *Niccolò Niccoli*.
[93] Gherardi, *Statuti*, p. 248.
[94] *Tratte*, 80, f. 61v.
[95] *Tratte*, 78, f. 226v; 79, ff. 68r, 68v, 69r, 70r, 70v.

Defectuum officials when he died at the beginning of February 1437.

Four of Niccolò's brothers have not yet been considered: Giovanni, Bernardo, Piero, and Vettorio. Giovanni sat in the legislative councils only once, in the summer of 1394;[96] Bernardo appeared in the councils twice in one year, 1414, and probably on several occasions thereafter;[97] but the *Tratte* inventories never record the presence of Piero or Vettorio in those bodies. Vettorio, however, was once an emissary of the Republic. In July 1412, he was sent into the borderlands between Umbria and the Marches as an envoy to the *condottiere,* Braccio Fortebracci, who had seized Piero Niccoli near Foligno.[98] Having taken his money and cargo of horses and arms, the soldier had then cast Piero into prison. Vettorio's task was to work for his brother's release and the restitution of the confiscated goods. The Signoria's intervention in favor of Piero indicates something about the kind of influence available to the Niccoli when they made a concerted effort to exercise it.[99] Bernardo, the brother who appeared in the legislative councils twice in 1414, was given two diplomatic missions in the early 1420's. The first assignment, confirmed on 18 April 1421, took him to Messer Tommaso di Campofregoso, "Duke of Genoa."[100] His job was to get the Duke to assist in the recovery of two Florentine vessels, loaded with grain and English wool, which had been seized by the Genoese. The second assignment was on 23 July 1423, when Bernardo was appointed ambassador to Antonuccio di Camponeschi, Lord of Aquila (in the Abruzzo). His mission was to obtain promises concerning the safety of Florentine commercial goods in Aquila, for Antonuccio seems to have threatened their seizure.[101] The fact that

---

[96] *Tratte,* 145, from 1 May 1394, under "nicchii" in S. Spirito.

[97] *Tratte,* 151, ff. 106r, 127v.

[98] *Leg. Comm.,* 6, ff. 21v-22r. Vettorio was also to speak to the Priors of Todi, to Ridolfo of Camerino, and to the lord of Foligno. The brief begins: "Nota et informatione a te, Vettorio di Bartolomeo Niccoli, di quello che ai a fare con Braccio Fortebracci e altri come ambasciadore del Comune di Firenze."

[99] This observation is also based on the tax indulgences which they successfully petitioned from the Commune: ASF, *Provv.,* 90, ff. 338v-340v (dated 23 Dec. 1401); *Lib. Fab.,* 46, ff. 46v, 47v (14-15 Oct. 1398); 48, f. 99r (26 Feb. 1406); 52, ff. 185v, 186v (30 Oct. 1422).

[100] *Leg. Comm.,* 6, ff. 117v-118r.

[101] *Leg. Comm.,* 7, f. 30r/v.

Bernardo was selected for this embassy was not accidental: he himself had been a merchant in Aquila for years,[102] so that he was familiar both with the city and the people.

It is very difficult to explain the absence of civic ambitions in the Niccoli brothers, particularly as they were sometimes in great need of political power. For not only did they dissipate an enormous patrimony, but also—like even the greatest families—they occasionally fell victim to the partisan nature of Florentine tax administration. Furthermore, they reached their political majority in the late 1380's and early 1390's, precisely as the oligarchy regained control of the state and as public office became one of the surest means of social survival in upper-class Florence. But strangely enough, none of this proved a sufficient stimulus to incline the brothers toward public life. Since custom in Florentine families made the eldest son the first heir to the family's political fortunes,[103] it was up to the humanist, Niccolò, to lead the family in vying for political office. This he failed to do. The responsibility then passed to his brothers, but they too refused. Why? What prevented them? The fact that they were upstarts? That *was* a handicap. But they had ties of marriage with the Brancacci of S. Spirito and the Del Toso of S. Maria Novella, strong bureaucratic families with good connections.[104] Niccolò himself was known to be a clever and persuasive speaker and such a talent in Florence was an asset of the first order.[105] In support of his eloquence, moreover, and prepared to serve the family's political advantage, there were the influential people in Niccolò's circle of friends: Coluccio Salutati, Bindo de Messer Jacopo Guasconi, two of the Corbinelli brothers, Messer Agnolo Acciaiuoli, Cosimo and Lorenzo de' Medici, Messer Guglielmo Tanagli, and others. There is no evidence that Nic-

---

[102] ASF, *Notarile antecosimiano*, F 329, i, f. 127r (19 June 1402). Contains the protocols of the notary, Ser Filippo di Michele da Poggibonsi.

[103] For example: Cosimo (for the Medici), Neri di Gino (for the Capponi), Bartolomeo di Tommaso (for the Corbinelli), Jacopo di Messer Rinaldo (for the Gianfigliazzi), Messer Giuliano di Niccolò (for the Davanzati), Ugolino di Niccolò (for the Martelli), and Nicolaio di Ugo (for the Alessandri).

[104] A first cousin of the brothers, Lorenza, married Zanobi di Lapaccino del Toso: ASF, *Catasto*, 378, f. 262r. Vettorio Niccoli married Nanna di Bartolomeo di Silvestro Brancacci: ASF, *Carte Ancisa*, MM, f. 583r.

[105] Santini, *Firenze*, passim.

colò ever tried to use his friends in order to advance himself politically, except possibly in connection with the office he obtained at the end of his life. At the height of the political and military crisis around 1400, caused by the Duke of Milan's ambitions against Florence, the humanist appeared and reappeared in the legislative councils. But apart from the few offices assigned to him, he made no other attempts to involve himself in public affairs.

Thus, Niccolò Niccoli was the one member of the Florentine humanist circle—Rossi's situation was ambiguous—who really seems not to have been interested in holding public office. Indeed, as his detractors claimed, he may sometimes in annoyance have scorned it. But if we choose to emphasize this view, we must find a way to explain Niccolò's early presence in the legislative councils, as well as his appointments to the *Defectuum* officials and to the office on the reduction of the public debt.

Dr. Baron has observed that one of the inherent dangers in the revival of classicism was the trend in some quarters to sacrifice civic responsibility to a full-time concern for classical languages and literature.[106] The danger was certainly present and Niccolò may well have exemplified this tendency. After having examined the administrative record of the family, however, it appears that all its members—Niccolò, his father, and his five brothers—were lacking in forceful political and administrative ambitions. Consequently, Niccolò's civic indifference may have been a product of his immediate family background (hard as this is to explain in the context of upper-class Florence), rather than of the way he elected to regard his humanistic studies.

4. LIONARDO BRUNI

When Cosimo de' Medici returned from exile in the fall of 1434 and the Medicean partisans seized control of the state,[107] the first secretary of the Florentine Republic, Lionardo Bruni, cannot have been entirely without anxieties. At the end of 1427 he had replaced in the chancellery one of the leaders of the anti-Medicean faction, Ser Paolo di Ser Lando Fortini. Bruni seems

---

[106] Baron, *The Crisis*, I, 284ff.
[107] Cavalcanti, *Della carcere*; also Gelli, "L'esilio di Cosimo de' Medici," pp. 53-96, 149-169.

to have been a compromise candidate, a man whose great humanistic renown was perhaps thought to put him above factional prejudice. As a compromise chancellor, accordingly, he was apparently not a Medicean; when Cosimo and others of the sect were exiled in October 1433, he retained his government post. The records of the time betray nothing about Bruni's movements. Quietly, it seems, he tried to walk a tightrope between the two factions. But when the pro-Medici forces returned to the political foreground a year later, it is not unlikely that there were men in the winning sect with suspicions about Bruni's unobtrusive conduct in office during the past year.

All around him friends were imprisoned, fined, and banished. In 1431 the humanist had contracted a marriage for his only son with one of the leading Castellani households. The marriage was clearly (see Ch. V, 1) a social and political maneuver on Bruni's part. But with the return of Cosimo all the leaders of the Castellani clan were exiled from the city.[108] Banished too was Palla di Nofri Strozzi, a man who had studied Greek with Bruni under the tutelage of Chrysoloras and who became one of Bruni's close friends. The leading exile was Rinaldo degli Albizzi, to whom the humanist dedicated his *De Militia* in 1422[109] and with whom ten years later he was still on amicable terms.[110]

But Bruni maintained a discreet silence in all these cases. Wealthy, distinguished, a parvenu, he had no choice but to hold as best he knew to the place he had made for himself in Florentine society. The great polemicist and humanist, Francesco Filelfo, tried very hard in the *Commentationes Florentinae de Exilio* to taunt him into declaring his position on the conflict between the factions, but the chancellor held his tongue. These observations point to a man who was prudent, practical, and possibly something of an opportunist; at any rate, a man tenacious about his place in public life.

Nothing in Bruni's background enabled him to claim a Florentine political tradition. He was the son of a small grain dealer from Arezzo, where the family had occupied an undistinguished

---

[108] Cavalcanti, *Istorie*, I, 601-602.
[109] Bruni, *Epistolarum libri viii*, p. lix.
[110] *Commissioni di Rinaldo degli Albizzi*, III, 549.

social and political position.[111] At an early period his father may have thought of sending him into trade, but this perhaps required more capital than the family could manage. The boy, therefore, had to enter one of the professions: he chose law, the field nearest his literary inclinations. In the mid 1390's he was studying law in Florence, where he was taken up by the Republic's chancellery head, Coluccio Salutati. When Chrysoloras went to Florence at the end of 1396, Bruni for a time abandoned his legal studies to learn Greek. It was in the Chrysoloras circle that he met men like Roberto de' Rossi, Palla di Nofri Strozzi, Niccolò Niccoli, and possibly Antonio Corbinelli. These early friends extended his connections in Florence, but it was with the concrete support of Salutati that he managed in 1405 to secure a secretarial dignity in the papal curia. There, in a court where meeting the highest prelates of the Church was a quotidian experience, he served popes Innocent VII, Gregory XII, Alexander V, and John XXIII. Bruni seems to have been gifted at courting and winning the support of influential people.[112] Had he finally decided on an ecclesiastical career, there is no doubt that he would have risen to one of the major prelacies. He had joined the pontifical court in 1405, and in 1407, when he was named one of the Florentine cathedral canons, he took the place vacated by Monsignore Antonio Casini, who then became Bishop of Pesaro.[113] Bruni was afterwards to become chief representative of the Florentine cathedral chapter at the Council of Constance, although he renounced his canonical dignity in 1409.

Meanwhile, his literary fame had spread and his contacts in the Church served to widen his social connections. In fact, he must already have reached a stage where he could expect superior dignities, for the year after he left the Church he was appointed Florence's chancellery head for a period of one year.[114] But three

[111] The only reasonably accurate life of Bruni has been briefly sketched by Santini, *Leonardo Bruni Aretino*, pp. 3-129. See also the very important "Aggiunte e correzioni" by G. Mancini in his edition of Bruni, *Istoria fiorentina*, I, 29-45.

[112] There is an excellent summary description of Bruni's first arrival at the papal court in Weiss, "Jacopo Angeli da Scarperia," pp. 815-817.

[113] Salvini, *Catalogo cronologico*, pp. 30-32.

[114] Marzi, p. 159.

months later he abandoned the office and went back to Rome. Though it was one of the highest-paid offices in the Republic, it had not put an end to Bruni's discontent. In 1415, he finally returned to settle in Florence. There, using his powerful friendships, he got the Republic to grant him Florentine citizenship and a tax indulgence such as only six or eight others in the city could claim.[115]

After his brief appointment as chancellor at the end of 1410, Bruni did not again accept a civic dignity until late in May 1426.[116] He was then, together with Francesco di Messer Simone Tornabuoni, made ambassador to Pope Martin V. Francesco captained the powerful Tornabuoni family, later closely tied to the Medici by bonds of marriage. The two men started out from Florence on 30 May. Their mission in Rome was to negotiate a peace with the Duke of Milan's ambassadors. Pope Martin was to arbitrate the colloquies. Bruni and Tornabuoni were also to ask the Pope for the restitution of certain Florentine fortresses in the Romagna; they had been taken from the Florentines by the papal governor of Bologna, the Archbishop of Arles.

The Signoria's correspondence to the two diplomats was mainly addressed to Bruni, who seems to have been the senior member.[117] Moreover, sometime before the Rome meetings were terminated, probably several weeks before, Francesco withdrew from the mission. Consequently, the concluding sessions with the Milanese legates were negotiated by the humanist alone. All told the assignment lasted four months. Bruni drafted his final report to the Signoria on 29 September 1426, the day he returned to Florence. He reported that the Pope promised to have the Florentine forts surrendered to the Republic, but that the Duke of

---

[115] In 1427 the following citizens possessed tax privileges: Alessandro di Ser Filippo Borromei, Francesco Nerli, Vinanzo (?) Pieruzzi da Camerino, Madalena di Carlo Strozzi (widow of Luchino Visconti), Giovanni and Benedetto di Messer Piero Gaetani, and Bartolommeo di Gherardo da Bologna. No scholarly work has been done on the nature of the tax indulgence in Florence.

[116] *Leg. Comm.*, 7, ff. 51r-53v.

[117] The documents of the mission are printed in Monzani, "Di Leonardo Bruni Aretino." The first letter begins: "Nota et informatione a voi messer Leonardo da Arezo et Francesco di messer Simone Tornabuoni," etc. The other letters read: "Domino Leonardo de Aretio et Francisco de Tornabuonis."

Milan had refused to compromise on several major items. Hence Florentine relations with Milan were left unsettled.

On 30 March 1425 Bruni was matriculated in the *Calimala* guild.[118] Since his catasti (see Ch. III, 7) do not show that he was then directly involved in the importing and resale of foreign cloth, it may be that he entered the guild for political reasons. What specifically suggests this is that the first step in political mobility for a "new" man was to gain admittance to one of the city's seven major guilds. Bruni reinforced his guild status before 1429 by enrollment in the lawyers' guild.[119] For years now (from at least the time of his first election to the chancellorship) *Messer* or *Dominus* had been regularly prefixed to his name. According to the custom of the period, only knights and jurists were permitted the use of this title.[120] Bruni's entry into the lawyers' guild as a *iudex* denotes that he may have been a doctor of law, for most judges in the guild possessed degrees either in civil or canon law.

He entered the guild of the wool merchants in March 1434. Some years later he obtained formal entry into the silk guild.[121] In the end, therefore, he could claim membership in four of the seven major guilds, having thus given himself a broad basis for political action. But he himself was active only in the consulate of the lawyers' guild. He appeared as an advisor in that directory in 1429, 1431, and 1437. On eight other occasions, however, he sat as one of the eight voting consuls: in 1430, 1431, 1435, 1438, 1439, 1441, 1442, and 1444.[122]

Attention has already been called to his second and final appointment as head of the Republic's chancellery in November 1427. The historian of this department of Florentine government

[118] *ASF, Calimala*, 6, f. 32v.
[119] The records of the lawyers' guild are in an extremely bad state of preservation. We know, however, that Bruni entered it before 1429 because in that year he first appeared as an advisor to the guild consulate. *ASF, Proconsolo*, 26, f. 71r.
[120] I know of two exceptions only: Coluccio Salutati and Poggio Bracciolini. Both were *notai* and hence the title *Ser* was their proper designation. From the time of Salutati's death, however, he became known as *Messer* or *Dominus* in the official records. Perhaps as "Poet Laureate" he was entitled to this. Poggio enjoyed the titles *Messer* and *Dominus* for two decades before his death.
[121] *Lana*, 21, f. 122v; also *Seta*, 8, f. 132v.
[122] *Proconsolo*, 26, ff. 24v, 25r, 26r, 27r, 27v, 28r/v, 29r, 71r, 72r, 75r.

observed that Bruni would not have accepted the office if he had not been offered more privileges and powers than in 1410.[123] At any rate, his chief duties remained those of overseeing the lists of men eligible for office (given up in 1435), sitting in on the Signoria's executive councils, and dictating the Republic's foreign correspondence. During his first ten years in this office, Bruni seems to have attended mainly to chancellery business. The probable reasons for this caution have already been explained. Chosen as a compromise chancellor, he could not at once take sides in the factional struggle. In 1431 his son's marriage to one of the Castellani girls was a move away from the Medici circle. The party strife then came to a head and the Medici were temporarily vanquished. But Bruni, whose letters betray a great deal of political sensitivity, avoided any overt commitment to the anti-Medici forces. In all probability he correctly estimated the preponderant power of the Medici even during their year's exile. And when they returned, he appeared not to have compromised himself, at any rate not in such a way as to have done himself any lasting harm. His next task was to win back the full confidence of the ruling set. This would not have been difficult for a man of his resources, and was quietly accomplished in about two years.

In 1436 he penned a letter to the Sienese government against Florentine exiles. In June 1437 he managed to obtain a seat in the *Dodici Buonomini*,[124] so that now for the first time he appeared in the executive councils as a full-fledged member. But he had nothing to learn, for as chancellor he had attended these meetings during the past ten years, recording the debates. At the end of January 1438 he was made one of the four *sindici* of the Six on Commerce.[125] The job of the syndics was to examine the official behavior of, and possibly review the cases tried by, the magistrates of Florence's highest commercial tribunal.

Once the humanist became convinced that he had won back the oligarchy's confidence, he began to exert a continuous pres-

[123] *Marzi*, p. 191.
[124] *ASF, Mss.*, 265, f. 123. He entered the *Dodici* on June 15th. A term here was for three months.
[125] *Tratte*, 80, f. 243r.

sure in all that concerned his interests and advancement. His sense of timing did not deceive him. In February 1439 he confronted the legislative councils with a petition to extend his tax privilege to his direct male descendants.[126] Since the bill reduced their direct income taxes to a bare minimum, debate on the measure was sure to be heated, particularly since taxation in the city was one of the two focal points of contention.[127] Furthermore, Bruni had to overcome any hostility aroused by his condition as a *nouveau riche*, or by the fact that he had already enjoyed a fiscal indulgence during more than twenty years. The bill went before the Council of the People on 7 February 1439, and was passed. Two days later it was put to the vote in the Council of the Commune, which on that occasion numbered 146 councillors. A two-thirds vote was needed to pass it. The final count was ninety-eight votes in favor of the measure to forty-eight opposed.[128] Was it coincidence that passage of the bill was obtained by a majority of only one vote? What kind of canvassing had the humanist done? Of the eighteen measures proposed in the Council of the Commune on 9 February, the bill favoring Bruni's heirs received the heaviest negative vote, so opposition to it must have been very considerable. But strong though the opposition was, Bruni's good name triumphed. The fact that he had got such a petition into the councils at all (a step which required the approval of the Signoria and colleges by a two-thirds vote) was already indicative of his distinction. It was more remarkable still that the petition should have been favorably acted on in the legislative councils.

Bruni's efforts to obtain superior public dignities seem to have been unremitting. On 1 June 1439 he was made one of the *Decem Baliae* (Ten of War).[129] The appointment was for six months. Almost a year later, on 1 May 1440, the appointment

---

[126] *ASF, Lib. Fab.*, 58, f. 35f. The original privilege was granted in 1416 and greatly reduced his direct property and income taxes. See above Ch. III, n. 117.

[127] E.g., *ASF, Consulte*, 44, ff. 113v, 136v-137r (date: 1421). The other issue involved the method of drawing up the lists of eligibility for public office. See the debates in Pellegrini, *Sulla repubblica fiorentina*, pp. xxxiiiff., cxlvii.

[128] *Lib. Fab.*, 58, f. 35f.

[129] *Tratte*, 80, f. 441v.

was renewed, and it was given to him a third time in June 1441.[130] But what did these appointments mean?

Although strictly speaking the Ten of War were set up for the first time in 1384, similar commissions had appeared and functioned alongside the Signoria in the earlier fourteenth century.[131] The Ten, at all events, were only convened in time of war or preparation for war. But as the resurgence of the oligarchy in the 1380's and 1390's meant the reappearance of an aggressive ruling set eager to perpetuate small, powerful commissions, and since the war years outnumbered the years of peace, the Ten of War soon began to take on the semblance of a permanent commission. As the name suggests, they were a special-powers commission set up to conduct the Republic's wars. First of all, the Signoria ceded power to the Ten.[132] Included in the delegated power was the right to make agreements or alliances with any commune, lord, or principality which had already been approached by the Signoria in a friendly fashion. The Ten could declare war on Florence's enemies, dispatch spies and ambassadors into any region or court, but not to the Pope, the Emperor, or a king. They also conferred with the Signoria on the hiring of troops, and by appointing one of the Ten as first commissioner in the field, they swiftly took over the complete supervision of Florentine armies in time of war.[133]

Since a place in the Ten of War was more highly coveted than a seat in any other magistracy, appointments to the commission were jealously guarded by the oligarchy. Only the special dignity of the Gonfalonier of Justice was deemed superior, so that preferment even in the Signoria could not match an appointment to the Ten. Let us clarify this: election to the Priorate, the *Dodici Buonomini*, or the *Sedici Gonfalonieri* tended to be based on a system of rotation. If a man's forebears had appeared in the Signoria, and if the family had not afterwards fallen into political disfavor or troubles preventing tax payment, then he could fully

[130] *Ibid.*, ff. 441v, 454r; *ASF, Mss.*, 271, by dates.
[131] Marzi, pp. 176-177.
[132] *Statuta*, III, 25ff., on the powers of the Ten.
[133] E.g., when Florence took Pisa in 1406 two members of the Ten were at the head of the Florentine army, Gino Capponi and Bartolomeo Corbinelli. See Capponi, *Commentari*, in *Cronichette antiche*, pp. 251-281.

expect to be entered in the Signoria's eligibility purses. How often he was entered in the purses depended on the power of his family; and how often he was actually drawn for an office was determined by the number of names in the purse. But an assignment to the Ten of War was something else: only favorites of the oligarchy or outstanding figures could hope to obtain a place there. The technique of control over the membership was relatively simple: the ten places were filled by appointees who were drawn from a special purse and who must receive the approval of the *Consiglio degli Ottantuno* by a two-thirds vote. This council consisted of the Priors, the *Sedici*, the *Dodici*, the nine Captains of the Guelf Party, the Eight on Security, the Six on Commerce, and twenty-one guild consuls.[134] Since election to each of these bodies was also screened, the ruling party had no trouble regulating membership in the Ten of War.

Prominent as he was in the Ten of War, Lionardo Bruni continued to press for assignments to other commissions. Thus, on 1 May 1441 he began a term in the Eight on Security (*Octo Custodiae*).[135] But he took part in the deliberations of this body for only one month, for it was illegal to hold a post there contemporaneously with an appointment to the Ten of War. Set up in 1378, the Eight on Security, like the Ten of War, grew into a powerful magistracy, largely through the process of encroachment. It took military prerogatives from the Signoria and the *Conductae* officials; it looked after civil defense; it censored all suspect correspondence entering and leaving the city;[136] but it was particularly designed to deal with questions of political loyalty and conspiracy.[137] After 1433 the Eight on Security also began to send special directives to the three major Florentine judges (i.e., the *Podestà*, the *Capitano del Popolo*, and the *Esecutore*), so determined were they to influence judicial decisions. Illegal

---

[134] See the *provvisione* setting up the *Decem Baliae* of 1393, in Pellegrini, pp. i-v. Note that sixteen of the consuls were from the major guilds; the others were *minori*. Furthermore, the *Decem* must always include seven members of the major guilds, two *minori*, and one *magnus*. One of Cosimo de' Medici's letters perfectly exemplifies the patriciate's attitude towards membership in the *Decem*, also in Pellegrini, pp. xvii-xviii.

[135] *Tratte*, 80, f. 15v.

[136] Strozzi, *Lettere*, p. 143.

[137] Antonelli, "La magistratura degli Otto di Guardia."

though this pressure was, it gradually became legal and the Eight finally disposed of genuine judicial powers.

February 3, 1442: the humanist accepted an appointment to the ten *Sindici Potestatis*.[138] They were an investigative group convened on the completion of the *Podestà's* term on the bench, normally twice yearly. In Bruni's time the office of syndic was exercised by men like the prominent Messer Agnolo Acciaiuoli, Piero di Cosimo de' Medici, Bartolommeo di Lorenzo de' Bardi, Messer Giuliano Davanzati, and Bartolommeo di Ugo degli Alessandri.[139] About three months after leaving this commission, Bruni began a tour of duty as one of the Approvers of the Guild Statutes.[140] He represented the lawyers' guild and his term ran from 5 May to the end of December 1442. The Approvers were composed of eight officials, seven from the major guilds and *scioperati* and one *minori*. They were responsible for "the revision, correction, cancellation, approval, or disapproval, of all guild statutes and ordinances."[141] Set up on a yearly basis, the purpose of the commission was to detect breaches of the Florentine constitution. Citizens were selected for the *Approbatores Statutorum* by the drawing of names from an eligibility purse; the purse was assembled by the Priorate, the Sixteen, the Twelve, the Six on Commerce, and the nine Guelf Captains.[142]

It must be remembered that during the late 1430's and early 1440's Bruni continued as the first secretary of the Republic. This dignity was his until he died in March 1444. But before his death he added still another office to his career. On 1 September 1443 he entered the Priorate,[143] Florence's chief executive body. One of the major tasks confronting the Priorate of Bruni's term was that of raising additional revenue. It was decided to try levying a tax of four *decine*.[144] Such an impost, however, required

[138] *Tratte*, 80, f. 215v.
[139] *Tratte*, 80, ff. 215r/v, 216r/v.
[140] *Ibid.*, f. 289r.
[141] *Statuta*, III, 20. Their decisions were good for one year: "et quidquid per eos factum fuerit in cassando, corrigendo, emendando, improbando, vel approbando dicta statuta, seu capitula in eis contenta obtineat plenum robur, et duret per annum."
[142] *Ibid.*, II, 656.
[143] ASF, *Priorista del Palazzo*, f. 187v.
[144] A variation of the catasto. The term *decine* referred to the type of officialdom involved in collecting the impost. See Canestrini, pp. 178ff.

a legislative act and stiff opposition was expected. Being a fiscal measure, the bill had first to pass through the Council of the Two Hundred by a two-thirds vote. Only then could it be introduced into the Councils of the People and Commune. The gravity of the measure is indicated by the fact that all councillors absent on the days it was debated had to pay a fine of 2.00 florins per absence,[145] a step taken only in the case of important legislation.

Lionardo Bruni put the bill before the Two Hundred on September 23, 1443.[146] Four prominent Florentines then addressed the body, calling for approval of the bill—Giovanni di Jacopo di Lutozzo Nasi (for S. Spirito), Alamanno Salviati (S. Croce), Messer Palla di Messer Palla Strozzi (S. Maria Novella), and Neroni di Nigi di Dietisalvi Neroni (S. Giovanni). But the bill was not passed and the humanist proposed it again on the following day. Again it was refused. There ensued some three weeks of debate. In the meantime a less ambitious tax bill was prepared. Bruni's prestige and influence were apparently being enlisted to secure its passage. Then on October 16, 17, and 18 the old and venerable humanist again went before the Two Hundred and repeatedly confronted them with the modified measure.[147] Bruni softened the opposition. On October 19 the bill was proposed by a modest figure, Bartolommeo di Gherardo Maruscelli, and this time it was driven through.[148]

This completes the picture of Bruni's career in public office. He attained the city's leading magistracies first by establishing a reputation in Florentine literary circles, then through his contacts in the Church, and finally by extending his political and social connections during his tenure of the Republic's chancellorship. By 1410, as his ecclesiastical preferment and first assignment to the chancellery disclose, he was no longer just a literary figure, but rather a high-ranking administrator. Correctly enough, therefore, when after 1434 Filelfo sat down to write his *Commentationes Florentinae de Exilio*, he placed Bruni on an equal footing with men like Rinaldo degli Albizzi, Palla di Nofri Strozzi, Ridolfo di Bonifazio Peruzzi, and Francesco di Messer Tommaso

---

[145] *Lib. Fab.* 59, ff. 89r *et seq.*
[146] *Ibid.*
[147] *Ibid.*, ff. 96r/v, 97r.
[148] *Ibid.*, f. 97v.

Soderini. For Bruni was himself a leading member of the Florentine patriciate. The summit of his civic career consisted in his appointments to the *Decem Baliae*. His colleagues in this commission were the leading Florentine statesmen of the day—Cosimo de' Medici, Neri di Gino Capponi, Messer Agnolo Acciaiuli, Alessandro di Ugo degli Alessandri, Messer Lorenzo Ridolfi, Messer Piero Beccanugi, and others.[149] He sat with all of them around the conference tables between 1439 and 1441. And the place he created for the Bruni family in Florentine society later enabled his only son, Donato, to enter the Priorate, the Sixteen, the Twelve on two occasions, and to hold a variety of other important offices.

5. GIANNOZZO MANETTI

The traceable origins of the Manetti family go back to the early thirteenth century.[150] We know nothing of them before that time. In the fifteenth century there were various branches of the family in different parts of the city—in S. Spirito, S. Giovanni, and S. Croce; but the ties of kinship between some of them were already far removed in time. Clarification of this point will depend on further research in the early notarial protocols, preserved in the State Archives of Florence and still to be given careful study.

During the early fifteenth century the Manetti of S. Croce were moderately active in political society, but they were not well known. Tuccio di Marabottino and Nozzo di Vanni, who captained two branches of the Manetti of S. Spirito, were much more active in civic affairs. They were administrators of moderate rank, civil servants who helped to staff the wide range of offices in Florentine government.[151] At the head of the system were the Republic's key offices: the Signoria and colleges, the Ten of War, the Eight on Security, the Six on Commerce, the Captains of the Guelf society, and the guild consuls.

In the early fourteenth century Giannozzo's branch of the family, also a S. Spirito house, contracted marriages with the

---

[149] *Tratte*, 80, ff. 441v, 454r.

[150] *BNF, Mss. Passerini*, 189, insert 33, "Manetti."

[151] Several score families furnished the men of this type: e.g., the Lorini, Della Fioraia, Anselmi, Ceffini, and on a higher level families like the Filicaia, Riccialbani, Raffacani, Sassolini, and Serzelli. See *Tratte*, 78-80, passim.

Frescobaldi, Ricci, Strozzi, and Rucellai. Consequently, even then the social position of the Manetti must have been relatively high, for these families had large commercial, banking and real-estate fortunes, and three of them were moving towards their political apogee—the Ricci, Strozzi, and Rucellai. Giannozzo Manetti's grandfather, Giannozzo di Lambuccio, may have been the first of his family to go into banking on a moderate scale, and he appears to have done so with success; for he managed to obtain appointments to the directory of the *Cambio* guild. His last appearance as a consul of the *Arte del Cambio* was in the summer of 1359.[152] The year before, during the November-December term, he had sat in the Priorate; he was thus the first Manetti to attain this dignity.[153] With this achievement, the Manetti made their major début in public life.

In the next generation the family destinies passed into the hands of the humanist's father, Bernardo (born ca. 1347). Although Giannozzo di Lambuccio seems to have prospered as a banker and currency exchanger, something probably went wrong. For at the end of his life he had little to show for it: his son Bernardo inherited a small patrimony, but spent most of his life amassing an enormous fortune. He made some of his wealth abroad, in Naples, Spain and Portugal, from which we gather that he lived a good deal of his life away from his native land. This would go far in explaining why he took so little part in the civic life of Florence. He occasionally appeared in the legislative councils: in 1382, 1405, 1407, 1412, and 1417.[154] But it was only in 1412, as a man about sixty-five years old, that he was chosen for one of the more responsible offices, a *podestería* in the dominion.[155] The only other office connected with his name in the records was that of Studio trustee in 1429, at the end of his life.[156]

The meagre administrative record of the humanist's father and grandfather did not offer a strong background to recommend him in political circles. But this was not an insuperable difficulty. In

---

[152] *ASF, Mss.*, 544, entitled "Matricole dell' arti maggiori mercatanti e cambio," f. 911r.

[153] *ASF, Priorista Mariani*, iii, f. 600r.

[154] *Tratte*, 142, under 1 Jan. 1382; 147, under 1 Sept. 1405; 148, under 1 Feb. 1407; 151, f. 66r; 152, f. 117v. *Tratte* registers 151 and 152 are paginated; the others are not.

[155] *Tratte*, 66, f. 133r.   [156] Gherardi, *Statuti*, p. 221.

the 1420's his father's gradual accumulation of wealth made them the second richest family in S. Spirito and one of the first ten in Florence. Giannozzo was matriculated in the guild of bankers and money changers in 1425.[157] At the same time the Republic's internal political struggle was intensified and the schism in the governing class moved towards a crisis. Confronted by that struggle, what was the proper course of action for an upper-class Florentine? He might try to avoid commitments to either side; like Bruni, he could angle to wait for the outcome; or he might even try to shun election to the principal offices. But these alternatives were not the same as avoiding public office altogether. And in any case it was next to impossible for a wealthy family to stay entirely out of politics. The Florentine system of privileges and forced loans, the habit of official tampering with government securities through manipulation of the public debt, the exertion of powerful pressures on the law courts and the Six on Commerce—these forces and practices ruined and elevated families. Not to go into politics was to gamble with economic and social survival. This in the end was the coercive factor behind the Florentine readiness to enter public life. Consequently, if a rich and prominent house like the Panciatichi or Rinuccini failed to get members of the family into the Republic's governing councils, the reason was not in their unwillingness to serve the Commune, but rather in the organized, or at any rate effective, opposition directed against them.

Such was the political climate of Giannozzo Manetti's youth. The intellectual life of the times must have seemed more benign. Humanism was capturing the intellectual centers of Italy and Florence stood in the foreground. Giannozzo diligently pursued his humanistic studies; yet he also prepared to go into the marketplace of politics.

His first appearance in office was impressive: he was given a term of office in the *Dodici Buonomini*, beginning on 15 June 1429.[158] It was very unusual for a young man to begin his civic

---

[157] *ASF, Cambio,* 12, f. 93v.
[158] *ASF, Mss.,* 265, f. 6r. Periodic membership in the legislative councils was the birthright of all male citizens who enjoyed political rights. Therefore, Giannozzo's appearance in those bodies will not be considered. He first appeared in one of the councils in 1425: *Tratte,* 153, f. 207v.

career as a participant in the deliberations of the Signoria. Hence Giannozzo's connections must have reached into the highest circles of Florentine government. The importance of the *Dodici* has already been explained. It will be enough to add here that they composed one of the essential bodies involved in the drawing up of the eligibility lists for such powerful offices as the Ten of War, Eight on Security, and the commission for the catasto. When Giannozzo left the *Dodici* he took no other offices for six years. Meanwhile, he contracted marriage; his father died; he was matriculated in the silk merchants' guild;[159] and for a few years he devoted himself more fully to the study of classical literature, Latin, and Greek.[160] Then in 1435, with the Medici partisans in the full breadth of their recent victory, he was made one of the Studio trustees.[161] In the late autumn of the same year his name was drawn from the purses for the *Grascia* Commission.[162] This office, we noted, administered government policy on the prices and quality of food staples and on the products of artisans and small craftsmen. The humanist sat among the *Officiales Grasciae* for four months. From now on he became very active in the affairs of state, and he was to remain so for the next eighteen years.

Two weeks after leaving the *Grascia* Commission Giannozzo was made Treasurer of the Tower Officials and of the Commission on Jails ("camerarius turris et stincarum"). The office began on 1 April 1436 and was to last for six months. But he held this post only until 7 May 1435, as on the following day he began a tour of duty as one of the *Sedici*.[163] According to Florentine law, no member of one of the three major offices (the Priorate, the *Sedici*, and the *Dodici*) could at the same time serve in another office.[164] When Giannozzo ended his term in the *Sedici* on 7 September 1436, he was immediately confirmed as one of the six Consuls of the Sea (*Consules Maris*) for one year.[165] Three of the Sea

[159] *Seta*, 8, f. 87r, as a "setaiuolus grossus" on 6 August 1433.
[160] Naldi, p. 131.
[161] Gherardi, *Statuti*, p. 251.
[162] *Tratte*, 80, section not paginated; see *Grascia* under 18 Nov. 1435.
[163] *Mss.*, 265, entitled "Biscioni: gli dodici buonomini e gli sedici gonfalonieri," f. 6r. On the Grascia office see *Tratte*, 80, f. 327r.
[164] *Statuta*, II, 780. The exceptions made were for men like Bruni.
[165] *Tratte*, 80, f. 390v.

Consuls were stationed in Florence, the others in Pisa on a rotating basis. The six were responsible for the fortresses of Livorno, Motrone, and the citadel of Pisa. They were charged with the building and maintenance of Florentine vessels and they also screened the merchandise entering Florentine ports from all parts of the world. The silk merchant, Dati, said that the Sea Consulate "is more comely and esteemed a dignity than any which goes out of Florence."[166] This assertion is supported by the type of men who appeared in the office. For example, Andrea de' Pazzi was a *consul maris* in 1434, Lorenzo de' Medici in 1435, Agnolo Pandolfini in 1436, and Tommaso di Giannozzo degli Alberti in 1437.[167] They were not the kind of men who dispersed their energies in offices of little worth. At any rate, on leaving the Sea Consulate in September 1437, Giannozzo did not again appear in office for almost ten months. He was then assigned to the *Regulatores*.[168] They kept a strict account of the income and expenditures of the Commune. Since in addition they recorded all the state's credits and debits, they also submitted reports on citizens ineligible for civil office because of failure to pay taxes.[169] Almost at once, however, the humanist was forced to give up his place in the Regulators, for on 10 July 1438 he was made one of the Twelve Good Men (*Dodici*) for the second time.[170] From this point on he passed through a long period of administrative activity which was still more concentrated and more important than before.

Giannozzo was released from the Twelve Good Men in the middle of September 1438. Two months later he took office as one of the *Ufficiali delle vendite*,[171] officials charged with collecting the fines on back taxes by confiscating and selling the goods of the state's debtors.[172] He kept that post for eight months. At the beginning of January 1439, concurrently with his assignment in the Officials on "Sales," he was elected to the consulate of the silk merchants' guild.[173] Like other guild consulates,

---

166 Dati, *L'Istoria*, p. 154, "ed è un bello e onorato ufficio quanto niúno altro che esca di Firenze."
167 *Tratte*, 80, ff. 390v, 391r.
168 *Ibid.*, f. 24r. His term began early in July 1438.
169 *Statuta*, III, 267ff.　　170 *Mss.*, 265, f. 6r.　　171 *Tratte*, 80, f. 446r.
172 Rezasco, p. 1235, under "Ufficiali delle vendite."
173 *Seta*, 246, f. 19v.

the directory of this guild discussed and enacted the measures pertaining to the guild craft and trade. But once again Giannozzo was forced to abandon the office long before the expiration of its term, for he was selected as one of the Approvers of the Guild Statutes on 19 January 1439.[174] This office, which was to last for one year, was interrupted on 17 September, when he began a six-month term in the *Conservatores Legum*.[175] Founded at the outset of 1429, the commission consisted of ten citizens and was designed to compel public officials to observe the laws of the Commune. It had extensive powers of investigation, certain judicial powers, and was the tribunal to which all petitions were submitted requesting the right to enter public office.[176] The Defenders of the Laws were selected from an eligibility purse which excluded all names except those of men who had appeared in the Council of the Two Hundred. This council in turn was open only to Florentines eligible for service in the Priorate, the *Sedici*, or the *Dodici*.[177] Consequently, election to the Defenders of the Laws was largely controlled by the oligarchy. Nevertheless, since the Defenders had to be confirmed in their dignity by a two-thirds vote of the Councils of the People and Commune, service in the commission was to some extent an index of political popularity. Cosimo de' Medici and Rinaldo degli Albizzi served there in 1429, Alessandro degli Alessandri in 1430, Lorenzo de' Medici in 1431, Giannozzo Pandolfini in 1432, Lorenzo Ridolfi in 1433, Matteo Strozzi in 1434, Luca Pitti in 1437, and Giannozzo Manetti in 1439.[178]

Two weeks after Giannozzo ended his term in the *Conservatores Legum* he went into the dominion, and on 2 April 1440 assumed the governorship of the Val di Nievole (*Vicarius Vallisnebule*), a rich agricultural region stretching between Pistoia and Lucca.[179] His office was to administer justice for a period of six months. Attached to this dignity was a staff which included one licensed judge, a notary, one knight, four attendants, and

---

[174] *Tratte*, 80, f. 289r.
[175] *Ibid.*, f. 418v.
[176] *Provv.*, 120, ff. 7v–11r, being the bill which established the office. See also Ammirato, v, 145; and Rezasco, pp. 555ff.
[177] *Priorista Mariani*, i, Introduction.
[178] *Tratte*, 80, ff. 416r–418v.
[179] *Tratte*, 67, f. 26v.

fifteen footmen. The post was one which would have stood out in the career of nearly any leading Florentine. A month after his return from the Val di Nievole the humanist was sworn into the powerful Eight on Security.[180] This meant giving the months of December and January to military and police affairs. He spent February looking after his own domestic and commercial interests. But on 1 March 1441 he was in the service of the state again—a commissioner in one of the Republic's principal fiscal offices, the Monte directory.[181] The offices of the Monte were the Commune's central security exchange: here government securities were bought and sold, the interest on them was paid, and investments were put into the dowry fund. The chronicler, Dati, observed that most of Florence's revenue passed through the Monte coffers.[182] Considering that the bulk of the great Florentine families had vast sums of money invested in the public debt,[183] it is not surprising to learn that service in the Monte Commission distinguished the public lives of most of the city's wealthy men. Giannozzo concluded his year's term there at the end of February 1442. Like the year before, he took another month away from government activity. His next assignment involved a place in the commercial tribunal, the Six on Commerce.[184] On 1 July 1442 he was free again. A year later he was appointed to the *Grascia* Commission for the second time. The term expired before the end of November 1443.[185] From 8 January to 8 May 1444, he took part in the deliberations of the Signoria as one of the Sixteen *Gonfalonieri*,[186] where he represented the *Drago* section of the city's S. Spirito quarter. The following September he was re-elected to the directory of the silk guild.[187] On this occasion he served all but the last two weeks of the term, for on 15 December 1444 he entered the *Dodici* for the third time.[188] When he left the *Dodici* in mid-March 1445, he was free to accept another appointment to the Studio trustees,[189] which of all the Commune's dignities put him closest to

---

[180] *Ibid.*, f. 15v. A term in the Eight was for two months.
[181] *Ibid.*, f. 393v.   [182] Dati, *L'Istoria*, pp. 153-154.
[183] *Vide* e.g., ASF, *Monte*, num. prov., 358 (date: 1412), passim.
[184] ASF, *Mercanzia*, 129, not paginated. See under 1 April 1442.
[185] *Tratte*, 80, f. 75r.   [186] *Mss.*, 265, f. 6r.
[187] *Seta*, 246, f. 19v.   [188] *Mss.*, 265, f. 6r.
[189] *Tratte*, 80, f. 430r. He entered this office on 4 April.

his humanistic interests. But although he was supposed to retain the Studio post for one year, he spent a good deal of that year away from the city; for he now entered a period rich in diplomatic experience.

Giannozzo's activity in the Republic's foreign service was very different from his activity in domestic offices and will therefore be treated separately. We must first of all, however, complete the review of his magistracies in and around Florence.

Since his reappearance in 1445 among the trustees of the Studio Fiorentino did not prevent his holding other offices contemporaneously, Giannozzo was appointed for the second time to the commission on collecting back taxes through the sale of confiscated goods.[190] His term in this office ran from the end of November 1445 until the end of the following May. In the fall he was taken out of the city by an assignment to one of the Republic's most honored dominion offices, the Captaincy of Pistoia.[191] He arrived in this Tuscan city a day or two before 1 October 1446, accompanied by a staff of thirty-one men: one judge (usually a doctor of law), one knight trained in law, two notaries, twenty-five footmen, and two trumpeters. This office, like nearly all the dominion rectorships, was held for six months. Giannozzo's task as Captain of Pistoia was to try all cases entailing crimes against the state. It was the *Podestà* of Pistoia who was invested with judicial powers over civil litigation and ordinary criminal cases.

7 July 1447: Giannozzo was confirmed as one of the six *Noctis Officiales*.[192] All nocturnal movement and crimes, sodomy especially, came under their jurisdiction,[193] and no man could be taken from the Nocturnal Officials in order to serve somewhere else, the one exception being election to the Signoria. The humanist was supposed to remain in this office for one year, but in violation of one of the Commune's regulations he was permitted to abandon it early in September in order to accept a place for

---

[190] *Ibid.*, f. 479r. The importance of the office is indicated by the fact that the Signoria was the only magistracy to which the above commission could release its officials.

[191] *Tratte*, 67, f. 9v.

[192] *Tratte*, 80, f. 420v.

[193] Their powers to some extent seem to overlap with those of the *Honestatis Officiales*.

the second time as one of the Consuls of the Sea.[194] Although here again the appointment was supposed to last for one year, in February, or possibly sooner, the Signoria took him from his maritime duties and sent him on a diplomatic mission.

Giannozzo had now reached the summit of his political career. Both at home and abroad, as we shall see when considering his various diplomatic assignments, he was deemed one of Florence's leading statesmen. And if he was favored with important offices very early in his career, from now on he was to appear in dignities of the highest rank only. Thus he returned to the aggressive and potent Eight on Security during the July-August term of 1449.[195] On this occasion he was sent into the region between Pistoia and Volterra together with the knight, Messer Agnolo Acciaiuoli (see App. I, 27), to suppress an uprising at S. Miniato al Tedesco. The disorder had been provoked by the Duke of Urbino and a *condottiere* of the Orsini clan.[196]

A week after having finished his term in the Eight the humanist was sworn into the *Sedici*,[197] his third tour of duty there. Hence he participated in a Signoria which offered feckless promises to the Ambrosian Republic, friendship to Venice, placatory words to the King of Naples, and realities to Francesco Sforza. In December 1451 he made his fourth appearance in the *Dodici*.[198] Of offices in the city proper, this was to be his last important one among those in the ordinary circuit of preferment. The following summer he was sent into the dominion as Governor of the Mugello (*Vicarius Mugellis*),[199] a strip of territory at the foot of the Apennines just northeast of Florence. This too was one of the highly coveted dignities, passed back and forth between families like the Altoviti, Serragli, Martelli, Pandolfini, Pitti, Corsini, Bardi, and others of this sort.[200] Giannozzo entered the Mugello about 1 August 1452 with a staff of thirty-one men. Then, rather less than a year later, he terminated his political career with an appointment to the Ten of War.[201]

---

[194] *Tratte*, 80, f. 391v.
[195] *Ibid.*, f. 18v.
[196] Naldi, pp. 131-133.
[197] *Mss.*, 265, f. 6r.
[198] *Ibid.*
[199] *Tratte*, 67, f. 21v.   [200] *Ibid.*, f. 21r/v.
[201] ASF, *Mss.*, 271, by date, from June to December 1453.

Public Office in the Humanist Circle

His Foreign Service. Giannozzo Manetti's diplomatic career was chiefly concentrated in the years between 1448 and 1453. This was the period during which, following Filippo Maria Visconti's death (1447), Milan temporarily turned to a republican form of government, while both King Alfonso and the Venetian Senate worked to annex the Milanese lands.[202] For reasons of economic and political security, however, Florence determined to keep both king and republic out of Lombardy at all costs, and accordingly favored the ducal pretensions of Francesco Sforza. To be sure, the Florentines gave assurances of friendship and sympathy to the Ambrosian Republic. But when Milan surrendered to Sforza (February 1450), the aim of Florentine diplomacy at once became to secure Venetian and Neapolitan recognition of Sforza as Duke of Milan.

Giannozzo Manetti took a leading part in these events. According to a fifteenth-century biographer, the humanist's diplomatic activity began with an embassy to Genoa in 1437,[203] and the same source noted that in 1443 he was sent as an envoy to the Kingdom of Naples. But he is first encountered in the diplomatic correspondence on 10 May 1445, when the Signoria dispatched him to King Alfonso's court for the second time.[204] Manetti was to represent Florence at the wedding ceremonies of the King's son, Ferrante. The question of the Milanese succession was already in the air (Filippo Maria was without a legal heir), and the humanist was expected to justify the Republic's friendly attitude towards the *condottiere*, Francesco Sforza. On his return from Naples, the ambassador carried out an assignment in the pontifical court. In addition to soliciting the Pope's support of Sforza, he asked that Florentine power to tax the clergy be prolonged for two years and begged that the city be given more time to pay the interest on the Pope's investments in the Monte.[205] Giannozzo was finally called back to Florence on 8 July 1445. His legation had lasted two months.[206]

---

[202] See the collaborative work, *Storia di Milano*, vi, *Il ducato visconteo e la repubblica ambrosiana* (Milano, 1955), parts i-iii, by Francesco Cognasso, esp. pp. 390, 400, 416, 421.
[203] Naldi, pp. 131-138.
[204] *ASF, Leg. Comm.*, 11, ff. 56r-57v, 58v, 59r, 63v, 64r, 66r/v.
[205] *Ibid.*, f. 66r.
[206] *Ibid.*, f. 70r/v.

Public Office in the Humanist Circle

When Tommaso da Sarzana, once a tutor in the Albizzi household, became Pope Nicholas V in March 1447, six Florentine ambassadors were delegated to convey the Republic's felicitations and encomia: Messer Agnolo Acciaiuoli, Messer Giovannozzo Pitti, Neri di Gino Capponi, Alessandro degli Alessandri, Giannozzo Manetti, and Piero di Cosimo de' Medici.[207] Manetti was chosen to deliver the legation's opening oration.[208] Four of the envoys were soon withdrawn from the mission; but Acciaiuoli and Manetti, knight and humanist, remained in Rome until the middle of April. They conferred with the Pope, with King Alfonso, and with the emissaries from Bologna and Faenza.[209] This assignment over, late in that year or early in 1448 the humanist was sent to Sigismondo Malatesta to wean him from King Alfonso's payroll and to buy his services for Florence. The mission was successful.[210] His next embassy took him to Siena.[211] The *Legazioni* and *Commissarie* correspondence in the State Archives of Florence contains no record of this mission, but its purpose was probably to keep Siena from joining either King Alfonso or the Venetians in their designs against the Ambrosian Republic.

Some time after the Sienese embassy, and more exactly on 27 August 1448, Manetti was appointed ambassador to Venice. His task—to solicit Venetian aid against Alfonso's ambitions in Lombardy[212]—was a delicate one. He must turn the Venetians against their ally, proffering friendship and vague promises; yet he must not go so far as to give the impression that Venice could then have a free hand in Lombardy. The Venetian colloquies were prolonged. In November it was discovered that Venice had negotiated a league with Francesco Sforza,[213] whereupon Manetti was immediately ordered to seek a place for Florence in the

[207] *Ibid.*, ff. 185v-188r.
[208] Ammirato, v, 300.
[209] *Leg. Comm.*, 12, f. 3v.
[210] Naldi, p. 131; Ammirato, v, 305. I have been unable to find the documents pertaining to this mission.
[211] Naldi, *ibid.* I follow Naldi here, somewhat securely, for all the archival material so far disclosed fully supports him in the areas of duplication. Future research will almost certainly bring forth additional material.
[212] *Leg. Comm.*, 12, ff. 56v-60r, 61v-62r, 63r/v, 65r/v, 66r/v. Some of the Signoria's letters to the humanist were published by Luigi Rossi, "Firenze e Venezia dopo la battaglia di Caravaggio," A.S.I., ser. 5, xxxiv (1904), 158-179.
[213] Rossi, *ibid.*, p. 173.

alliance. Meanwhile, domestic necessities made him anxious to return home; he therefore requested the Signoria to relieve him of his duties. On 22 December 1448, after a stay in Venice of nearly four months, Giannozzo was informed that two new ambassadors were being sent out to replace him. They were well-known members of the oligarchy, Messer Bernardo Giugni and Dietisalvi Neroni.[214]

Early in February 1450 Giannozzo was sent to Venice for the second time.[215] He relieved Messer Giovannozzo Pitti, one of the most active Florentine statesmen of the day. Another legate, Luca di Messer Maso degli Albizzi, was already in Venice waiting for the humanist. Since Florence had concluded an accord with the Ambrosian Republic, the task of the Florentine ambassadors was to persuade Venice and Sforza to enter an alliance with Florence and this short-lived republic. But on 26 Feburary, after a long siege and heroic resistance, the Milanese capitulated to Francesco Sforza, who became the new Duke of Milan. Luca degli Albizzi was released from the Venetian mission before March 9 and Giannozzo was left alone to seek Venetian acquiescence in Sforza's usurpation. The humanist's negotiations with the Venetians were very lengthy and finally, on June 6, Neri di Gino Capponi and Piero di Cosimo de' Medici were sent out to join him.[216] According to Machiavelli, Neri Capponi was then one of Florence's most authoritative statesmen, distinguished enough to count as Cosimo de' Medici's chief adversary.[217] The three ambassadors now worked on the Venetians with a new vigor, pressing for an accord with Sforza. They were still negotiating in July.[218]

The following January Giannozzo was dispatched to Naples as Florentine ambassador to King Alfonso.[219] It was his third trip to the Neapolitan court. His mission on this occasion involved the whole of Florence's political security: the Venetian Senate

[214] *Leg. Comm.*, 12, f. 66v.

[215] *Ibid.*, ff. 119r-120r, 122v-123v, 124r, 125v-126r, 128r, 132r/v, 134r/v, 135r/v, 136r-137r, 137v, 140v, 141r/v, 142r, 151v-152r, 154v, 160r/v, 162r.

[216] *Ibid.*, f. 154v.

[217] *Istorie fiorentine*, pp. 232, 271.

[218] *Leg. Comm.*, 12, f. 162v.

[219] *Leg. Comm.*, 13, ff. 3r-4v, 5r/v, 11r-12r, 12v-13r, 13r-14r, 15v-17v, 18v-21r.

and King Alfonso had contracted a league, the particulars of which were concealed from the Florentines. It was perfectly clear, however, that they hoped to intimidate Florence into breaking her alliance with Milan, thereby isolating Francesco Sforza and clearing the way for their own aggrandizement in Lombardy. And it was to prevent this that Giannozzo's diplomatic skills were turned on Alfonso. There was also an economic mission connected with the humanist's assignment: nearly every letter to him from the Signoria contained directives urging the damage claims of Florentine merchants in the royal domain. Particularly prominent were the losses suffered years before in the territories of Barcelona and Valencia.[220] In order to cover these claims, Florence wanted royal consent to tax all goods entering the Florentine dominion from the King's realm. The tax was to be levied for a period of at least twenty years.[221]

Giannozzo had arrived in Naples at the end of January 1451. Late in May he was anxious to get back to Florence. A legation which lasted four months was considered onerous, especially for a merchant with family and trade interests to look after. Consequently, on 11 June the Signoria prepared to relieve the humanist by turning the assignment over to Messer Giovannozzo Pitti.[222]

Eight months later Giannozzo went into the field again. Together with Messer Bernardo Giugni and Messer Carlo Pandolfini, he took part in the Florentine delegation which accompanied the Emperor-elect, Frederick III, on his way to Rome and the coronation.[223] The procession was to make a temporary stop in Siena, and the Florentines were ordered to keep the Venetian ambassadors under a careful surveillance. It was feared that the Venetians might try to persuade the Emperor to use his influence on the Sienese in order to draw Siena into the Aragonese alliance. In Rome the Florentines made special pleas for the peace of Italy. They tried to obtain the Pope's permission to levy

---

[220] *Ibid.*, f. 12r/v, letter dated 20 March 1450 (Florentine).

[221] The correspondence consulted by the author does not show that the Republic managed to get the King's consent for this tax.

[222] *Leg. Comm.*, 13, ff. 19r-21r, 23v. The assignment was finally turned over to Pitti on 28 June.

[223] Rinuccini, *Ricordi storici*, p. lxxvii. The documents of the mission are in *Leg. Comm.*, 13, ff. 32v-35r/v.

a special tax on the Florentine clergy; and Manetti, known to be one of Nicholas V's humanist favorites, was individually requested to solicit the Pope's intervention in a wrangle between two Florentine families over a lucrative benefice.[224] The three-man legation was still in Rome in mid-March 1452.

23 February 1453: Messer Giannozzo Manetti (knighted the year before) and Messer Otto Niccolini (a doctor of law) were appointed ambassadors to the Pope.[225] Once again Florence sought the peace of Italy through the maintenance of the *status quo*. The primary objective of the Republic's diplomacy remained that of obtaining universal recognition for Francesco Sforza as the rightful Duke of Milan. When the Florentine ambassadors appeared before the Pope, they stressed the warlike conduct and bad faith of the Venetians and King Alfonso, their abuse of Florentine merchants, and their unprovoked attacks on Milanese territory.[226] At the end, however, Manetti and Niccolini were to press for a "just and honorable" peace. But that peace was not to be negotiated until the following year.

This was the humanist's last formal embassy. He had of late alienated some of Florence's leading political figures and that spring, the spring of 1453, they set out to disgrace and if possible destroy him.[227] His chief enemies were his brother-in-law (Messer Agnolo Acciaiuoli),[228] Luca Pitti, Dietisalvi Neroni, and Niccolò Soderini. He was alerted to the danger by a close friend and political associate, Neri di Gino Capponi. Crippling taxation was the device his enemies used, followed by accusations of treason.[229] Now in view of Giannozzo's friendship with Neri di Gino Capponi, it is not unreasonable to assume that Cosimo de' Medici may have given some support to the group which sought to remove the humanist from public life. For in the late 1440's and early 1450's, Neri Capponi was Cosimo's foremost political adversary. They were particularly divided over the question of Sforza's legitimacy. Neri believed that any triumph for Sforza automatically enhanced Cosimo's power in Florence. Soldier and

---

[224] *Leg. Comm.*, 13, f. 35r/v.
[225] *Ibid.*, ff. 41r-42r.
[226] *Ibid.*, f. 41v.
[227] Naldi, pp. 133-134.
[228] On this bond see Della Torre, *Accademia*, pp. 233-235.
[229] Vespasiano, p. 285.

banker were linked by the fact—and it was widely known—that Cosimo was personally committed to Sforza in his whole outlook on the Lombard question.[230] For this reason Neri had urged a strong Milanese Republic, hoping thereby to keep the *condottiere* a military rather than a political figure. Giannozzo Manetti seems to have had some sympathy for this view. Worse still, his friendship with King Alfonso was public knowledge, for he had dedicated to Alfonso his *De dignitate et excellentia hominis.* Executed at the request of the King himself, the work was written in 1451-1452, at the height of Florence's struggle against Alfonso.[231]

It was in the early spring of 1453, while negotiating his last mission as an ambassador, that Manetti learned of his enemies' machinations. Fearing their power, he turned his mission at the papal court into a pretext for remaining in Rome, out of the reach of his foes. Nicholas V then made him a papal secretary.[232] News of this had no sooner reached Florence than he was summoned to appear before the Signoria within ten days. Giannozzo set out at once, but he was arrested in Siena and taken to Florence under escort.[233] There he was charged with treason because of the book he had dedicated to King Alfonso. And though he was officially a papal secretary, he was forced to defend himself as a private citizen. Surprisingly enough, he managed to win over more than two-thirds of the Signoria, and obtained his release. Apparently he had called on the popularity he still enjoyed in Florence, built up across the years by his activity as a statesman and humanist. Indeed, reaction to his defense went so far in his favor that in June he was given a place in the Ten of War. The appointment was for six months. It was the highest sign of confidence that could be shown him and, as stated in the section on his domestic offices, was his last public dignity.

Alas, however, he no longer felt safe in Florence. In 1454 he went into voluntary exile, going first to the papal court, then to the Kingdom of Naples. There the Signoria occasionally commissioned him to solicit Alfonso's intervention on behalf of

[230] Machiavelli, pp. 249-250.
[231] Dates of the work given by Garin, *Prosatori latini del quattrocento,* p. 421.
[232] Naldi, p. 133.
[233] Vespasiano, p. 286.

various Florentine commercial companies. He is found negotiating the Signoria's requests in the summer of 1456 and early winter of 1458.[234] In exchange, the Signoria tried to get King Alfonso to exert some pressure in favor of a law suit involving the humanist.[235]

Giannozzo Manetti's career in politics ended with these events. From about 1447 onwards he was one of the men most prominently in the public eye. In 1453 he clashed with a powerful clique, but managed to hold his own where a lesser man would almost surely have gone under. Much as the clique desired Giannozzo's ruin, his reputation as a humanist and statesman was such that, standing before the *Signori*, he could turn it to his account, save himself, and even secure a seat in a commission which now and then overrode the Signoria—the Ten of War.

6. MATTEO PALMIERI

Two young contemporaries of Matteo Palmieri, Vespasiano da Bisticci and Alamanno Rinuccini, are responsible for the traditional assumption concerning his family background: namely, that it was relatively modest.[236] Vespasiano also said that Matteo was the "founder of his house." If true, one obvious assumption might be that before Matteo's time the Palmieri were mere druggists and confectioners on a relatively low level. This misleading literary impression was partly corrected by an Italian scholar at the end of the last century.[237]

Making extensive use of archival materials, Antonio Messeri summarily indicated some of the public offices held by Matteo's father and uncle. Then he passed on swiftly to his main interest: a full record of the offices Matteo himself occupied. One of our tasks, therefore, will be to summarize Messeri's research, with an eye to bringing out its implications for this study. But as Messeri

[234] *Leg. Comm.*, 14, ff. 24v-25r, 62r-63v.
[235] *Ibid.*, f. 28v, being a letter to the Florentine envoy, dated 2 December 1456. See the part beginning, "Lo spectabile cavaliere Messer G. Manetti nostro citadino ha una causa a Napoli. Pare che la parte adversa vorrebbe transferire il giudicio ad altro giudice che dove essa causa e cominciata e contestata la lite," etc.
[236] Alamanno Rinuccini, *Lettere ed orazioni*, p. 80; Vespasiano, p. 302, "nacque di parenti di mediocre condizione, dette principio alla sua casa, e nobilitòlla per le sua singulari virtù."
[237] Messeri, "Matteo Palmieri," pp. 256-340.

did not examine Matteo's family background in political and administrative terms, our chief aim will be to present a fuller picture of that background by examining the political careers of his father, uncle, and maternal grandfather.

Born in 1406, Matteo Palmieri was active in public life from 1432 to 1475. He was one of the era's outstanding public servants. During those forty-three years he negotiated eight diplomatic missions for the Republic and took office at least sixty-three times. This record excludes his appearances in the legislative councils, where a term of office lasted four months. In the Council of the Two Hundred a term was for six months.[238]

Matteo's foreign missions were assignments of the first order. Four of them, for example, took him to the papal court, where he represented the Republic before Calixtus III (1455), Paul II (twice: in 1466 and 1468), and Sixtus IV (1473).[239] Another took him to King Alfonso in Naples (1455), and a sixth to Bologna (1466). Seven of the sixty-three domestic offices involved posts in the Florentine dominion. Of the seven, only one can be said to have been a lesser dignity, his governorship of Firenzuola (1464), and this office was merely one rank below that of the major posts in the dominion.[240] The other six were of the type normally monopolized by members of the great ruling families: the offices of Captain of Livorno (held in 1445), Vicar of the Val di Nievole (twice: 1451 and 1471), Vicar of the Mugello (1455), Captain of Pistoia (1460), and Captain of Volterra (1474).

Turning to the city proper, Messeri's researches show that the humanist was elected or assigned to fifty-six offices, sixteen of which were truly of major importance. In 1453, during the September-October term, he was Gonfalonier of Justice. He sat in the Priorate in 1445 and 1468; in the *Sedici* in 1437, 1440, and 1452;[241] in the *Dodici* in 1442, 1454, and 1474. He was one of the

[238] Messeri entirely overlooked this aspect of Matteo's participation in public affairs. Indeed, the whole question of representation in the legislative councils is untouched in Florentine historiography. The lists of the members of these councils are conserved in *Tratte*, 140 *et seq.*

[239] Messeri, pp. 291, 301, 309, 314.   [240] *Tratte*, 66, f. 31r; 67, f. 30r.

[241] This is Messeri's tally of Matteo's terms in the *Sedici*. But the appropriate archival source mistakenly attributes a fourth term to the humanist in 1478, three years after Matteo's death. See *ASF, Mss.*, 266, f. 79r.

Ten of War during the second half of 1467. His colleagues in this commission were the following notables: Tommaso Soderini, Bernardo Corbinelli, Niccolò Giugni, Mariotto Benvenuti, Bongianni Gianfigliazzi, Piero di Cosimo de' Medici, Bartolommeo Lenzi, and the minor guildsmen, Zanobi Buonvanni and Antonio Lenzoni.[242] Finally, on six occasions he was appointed to the powerful commission on political and military security, the *Octo Custodiae*: in 1449, 1454, 1462, 1467, and 1475.

The offices listed above mark the high points of Matteo's career as a civil servant. Messeri gave an account of most of his other dignities; it would be superfluous to record them here. The account includes tours of duty in different fiscal offices, in various commissions for the screening of eligible government personnel, in guild consulates, the Five on Pisa, the Consuls of the Sea, and the Guelf Captains.

The fifteenth-century biographer, Vespasiano da Bisticci, stated that Matteo earned his prominence in public life entirely by his own means, without the aid of family. But great as his virtues were, this is not what happened. For we shall see that Matteo was the heir, literally speaking, to the political fortunes of a family which attained a solid place in the bureaucratic life of the city before he was old enough to hold public office. Furthermore, his mother's family, the Sassolini, were an added buttress to his political ambitions. A review of this background will clarify the political station to which he was born and from whence he was able to move with ease and success.

Marco, the humanist's father, was matriculated in the guild of doctors and apothecaries, where he became a man of some prominence. He was appointed a guild consul on nine occasions between 1409 and 1427.[243] Since the *Arte dei Medici e Speziali* was one of the seven major guilds, it was not likely constantly to re-elect an obscure and "low-born" man to its governing body. For one thing, there was the fact—it was worth considering—that the consuls of all the guilds were voting members of the Council of the People.[244] But periodically Marco Palmieri also entered

---

[242] Messeri, p. 307.

[243] ASF, *Medici e Speziali*, 46, ff. 35v, 36v, 38r, 39r, 40r, 41r, 42v, 43v, 44v.

[244] *Statuta*, II, 661.

the legislative councils in a private capacity, by right of his family's political franchise. He first sat in the Council of the People in February 1403, and during the rest of his life—he died in 1428—was regularly chosen for service both there and in the Council of the Commune.[245] In the 1420's we also find him serving in the Council of the Two Hundred.[246] This was the Republic's senatorial body, whose approval was required for the enactment of all measures bearing on taxation and important phases of foreign policy. Membership in this council presupposed that a citizen was eligible for election to the Priorate, the *Sedici*, or the *Dodici*. Matteo's father served in the Priorate only once, during the November-December term of 1427. More than ten years earlier, however, in 1416, he had already appeared in the executive councils as one of the *Sedici Gonfalonieri*. He was selected for the *Dodici Buonomini* twice, in 1420 and 1423.[247] One other major assignment distinguished his career—his appointment in 1424 to the Eight on Security.[248] The rest of his offices were mainly small dignities, two of them minor rectorships in the dominion.[249]

Although Marco's record as a civil servant was by no means spectacular, it was substantial. After all, he was a younger son; he was groomed to run the family business; and the offices doled out to the Palmieri would be given mainly to his elder brother, Francesco. Custom in Florence made the elder or eldest son the direct heir to the family's political and administrative responsibilities. If the heir defaulted, then responsibility passed to another son. But Francesco, the humanist's uncle, did not default. He seems to have entered public life with alacrity and evidently demanded his share of offices, for in the thirty-eight years from 1401 to 1439 he took office upwards of sixty times.[250] This figure excludes his terms in the legislative councils, where his presence is encountered again and again throughout the first four decades

[245] *Tratte*, 147, under 1 Feb. 1403, 1 Oct. 1403, 1 Feb. 1406; 148, 1 Sept. 1406, 1 Feb. 1407, 1 Jan. 1408, 1 June 1408, 1 Sept. 1409, 1 Feb. 1410, etc.
[246] *Tratte*, 153, e.g., ff. 4v, 71r, 177v, 215r. These citations refer to the years 1420, 1422, 1424, and 1425.
[247] *Mss.*, 266, f. 79r.   [248] *Tratte*, 79, f. 20v.
[249] *Tratte*, 66, ff. 122r, 131r, the *podesterie* of Tizzana and Scarperia.
[250] My tally.

of the fifteenth century;[251] it also excludes his appearances among the Guelf Captains.[252]

Francesco Palmieri was elected a guild consul no less than sixteen times between 1403 and 1436.[253] He is found in the Priorate in 1404, 1408, 1420, and 1431. On four occasions in the years from 1406 to 1432 he sat among the *Sedici*, where he participated in the executive councils of the Republic.[254] In 1401, 1411, and 1435 he was one of the *Dodici Buonomini*. Three times he was elected to the Commune's supreme commercial tribunal, the Six on Commerce;[255] and twice he was sworn into the Eight on Security, in 1418 and 1423.[256] Of the five rectorships ascribed to him in the records, two ranked as first-class dignities, his *podestería* of Prato (held in 1427) and his Captaincy of Volterra (1430).[257]

These magistracies represent the most distinguished offices in Francesco's career as an administrator and statesman. It will be unnecessary to specify some thirty others[258] which entailed tours of duty in various fiscal, investigative, judicial, screening, and planning commissions: for example, the Ten on Liberty, the Tower Commission, the Treasury Directory, the Syndics of the Podestà, the Approvers of the Guild Statutes, and others.

Francesco had a son, Giovanni (Matteo Palmieri's first cousin), who appeared in a half dozen offices, but none of major importance.[259] The family's political fortunes ought to have passed

---

[251] E.g., *Tratte*, 147, by date under S. Giovanni in "Chiave," 1 Jan. 1403, 1 Jan. 1404, 1 Sept. 1404; 148, 1 Sept. 1408, 1 Oct. 1409; 151, 1 Feb. 1412; 153, 6 Jan. 1421 (f. 29r).

[252] *ASF, Capt. Guelforum*, n. rossi 5, ff. 71r-72v, listing Francesco's son, Giovanni, as an "arroto," which indicates that Francesco himself was a prominent Guelf. The Guelf papers passed into the Florentine Archives in a very incomplete state.

[253] *Medici e Speziali*, 46, ff. 32v *et seq.*, passim.

[254] E.g., *Consulte*, 41, f. 59v; 43, f. 180v.

[255] *Mercanzia*, 129, by date: 1 July 1412, 1 April 1430, and 1 Oct. 1433.

[256] *Tratte*, 79, ff. 18v, 21r.

[257] *Tratte*, 67, ff. 8r, 40r.

[258] E.g., *ibid.*, ff. 57r, 105v; *Tratte*, 66, f. 128r; 79, ff. 41r, 47r, 50r, 62r, 85r, 87r, 99r, 108r, 109v, 148r, 156v, 280v, 375r; 80, ff. 36r, 96v, 140v, 199r, 288v, 289r.

[259] *Tratte*, 80, ff. 40r, 52r, 61v, 296r; *Capt. Guelforum*, n. rossi 5, ff. 71r-72v; *Tratte*, 67, f. 79v. These citations show Giovanni in the following offices: *Provisor Regulatorum*, *Decem Libertatis*, the *Conductae* and *Defectuum* officials, the screening board of the Guelf Captains, and the *podestería* of Monte S. Sevini.

to Giovanni, but he seems to have been little interested in civic affairs. Perhaps he was sickly, or possibly his manner did not lend itself to public life. He was, at any rate, overshadowed by his brilliant cousin, and consequently the family's political future passed to the other branch. Matteo thus became sole heir to the position which both his uncle and father had earned for the Palmieri in government circles. In some ways Francesco's record was not unlike Matteo's. Like his humanist nephew, Francesco took office on more than sixty occasions; like Matteo again, sixteen of his domestic offices were dignities at the highest levels of government—the Signoria, the Eight on Security, and the Six on Commerce. Only two of Francesco's five governorships were leading dignities, whereas of the seven Matteo filled six were first-rate. From this point on their careers exhibit the difference between a major public figure and a prominent administrator who was only a minor statesman. The humanist's offices at just below the level of the Signoria were powerful posts, more distinguished than those of Francesco. For the former sat among the Defenders of the Laws (during four terms), the Consuls of the Sea (twice), and the Five on Pisa (twice); the latter was appointed to none of these commissions. Unlike Francesco, Matteo attained the city's chief dignity, Gonfalonier of Justice. He also served a term in the Ten of War, which his uncle did not; and he was the first of the Palmieri to enter the Republic's diplomatic corps.

Matteo's humanistic studies took him into a circle of socially prominent Florentines: Agnolo Pandolfini, Neri di Gino Capponi, Alessandro degli Alessandri, Luigi Guicciardini, and Franco Sacchetti. These were strategic friends because of their standing in the administrative and political life of Florence, and Matteo could draw on their influence for his preferment. In addition, he possessed unusual powers of oratory, which placed him in the ranks of those occasionally invited to manage the Republic's embassies. These then were the factors—his humanistic interests, his eloquence, and through these his friends—which enabled him to attain Florence's major dignities. But he began from the solid foundations built by his uncle and father. They were the first Palmieri to enter the Signoria, not Matteo; they founded the family's place in the public life of the city, not Matteo. He buttressed his virtues and built his career on their achievement. And finally, he had his mother's side of the family to lean on; here too he could count on immediate bureaucratic connections.

The humanist's mother, Tommasa, was a daughter of Antonio di Marignano Sassolini.[260] Antonio was matriculated in the silk merchants' guild. He was not a very wealthy man, judging by the tax records of the period,[261] but this did not deter him in his career: he became a prominent figure in the guild directory, and from about 1380 onwards he was elected to his guild consulate with great frequency and regularity.[262] In 1383 he won a place in the city's supreme commercial tribunal, the Six on Commerce, and he reappeared there in 1391, 1396, 1400, 1402, and 1407.[263]

A citizen who was prominent in the silk merchants' guild, and who frequently sat in the Commune's chief business tribunal, was already a man with political inclinations, bound to be active in the affairs of state. This description perfectly accords with Matteo's maternal grandfather. From 1380 to about 1410 Antonio Sassolini was one of the most frequent participants in Florence's legislative councils.[246] He made his début in the Priorate in November 1385, returning there for a second term in January 1406. On three occasions he was drawn for duty in the *Sedici*—1393, 1400, and 1412.[265] He was confirmed in the *Dodici* only once, in 1409. Outside the city proper his administrative activity was equally intense: between 1387 and 1408 he was given thirteen magistracies in the dominion.[266] Four of the thirteen were major posts; the others are recorded in the *Tratte* lists as second-

---

[260] *ASF, Notarile antecosimiano*, P 282, under 7 Sept. 1422, not paginated. This register contains some of the acts of the notary, Ser Ugolino Pieruzzi. Registered under the indicated date is Marco Palmieri's will, naming his wife, the nature of her dowry, his heir, and so forth.

[261] *ASF, Prest.*, 1262, 2000 (dates: 1390 and 1403), for the S. Spirito quarter, alphabetically arranged by Christian name. Antonio di Marignano Sassolini is entered under "Scala." I indexed the first 15 per cent of all taxpayers here, and Antonio was not near this level.

[262] *ASF, Seta*, 246, ff, 2r/v, 3v, 4r, 5r/v, 7r/v, 8v.

[263] *Mercanzia*, 129, not paginated. Consult by date.

[264] E.g., *Tratte*, 140-145, under "Scala" in S. Spirito, passim; *Tratte*, 147, (by date) 1 Feb. 1404, 1 Sept. 1404, 1 Sept. 1405; 148, 1 May 1406, 1 Sept. 1408, 1 May 1409, 1 Oct. 1409, 1 May 1410.

[265] *Mss.*, 265, f. 42r.

[266] *Tratte*, 65, ff. 32v, 40r, 43r, 53r, 75r, 77r, 86r, 88v, 96r, 121v, 126v; 66, ff. 46r, 160r.

class dignities. Altogether he took office some seventy times during a period of about thirty years,[267] not including his terms in the legislative councils. His offices reveal that he went through an ordinary pattern of preferment in the Republic's various fiscal and regulative commissions.

The Palmieri and Sassolini were upper middle-class families of the type prominent in administrative circles. They did not rank with "historic" families like the Strozzi and Albizzi. Their place in the social and political hierarchy was below that of the great ruling families. Like the Serzelli, Cresci, Morelli, Covoni, and others, the Palmieri and Sassolini were *bureaucratic* families. They stood out among those who staffed the Republic's administrative cadre, but they were neither strong enough nor distinguished enough to hold places of importance within the factions, let alone to captain the factional strife. This kind of leadership required families like the Acciaiuoli, Capponi, Castellani, Strozzi, Pandolfini, and Alessandri. The bureaucratic families might be courted or protected, or when in a combine even feared, by powerful families such as the Medici, Uzzano, Albizzi, or Peruzzi. Separately, however, they were powerless to affect the structure of government or determine policy. Yet whatever faction or fraction won out in the struggle within the oligarchy, the bureaucratic families would survive, ready to take up once again the administration of the state.

Matteo Palmieri drew his traditions from two bureaucratic families. But his virtues and circle of friendships enabled him to enter the world of statesmanship.

---

[267] This sum includes the offices already specified. Others are found in *Tratte*, 78, ff. 12v, 52r, 87r, 96r, 99r, 101r, 104r, 123r, 132r, 147r, 158r, 215v, 222v, 225r, 229r, 231r, 244v, 245r, and 281r.

CHAPTER FIVE

HUMANIST MARRIAGES:
A STUDY OF FIVE FAMILIES

1. THE CASTELLANI

ON THE ruling sectors of Florentine society, as we have already seen, marriage was a political, social, and economic bond; it was contracted with an eye to maintaining or improving the total situation of the family. We shall do well, therefore, to describe the place in society of five families connected by marriage with the humanists.

Of the humanists who gathered around Coluccio Salutati about 1400, the first to marry was Lionardo Bruni. Two members of the circle, Roberto de' Rossi and Niccolò Niccoli, did not marry; another, Pier Paolo Vergerio, resided in Florence for only a very short time and was not a Tuscan; and for a third, Jacopo da Scarperia (see App. I, no. 3), there is too little social evidence for comment here.[1] Bruni celebrated his marriage in 1411. The marriage does not seem to have been held in Florence[2] and the identity of his wife's family is still a mystery. One known fact, however, clearly discloses their wealth. When Bruni drew up his last will and testament in March 1439,[3] he included a clause leaving his wife, Tommasa, the original sum of her dowry, 1100 florins. A dowry this size in 1411 denoted the backing of a family with superior means. This may be discerned by comparing Tommasa's dowry with the dowries of the Medici house during the fourteenth century. In some cases as little as from 10.0 to 100 florins were involved. Large Medici dowries varied from 500 to

[1] On Jacopo see Salutati, *Epistolario*, III, 129, 403, 520-523; IV, i, 111-112. Jacopo lived in the S. Giovanni quarter of Florence (hitherto unknown), at all events when he was in the city. See *ASF, Prestanze*, 1999, f. 181v.

[2] This statement is based on the fact that the marriage is not recorded in the Ancisa papers of the State Archives of Florence, possibly the only trustworthy (though not the only existing) *spoglia* of marriages contracted in Florence during the fifteenth century. The *Carte dell' Ancisa* were made from the accounts, now destroyed, of the tax imposed by the Florentine state on every contract of marriage.

[3] *ASF, Notarile antecosimiano*, B 74 (1426-1456), ff. 133r-137r, being three original copies of the will. This *filza* contains the notarial acts of the notary, Ser Mariotto Baldesi.

1200 florins. And "The largest recorded dowry received by any of the Medici in the fourteenth century was the sum of 1,500 florins brought to Giovanni di Bicci by his bride, Riccarda Bueri, in October 1385."[4]

The foregoing figures are entirely consistent with general Florentine practice among the dominant families during the first three or four decades of the fifteenth century.[5] Thereafter, changes in social life introduced a greater emphasis on larger, even ostentatious dowries.

Since the absence of additional information regarding Tommasa's background prevents our making further comment about her family, we will consider at some length, instead, the family of the woman given in marriage to Lionardo Bruni's son in 1431.[6] Donato Bruni, twenty years old, was marrying at an early age by Florentine standards.[7] As with all Florentines of his condition, however, his father chose his betrothed. Such items as dowries and the time and place of marriage were decided by the heads of the two families. And if the humanist was willing to see Donato married so early in life, the match must have promised concrete advantages, social or economic, for both families.

It has been shown in Chapters III and IV that Lionardo Bruni, born in Arezzo, was one of Florence's richest and most illustrious citizens in 1431. What type of Florentine marriage, therefore, could he aspire to for his son? Certain considerations were of primary importance. Since Donato was his only son, the future of the Bruni house was at stake; hence Lionardo would surely give great care to his decision. Next, as the humanist was a prominent parvenu, he must think of a family with a distinguished place in the political life of Florence, a family of old wealth and old traditions. Furthermore, in order to derive full advantage from such an alliance, the family selected must reside in the S. Croce quarter,[8] where the Bruni themselves had settled.

---

[4] Brucker, "The Medici in the Fourteenth Century," p. 11.
[5] See Ch. II, 1 above.
[6] *ASF, Catasto*, 661, f. 687r; 662, ff. 656r-659v.
[7] Men in Florence usually married between the ages of twenty-five and thirty-five, women between the ages of fourteen and eighteen. These estimates are based on a familiarity with the reports in *Catasto*, 64-69, 72-81, passim.
[8] On the sagacity of establishing bonds of marriage with a family of the same precinct or quarter see Morelli, *Ricordi*, p. 263.

True to his political acumen, a talent refined in the Republic's executive councils, the humanist arranged a brilliant match for his son: the girl was Alessandra di Messer Michele di Messer Vanni Castellani.

The Castellani were one of the most powerful clans of the oligarchy that ruled Florence in the four or five decades before 1434. They came of old stock, were divided into several strong households, associated with a tradition of commercial wealth and knightly dignity, and connected by marriage with at least a dozen houses of equivalent stature. It will be useful to consider these features in some detail.

The name of the family, Castellani, suggests that they may once have been the wardens of a castle or fort. This possibility is not at variance with their antiquity and subsequent interest in the profession of arms.[9] The first recorded mention of the family involves a certain Ioseppo, who lived around 1197.[10] In 1210 they appeared among the families listed as resident in the S. Piero–Scheraggio section of Florence.[11] During the middle and later decades of the thirteenth century, Ser Alberto Castellani and his son, Lotto, practiced *notaria*. This associated them with the city's most honored guild, *l'Arte dei Giudici e Notai*. The major Castellani households of the fifteenth century traced their origins back to Ser Lotto. The first of the house to enter the Signoria was Vanni di Ser Lotto, who became a prior in June 1326. After that, until their clash with the Medici in 1434, they often appeared in the chief magistracy. Between 1326 and 1400 they obtained a place in the Priorate on twenty-three occasions, or an average of nearly one triennially.[12] During the same period the Pitti sat in the Priorate fourteen times, the Capponi seventeen, the Acciaiuoli twenty-four, the Medici thirty-one, and the Strozzi fifty times.[13]

---

[9] The clan had four knights in the early fifteenth century: Messer Lotto, Messer Vanni, Messer Michele, and Messer Matteo. On Lotto's military background see *ASF, Leg. Comm.*, 5, f. 5v.

[10] *ASF, Carte Pucci*, 29, iv, "Castellani"; *BNF, Mss. Passerini*, 186, "Castellani."

[11] *Delizie degli eruditi toscani*, ed. Fr. Ildefonso di San Luigi (Firenze, 1770-1789), vii, 160.

[12] *ASF, Priorista Mariani*, iii, f. 554.

[13] *Ibid.*, i, ff. 55r, 172r, 26r, 234r, 94r.

Humanist Marriages

Bruni's daughter-in-law, Alessandra, grew up in the S. Croce quarter. It is there the Castellani had their *palazzi*, not far from the Baroncelli and Cavalcanti houses in the Carro district. Precisely when they entered banking and money-lending on an international scale is not clear; it cannot have been very early, as their renown in business circles around 1300 was not as extensive, nor nearly as old, as the commercial fame of their neighbors, the Baroncelli and Cavalcanti.[14] A generation later, however, the Castellani operated one of the Commune's biggest banking firms. For in 1342 Giovanni Villani, recording the startling financial failures of that year, included the Castellani in the list of the city's greatest banking houses: the firms of the Peruzzi, Acciaiuoli, Bardi, Buonaccorsi, Cocchi, Antellesi, Uzzano, Corsini, Castellani, and Perondoli.[15] All these families, with the single exception of the Perondoli, long survived the crisis of the 1340's.

The Castellani went on to become a power of the first order in politics and administration, and they built up new commercial fortunes. Part of this new wealth was made—in some cases for the second time—in the cloth trade, the specialty of the Castellani household connected with Bruni. Alessandra's father and grandfather were matriculated in the guild of the international cloth merchants, the *Arte di Calimala*. Messer Michele, her father, appeared in the guild consulate in 1419 and 1423. Her grandfather, Messer Vanni, took office as a consul in 1385, 1391, 1396, 1400, 1403, 1408, and 1417.[16] Between 1385 and 1420 the same Vanni received ten different appointments to the city's supreme commercial tribunal, the *Sei di Mercanzia*.[17] And on five occasions between 1388 and 1418 he was selected to represent the *Calimala* guild among the officials of the mint.[18] The prominence of the Castellani in their guild directory and their frequent representation in the chief commercial tribunal were

[14] On the Baroncelli see Malespini, *Storia fiorentina*, I, 142. The Cavalcanti appeared in the governing body of the *Calimala* guild as early as 1192, G. Filippi, *L'arte dei mercanti*, p. 187.

[15] Villani, *Cronica*, III, 375.

[16] *ASF, Mss.*, 544, ff. 600v, 605r, 614v, 622v; *ASF, Calimala*, 8, ff. 29r, 33r, 39r.

[17] *ASF, Mercanzia*, 129, paginated by date. Messer Vanni's first term began on 1 April 1385. Messer Lotto Castellani was another very prominent appointee to this tribunal.

[18] *ASF, Tratte*, 78, ff. 71r-v, 113r-v; 79, f. 200r.

distinctions they shared with the richest and best-known of the *Calimala* families: the Uzzano, Strozzi, Peruzzi, Alessandri, and Tornabuoni. Whether or not the Castellani, like these families, really possessed much wealth around 1400, may be established by turning to the Republic's fiscal records.

According to an *estimo* of about 1390, Messer Vanni Castellani and three of his brothers were prescribed the highest tax in the Carro district of S. Croce.[19] Two of the Cavalcanti households were assigned the second and third levies, and the fourth (45.0 florins) was put down to Messer Lotto Castellani, Messer Vanni's uncle. Moving from the level of *gonfalone* to that of the quarter, we find that the Castellani of Messer Vanni's household were rated as S. Croce's fourth family. The three wealthiest houses in the quarter were headed by Messer Antonio di Messer Nicolaio degli Alberti, Ricciardo di Messer Benedetto degli Alberti, and Messer Giovanni di Messer Francesco Rinuccini.[20]

To judge by the regrouping of names in the upper 5 per cent of the Commune s tax lists, it appears that for several decades after 1390 the distribution of wealth in Florence underwent a notable change. Thus, in 1427 the first houses in the Carro district were those of Bernardo di Lamberto Lamberteschi and Jacopo di Piero Baroncelli. The third household was captained by a brother of the old Messer Vanni Castellani, with gross assets of 17,992 florins.[21] But despite this sum, after having been the fourth family of all S. Croce in 1390, the first catasto reveals that by 1427 the richest of the Castellani had fallen to the eleventh place in the quarter. They continued, nevertheless, to rank above the Salviati, Niccolini, Antellesi, Cavalcanti, and above most of the Baroncelli, Peruzzi, Alberti, and Busini households.[22]

In 1427 Alessandra's immediate family reported assets of medium value by the standard of families in the dominant social stratum. But they were very modest assets for a house which, like the Castellani, was judged to be of the first political magni-

---

[19] *ASF, Estimo*, 183, f. 3r. [20] *Ibid.*, ff. 7r, 15r, 38r-v.

[21] *ASF, Catasto*, 68, ff. 114v *et seq.* Messer Matteo's net taxable assets totaled 13,234 florins; Baroncelli's totaled 17,883 florins; and Lamberteschi's 41,727 florins. Cf. also App. II, table v.

[22] The Salviati and Niccolini were domiciled in the Ruote district; the Antellesi and Cavalcanti in Carro; the Peruzzi, Alberti, and Busini in Leon Nero. See the alphabetical indices in *Castasto*, 68, 72, 73.

tude. Alessandra's grandfather, Messer Vanni, had just died, leaving a legacy in farms and houses of 3912 florins,[23] to be divided equally between five heirs. Messer Michele, her father, who died in 1424, left a legacy still to be settled in 1427. Its gross value amounted to 2393 florins, including a one-fifth portion of Messer Vanni's estate.[24] But the deductions and debts attached to Messer Michele's bequest so diminished it, that the accounts finally showed liabilities of 1554 florins.[25] On paper at least, Michele's heirs thus found themselves in a condition of acute economic need, and this perhaps was why his widow, Barto-lommea, eagerly negotiated a marriage for Alessandra in 1431 with the younger Bruni. The girl was fourteen years old, but the match established a connection with the heir of a wealthy states-man, lawyer, and renowned humanist. Noting these advantages, the Castellani had no trouble overlooking the fact that the Bruni were parvenus. Bruni also gained by the alliance: it drew around his own family, still new and unsteady, the traditions of a house identified with the most conservative current in the political life of Florence.[26]

Alessandra, moreover, was not given in marriage with a small dowry. In spite of the family's meager finances in 1427, four years later she was promised with a dowry of about 1000 florins or more,[27] a sum fully in keeping with the accustomed dowries of the Republic's ruling families. But the entire dowry was not made over at once, and after the banishment of the Castellani in 1434, the Commission on Rebels, responding to a request from the humanist, allotted some of the family's estates to the Bruni,[28] in

[23] *Catasto*, 68, ff. 53v-57r. This bequest rated ninth in Carro's vertical tax distribution.

[24] *Ibid.*, ff. 309v-311r.

[25] *Ibid.*, f. 309v, for Otto's catasto inventory. Most of the Castellani estates were located along the Lower and Upper Valdarno: at Vinci, Cetina-Vechia, Altomena, and Cancelli. See Repetti, *Dizionario*, I, 76, 677; V, 785.

[26] Rinaldo degli Albizzi was one of the chiefs of the ultra-conservative faction. Messer Matteo Castellani supported him in agitating against the political participation of the parvenus and artisans. See Cavalcanti, *Istorie*, I, 90-92.

[27] Estimated on the evidence of the following reports, *Catasto*, 662, ff. 656r-659v; 801, ff. 1195r-1198v. The Castellani farms listed among the Bruni properties comprised only part of the promised dowry.

[28] E.g., *ASF, Notarile antecosimiano*, L 144 (dates: 1432-1440), ff. 96r-v, 182r. Protocols of Ser Gabrielle Leoni, awarding one of Otto Castel-lani's farms to Lionardo Bruni.

addition to a first option on the purchase of certain other Castellani lands.

The matrimonial alliances of the Castellani reflected the family's antiquity and economic traditions. During the half century or more preceding the Bruni negotiations, they established bonds of marriage with three illustrious *magnati* houses: the Bardi, Frescobaldi, and Ricasoli.[29] Although the Ricasoli, a baronial family, were the oldest of the three, the Bardi and Frescobaldi were already celebrated international bankers in the mid-thirteenth century.[30] The *popolani* side of the Castellani marriages involved powerful merchant families: the Altoviti, Davanzati, Del Palagio, Guidetti, Peruzzi, Salviati, and Strozzi.[31] Looking at Alessandra Bruni's immediate background, we find that her grandfather, Messer Vanni, married Francesca di Bettino Ricasoli, and her father, married first to a Panciatichi,[32] then married a woman of the Gambacorti family, an ancient Pisan house.

Let us consider next the political and civic importance of the Castellani. Their formal entry into public life began with an appointment to the Priorate in 1326. In 1366 Alessandra's great-grandfather, Michele di Vanni, was the first of the family to be confirmed in the Commune's leading dignity, Gonfalonier of Justice. He was drawn for the dignity a second time in 1372. In the next generation Messer Vanni was elected Gonfalonier on four occasions: in 1388, 1398, 1406, and 1414.[33] This record compared favorably with those of some of the Commune's most authoritative statesmen. Maso degli Albizzi, for example, held the office three times, Messer Lorenzo Ridolfi four and Cosimo de' Medici three times.[34]

Alessandra's father, Messer Michele Castellani (ca. 1375-1424)

---

[29] *ASF, Carte Pucci,* 29, iv; *BNF, Mss. Passerini,* 186; on the Ricasoli see L. Passerini, *Genealogia e storia della famiglia Ricasoli* (Firenze, 1861).

[30] See a contemporary's view of the Bardi and Frescobaldi in *Historia antica di Ricordano Malespini* (Fiorenza, 1568), p. 75.

[31] *Carte Pucci,* 29, iv; *Mss. Passerini,* 186. One of Alessandra's sisters, for example, was married to Niccolò di Andrea di Neri Lippi del Palagio. She left a bequest of 100 florins for Alessandra's dowry: *Notarile antecosimiano,* P 282, under the acts of 6 April 1422. Not paginated.

[32] On the Panciatichi see above Ch. II, 5.

[33] *Mariani,* III, f. 554r.

[34] *Ibid.,* I, ff. 49r, 234r; III, f. 535r. On the other hand, Cosimo's great opponent, Rinaldo degli Albizzi, sat in the Priorate only once, and he was never chosen Gonfalonier of Justice.

took his first important executive office in 1413, when he was appointed a member of the Eight on Political and Military Security. In 1418 and 1421 he sat among the Twelve Good Men. He also held three provincial governorships, several other domestic posts, and—like most Florentines of his condition and station—he was often found in the Councils of the People, the Commune, and the Two Hundred. His record as a civil servant, however, did not eventually include a term in the Priorate, and so it would appear that Messer Michele's career was modest.[35]

But in his case, as with all men from the leading Florentine families, it is misleading to assess political stature merely by counting the offices they held or weighing their importance. For one thing, when six or eight members of the same clan were active in government circles (and this was true of the Castellani), the number of times each could appear in office was inevitably reduced. Particularly affected were appointments to the Signoria and to the important commissions, dignities apportioned to the political families in such a way that a pattern of rotation is evident.[36] Moreover, prominent members of the ruling families sometimes specialized in certain departments of government: finance, military affairs, foreign relations, questions of administration, and so on.[37] For these reasons, to appear infrequently in the Commune's standard run of important offices was not necessarily an index of modest political standing. Furthermore, the vast inventories (*Tratte*) of the holders of public office do not record embassies, temporary investigative and fiscal commissions, special electoral committees, to say nothing of participation in the executive councils.

Thus, although Messer Michele did not often appear in the

[35] Messer Michele's offices are recorded in *ASF, Mss.*, 265, f. 60r; *ASF, Tratte*, 78, f. 115r; 79, ff. 15r, 70r, 147r; 66, f. 15r; 67, ff. 27r, 30r; 147 (paginated by date), 1 Sept. 1401, 1 Jan. 1402, 1 Sept. 1402, 1 May 1403, 1 Jan. 1405; and, for example, *Tratte*, 152, ff. 4r, 21r, 46r, 134v, 159r, 163v.

[36] Although archival material is voluminous on this aspect of the question of public office, it has not been studied. Properly done, such a study would involve several stages of work: inquiries into the *scrutinio* procedure, *imborsazione*, and frequencies in office of major and minor political figures.

[37] For example, Messer Lotto Castellani was the family expert on military affairs. He sat in the Ten of War no less than nine times between 1384 and 1406. Messer Vanni, on the other hand, did not serve in this commission. See *ASF, Manoscritti*, 274, entitled "Decem viri baliae." Paginated by date.

obvious circuit of offices, he took an energetic part in political affairs and developed something of a reputation as a statesman. His list of embassies made him one of the more active of Florence's younger diplomats. In 1407, for example, he was sent as an envoy to the Lord of Foligno, Messer Corrado de' Trinci. The following year he led an embassy to Siena, and in June of 1413 he was appointed one of the four ambassadors to the papacy.[38] Five years later, accompanied by Luca di Maso degli Albizzi, he conducted an embassy to Pope Martin V. He was in the field again in the autumn of 1421, with instructions on coming meetings with King Louis, Giovanna of Naples, and Martin V.[39] Finally, early in 1424, he made a trip to Bologna and there negotiated his last foreign assignment.[40] He died the following November. Those who mourned his death (Rinaldo degli Albizzi, for one) may have remembered his political skill and informed participation in the governing assemblies.

When, in the course of sponsoring bills, the Signoria met opposition in the legislative councils, the priors often reacted by soliciting the support of influential citizens. These citizens went before the councils to explain or justify the proposed legislation, to urge its adoption, to ask for a modified bill, or even to call for further debate. A citizen who made such recommendations in the councils was usually designated as representing one of the city's four quarters or a special-powers commission, the Guelf Party, or one of the guilds. Messer Michele Castellani, like his father and uncles, was occasionally recruited to comment on pending legislation in an effort to influence the councils. The *Libri fabarum* record his acting in this capacity in 1406, 1412, 1418 (on seven occasions), 1420, 1422, and 1423.[41] He dealt with measures pertaining to public finance, the drafting of new lists of the men eligible for public office, and the setting up of a Ten

[38] The other three were Messer Filippo Corsini, Messer Jacopo di Giovanni Gianfigliazzi, and Bernardo di Vieri Guadagni. See Ammirato, v, 29, n. 2.

[39] His coadjutant on this occasion was the feared and much talked-about Rinaldo degli Albizzi.

[40] ASF, *Leg. Comm.*, 4, ff. 37r-v, 68r-v; 6, ff. 31v, 96r, 127r; *Commissioni di Rinaldo degli Albizzi*, I, 312, 380. It is not unlikely that future research will uncover other of Messer Michele's embassies.

[41] ASF, *Lib. Fab.*, 48, f. 149r; 50, f. 71r; 51, ff. 219v, 220r, 223r, 231r, 239r, 240r, 241r; 52, ff. 38v, 198r (?), 218v.

of War. But his pronouncements in the legislative councils did not comprise the whole of his counseling activity in Florence. During the twelve or fifteen years before his death, he often took part in a set of small councils at the executive level of government, the very councils where the authority of the city's major political figures was most in evidence.

The Signoria's most important deliberations, called the *Consulte e Pratiche*,[42] were normally held by the Priorate sitting in secret consultation with the Sixteen Gonfaloniers, the Twelve Good Men, and a special group of advisors termed a *pratica*. Generally speaking, a *pratica* varied in size from eighteen to two-score advisors. These advisors gave counsel in their capacity either as private citizens, as representatives of one of the four quarters, or as spokesmen for one of the departments of government. Plenary sessions of the Signoria and its counselors were held irregularly: daily, two or three times a week, or several times monthly, depending on the issues at hand. Statesmen and administrators of secondary importance regularly attended the sessions, but discussion itself was often monopolized by the dominant political personalities. Therefore, to participate in these deliberations denoted a certain (and not an insignificant) political or administrative reputation. And although a Florentine might take office very infrequently, if for one reason or another he was thought to be of some importance in public life he was almost certain to appear in the *Consulte e Pratiche*.

Four members of the Castellani family, all knights, distinguished themselves in the executive councils of the first quarter of the fifteenth century: Messer Lotto di Vanni,[43] Messer Vanni di Michele,[44] Messer Matteo di Michele,[45] and Alessandra Bruni's father, Messer Michele di Messer Vanni.

The junior member, Alessandra's father, was the least prominent of the four, but even so the nature and frequency of his

---

[42] F. Gilbert, "Florentine Political Assumptions in the Period of Savonarola and Soderini," *Journal of the Warburg and Courtauld Institutes*, xx (1957), 187ff. A *pratica* was also an executive session on a given theme.

[43] See, e.g., ASF, *Consulte*, 34 (19 July 1400-20 May 1401), passim.

[44] *Consulte*, 35 (24 May 1401-23 November 1402), passim.

[45] *Consulte*, 44 (1 April 1420-8 April 1422), passim.

recommendations in council made him one of the Republic's important statesmen.[46] During the years 1411-1413, for example, Michele's recommendations were primarily concerned with foreign affairs and public finance,[47] and these were the themes to which he returned in 1414, 1415, and thereafter.[48] His participation in the executive deliberations was somewhat irregular, and this was caused by the obligations of his foreign assignments, by sickness, by the presence in the *pratiche* of his father or uncle, and on three occasions, each lasting six months, by his holding rectorships in the dominion. But he took part in the deliberations when he was able and when the Signoria invited him to do so. He was especially active in the *consulte* of 1423;[49] hence he served the Republic in the councils of state until almost the year of his death.

Although the last member of the clan to exhibit individual power in the councils, Messer Matteo di Michele, died the year before his grandniece became Lionardo Bruni's daughter-in-law, the younger Castellani were already beginning to appear in leading offices, evidently preparing to assume their traditional leadership in the affairs of state.[50] Their name was then associated with a political future of the first order and it was untouched by scandal such as disfigured the Serragli, Brancacci, Biliotti, Guicciardini, and others.[51] But when the rivalry and hatred between the ruling families came to a head in the autumn of 1433, the Castellani threw in their lot with the forces opposed to the Medici and

[46] *Consulte*, 41, 42, passim.
[47] *Consulte*, 41, ff. 27v, 28v, 35v, 39r-v, 41v, 124r, 129v, 136r, 155v, 161r, 169v, 171v, 175v.
[48] *Consulte*, 42-44, passim.
[49] *Consulte*, 45, ff. 54v, 56r, 63r, 65r, 66r, 71v, 77r, 81r, 82v, 116r, 121r, 124v, 126v, 131r, 134r, 136v, 141r, 144r.
[50] Messer Matteo died in September 1430. See *ASF, Notaio di Camerauscita*, 1 (dates: 1426-1430), f. 96v. This rarely-used source records the government's expenses for his public funeral. The clan's chief office holders then became Jacopo and Piero di Messer Vanni: see e.g., *ASF, Mss.*, 265, f. 60r-v; *Mariani*, iii, f. 554r. In 1427 they were respectively only thirty-one and thirty-eight years of age; see *Catasto*, 68, ff. 102v-103v, 146v-148r.
[51] Vannozzo di Giovanni Serragli was fined 30,000 florins for fraudulence in office in 1430; he died in prison in 1433. See *Catasto*, 490, f. 431r-v. Felice Brancacci was fined 6,000 florins for a similar crime, or as he said, "pro chagione del caseraticho della camera," *ibid.*, f. 147r. On the Biliotti, Arrigucci, and Guicciardini see Ammirato, v, 25; Cavalcanti, *Istorie*, ii, 571.

a year later were banished from Florence.[52] From that time on they never counted as a political force.

2. THE BUONDELMONTI

On January 19, 1436 Vaggia di Gino Buondelmonti was married to the celebrated humanist, Poggio Bracciolini.[53] Considering that social place deeply affected decisions about marriage and that the Buondelmonti constituted one of the city's oldest and most noble houses, did Vaggia's family weigh the matter of Poggio's social origins, or hesitate to let her contract what might well be deemed a lowly match? It is safe to assume that in view of Poggio's position in 1436, Vaggia's father, Gino, dismissed as irrelevant the fact that the humanist was the son of an humble apothecary. For Poggio, bearing the title *Messer* or *Dominus*, was a papal secretary and lawyer who had already earned an international reputation as a man of letters. He conducted an extensive correspondence with temporal and ecclesiastical princes, and his Florentine friends belonged to the dominant social sector. As a matter of fact, it was to him that the Buondelmonti eventually turned for favors: for example, when he recommended his brother-in-law, Manente, in a letter to Novello Malatesta: "Manentes adolescens nobilis, uxoris meae frater, ad te deferet aliqua opuscula mea. . . . Eum tibi majorem in modo commendo,/ et tu in tuis, quod commodo tuo fiat, suscipias oro."[54] Later he used his influence at the Pontifical Court to obtain a Florentine prebend for Manente.[55]

Although Poggio often assailed the idea of a blood nobility, he was proud of the ancient traditions of the Buondelmonti and his letters to non-Florentine friends sometimes reminded them of Vaggia's noble ancestry.[56] According to Litta,[57] the family went back to the first half of the tenth century, to a certain Sichelmo,

[52] Cavalcanti, *Istorie*, I, pp. 601-602. Though only the leaders of the clan were banished, it was enough to break their power permanently. Otto, Alessandra Bruni's half-brother, was one of the exiles.

[53] Walser, doc. 43, p. 353.

[54] *Epistolae*, II, 325-326. Letter dated 1446 by editor.

[55] Walser, doc. 76, p. 380, "Reservatio pro Manente cognato domini Poggii de uno canonicato florentino cum derogatione omnium aliarum etc."

[56] *Epistolae*, II, 80, 169.

[57] P. Litta, *Buondelmonti di Firenze*, 6 tavole (Milano, 1850).

who appears to have been the patron of the monastery of St. Michael at Passignano. The native ground of the Buondelmonti was just south of Florence, along with the Val di Greve at Montebuoni,[58] where they originally possessed a feudal castle. At an early period—their castle destroyed by the Florentine burghers[59]—they settled in Florence and there distinguished themselves as leaders of the Guelf nobility. In the course of the thirteenth century they came to the fore as international bankers; at the same time they continued to hold large rural estates, though in the city itself the family seat was one of the typical tower-like fortresses.[60]

When in the late thirteenth century the key offices of state were closed to the ancient feudal houses and to many of the old business families,[61] the Buondelmonti were forced to surrender their accustomed pre-eminence in public life. But in some ways the process was a slow one, and the family remained a political force throughout the fourteenth century. For the Buondelmonti stood out in magnate circles, the magnates exercised a great deal of control over the Guelf society (*Parte Guelfa*), and the society in turn exerted considerable influence on the direction of Florentine politics during much of the century.[62] Nevertheless, the Buondelmonti and other magnates lost the chief magistracies to the upstart families of the 1280's and 1290's: the Albizzi, Corbinelli, Medici, Rucellai, Strozzi, and so on. In the first third of the fifteenth century Vaggia's father and grandfather appeared in only those offices which the Florentine constitution had left open (or periodically opened) to the *magnati*.

Before sketching in the relative civic importance of Vaggia's immediate family, let us get some idea of their material condition and marriage connections.

Most of the Buondelmonti houses in 1400 were in the S. Maria Novella quarter.[63] Vaggia's family, however, resided in the

---

[58] Repetti, *Dizionario*, III, 327.   [59] Malespini, *Storia fiorentina*, I, 137.
[60] Salvemini, *Magnati e popolani*, pp. 376-377.
[61] Causing Messer Berto Frescobaldi to say that "i cani del popolo aveano tolto loro gli onori e gli ufici," Dino Compagni, *Cronica fiorentina* (Livorno, 1830), p. 35.
[62] The best analysis of the *Parte Guelfa* in the politics of Trecento Florence is in Brucker, *Florentine Politics and Society*, Chs. II-VI.
[63] *ASF, Prest.*, 1996, passim.

Chiave district of S. Giovanni—home of the Albizzi, Pandolfini, and Pazzi. The economic situation of the clan varied from household to household. Richest of all was Andrea di Messer Lorenzo, whose prestanza of 24.7 florins in 1403 was the eighteenth levy in a distribution of 1492 levies for the whole of S. Maria Novella.[64] Well-known names stood above his on the taxrolls: the Strozzi (two households), Ardinghelli (two), Davanzati (two), Della Luna, Gianfigliazzi, Gondi, Tebalducci and Tornabuoni.[65] The other Buondelmonti of the district[66] were assessed prestanze which on the whole associated them with the economic means of the small landholding type. In the S. Giovanni quarter Vaggia's father was prescribed a levy of 2.00 florins. This was a modest sum but it rated near the first 12 per cent of all levies in the area, and hence stood above the medium level of S. Giovanni's middle-class families.[67]

In 1427 Vaggia's father, Gino, claimed one large house with a courtyard and shop, two cottages, four farms, various land parcels, and some livestock.[68] His remaining assets included an outstanding credit of 858 florins and government bonds with a market value of 118 florins. Altogether his gross capital came to 2424 florins. The debts on this estate amounted to 500 florins,[69] and rental and subsistence deductions reduced Gino's taxable capital to 336 florins. Consequently, Poggio's match with Vaggia was hardly contracted with an eye (on his part) to forming an alliance with a moneyed family. Nevertheless, she brought him a dowry whose value, 600 florins,[70] conformed with the dowries customarily given by the political families of medium stature, or

---

[64] See App. II, table III.

[65] The other six were Giovanni di Bartolomeo di Ser Spinello, Marco di Tommaso Bartoli, Zanobi di Francesco Agolanti, Ambrogio di Meo Boni, Zanobi di Ser Benozzo, and Domenico di Antonio Allegri.

[66] E.g., Gherardo di Gherardo, Lorenzo di Messer Gherardo, Niccolò di Andrea, and the heir ("Rede") of Niccolò di Rosso.

[67] *Prest.*, 1999 or 2002, paginated alphabetically by Christian name. The totals and percentages are my own. 296, or nearly 12 per cent, of S. Giovanni's 2500 prestanze were for amounts of 3.00 florins or more. Therefore, a levy of 2.00 florins stood just under the percentage designated.

[68] *Catasto*, 80, f. 174r.

[69] 150 of which were owed to the convent of S. Apollonia, where Gino had just sent his daughter, Nanna, age seven. Nanna's dowry of 150 florins would be invested by the convent, for each girl or nun was supposed to live on the income from her dowry.

[70] Walser, p. 353.

by the distinguished old families (somewhat down at heel) whose major social virtue was their blood.

In gentle blood the Buondelmonti were distinguished enough, and for generations they had not feared to unite in marriage with purely bourgeois or mixed houses. Two of Vaggia's sisters, for example, were married to a Strozzi and a Guadagni.[71] One of her brothers, Pier-Antonio, married Oretta di Antonio de' Medici. Vaggia's mother, Papera, was born into an old administrative clan from the far side of the Arno, the Sassolini. The immediate noble connections of the Buondelmonti included the Bardi, whose blood Vaggia claimed through her paternal grandmother. Her great-grandmother was a Quaratesi,[72] while Vaggia's brother, Giambattista, married a Ricasoli.[73]

Turning next to the family's record in public office, it is essential to remember that because of their status as magnates, they could not match the striking records of powerful merchant families like the Rucellai or Corbinelli. But they entered all offices open to *magnati* and were as active in this regard as the most energetic of the great noble houses: the Agli, Bardi, Frescobaldi, Gherardini, Ricasoli, and Rossi.

Taking Vaggia's family alone—and they were not the most prominent of the Buondelmonti—we find that her grandfather, Manente (d. 1417) occupied nearly a score of government offices between 1390 and 1416.[74] On one occasion he was dispatched to the *condottiere*, Bernardino dalle Serre.[75] In 1396 he entered the Republic's most powerful commission, the Ten of War, where he represented the nobility. But with these exceptions, his offices entirely involved administrative functions in the city and rectorships in the Florentine dominion.

[71] The Guadagni were old *popolani*, already active in Florentine government in 1202. They first entered the Priorate in 1289, *Mariani*, I, f. 202r.

[72] The Quaratesi came from Quarata near Galluzzo. They obtained their first seat in the Priorate in 1317, *ibid.*, II, f. 470r-v. Judging by one of Dino Compagni's observations, they were coming into prominence around 1300, *Cronica*, p. 157.

[73] On all the above-mentioned marriages see Litta, *Buondelmonti*.

[74] *Tratte*, 65, ff. 37v, 86r; *Tratte*, 66, ff. 27r, 85r, 106r, 119r; *Tratte*, 78, ff. 15r, 23r, 27r, 29v, 48v, 61v, 117v, 222r, 227v; *Tratte*, 79, ff. 47v, 118r; *Delizie degli eruditi toscani*, XIV, 289.

[75] ASF, *Leg. Comm.*, 1, f. 144r. Manente was given this commission on 25 May 1399. Bernardino was to be hired for six months and possibly a year. The salary offered him was 500 florins monthly.

Poggio's father-in-law, Gino (b. 1390), served in a dozen offices of the better sort.[76] The record included, apart from three rectorships, appointments to the Ten on Liberty, to the commission entrusted with the hiring of troops, and to the office which managed the *Parte Guelfa* properties. On three occasions he was named one of the five treasury officials, a fact suggesting that Gino canvassed for these reappointments, as only one of the five places in the commission was open to noblemen. In 1427 his name was drawn from the eligibility purses for duty in the Ten of War. He was reassigned to this office in 1431 and possibly a third time in 1437.[77] The powers of the Ten of War were military, diplomatic, and executive, so that Vaggia's father had the opportunity here to exercise the highest functions of state. But being a nobleman, he must have been urged to moderate his conduct. In recent years the *magnati* chosen for the Ten had provoked sharp criticism by their arrogance and boldness,[78] and the merchant oligarchy had reacted by selecting the commission's single nobleman with increased caution. That Gino was chosen more than once for this office indicates something of the favor he could draw on in the city's highest political sectors.

By comparison with the power they wielded in the thirteenth century, the Buondelmonti of the Quattrocento hardly represented a real political force. Yet Manente and Gino held on to as much of their political legacy as the age permitted. In Poggio's time they maintained a certain administrative distinction, and it is not unlikely that their illustrious traditions allowed them to invest their more ordinary offices with greater authority than other men.

3. THE TEBALDUCCI

When in 1427 the catasto revealed that the Manetti of S. Spirito were economic peers of the leading Medici and Strozzi families, Giannozzo Manetti was soon to celebrate his marriage with Alessandra di Tommaso di Giacomino Tebalducci.[79] To

---

[76] *Tratte*, 67, ff. 72r, 79r, 104r; *Tratte*, 79, ff. 4v, 48r; *Tratte*, 80, ff. 3v, 6v, 48r, 98r; *ASF, Capt. Guelforum*, n. rossi 6, f. 27r.

[77] *Delizie*, xiv, 299, 300, 302; also Litta, *Buondelmonti*, tav. ix.

[78] Cavalcanti, *Istorie*, i, 547-548.

[79] *ASF, Ancisa*, II, f. 227v; MM, f. 440r.

judge by the standard histories of Florence,[80] the Tebalducci were a family of little economic or social significance. In fact, the opposite was true.

Sometimes called the Giacomini-Tebalducci, they lived in the White-Lion district of S. Maria Novella. They were members of the *Cambio* guild and figured prominently in its governing body.[81] Their business interests were diversified, but currency exchange, loans, banking, and government securities were their principal spheres of interest. In 1427 the Tebalducci bank had branches in Venice and Genoa, as well as far-flung business connections in London, Bruges, Rome, Budapest, and other parts of the world.[82] The home branch in Florence carried some of the investment deposits of the Manetti, Panciatichi, Marsuppini, and Bruni. Conversely, the Tebalducci were creditors of the Salviati, Quaratesi, Guicciardini, Soderini, Tornaquinci, Acciaiuoli, Altoviti, and others.

In 1403 the tax officials assigned Alessandra's father, Tommaso di Giacomino, a levy of 58.0 florins per prestanza.[83] It has already been observed that in that year S. Maria Novella had some 1492 registered payers of forced loans. Tommaso's levy was the fourth highest.[84] Looking at other sections of the city in order to extend the significance of Tommaso's prestanza of 58.0 florins, it may be noted that Messer Maso degli Albizzi was prescribed 17.5 florins, Gino Capponi 6.00 florins, Giovanni di Bicci de' Medici 37.5 florins, and Niccolò da Uzzano 20.0 florins.[85]

In 1427, shortly before Giannozzo Manetti was married to Alessandra Tebalducci, a report of her father's assets, drafted

---

[80] They are not mentioned in the following: G. Capponi, *Storia della Repubblica di Firenze*, 2 vols. (Firenze, 1888); F.-T. Perrens, *Histoire de Florence*, 6 vols. (Paris, 1877-1883); F. Schevill, *History of Florence* (New York, 1936).

[81] *ASF, Mss.*, 544, e.g., ff. 966r, 974r, 979r, 988r, 993r, 1011r, 1024r. Alessandra's great-grandfather, Goggio, was matriculated in the *Arte del Cambio* in 1333, *ibid.*, f. 878r.

[82] *Catasto*, 47, ff. 594r-614v; *Catasto*, 77, ff. 190v-195r.

[83] *Prest.*, 1996, paginated alphabetically by Christian name. Read: Tommaso and Jacopo di Giacomino.

[84] See App. II, table III.

[85] On Albizzi and Medici see *Prest.*, 1999, 2002, alphabetically by Christian name. On Capponi and Uzzano see *Prest.*, 1994, 2000, alphabetically. Read: Cappone and Gino di Neri, and Niccolò and Angelo da Uzzano. Cf. also App. II, tables II and IV.

for the catasto commission, made him the city's twenty-third highest taxpayer and head of S. Maria Novella's fifth household.[86] Since Florence was one of Europe's most advanced commercial centers, Tommaso's position in this city made him one of Europe's wealthiest men. Parenthetically, the same was true of three other men whose fortunes we have already examined: Giannozzo Manetti, Carlo Marsuppini's father, and Lionardo Bruni.

The Tebalducci fortune was divided three ways: part in real estate, part in commercial and finance capital, and part in government securities. Real estate accounted for some 3920 florins, chiefly in lands along the Val di Pesa and near the Badìa of Ripoli.[87] Although the corpus of Tommaso's commercial and finance capital was estimated to be between 3500 and 4000 florins, his accounts dealt in many times this amount. The bulk of his wealth was in government securities, worth 19,218 florins in real market value.[88] Financiers of Florence's toughest sort,[89] the Tebalducci had amassed a fortune which could not be rivaled by some of the city's most celebrated political families—the Albizzi or Castellani, the Corsini or Soderini, the Gianfigliazzi, Pitti, Ridolfi, or Salviati.

But the family's brilliant financial leadership did not last: they went bankrupt early in 1431.[90] Tommaso and his brothers had bought a large merchant vessel on credit from the Republic, expecting to pay for it with subsequent trade earnings. The vessel was to make trade runs to Sicily and Barcelona and its control vas largely in the hands of the Tebalducci company of Genoa. or reasons still obscure, however, the Genoese company, as ll as the family company in Venice, were very badly managed. r currency exchanges accounted for part of their losses. The lian and Barcelonian ventures were unsuccessful, and to matters worse the Florentine state suddenly demanded nt for the vessel. Tommaso was then forced to sell a large ty of government securities. Their worth in nominal values

sto, 77, ff. 190v-195r.

o, 47, ff. 594r-614v; *Catasto,* 77, ff. 190v-195r.
aso's brothers, Lionardo and Giovanni, were also prominent *atasto,* 77, see index for folio numbers.
ovv., 122, ff. 62r-63v. His brothers were also involved in the *bid.,* ff. 362v-363v.

came to about 36,000 florins; their market value varied from one-third to one-fourth this sum. But owing to unfavorable Monte fluctuations, retarded interest payments, and taxes of various kinds, Tommaso lost very heavily. On investigation the government discovered that all told he had suffered losses of 18,340 florins. In May 1431 the inquiry into his finances revealed that his taxable assets had fallen to 2500 florins. His tax rate was then reduced from 107 florins to 12.5 florins per catasto.[91]

The family did not thereupon disappear from the economic and social life of Florence. Other Florentine families had faced bankruptcy and survived; so too did the Tebalducci, whose saving good fortune was that they succeeded in holding on to their landed possessions. In 1458 Tommaso's heirs reported the ownership of large new properties, as well as the old family estates in the Val di Pesa and Ripoli areas.[92] These lands, together with the family's workshops and urban real estate, were given a value of 6133 florins. It is worth noting that this figure surpassed by one-third Tommaso's real estate assets of 1427. Once again, therefore, the Tebalducci ranked with the city's leading taxpayers.[93]

Turning next to the traditions of this family, we do not find that they were parvenus, as their type of wealth might lead us to expect. On the contrary, they were an old family of landowners whose existence as a distinct house went back to the middle of the twelfth century and who, before that time, carried the name of one of the city's oldest and best-known Ghibelline families, the Malespini.[94] The titles (*Messer*) of the family chieftains down to the end of the thirteenth century indicate that the Tebalducci long preserved a knightly and military tradition.[95] In the mid-fourteenth century they were connected by marriage with the Filicaia and Sassetti households. The Sassetti were one of the leading old families grouped around the Cavalcanti during

---

[91] *Ibid.*, ff. 62r-63v.

[92] *Catasto*, 818, ff. 549r-557r; *Catasto*, 819, ff. 185r *et seq.*

[93] Their catasto of 14.5 florins may easily be compared with all the S. Maria Novella assessments of the same year. See the "sommario," *Catasto*, 836.

[94] *Historia antica di Ricordano Malespini*, p. 72. The Gugialferri, like the Tebalducci, were also a branch of the Malespini.

[95] *Mariani*, vi, f. 1311r. The title *Messer* also applied to *doctores legum*. But the Tebalducci family connections were with the warrior nobility.

the civil disorders of 1304;[96] the Filicaia, related to the ancient clan of the Tedaldi,[97] first sat in the Priorate in 1284 and for the next two centuries were very active in political and administrative affairs.

Alessandra Manetti's grandfather, Giacomino di Goggio, was married to Cilia di Vieri Altoviti in 1371 and to Saracina de' Donati in the 1380's.[98] Cilia's family made their initial appearance in the Priorate the year of its establishment, 1282, and according to the *Priorista Mariani* they already had a distinguishable identity in the early eleventh century.[99] Saracina's family, as is well known, played an historic part in the political events of Dante's time: they were the noblemen who led the Blacks in the acrimonious Black-White conflict.

Alessandra's father and his generation negotiated an interesting series of marriages.[100] In 1401, for example, Tommaso married Ghostanza di Agnolo degli Alberti, of the famous family of international bankers. Widowed, he married one of Cino Rinuccini's nieces.[101] Alessandra's aunt, Bartolommea, was given in marriage to one of the city's influential statesmen of the years 1395-1412, Messer Bartolommeo Popoleschi, a doctor of law.[102] The Popoleschi took their "democratic" name in 1282, when they repudiated the elder branch of their house, an unruly noble clan, the Tornaquinci.[103] Alessandra had three other aunts who married into the Albizzi, Arrighetti, and Salviati families, and one of her uncles married a Ridolfi. While the Arrighetti gave their name to a house which once had claimed feudal jurisdiction, the other three ranked with the principal merchant families of the oligarchy during the fifteenth century.

In Alessandra's generation we find a group of marriages similar to those of the previous period. Alessandra, as we said, was mar-

---

[96] Compagni, *Cronica*, p. 158.
[97] Malespini, *Historia antica*, p. 74. They may also have been related to the Gherardini and Aldobrandini, *Mariani*, I, ff. 108r.
[98] *ASF, Carte Pucci*, xx, 6.
[99] *Mariani*, I, f. 15r.
[100] *Carte Pucci*, xx, 6; *BNF, Mss. Passerini*, 188, 19.
[101] On the Rinuccini see Chs. II and III above.
[102] See e.g., *Consulte*, 40 (date: 1409-1410), passim; *Leg. Comm.*, 1, ff. 78r, 89r; 2, ff. 28r, 45v, 64r; 3, ff. 34v, 69r; 4, ff. 70v, 74r, 75r-v, 114r, 136r, 140r, 141r; 5, ff. 1r, 2r, 74r; 6, ff. 1r, 17r.
[103] Ammirato, I, 293.

ried to Giannozzo Manetti. Her sister, Saracina, was married to a swiftly rising young knight, Agnolo Acciaiuoli (see App. I, no. 27), who became one of Florence's most authoritative statesmen during the middle decades of the century.[104] Another sister, Antonia, became the wife of Bartolommeo di Piero Capponi. The commercial traditions of the Capponi associated them with the silk trade and probably they were already engaged in it when they emigrated to Florence from Lucca in 1216.[105] They obtained their first seat in the Signoria in 1287.[106]

The political alliances which ensued from these matches were strengthened by the marriages of Alessandra's brothers, Jacopo and Giacomino. Jacopo was married to Giovanna di Niccolò Giugni, Giacomino to Ginevra di Francesco Quaratesi. The Giugni were a S. Croce family—wealthy, numerous, and already venerable in the thirteenth century.[107] The Quaratesi of S. Spirito were one of the richest clans in Florence. Noblemen who secured popolani status in the early *Trecento*, they gained entry to the Signoria in 1317, but demonstrated their solidarity with the *magnati* in 1343, when they took the Bardi into their houses to protect them from the fury of the mob.[108]

The Tebalducci took an active part in the public life of Florence before the general constitutional changes of the late thirteenth century.[109] Their standing as magnates then excluded them from political society for about a century. They probably tended to avoid political agitation and *consorterie* (cabals), for they go unmentioned in the Compagni and Villani chronicles.

[104] Vespasiano da Bisticci, pp. 486ff.

[105] *Mariani*, I, f. 172r. On the family's political chieftain in the early fifteenth century see M. Mariani, "Gino Capponi nella vita politica fiorentina dal 1393 al 1421," *A.S.I.*, IV (1957), 440-484.

[106] *Mariani*, I, f. 172r. On the outstanding Capponi of the mid fifteenth century see I. Bencini, "Neri Capponi," *Rivista delle biblioteche e degli archivi*, XVI (1905), 91-100, 138-154, 158-174; also Bencini, "Note e appunti tratti da documenti sulla vita politica di Neri Capponi," *Rivista delle biblioteche e degli archivi*, XX (1909), 15-31, 33-56.

[107] The Giugni were a branch of the Galigai, once a powerful feudal family. Malespini, *Storia fiorentina*, I, 141.

[108] *Mariani*, II, ff. 470r-471v.

[109] Duccio di Messer Cherico Tebalducci, for example, was a grain commissioner for the Florentine armies in 1260, *Mariani*, VI, f. 1311r. See also A. Gherardi, ed., *Le consulte della repubblica fiorentina*, 2 vols. (Firenze, 1896), I, 134; P. Santini, ed., *Documenti dell' antica costituzione*, pp. 99, 164.

The first member of the house to enter office in our period appears to have been Alessandra's grandfather, Giacomino di Goggio, whose career was crowned by an appointment to the Ten of War at the height of the Florentine struggle with Giangaleazzo Visconti.[110] The next heir to the family's political fortunes, Jacopo di Giacomino, obtained a place among the Sixteen Gonfaloniers in 1413, in the Priorate a year later, and the Twelve Good Men in 1415.[111] But he died shortly thereafter and responsibility passed to Alessandra's father, Tommaso, soon to become a major administrative figure and a tireless seeker of public office. He served in practically every one of the standard offices,[112] including those at the head of government. In 1417 he represented the White-Lion district in the Sixteen; four times between 1421 and 1435 he took office as one of the Twelve; and in 1419, 1423, and 1427 he sat for S. Maria Novella in the Priorate.[113]

Let us end by noting that Giannozzo Manetti's father-in-law, Tommaso, entered office more than fifty times between 1405 and 1436, not counting his numerous appearances in the legislative councils.[114] Comparing this record with that of one of the age's major political figures, Neri di Gino Capponi, we find—since Neri took office some seventy times in the period 1412 to 1454[115]—that Tommaso could scarcely have had a busier career in public life, especially in view of his business obligations. The similarity between the two careers, however, terminated there. Everything else was different: the nature of their offices, their stature in the

[110] *ASF, Mss.*, 544, ff. 931r, 954r; *Tratte*, 78, ff. 18v, 64r, 64v, 71v, 103r; *Mss.*, 266, ff. 64v-65r; *Delizie*, XIV, 290.

[111] *Mss.*, 266, ff. 64v-65r; *Mariani*, VI, f. 1311r.

[112] *Mss.*, 544, ff. 966r, 974r, 979r, 988r, 993r, 1011r, 1024r; *ASF, Mercanzia*, 129, paginated by date, read 1 July 1419, 1 Oct. 1424, 1 Oct. 1429, 1 April 1431; *Tratte*, 67, f. 14v; *Tratte*, 78, ff. 94r, 234r; 79, ff. 69v, 77v, 87v, 108r, 130r, 146v, 200r, 205r, 218v, 238r, 281r, 382r, 388v; 80, ff. 10r, 37r, 149r, 172r, 188v, 233r, 243v, 297r, 390r, 402r.

[113] *Mss.*, 266, ff. 64v-65r; *Mariani*, VI, f. 1311r.

[114] E.g., *Tratte*, 147, under Leon Bianco in S. Maria Novella, read 1 Jan. 1401(2), 1 Oct. 1402, 1 May 1403, 1 June 1404, 1 Jan. 1404(5); *Tratte*, 152, ff. 13r, 30r, 47v, 69r.

[115] E.g., *Tratte*, 79, 80, passim; *Tratte*, 67, ff. 8r, 9r, 9v, 24r, 39r, 40v; *ASF, Lana*, 39, ff. 17r, 19r, 32v, 43r; *Mariani*, I, f. 172r. So far as one can tell, Tommaso was never given a diplomatic assignment. But Neri was one of the Republic's leading diplomats during the middle years of the fifteenth century.

Humanist Marriages

Consulte e Pratiche,[116] their political traditions, and their personal interests. Neri was a man of state very nearly without a peer in Florence. Tommaso, on the other hand, like scores of his contemporaries, was not a statesman but an administrator, though a prominent and influential one. His place in government was strong enough to insure the political and social status of the Tebalducci. But if ever it proved inadequate, the family might then draw on the support of houses connected with them by marriage. There is enough evidence in the legislation on the Tebalducci bankruptcy to establish the family's influential position in the highest sectors of government: without the intervention of the state on that occasion, they would have been financially ruined.

4. THE CORSINI

Carlo Marsuppini was married to Caterina di Gherardo di Messer Filippo Corsini in 1435.[117] Before the end of the year he was appointed lecturer in rhetoric and poetry at the University of Florence, and nine years later he succeeded Lionardo Bruni as head of the Florentine chancellery. Carlo's contemporaries were not likely to forget that he had powerful connections: he was one of the best-loved friends of the Medici,[118] and in all probability Cosimo's influence had been used to help him obtain the senior chancellery post. Yet no Florentine could truly say that Carlo needed the Medici for his material or social advancement. For it has already been shown that the Marsuppini, old Aretine nobility, were the richest of Arezzo's families in Carlo's generation. Moreover, in Florence proper, where they also maintained a fixed residence, their tax returns exhibited more assets than those of any single household of the Albizzi, Acciaiuoli, Capponi, Cavalcanti, Corbinelli, Rucellai, Salviati, or Soderini families. Not surprisingly, therefore, as the elder Marsuppini

---

[116] Tommaso rarely spoke in the executive councils. But see *Consulte*, 43, ff. 131r, 136r; 44, f. 143v; 45, f. 45v; 46, ff. 45v, 179r. Neri, on the other hand, was one of the Signoria's most authoritative and prominent counselors, *Consulte*, 50-51, passim.

[117] ASF, *Ancisa*, MM, f. 472r.

[118] This is best seen in Carlo's consolatory letter on the death of Cosimo de' Medici's mother, *Biblioteca Laurenziana di Firenze, Mss. Laur.*, LIII, 20; LIV, 10. Published by P. G. Ricci, "Una consolatoria inedita del M.," *Rinascita*, III (1940), 363-433.

proudly said, Carlo could devote himself to the study of "poetry, philosophy, Greek, and Latin . . . branches of knowledge which bring honor rather than money."[119]

When we consider Carlo's marriage in the light of Florentine mores, keeping in mind his brilliant social position, the question of the social identity of Caterina's family automatically arises. Who were they and what traditions did they represent?

Many of the Florentine families of the fifteenth century rose to prominence during the later thirteenth century. In 1282, the year the Priorate was established, such families were considered newcomers by the urbanized nobility and the old merchant houses. Already known *ab antico* in Florentine commercial circles were the Baroncelli, Buoninsegni, and Cavalcanti.[120] The old baronage included the Adimari, Agli, Buondelmonti, Chiaramontesi, Galigai, Malespini, Pazzi, Scolari, Uberti, and so forth. Another class of families was made up of the Bardi, Cerchi, Frescobaldi, Mozzi, and Rossi: these distinguished themselves in the early thirteenth century, largely through brilliant commercial and banking ventures.[121] Among the unmistakably parvenu families in 1282 were the Albizzi, Capponi, Corbinelli, Medici, Rucellai, Strozzi, and others of the same type who, in their turn, were to form the old established houses of the fifteenth century.[122] It is to this group of families, the upstarts of the 1280's and 1290's, that the Corsini were connected by reason of their origins, wealth, and political traditions.

According to their historian,[123] the Corsini originated among the plebs of Castelvecchio di Poggibonsi, a point above and halfway between Siena and Volterra. They entered Florence about

[119] *Catasto*, 203, f. 647v, "Carlo e d'eta de anni xxviiii. Studia in poesia, philosophia, et altre scientie, et in greco et latino, le quali scientie sopradecte sono d'onore et non di guadagnio." Date: 1427.

[120] Malespini, *Storia*, i, 142; G. Filippi, *L'arte dei mercanti*, p. 187, where we find the Cavalcanti and Buoninsegni in the *Calimala* consulates of the 1190's.

[121] In another edition of the Malespini chronicle, *Historia antica* (Fiorenza, 1568), p. 75. According to Malespini, even the Cavalcanti were part of this group.

[122] On some of these families see Passerini, *Albizzi di Firenze*, and Litta, *Strozzi di Firenze*, in Litta, *Famiglie*; Brucker, "The Medici in the Fourteenth Century"; Passerini, *Genealogia e storia della famiglia Rucellai*. The Rucellai did not enter the Signoria until 1302, *Mariani*, ii, f. 373r.

[123] Passerini, *Genealogia e storia della famiglia Corsini*.

the middle of the thirteenth century and settled in S. Spirito. Neri, the first outstanding member of the family, was a dyestuffs merchant.[124] He appeared in the Priorate no less than nine times during the period from 1290 to 1315. True to the family's relatively late origins, he seems to have fought hard to break the power of the *magnati*.[125]

At the outset of the fourteenth century, or possibly earlier, the Corsini branched out into banking and money-lending. In the 1320's and 1330's they ran one of the largest banking houses in Florence, for Giovanni Villani, when recording the great banking failures of 1342, included their firm with the firms of the Peruzzi, Bardi, Castellani, and the city's other half dozen leading houses.[126] With the exception of the Perondoli, all the families involved in these bankruptcies retained their prominence in public life. And from about 1380 to 1418, under the leadership of Caterina's extremely able grandfather, Messer Filippo, the authority of the Corsini in the executive councils was not far inferior to that of the leading Albizzi, Medici, Strozzi, or Uzzano households.

Although political power in Florence tended to gather around wealth, especially older wealth, the connection between the two was of course neither inevitable nor mechanical. During the first half of the fifteenth century, the Corsini were not one of the city's richest families. They ranked among the upper 2 or 3 per cent of the populace, but not among the first 100 families. In 1390, for example, when Messer Filippo was assigned a prestanza of 50.0 florins, forty-one of the 1430 levies in his quarter, S. Spirito, were greater than his.[127] The family's inventories for the catasto of 1427 were drawn up by Caterina's father, Gherardo di Messer Filippo.[128] They reveal that in the years after 1413 the family may have passed through a period of financial

[124] A. Sapori, *Una compagnia di calimala ai primi del Trecento* (Firenze, 1932), p. 334, where we find Neri in the Bardi accounts as a merchant of "grana di vespida."

[125] *Mariani*, ɪ, f. 212r; Passerini, *Corsini*.

[126] Villani, *Cronica*, ɪɪɪ, 375.

[127] *Prest.*, 1262, f. 82v; *Prest.*, 2000, alphabetically by Christian name; *Prest.*, 2901, f. 57r. The above totals are based on my own counts. Messer Filippo later received a "sgravo" (i.e., a reduction) of 7.00 florins on his prestanza of 1413. Cf. App. ɪɪ, table ɪᴠ, no. 43.

[128] *Catasto*, 66, ff. 61v-63v.

distress,[129] for on this occasion 129 of the district's 2900 reporting households declared taxable assets greater than those of the Corsini. Gherardo's report, showing a family of six, revealed that they lived on the income from four farms, a small commercial investment, and 1248 florins (real values) in government securities. Not included were Gherardo's earnings as a civil servant— he was one of the period's important office holders—but such income was not normally reported in catasto returns. The trade investment, taxed on the assumption that it drew an interest of 7 per cent yearly, was deposited with one of the firms of the wealthy Isau Martellini. Gherardo's estates were in the town of S. Casciano, halfway between Florence and Poggibonsi. He added another farm to his lands in S. Casciano before 1446 and the income from half a farm in Certaldo. The S. Casciano farm he inherited from his brother, Messer Amerigo Corsini, the late Archbishop of Florence.[130]

Although the Corsini did not recover from the citywide banking crisis of 1342, they continued, as we have said, to figure prominently in Florentine public life. A summary look at the career of Caterina's grandfather will illustrate this point.

Messer Filippo Corsini (1334-1421) was so closely connected with politics, diplomacy, and civil administration in the years between 1370 and 1418, that a full biography of his life would constitute a history of Florence during those years. A knight and doctor of law, he grew up and entered middle age during the half century of the most democratic government in the history of Florence. But he had no taste for the political rights or action of the lower classes. Twice, in 1378 and 1382, his house was put to the torch by mobs of political demonstrators.[131] Understandably, therefore, in the 1380's, after the last serious popular attempts to widen class participation in government, Messer Filippo came to the fore as an ardent exponent of restricted government and

[129] The fact that in 1416, 1419, and 1421 Messer Filippo held governorships in the dominion suggests that he may have been faced with financial troubles, for such offices were among the most lucrative. Besides, the legist was about eighty-six years old in 1421 and a six-month term of judicial duties in the provinces would not have been easy for a man his age.
[130] *Catasto*, 650, ff. 217r-219r.
[131] Rado, *Maso degli Albizzi*, p. 73; Rinuccini, *Ricordi storici*, p. xxxiv.

became one of the architects of the pre-Medicean oligarchical settlement.

He was Gonfalonier of Justice five times between 1368 and 1417.[132] On six occasions between 1371 and 1410 he sat among the Twelve Good Men and Sixteen Gonfaloniers. In 1403, just after the culmination of the Florentine struggle for independence against the Duke of Milan, Messer Filippo was appointed to the powerful extra-powers commission, the Ten of War.[133] No other contemporary had managed to occupy so many primary dignities in a single lifetime.

A practicing lawyer, Messer Filippo was matriculated in the *Arte dei Giudici e Notai*, where for many years he stood out in the consulate.[134] He also took out membership in the *Calimala* and *Lana* guilds.[135] But he did not occupy himself with their internal affairs because, like all Florentines of his station and interests, most of his time was spent in the Republic's elaborate run of offices: judicial, military, and fiscal commissions of various types, investigative committees, small executive groups, embassies, and so forth.[136] Participation in the executive debates and his key offices occupied him above all. High among these offices were his diplomatic assignments, which took him all over Italy and France, particularly during the years 1386-1413.[137] On most of these missions Messer Filippo was accompanied by one or two other legates, but he was usually the man in charge, above prominent figures like Messer Cristofano Spini, Messer Jacopo Salviati, Messer Rinaldo Gianfigliazzi, and younger men like Matteo Castellani and Rinaldo degli Albizzi.[138]

---

[132] *Mariani*, I, f. 212r. Maso degli Albizzi held this dignity only three times; Gino Capponi held it twice, Messer Rinaldo Gianfigliazzi four times, Cosimo de' Medici thrice, and Messer Lorenzo Ridolfi four times.

[133] *Delizie*, XIV, p. 291; *ASF, Mss.*, 265, f. 75r-v.

[134] *ASF, Proconsolo*, 26, ff. 10r *et seq.*

[135] E.g., *Lana*, 20, f. 21r.

[136] *Tratte*, 66, f. 17r; 67, ff. 20r, 23r; *Tratte*, 78, ff. 15v, 28v, 72v, 73v, 77v, 103v, 105r, 106v, 216r, 219v, 227r, 229r, 231r, 236r, 246v, 248r, 276v, 280v, 281r; 79, ff. 38r, 84r, 108r, 218r, 280v.

[137] Ammirato, IV, 13; *Delizie*, XIV, 63; XVIII, 87-88, 112, 113, 230, 273; *Commissioni di Rinaldo degli Albizzi*, I, 8, 153, 199; *ASF, Leg. Comm.*, 1, ff. 2r-3v; 2, ff. 7v, 21r-22r, 35v, 42v, 44v-45r; 3, ff. 40r-v, 59v; 4, ff. 14v, *et seq.*, 26v *et seq.*, 91v-93r.

[138] See e.g., *Consulte*, 40, passim, for Messer Cristofano's prominence in the executive councils; *Consulte*, 37, passim, on Salviati; *Consulte*, 37-40, passim, on Gianfigliazzi.

The career of this important Florentine suggests that he must have been one of the Signoria's outstanding counselors. Turning to the appropriate source,[139] we find that only four or five of his contemporaries consistently matched, or now and then slightly surpassed, his standing in the executive deliberations. They were Messer Maso degli Albizzi, Messer Rinaldo Gianfigliazzi, Niccolò da Uzzano, Messer Lorenzo Ridolfi, and possibly Bartolommeo di Niccolò Valori. Messer Filippo's counsels, like theirs, normally concerned the important questions of state, but generally speaking foreign affairs and public finance outweighed all other topics.[140] Messer Filippo was deemed an expert in both areas and an authority on municipal administration. Counting on his great skill and reputation, therefore, the Signoria sometimes solicited his help in getting difficult bills through the legislative councils.[141]

Such, in brief, was the career of Caterina Corsini's grandfather. He took his last office, the governorship of Anghiari, on 14 April 1421, and died the following September, a few weeks before his term expired. Florence responded by honoring his memory with an elaborate public funeral.[142]

The foregoing account suggests that Carlo Marsuppini's father-in-law, Gherardo di Messer Filippo, came into a political fortune the keeping of which required a statesman of genius. For in Florentine public life there was no room at the top for the leadership of men with mediocre political talents: rivalry was too keen, place too important. If a family sought to preserve a strong tradition of leadership, it must strive in each generation to produce one man capable of transmitting his political inheritance. Cosimo de' Medici, for example, had to be a consummate politician in order to foster his father's political estate. His banking empire was very helpful, particularly since many of the ruling families appeared in the Medici account books. As a political weapon, however, *haute finance* by itself did not suffice. We can

---

[139] *Consulte*, 37-41, passim.

[140] As in *Consulte*, 41, ff. 4v, 5v, 6r, 7r, 7v, 8v, 13r, 13v.

[141] E.g., ASF, *Lib. Fab.*, 44, ff. 19v, 51v-52r, 166v; 45, f. 48r; 47, ff. 58v, 101r-v, 102v.

[142] *Lib. Fab.*, 52, f. 112v. A special money bill was passed empowering the government to honor "corpus domini Filippi de Corsinis defuncti de signo populi florentie in targia pennone veste," etc.

see this inversely by noting that although Neri di Gino Capponi could not claim the thirtieth part of the Medici wealth, his political ability was so great as almost to enable him to rival Cosimo de' Medici in the 1440's and 1450's. The power of the Albizzi family survived the death of Maso partly because two of his sons, Luca and Rinaldo, were greatly endowed politically. Similarly, the prominence of the Ridolfi family during the first third of the fifteenth century was fostered in the succeeding generations by highly skilled descendants. The Pandolfini were kept in the oligarchy's innermost circle by three generations of brilliant statesmen. And in Messer Alamanno the Salviati house had a leader who forcefully maintained the political reputation founded by his father, Messer Jacopo.

But with the death of Messer Filippo, the Corsini gradually lost their place among the first half-dozen ruling families. Interested as he was in public affairs, Caterina's father, Gherardo, does not seem to have been a gifted statesman and so could not step into his father's place. The family's political pre-eminence thus temporarily faded, but they nevertheless managed to retain their position among the oligarchy's first fifty or sixty houses. Although Gherardo did not stand out in the framing of domestic or foreign policy, he kept the family's tradition of public service very much alive by becoming one of the Republic's most active office holders.

Gherardo di Messer Filippo (1376-1456)[143] took his first major office, as Treasurer of Pisa, in 1409. Carrying a term of six months, the post was exceedingly important, for Pisa had only recently come under Florentine rule (1406) and Gherardo's immediate successors were the well-known Rinaldo degli Albizzi and Gino Capponi.[144] His other offices in the years immediately following the Pisan appointment[145] indicate that his early preferment was in the care of someone at the summit of Florentine government— his own father. But the elder Corsini died in 1421 and Gherardo did not enter the Priorate until 1424. Thereafter he sat only once

[143] Passerini's dates, 1380-1457, are incorrect, *Corsini*, tav. viii. See *Catasto*, 650, f. 219r. On his death see *Tratte*, 80, f. 109v.
[144] *Tratte*, 78, f. 140r.
[145] Vicar of the Upper Valdarno, one of the *Octo Custodiae* and *Decem Libertatis*. See *Tratte*, 66, f. 33r; 79, ff. 15v, 46r.

in one of the colleges, the Twelve Good Men in the 1428-1429 winter quarter.[146]

Excluding his appearances in the legislative councils, Gherardo took office some sixty times during the period 1409 to 1455.[147] He occupied some offices more than once, such as the Eight on Security and Ten on Liberty; others he held on only one occasion, such as the various commissions on salt, wine, meat, contracts, and the city gates. Prominent in his career was a high percentage of rectorships in the Florentine dominion. The average number of such offices for a man of his background was four or five; he held thirteen and hence stood out in the provinces as one of the Republic's most experienced magistrates. Can it be that Gherardo canvassed for this type of office, owing to financial need? According to his first catasto report, we may remember, the family had a remarkably modest income for one with so outstanding a place in Florentine society. And in an age, in Florence at least, when the upper classes were spending more and more heavily, especially on such items as houses, dowries, and dress, the hardship produced by financial need must have become increasingly intense. Thus the propriety of pointing out here that the most lucrative offices available under the Republic were the dominion rectorships, particularly the larger ones. In time their abuse was to raise acid protests against the "fleecing" of Florentine territory.

We have yet to bring out the marriage connections of the Corsini.[148] Messer Filippo's mother was an Albizzi. Hence he was cousin to Maso degli Albizzi, which made all the more fitting the lawyer's leading position in the pre-1434 oligarchy. Filippo himself was married to Lisa di Messer Barna de' Rossi, born to an illustrious old *magnati* family of S. Spirito. Among the *magnati* houses of that quarter, the Rossi were surpassed in strength and numbers only by the Bardi. Caterina's father, Gherardo, born of this union, espoused Bartolommea di Antonio degli Alessandri.

[146] *Mss.*, 265, f. 75v; *Mariani*, I, f. 212r.

[147] *Tratte*, 66, ff. 33r, 106r; 67, ff. 6v, 9r, 15r, 21r, 22r, 25v, 41v, 42r, 59r, 66r, 67r; *Tratte*, 78, f. 140r; 79, ff. 15v, 20v, 41v, 46r, 63r, 86r, 87r, 119r, 147r, 185v, 205v, 251r, 381r, 391r; 80, ff. 13v, 26v, 35r, 41v, 86r, 89v, 109v, 116r, 132v, 148r, 175v, 199v, 280r, 409v, 425r; ASF, *Capt. Guelforum*, n. rossi 6, 1r; 7, 26r-27v; *Lana*, 32, ff. 36r, 37r, 39v, 41v, 43v, 47r; *Lana*, 39, ff. 19v, 24r, 27v, 42v.

[148] The marriage lines are recorded in Passerini, *Corsini*, tav. VII.

A branch of the Albizzi, the Alessandri broke from them in 1372,[149] changed their name and from that time on promised to avoid all *consorterie* (cabals). During the fifteenth century they ranked among the first fifteen or twenty political families and among the first fifty in terms of wealth.[150]

Gherardo's brother, Piero, married Caterina di Albertaccio degli Alberti; another brother, Messer Amerigo, became the Archbishop of Florence; and his sister, Ghita, was given in marriage to Salamone di Carlo Strozzi.[151] The Alberti and Strozzi had few social peers in Florence, owing partly to the fact that Florentine history during the second half of the fourteenth century had been closely connected with their political fortunes. But most branches of the Alberti were harshly persecuted by the pre-1434 oligarchy, and it is very likely that Piero Corsini's match with Albertaccio's daughter was one of those mutually advantageous arrangements, with the Corsini offering political protection and the Alberti offering a large dowry.

The Albizzi, Alessandri, Alberti, and Strozzi marriages associated the Corsini with some of the oldest and most conservative houses of the merchant class. But so far as political grievances went, there was no perfect security. The fact that Gherardo did not reappear in the Signoria after 1424, although he was an active office-holder until 1456, suggests that he may have been the partial victim of political vendetta. His daughter's match with Carlo Marsuppini may thus have been an indirect political bid. For the Marsuppini, and especially Carlo, were intimate friends and commercial *creditors* of the Medici.

5. THE SERRAGLI

Matteo Palmieri, a druggist by trade, a humanist by avocation, and by ambition a statesman, was descended from a family which already paid taxes in Florence in about 1200.[152] During the first quarter of the fifteenth century, the Palmieri became one of the city's notable administrative families. On his mother's side Matteo

---

[149] Passerini, *Alessandri gía Albizzi di Firenze*, in Litta, *Famiglie*.

[150] *Prest.*, 2002, read alphabetically under Maso di Bartolommeo degli Alessandri; *Catasto*, 80, f. 73v. Cf. App. II, table VI, no. 16.

[151] Passerini, *Corsini*, tav. VII.

[152] *ASF, Acquisti e doni*, 7, f. 132r.

was related to an old and respected S. Spirito house, the Sassolini, who boasted venerable Guelf traditions: their proof—if such
were needed—lay in the fact that the Ghibellines had demolished
their "turrim cum palatio" in 1266.[153]

In 1433 Matteo married into the Serragli family of S. Spirito.[154]
His bride was Cosa (i.e., Niccolosa) di Niccolò di Agnolo de'
Serragli. The Florentine traditions of Cosa's family were not as
ancient as those of the Palmieri, but the Serragli had a more distinguished economic and political past. They were descended
from an old feudal clan by the name of Buonaiuti.[155] Their original seat was the castle of Pogna in the Val d'Elsa, a region
stretching between Siena and Empoli. When the castle was
destroyed by the Florentines in 1286, the Buonaiuti emigrated to
Florence. There, owing to the fact that they joined forces with
the old nobility and entangled themselves in the machinations
of secret political societies, they were declared *magnati*. The
founder of the Serragli, a notary named Ser Belcaro Buonaiuti,
settled in Florence around 1310.[156] To distinguish himself from
his unruly kinsmen, he changed his surname and obtained both
Guelf status and citizenship *pleno iure* for himself and his family.
In 1325 he entered the Priorate, the first of his family to sit in
the Commune's chief executive body.

At the end of the fourteenth century the Serragli were deemed
one of the city's principal merchant families. From time to time
they served in the ruling bodies of the *Lana* and *Por Santa Maria*
guilds. But the particular Serragli household which concerns us
here was especially active in the *Cambio* or money-changers'
guild.

Cosa's father, Niccolò di Agnolo (1369-1438?), was taken into
the *Cambio* guild in 1399. In 1406 he made his début in the guild
consulate, where altogether he served ten terms between 1406
and 1434.[157] Niccolò's popularity in the guild gradually earned
him a reputation as an expert on commercial policy. He enhanced
the impression by seeking terms in the city's chief commercial

[153] *Mariani*, II, f. 380r.
[154] *Catasto*, 490, f. 315v.
[155] *Delizie*, VII, iii *et seq.*   [156] *Ibid.*
[157] ASF, *Mss.*, 544, ff. 949r, 954r, *et seq.* The first citation records the
matriculation of the elder Serragli, Agnolo, on 18 March 1394.

tribunal, the Six on Commerce, where he sat a half-dozen times.[158] According to a silk merchant and chronicler of the time, only the distinguished and most experienced members of the trade guilds gained admission to the Six, and they, he observed, were normally the richest and best-known merchants in Florence.[159] Did Niccolò de' Serragli conform to this type?

The prestanza records of 1390 indicate that the Serragli were then a family of moderate means. That year Niccolò's father was prescribed a levy that did not figure among even the first 15 per cent of all levies distributed in the S. Spirito area.[160] By 1403, however, his levies rated in the upper 6 per cent.[161] Are we to understand that the thirteen-year lapse had seen a considerable gain in the house's fortunes? In view of the family's political distinction and noted social aggressiveness,[162] it is unlikely that they could have failed to rank at any point in this period among the first 15 per cent of the population. Moreover if, as it seems to us, the bulk of their wealth was tied up in commercial and finance capital, this might well account for their low rating in the designated prestanze. For the full sum of such capital came to the attention of the state with some difficulty. Nevertheless, since there was a continuing upward curve to the Serragli prestanze after 1390, we can probably assume that their accounts showed an increasingly greater intake.

Bankers, money-lenders, and currency exchangers, Niccolò and his father built up a successful firm during the years when powerful business interests brought about the conquest of Pisa and the purchase of Livorno. As he prospered—while not failing to take his large share of public offices—Niccolò increased his landed possessions, thereby raising the estimates which determined his forced loans. Thus in 1413 he paid 22.0 florins per prestanza and his levy was preceded by only ninety others in a total distribution for the S. Spirito area of 2154 levies.[163]

---

[158] *ASF, Mercanzia*, 129, paginated by date.
[159] Dati, *L'Istoria*, pp. 156-157.
[160] *Prest.*, 1262, paginated alphabetically by Christian name. The first 202 levies were for 20.0 florins or more. Niccolò's father, Agnolo, was not in this group.
[161] See App. II, table IV, no. 133.
[162] Ammirato, IV, 39, for a typical story of Serragli arrogance.
[163] *Prest.*, 2901, f. 131r.

Niccolò prospered for another dozen years. Then he plunged into a critical financial phase, in part connected with Filippo Maria Visconti's new threats to Florence.[164] We shall profit from looking at Niccolò's troubles for a moment, for we have a chance here, in Matteo Palmieri's father-in-law, to observe an example of how place and influence served to ward off financial ruin.

In the summer of 1426 Niccolò petitioned for (and received) a reduction of his forced-loan obligations.[165] But the relief was inadequate, for the following year his banking house failed.[166] His returns for the catasto of 1427 showed gross assets of 18,000 florins.[167] Leaving all other expenses aside, his business debts alone amounted to about 15,500 florins. His major creditors were men like Bernardo Manetti (Giannozzo's father), Averardo de' Medici, Niccolò da Uzzano, Neri di Gino Capponi, Giannozzo degli Alberti, and Paolo Vettori.[168] Manetti, Vettori, and an impartial third person, Ridolfo Peruzzi, were appointed trustees of the properties surrendered by Niccolò to meet the demands of his creditors. But only the equivalent in lands of 4000 florins was appropriated. He was allowed to keep eleven farms, thirteen houses, and an unspecified number of land parcels, worth altogether some 4300 florins. Niccolò apparently had the indulgence of the trustees. Then in 1431 the legislative councils enacted two bills in his favor[169]—evidently he also enjoyed the support of men in high places. The report he submitted to the catasto commission of 1433 makes it perfectly clear that he had managed to hold on to most of his estates.[170] The turning point for Niccolò had come in 1431 when, on behalf of his defunct banking firm, he successfully petitioned the government for the payment of debts

[164] C. C. Bayley, *War and Society in Renaissance Florence*, pp. 82ff., for an admirable discussion of the strains produced in Florence by the Duke of Milan.

[165] *ASF, Provv.*, 116, ff. 147v-148v, 210v-211v.

[166] *Provv.*, 118, ff. 139r-142v, dated 19 December 1427. He had already been permitted to renounce a rectorship because "si ad dictum officium exercendum accederet sibi et suis creditoribus maximum incommodum resultaret," etc. *Ibid.*, f. 94r.

[167] *Catasto*, 67, ff. 86r-92v.

[168] *Catasto*, 347, ff. 353r-360v. Niccolò's report of 1430, including a list of his creditors not recorded in the catasto of 1427.

[169] *Provv.*, 122, ff. 65r-66r, 236r, 245v.

[170] *Catasto*, 490, ff. 311v-315v.

still owed to the firm, debts incurred by the Ten of War as far back as 1425.[171]

Since the Republic was very susceptible to the pressure of private interests, it must have been essential for Niccolò to command a certain political influence during the years involving his bankruptcy proceedings. In the early sixteenth century, Francesco Guicciardini was to accuse Lorenzo de' Medici of having so corrupted the membership of the *Sei di Mercanzia* that the partisans of the Medici inevitably won their commercial disputes.[172] But while membership in this high court took a cliquish turn as early perhaps as the end of the fourteenth century,[173] in the 1420's and 1430's the strife between the factions served to keep the tribunal free from absolute restraints. Besides, since Niccolò did not wish an unbiased judgment, he avoided letting final jurisdiction over his bankruptcy fall to the *Sei di Mercanzia*. This is where his political connections served him. First, he appears to have made a prior agreement with his main creditors. Then he took his case before the Signoria, which conducted its own inquiries (largely formal), decided what share of Niccolò's private estates should be put under trustee process, and appointed the trustees. This done, the case was drawn up as a private petition and sponsored by the government in the legislative councils. The measure was adopted, and Niccolò then followed it with further petitions favoring his case. Thus, by prolonging the proceedings, presumably with the collusion of his major creditors, he was finally able to keep the bulk of his estates from being absorbed into the bankruptcy.

Having briefly examined the family's antiquity and finances, it remains to consider their civil service and marriage connections.

The founder of the family, as we have seen, first appeared in the Priorate in 1325, and between that year and 1401 the Serragli contributed eleven priors to the Signoria.[174] During the period 1400-1437, when Niccolò di Agnolo was extremely active in

---

[171] *Provv.*, 122, ff. 65r-66r.

[172] *Dialogo e discorsi del reggimento di Firenze*, ed. R. Palmarocchi, p. 26.

[173] The trend begins in the 1380's. See *ASF, Mercanzia*, 129, not paginated. Consult by date.

[174] *Mariani*, III, f. 552r.

government, more than twenty members of the clan appeared in public office.[175] Although not all of them served in the leading dignities, to some extent they mutually affected their rate of appearance in office. The clan's best-known household was captained by Vannozzo di Giovanni, prior in 1390 and 1407, Gonfalonier of Justice in 1411 and 1425.[176]

Niccolò, Matteo Palmieri's father-in-law and the Serragli who most concerns us here, held nearly all the offices already familiar to us. He sat in the Signoria twice, in the colleges five times.[177] When the Medici returned from exile in the autumn of 1434, he was a member of the powerful Eight on Security. The commission's membership was dissolved and eight new men were installed in office.[178] But Niccolò's political future was not adversely affected: he held office thereafter. Like many other families, the Serragli may in some respects have temporized during the year of the Medici exile, but in 1433 a shrewd marriage (arranged partly by Cosimo de' Medici's brother, Lorenzo) associated them with the Martelli family,[179] who stood out among the staunchest supporters of the Medici cause.

Since Niccolò's banking experience qualified him as an expert on currency and fiscal questions, as a civil servant he excelled in the field of public finance. The offices connected with this aspect of government were the ones he most favored, the ones which predominated above all other offices in his career.[180] It was evidently because of this experience that Niccolò was invited on occasion to speak on fiscal measures pending in the legislative councils.[181] From time to time he also spoke up in the *Consulte e Pratiche*.[182]

---

[175] Cf. *Tratte*, 147, passim, in the rosters for the Drago gonfalon of S. Spirito; *Tratte*, 152, ff. 28v, 51v, 79r, 169v, 174v, 178v, 183r, 187v, 193v, 199v, 210v, 219v, 224v. All refer to attendance in the legislative councils, the only sure place to obtain a record of all the office holders.

[176] ASF, *Priorista di Palazzo*, consult by date.

[177] *Mariani*, III, f. 552r; *Mss.*, 265, f. 57r-v.

[178] *Tratte*, 80, f. 14r.

[179] Martines, "La famiglia Martelli," pp. 35, 40.

[180] *Tratte*, 78, ff. 133r, 260r; 79, ff. 99v, 331r; 80, ff. 1r, 41r, 200r.

[181] E.g., *Lib. Fab.*, 53, f. 88v (16 November 1425); 56, ff. 153r-154v (18-20 May 1434).

[182] *Consulte*, 41, f. 163v; 42, ff. 32v, 89r; 43, ff. 155v, 156v, 157r, 158v; 44, f. 10v.

In the years when Niccolò was struggling to keep the family estates from being drawn into his bankruptcy, he held only four government posts. Nevertheless, he was one of the busiest office holders of the age. Between 1401 and 1437 he took office more than sixty times,[183] excluding his terms in the legislative councils, in the ranks of the Guelf Captains, the commissions irregularly set up to decide on the citizens eligible for public office, or in other offices not listed in the official *Tratte* transcripts.[184]

How shall we judge the Serragli in the light of the foregoing account? Old Florentine lineage, honorable wealth, public office, and well-connected marriages: ideally, these were the main components of social place in Florence. Although the Serragli began to appear in public office somewhat more than a generation after the principal fifteenth-century families (e.g., the Albizzi and Strozzi), they threw in their lot with the proponents of close oligarchy as early as the late thirteenth century, and even after having been declared *popolani*, they continued to favor the older political element against the *gente nuova*.[185] The Serragli were thus associated with venerable traditions. Their wealth was made in banking, in the silk and wool trade, and probably in real estate speculation. Politically, they were one of the important families of the pre-Medicean oligarchy, as is indicated not only by the pattern of their preferment in the early fifteenth century, but also by the fact that they were regularly consulted about legislation on the screening of citizens for the chief magistracies.[186]

The Serragli were connected by marriage with some of the leading houses:[187] the Altoviti, Bardi, Bonsi, Corsini, Marchi, Martelli, Pugliese, Rucellai, and Soderini. The Altoviti and Soderini, old merchant families, first entered the Priorate in 1282 and

---

[183] Following are the references for most of the unspecified offices: *Tratte*, 65, f. 12v; 66, ff. 29r, 33r, 45r; 67, ff. 23r, 26r-v; 78, ff. 102v, 142r; 79, ff. 22v, 47r, 87v, 205v, 218v, 238r, 254r, 375v, 388r, 391r, 393r; 80, ff. 37r, 48r, 61r, 106v, 132r, 234r, 417v.

[184] The transcripts omit, for example, the *accoppiatori*, the prestanza officials, and the members of the *Tribunale di Mercanzia*.

[185] See Ammirato, IV, 39; also Brucker, *Florentine Politics and Society*, pp. 246, 247n.

[186] E.g., see *Lib. Fab.*, 47, ff. 101v, 102v; 52, ff. 35v, 38v, 176r.

[187] ASF, *Carte Ancisa*, FF, ff. 256r, 258r, 262r-v; II, f. 628r; LL, f. 529v; NN, ff. 186v, 364v, 397v, 398v.

1283; they appeared and reappeared in the major offices throughout the fourteenth and fifteenth centuries.[188] During the years associated with the Albizzi-Uzzano oligarchy, the Bardi were the wealthiest and strongest of the *magnati* clans of S. Spirito. As for the Marchi, they were prominent in legal circles, and the Bonsi, resident in S. Spirito, were very rich merchants.[189] More interesting were the Martelli: they were upstarts in 1350, important administrators in 1400, and by 1440 one of the ruling group's most powerful families. The Del Pugliese, on the other hand, active in Florentine public life as early as the middle thirteenth century, in the fifteenth century were great silk merchants.[190] More distinguished than most of the foregoing families were the Rucellai, outstanding wool merchants and bankers: they entered the Priorate in 1302 (twenty years after its founding), and in the course of the fourteenth century produced an astonishing number of priors—forty-seven—a record nearly matching the fifty Strozzi priors and easily surpassing the thirty-one priors of the Medici clan.[191]

Niccolò de' Serragli married twice. His first wife, Ginevra di Mariotto Banchi, came of pure merchant stock and a family not at all distinguished in political society around 1400. Lisa di Messer Jacopo Gianfigliazzi, Niccolò's wife by a second marriage,[192] was born into a family which in the early Quattrocento ranked with the first dozen or so houses of the oligarchy.[193] Their business traditions were more illustrious than those of either the Medici or Strozzi, for in the second half of the thirteenth century,

---

[188] *Mariani*, I, ff. 15r, 88r; Fiumi, pp. 387-439; Passerini, *Soderini di Firenze*, in Litta, *Famiglie*.

[189] Messer Tommaso Marchi, for example, was a prominent speaker in the executive councils of around 1400: *Consulte*, 34, passim. On the riches of the Bonsi see *Catasto*, 67, folios listed in the index under Donato di Ugolino Bonsi and Bernardo di Ugolino Bonsi. Altogether they had upwards of 30,000 florins in net taxable assets.

[190] *Mariani*, IV, f. 1434r.

[191] *Mariani*, II, ff. 374r-376r; also Passerini, *Rucellai*.

[192] ASF, *Notarile antecosimiano*, B 1542, see index there for references to Lisa's last will and testament. The register contains the notarial acts (dates: 1428-1453) of Ser Mariotto Bertini.

[193] This statement is based on Messer Rinaldo Gianfigliazzi's four terms as *Gonfaloniere* of Justice and on his and Jacopo's pre-eminence in the executive councils. See *Mariani*, V, f. 1075r; also *Consulte*, 34, 36-38, 40-42, passim.

well before these parvenus acquired a name in finance, the Gian-figliazzi already enjoyed international renown as bankers.[194]

Returning finally to Matteo Palmieri's marriage with Niccolò's daughter in 1433, we should note that whatever the humanist hoped to gain by this match in the way of political preferment fell through within a decade. Instead, it was he who attained a position enabling him to solicit favors for the Serragli. In 1437 his father-in-law obtained a sixth term in the extremely important Six on Commerce (*Sei di Mercanzia*).[195] This was Niccolò's last major office, for then came one of those turns in political fortune so common in Florence. The Serragli were drawn into a struggle for the control of the election purses and in the middle 1440's the entire house was excluded from the lists of the eligible office holders.[196] From this time on they ceased to count as a political force in the city, and more than ever Matteo Palmieri's prefer-ment was left to the resources of his own family background, his own virtues and friendships, rather than to any powers that once had been the distinction or pride of the Serragli.

[194] In the 1280's and 1290's, for example, the Gianfigliazzi appear to have been the leading bankers in southern France, especially in Dauphine and Provence. See Renouard, *Les Hommes d'Affaires Italiens*, p. 128.

[195] ASF, *Mercanzia*, 129, not paginated. Consult by date.

[196] Cavalcanti, *Istorie*, II, 192; Ammirato, v, 287. Who opposed the Serragli or why is still unknown. It is not enough to know the names of the *accoppiatores*, for one of them, Ugolino di Niccolò Martelli, was mar-ried to a daughter of Francesco di Vannozzo de' Serragli. Future research may uncover the obscure jealousies and issues involved.

CHAPTER SIX

THE FLORENTINE ATTITUDE TOWARDS
THE HUMANIST

1. INTRODUCTORY NOTE

ECAUSE the nature of primary source materials is a determining factor in historical study, we shall find it difficult to say what the ordinary shopkeeper or lowly worker in Florence thought of the humanists. But to wonder about such a question may be an unreal or false way of looking at the fifteenth-century world, especially if the question denotes a habit of mind peculiar only to the twentieth century. For why should the humble Florentine have left a record of his attitude towards the new men of letters, having left unrecorded many other things that concerned him with far greater immediacy? Our chief difficulty, of course, arises from the scarcity of extant diaries and letters, written by men of the lower classes. This material can never have been extensive; but even had it survived in considerable quantities, as did so many letters and diaries of the rich merchant class, we may assume that any references it might have made to the humanists would have been brief. After all, humanism played no part in the experience of the lower social orders; and besides, living conditions in Florence for the ordinary men of this estate were too onerous to provide them with opportunities to learn something about the discoveries and interests of the humanists.

Vespasiano da Bisticci, who left us an invaluable collection of fifteenth-century biographies, was a lowly stationer but no ordinary shopkeeper. Most of his portraits of the city's literati express an awe for the humanists—intellectual, social, and political awe. He is much impressed, for example, by Niccolò Niccoli's house, wealth, solemnity, friends, learning, and taste. He speaks with great esteem of Roberto de' Rossi as a literary host. With obvious admiration and deep respect he describes the wealth, prestige, political authority and accomplishments of Lionardo Bruni, Poggio Bracciolini, and Matteo Palmieri. And he tells the story of Giannozzo Manetti's life with scarcely less social veneration, scarcely less esteem, than when writing about men like Cosimo de' Medici, Agnolo Pandolfini, or Agnolo Acciaiuoli.

That Vespasiano regarded the humanists with veneration is not surprising, in view of the contrast between his own relatively humble place in Florentine society and the place of the humanists as set forth in the preceding chapters. Then too, he must have remembered, as we should, who the friends of the humanists were. The best known were great merchant-bankers and landowners like Palla di Nofri Strozzi, Cosimo de' Medici, and Domenico Buoninsegni; leading statesmen such as Agnolo Pandolfini, Franco Sacchetti, Lorenzo Ridolfi, Neri di Gino Capponi, and Agnolo Acciaiuoli; or men descended from the old families, Antonio Corbinelli, Jacopo di Niccolò Corbizzi, and Guglielmo Tanagli.

In short, the world of the humanist was circumscribed by the city's dominant social and political groups. He was best-known to the members of this class; it was here his civic and social standing were determined. Furthermore, since the official acts of the Florentine Republic expressed the will of the social class with political rights, the state papers adduced in the following pages ought to be considered in this light. When we speak of the Florentine attitude towards the humanists, we shall have in mind an upper-class attitude, the attitude of the peers of the humanists or, in some cases, of men even more highly placed. This attitude was a composite of the individual feelings of men who knew the humanists, and who followed their literary activity, gave them their daughters in marriage, and frequently appeared with them in public office.

2. THE TESTIMONY OF THE PUBLIC FUNERAL

The custom of holding public funerals to honor illustrious Florentines seems to have preceded the age of humanism by many years. Hence the rites sponsored by the Republic on the death of some of the humanists were not unusual; on the contrary, they were instances of a customary Florentine practice. The actual practice probably changed, becoming a fussier ceremony in the course of the fourteenth century. A description of the changes, however, would require an extensive study of *Trecento* legislation in Florence. All we are prepared to observe here is that during the second half of the fourteenth century Florence witnessed a series of costly and ostentatious funerals.[1] These were private affairs, arranged by the families of rich Florentines, and had nothing to do with state-sponsored burial rites; nevertheless, the expensive private funeral appears to have had some effect on civic practice.

During the first half of the fifteenth century, public obsequies were conducted as follows. First, the citizen involved must have been in the service of the state at the time of his death.[2] A bill on the estimated cost of the funeral was then sponsored by the Signoria in the legislative councils. Once the bill was approved, the Signoria was free to spend a sum of money (always stipulated in the bill) on such items as banners, uniforms, candles, attendants, religious offerings, and so forth. The civil aspect of the ceremony culminated with a procession through the city and occasionally an oration.

The amount of money spent by the state on individual funerals varied. In general, the rites of leading statesmen were assigned from 30.0 to 50.0 florins; those of lesser figures, even small tradesmen, from 15.0 to 20.0 florins.[3] But there was no way of telling beforehand the exact amounts which the legislative councils would approve, especially for the funerals of men who had been powerful in political affairs. Their importance in life sometimes left a trail of enemies, and hence resistance to a bill on their funeral expenditures could be very strong. But if a prominent man had managed to avoid the animosity of the factions, his death might well elicit a deep positive response.

Let us consider some examples. The death in 1414 of one of the most distinguished speakers in the executive councils, Messer Cristofano Spini, occasioned an expense for the state of 73.0

---

[1] See e.g., Monaldi, *Diario*, in *Istorie pistolesi* (Prato, 1835), pp. 510, 525, 528.

[2] The bills on funeral expenditures always stated that the subject died while in office. See the next note.

[3] *ASF, Lib. Fab.*, 48, f. 54v; *Lib. Fab.*, 50, f. 94r; 51, ff. 179r, 179v, 242r, 265v; 52, f. 112v; 53, f. 31v; *ASF, Notaio di Camera-uscita* (1426-1430), 1, f. 96v.

florins. Three years later Maso degli Albizzi's funeral cost the Republic 40.0 florins. In 1421 the councils voted to spend not more than 30.0 florins on Messer Filippo Corsini's rites. The ceremonies for Messer Giovanni Guicciardini were assigned 60.0 florins.[4] Only 30.0 florins were disbursed for Giovanni di Bicci de' Medici in 1429. When Lorenzo de' Medici (Cosimo's brother) died in 1440, the councils enacted a bill for an expenditure of 30.0 florins. But in August 1441 a petition to sponsor a funeral for Piero di Messer Luigi Guicciardini, a very prominent office holder, was rejected by the legislative councils.[5]

All the men named above were prominent Florentines, and the first five figured among the city's most influential statesmen during the first quarter of the fifteenth century. To take these men as examples of the distinguished public type is to set up a severe standard. Nevertheless, it will be seen that Florence honored the humanists with four state funerals which surpassed, in pomp and costliness, not only those mentioned above, but all others during the period covered by this study.

On the death of Coluccio Salutati in May 1406, large public ceremonies were held in the square (the Piazza de' Peruzzi) opposite his house.[6] All the knights and *legum doctores* of the city were present, including the Twelve Good Men, the Sixteen *Gonfalonieri*, various guild consuls, and representatives of the Commune of Buggiano. A brief laudatory address was delivered by the secretary in charge of Florentine legislation, Viviano di Neri de' Franchi. Salutati was crowned Poet Laureate and buried in the metropolitan church. Altogether the Republic spent between 200 and 250 florins in funeral expenses.[7]

In March 1444, Lionardo Bruni's death occasioned an elaborate public ceremony, greater than Salutati's. It was recorded by various chroniclers[8]—Rinuccini, Buoninsegni, Morelli, and others,

[4] Messer Giovanni died in 1427. He had distinguished himself in the struggle against the Duke of Milan. *ASF, Provv.*, 118, ff. 93r-94v.

[5] On the foregoing items see *ASF, Carte Strozz.*, 2a ser., 76, f. 368r; *Lib. Fab.*, 51, f. 179v; 52, f. 112v; *Notaio di Camera-uscita*, 1, f. 96v; *Provv.*, 131, ff. 190v-191r; *Lib. Fab.*, 58, f. 184 (?).

[6] Bartolommeo di Michele del Corazza, *Diario fiorentino* (1405-1438), in *A.S.I*, ser. 5, xiv (1894), 241; *ASF, Priorista del Palazzo*, f. 152r.

[7] Marzi, p. 149.

[8] Lionardo Morelli, *Cronaca*, in *Delizie*, xix, 172; Rinuccini, *Ricordi*, p. lxxiii; Buoninsegni, *Storie della città di Firenze*, p. 79.

so that it must have produced a vivid impression in the city and was manifestly taken to be an event of major public importance. The funeral was attended by the Republic's leading political figures, by knights and lawyers, as well as by the papal, imperial, and Aretine ambassadors.[9] One of the city's outstanding statesmen, a humanist and friend of Bruni, Giannozzo Manetti, was chosen to give the funeral oration. How expensive the death of this celebrity was for the Signoria we do not know, but the sum certainly exceeded that spent on Salutati's rites, for the government commissioned one of Florence's most gifted sculptors, Bernardo Rossellino, to execute a marble tomb for Bruni in the church of S. Croce.

Carlo Marsuppini, the third great humanist chancellor of the Republic, died in April 1453. The government spent 1500 florins on his funeral rites.[10] A committee of five men was appointed to make the arrangements for the ceremonies, and they were all prominent members of the pre-Laurentian oligarchy: Messer Giannozzo Manetti (recently knighted by Pope Nicholas V), Ugolino Martelli, Piero di Cosimo de' Medici, Matteo Palmieri, and Niccolò Soderini. The chronicler Cambi, who noted that the Twelve Good Men, the Sixteen *Gonfalonieri*, and other leading dignitaries participated in the ceremonies, also observed that the funeral procession flew the taffeta flags of the papacy and the banners of the King of France, the Duke of Milan, the Florentine Republic, the Commune of Arezzo, the Guelf Party, the University of Florence, and the lawyers' guild.[11] Carlo, like Lionardo Bruni, was buried in S. Croce; by order of the Signoria his tomb was designed by one of the greatest artists of the age, Desiderio da Settignano. The fact that chroniclers and private diarists recorded this event is an index of its contemporary importance.[12]

Another exponent of humanism, Poggio Bracciolini, would have been granted public obsequies had he kept his post as chancellor of the Republic. Appointed to this dignity when Carlo Marsup-

---

[9] Vespasiano da Bisticci, pp. 267-268; Marzi, pp. 197-198.
[10] Marzi, p. 215.
[11] Giovanni Cambi, *Istorie*, in *Delizie*, xx, 310-311.
[12] See e.g., mss. cited by Marzi, p. 215. The Salutati and Bruni funerals were also recorded by private diarists, Corazza, p. 241, and *ASF, Carte Strozz., 3a ser.,* 91, ff. 88v-89r, being extracts from the diary of a "donzello," Goro di Giovanni, kept between 1410 and 1471.

pini died in 1453, Poggio held it until the end of April 1458, when he resigned in order to pursue his private studies. He died eighteen months later, a private citizen, and the Signoria was powerless to sponsor a public funeral for him.

Of the humanists considered in this study, the last to receive public burial rites was Matteo Palmieri. The year before his death he held one of the Republic's leading rectorships, the Captaincy of Volterra, and on his death in April 1475 he was one of the powerful Eight on Security. Matteo's best-informed biographer did not list the government's funeral expenditures,[13] but here again the sum cannot have been small. The ceremonies were arranged and attended by some of the city's most authoritative citizens, including leading government officials, great merchants, the literati and learned men, and a large sector of the populace.[14] Matteo was buried in the Palmieri family chapel of S. Pier Maggiore, and Alamanno Rinuccini, scion of an old and wealthy house (cf. App. I, 42), delivered the funeral oration.[15]

What conclusions may be drawn from the impressive public rites described above? Since the expense and display connected with these ceremonies excelled all others of this type during the period between 1400 and 1475, the humanists in Florence must have been held in high esteem. Again, in showing favor to Salutati, Bruni, Marsuppini, and even Poggio in another regard, the state went so far as to suspend the law against the exhibition of individual portraits and private armorial bearings on public buildings.[16] Pictures of some of the humanists were placed in the offices of the lawyers' guild, and at least one portrait, Poggio's (possibly portraits of the others as well), appeared in the Palazzo della Signoria.[17] Thus, there can be no doubt of the enormous prestige of the early humanists in Florence, particularly in view of the relatively small sums (30.0 and 40.0 florins) spent by the government—and even that reluctantly—on the funerals of prominent statesmen from the Albizzi, Castellani, Corsini, and Medici households. Of course, no Signoria of the period could have

[13] Messeri, "Matteo Palmieri," pp. 256-340.
[14] *Ibid.*, p. 317.
[15] A. Rinuccini, *Lettere ed Orazioni*, pp. 78-85.
[16] Iodoco del Badia, *Miscellanea fiorentina di erudizione e storia* (Firenze, 1902), II, 48. The law was enacted in 1329.
[17] Marzi, pp. 149, 198, 223.

drummed up enough legislative support to associate the state with one of the party chieftains in a truly significant way. They were given public funerals, but to sponsor an elaborate ceremony for any one of them, as was done for the humanists, would have been to identify the state too intimately with one of the factions. The humanists, by contrast, were not party politicians; and if politics was sometimes a major interest for them, it did not become their dominant passion, as it did for men like Rinaldo degli Albizzi or Cosimo de' Medici. To be sure, the humanists inclined towards one or another of the factions (this was inevitable in Florence), but their literary acclaim often enabled them to be above party or factious dispute.[18]

We have noted that the Republic honored four humanists with public funerals. But four humanists were not *all* the humanists. What happened to the other men of the circle? Roberto de' Rossi did not die in government service. Cino Rinuccini, for all his civic fervor, held no offices of any distinction. Niccolò Niccoli was too insignificant an office holder to justify any action on the state's part at the time of his death. Leon Battista Alberti did not reside in Florence; moreover, he was a cleric. And Giannozzo Manetti died in Naples, five years after having left his last Florentine office.

The humanists who were given public funerals were representative: they shared the interests, skills, and most of the assumptions of their humanist contemporaries. Putting aside such things as wealth and family traditions, the early celebrity of the Florentine humanists rested on their literary and oratorical skills. And they all possessed these skills, Rossi as well as Manetti, Niccoli and Poggio, and of course Salutati, Bruni, Marsuppini, and Palmieri. So far as the Republic went, the main differences between the humanists concerned their actual service to the state: some devoted their lives to a career in public office, others did not. The humanist funerals, therefore, attested to an alliance between humanistic talent and the power of the state. The mak-

---

[18] There were two notable exceptions: Carlo Marsuppini's clash with Filelfo in the early 1430's involved rivalries between the Medici and anti-Medici factions; and in the early 1450's Giannozzo Manetti alienated the oligarchy for having appeared to follow an independent line in foreign policy.

ing of this alliance had been open to Rossi, Niccoli, and even Alberti. This is why the funerals described above, although there were only four, partly illuminate the position in society of most of the early Florentine humanists.

3. THE OFFICIAL VIEW ANALYZED

So far we have offered an idea, though not an explanation, of the public esteem enjoyed by the humanists. The succeeding pages will tell why the humanists were highly regarded and adduce further evidence of their place in the civic assumptions of the upper classes.

Of all the questions that still beset the study of early humanism, one of the most important actually preceded the rise of humanism in Florence by a very long time and had an existence independent of it: the question of why Florentines and indeed all other Italians attached such enormous importance to eloquence. Paul Oskar Kristeller has observed that in the art of speech-making the humanists were the heirs of the medieval rhetoricians or *dictatores* and that there was a tradition of "secular eloquence" in medieval Italy that went back to at least the eleventh century.[19] In the absence of specialized local studies we are largely in ignorance about specific rhetorical practice in the public life of medieval Florence, but for the later period, the later Trecento, all the material we have consulted points to a thesis first advanced by an Italian historian. While perfectly aware of the widespread tradition of medieval rhetoric and the very old interest in oratory, he noted that the end of the fourteenth century saw a new taste for public speaking develop in Florence, and that this taste "was not arbitrarily imposed by the erudition or whims of literary men, but answered, instead, to a vigorous need in practical life."[20] Let us try to account for this development.

Examining the new climate and turn of mind in Florence at the end of the fourteenth century, Hans Baron has directed at-

[19] *Studies in Renaissance Thought and Letters*, pp. 564-566.
[20] Santini, *Firenze e i suoi oratori*, p. 75, "si púo concludere che questa non era davvero qualche cosa di sovrimposto dovuto all' erudizione o al capriccio de' letterati, ma che soddisfaceva a un vivo bisogno della vita pratica."

tention to the Republic's struggle against the enveloping despotism of Giangaleazzo Visconti.[21] Wedded to a tradition of civic liberty and political independence, Florence in the fourteenth century had successfully resisted the encroachment of both internal and external tyranny, and had resisted the ambitions (or interests) of the papacy in central Italy during the third quarter of the century. Later, therefore, in isolated opposition to Giangaleazzo's brilliant advance into Tuscany, Florence rapidly evolved a view of its recent past and of its place in the present which bolstered municipal pride and civic responsibility in the hour of crisis. In that struggle the energies of the entire political class were brought into play; the cardinal importance of public life, the image of the distinguished public figure, and the value of each citizen's share in the struggle were all given a new emphasis— all combined to work a profound effect on the city's historical consciousness and intellectual climate.

In these summary observations we have the heart, I believe, of Baron's conception of the link between events and ideas in Florence at the end of the fourteenth century. The virtues afforded by this perspective, the light it throws on the new taste for oratory, will be clearly evident to the historian of the period and I shall discuss the view more fully in Chapter VII. In this part of the study, however, it seems advisable to take a somewhat different approach to the new stresses of around 1400, an approach fixed less on the crisis in foreign policy and more on domestic pressures and internal problems. We will revert to this approach in the next chapter, not only to examine it at greater length, but also, and chiefly, to see it in connection with a different set of problems.

After the various attempts in the 1370's and early 1380's to widen the class participation in government, a revitalized oligarchy restored political stability to Florence. The oligarchy took in a relatively large social sector: the bulk of the commercial upper class, part of the old nobility (not on the basis of proportional parity), and a certain fraction of the *bourgeoise moyenne*. Vespasiano da Bisticci, looking back to this period from about 1390 to the early 1440's, was to regard it as an age of political

---

[21] *The Crisis of the Early Italian Renaissance.*

good fortune, economic abundance, and intellectual achievement. Guicciardini, not always a critic of the Medici, looked at the era in very much the same way, except that he particularly admired its political virtues.[22] Speaking of the same period, Emilio Santini has noted that the Florentine republic "felt impelled to increase its wealth and trade, while the Guelfs or *grandi* sought to satisfy their personal ambitions. There was thus a need to break through the confined life of the Commune and get ever more entangled in the political affairs of others."[23] Between 1384 and 1430, accordingly, by means of conquest and purchase, Florence acquired Arezzo, Pisa, Cortona, Castrocaro, Livorno, Montepulciano, and finally opened a war of conquest against Lucca.

The success of the oligarchy enhanced its political optimism and economic energies. Out of success came passion for and confidence in political enterprise, until public life came to be the overriding preoccupation for men of the ruling families. To shape the destinies of Florence one had to hold public office; and in a climate of great political optimism, to hold office became a duty, a moral and social necessity. The question of eligibility for office was thus turned into one of the gravest issues of the day, and the anguish of being without a place in government, or of being barred from certain magistracies, was frequently reflected in contemporary diaries, letters, and chronicles.[24]

To give further proof of changes in the political and diplomatic life of Florence, we may note that transformations in foreign policy and in attitudes towards public life could not fail to affect the workings of the chancellery. For one thing, increasing paper work added a half-dozen new men to this office between about

[22] Francesco Guicciardini, *Storie fiorentine*, pp. 2-3. Guicciardini actually narrowed this "golden" age to the period 1393-1420. The first date refers to the year of Maso degli Albizzi's palace revolution; the second, 1420 and after, to a time when the city was increasingly torn by the divisions between the Medici and Uzzano-Albizzi factions.

[23] Santini, *Firenze*, pp. 129-130, "Il popolo sentiva il bisogno di accrescere/ la propria ricchezza, di allargare i propri commerci e la parte guelfa o i grandi di soddisfare alle ambizioni personali. Perciò tutto sollecitava a uscir fuori della vita ristretta del Comune e ad immischiarsi ancor più nella politica altrui."

[24] E.g., Morelli, *Ricordi*, pp. 197, 247, 341, 431, 500; Pitti, *Cronica*, pp. 189-195, 206; A. Strozzi, *Lettere*, passim.

1380 and 1450.[25] In the 1370's one of its sub-offices, the *Ufficio delle Tratte*, was given semi-autonomy, and from 1385 onwards inventories and lists of all civil servants were carefully kept.[26] This accorded perfectly with the growth and increasing complexity of the Republic's administrative machine. Next, the chancellery's section on foreign affairs was reformed. The dispatching of detailed instructions to Florentine ambassadors was old practice, but their thorough and permanent recording was not started until the late fourteenth century. At the beginning of the fifteenth century, another reform ordered all Florentine ambassadors to submit written reports to the chancellor on the completion of their missions, and new attempts were made to select only the best qualified citizens for the Republic's diplomatic work. Thus, "At no time have the official papers [of Florence] recorded a greater number of embassies than during the first third of the fifteenth century."[27]

As the new eagerness to hold civil office spread among the city's political class, the image of the ideal public figure became clearer. Apart from having such virtues as integrity and loyalty, he must be a "bello parlatore"—a gifted and experienced orator who could move audiences, persuade counselors, and charm rulers.[28] Appropriately enough, many of the leading figures of the day conformed to this public type: they were brilliant orators, writers, or trained debaters. Messer Filippo Corsini, for example, could expound a diplomatic assignment "with so much dignity, that all the lords of the council and many others wanted a copy of what he said."[29] The eminent Niccolò da Uzzano was a clever writer of political verses and a powerful speaker.[30] Rinaldo Gian-

[25] Marzi, pp. 106ff.; Dati, *L'Istoria*, p. 148. This section of the Dati chronicle dates from about the 1450's. Tallies should include assistants attached to the "notaio delle riformagioni."

[26] These records begin with *ASF, Tratte*, 78. The inventories before 1385 were kept in a disorganized and haphazard fashion.

[27] Santini, *Firenze*, p. 130, "Mai le carte pubbliche hanno registrato un numero maggiore di legazioni come nel primo trentennio del secolo xv."

[28] See Paolo da Certaldo's advice to the ambassador, *Libro di buoni costumi*, p. 159.

[29] Pitti, *Cronica*, p. 101. Pitti was referring to one of Messer Filippo's missions to the King of France. Messer Filippo spoke in Latin and was understood only by the chancellor, the prelates, and the Duke of Orleans.

[30] "Versi fatti da Niccolò da Uzzano," ed Canestrini, in *A.S.I.*, I, iv (1843), 297-300.

figliazzi "surpassed all other men in grace and humanity" and his "true eloquence made him worthy of being called *il gallo*."[31] Gino Capponi, one of the chief advocates of the war against Pisa, composed a chronicle which exhibits an exemplary clarity.[32] A prominent diplomat and bureaucrat, Buonaccorso Pitti, was a colorful diarist: his memoirs read like a picaresque novel.[33] Giovanni di Bicci de' Medici, on the other hand, who ought to have been a gifted speaker, "was not very eloquent, for nature had withheld the sweetness of good speaking from him."[34] But Puccio Pucci, Cosimo de' Medici's brilliant henchman, "was endowed with eloquence."[35] The highly influential statesman, Lorenzo Ridolfi, writer of a widely-read treatise on usury, often dominated the debates in the councils for long periods of time.[36] And one of the city's great political exiles, Palla di Nofri Strozzi, translated some works of Plato and Plutarch, in addition to various orations of Demosthenes, Aeschines, and Lysias.[37]

Before settling the main question raised by this section, the question of why the humanists were esteemed in political society, we will adduce additional evidence to show—for the connection was an important one—that the orator was highly valued as a public figure.

The fact that the Republic honored its lawyers with leading political dignities was not an accident. By reason of his forensic training, knowledge of the law, or now and then his preparation in the medieval rhetorical tradition, the lawyer was the man best equipped to engage in public debate. The fifteenth and early sixteenth century was, accordingly, the great age of political distinction for the Florentine lawyer. He was continually found in the three places which denoted maximum political stature: namely, in the executive deliberations, in the debates of the legislative

---

[31] Cavalcanti, *Istorie*, II, 461, "La sua autentica eloquenza il faceva degnamente essere chiamato il gallo."

[32] *Commentari dell'acquisto di Pisa*, pp. 251-281.

[33] Pitti, *Cronica*.

[34] Cavalcanti, *Istorie*, I, 267, "e non era molto eloquente, perchè dalla natura gli era negato la dolcezza del parlare."

[35] *Ibid.*, I, 5.

[36] *Archivio di Stato di Siena, Concistoro*, 1914, f. 98r, "fra gli altri Messer Lorenzo Ridolfi nel consiglio del popolo fe' uno sermone di piu d'una hora," etc.; Vespasiano, *op.cit.*, pp. 380ff.

[37] ASF, *Carte Strozz.*, 3a ser., 86, ff. 289r-290v; Santini, *op.cit.*, p. 157.

councils, and in the diplomatic service. Two of the statesmen mentioned above were lawyers, Filippo Corsini and Lorenzo Ridolfi. The other politically-important lawyers of our period were Bartolommeo Popoleschi, Marcello Strozzi, Piero Beccanugi, Giuliano Davanzati, Carlo Federighi, Alessandro Bencivenni, Nello di Giuliano Martini, Tommaso Salvetti, Guglielmo Tanagli, Otto Niccolini, and Domenico Martelli.[38]

The humanists played a part in the events described above. Their program and achievement could hardly have been more timely or fitting. For they developed and promoted the humanistic ideal of civic virtue. They held that the state was a positive institution, through whose means men practiced (or corrupted) the highest human virtues.[39] Often they buttressed their views by drawing attention to the writings of Plato, Aristotle, Cicero, Quintilian, and others. The force of what the humanists achieved is lost, however, unless we observe that by disseminating a code of public morality they satisfied the moral and ideological demands of the growing passion for holding public office, of the new feeling for an ardent commitment to the political affairs of the Republic.

How successful were the humanists? In 1428 a committee of citizens called for an expansion of the University of Florence, arguing that the liberal arts and other "honored" studies inculcated a sense of civic virtue and hence, by implication, prepared men to assume their responsibilities in the public life of the community.[40] Thus, the humanist emphasis on the pagan classics went far to give education a secular bent. The obvious advantage of this emphasis was that it permitted the systematic study of great historical figures in pre-Christian, or wholly secular, contexts. And insofar as the humanists studied man in a framework not immediately connected with a monolithic theological explanation of the world, so far was humanism the conveyor of a richer and wider outlook.

---

[38] These observations on the lawyer will be developed in a planned future work. They are based on my researches in the State Archives of Florence.

[39] The best student of this aspect of humanist thought is Garin, *Il Rinascimento italiano*, pp. 149ff.; cf. also the selections on civic virtue in his anthology, *Filosofi italiani del quattrocento*.

[40] Gherardi, *Statuti*, (Firenze, 1881), pp. 210-211.

Attitude toward the Humanists

The most immediate and influential achievement of the humanists derived from their stress on the study of grammar and rhetoric. They assumed that knowledge of the world had its foundation in Latin grammar,[41] that without it no one could learn anything of value about the nature of man, politics, history, or human institutions. Once a man had a firm grammatical foundation, he passed on to a rigorous study of rhetoric and oratory. To speak and write well were absolutely essential to a man of parts, above all to any man in public life. In this area Cicero and Quintilian were the appointed masters of the humanists, who in their turn greatly invigorated the study of oratory and were thus perfectly in accord with the new taste for public office and eloquence in Florence. In this connection, it is well to remember that the humanists were themselves highly-gifted debaters and orators.

We come back to the question, what were the reasons for the impressive public reputation of the humanists? They enjoyed their distinguished standing because they advocated a code of civic responsibility and gave education a broader and timelier basis; because they promoted the study of oratory and were themselves excellent speakers in a speech-conscious place and age; and finally, because their intellectual claim to the literature of antiquity was, in social terms, a highly restricted privilege.

But their immediate civic value for the Republic sprang from the Florentine assumption that their residence in the city, or better, their acceptance of appointments to office, was an honor for Florence. The rationale behind this view was simple: it was assumed that when a renowned literary personage took political office, he invested it (and so also the Republic) with his prestige. This is why the trustees of the University of Florence might justifiably observe that "no ancient city was ever world-famous, nor even worthy of being remembered, where the study of the different branches of knowledge had not gloriously flowered."[42]

In the following section, we will consider evidence of Florentine gratitude for the honor which the humanists brought to

[41] See for example Palmieri, *Della vita civile*, p. 24.
[42] Gherardi, *Statuti*, p. 211. "Però che, niùna anticha città fu mai famosa al mondo, o d'alchuna memoria degna, nella quale gli studii delle scientie gloriosamente non fiorissono."

the Republic. That so much can be claimed for them should not be surprising. For they knew how to turn their talents to different uses; and besides, from the moment they accepted public office, their eloquence ceased to be a mere literary endowment and became, willy-nilly, a political factor. How else should we assess humanistic eloquence, seeing it in the service of the state?

4. "THE HONOR OF FLORENCE"

When Coluccio Salutati was made chancellor of the Republic in 1375, he was already beginning to make a name for himself. He conducted an extensive correspondence with leading literary figures, among them Petrarch and Boccaccio, and soon his Latin epistles (widely sought in Western Europe) were taken to be models of stylistic excellence. Not surprisingly, therefore, in 1388, when it was resolved to renew Salutati's chancellery appointment, the Signoria stated that this "noted and illustrious man" was a disciple of that "fountain of eloquence," Cicero, and that Florence was honored the world over because of Salutati's elegant and sonorous letters.[43]

Eventually his private letters of recommendation carried a great deal of weight in the different Italian courts. We do not know whether or not, as Pius II and others reported,[44] Giangaleazzo Visconti truly feared Salutati's pen more than he feared a troop of horsemen. One thing, however, is clear: the essential judgment behind this anecdote was political, not literary. But even apart from this, there was no gainsaying the political turn of the humanist's mind: his letters reveal a keen political interest.[45] Marzi, the only student of Salutati's career as chancellor, called attention to the cynical nature of many of his political letters. He explained this by noting that the humanist "did not scruple much about means, given the end he had in mind; indeed, he was disposed to admit or concede anything, so long as he pleased the Signoria and served the interests of the state at all costs, by fair means or foul."[46]

---

[43] Salutati, *Epistolario*, iv, ii, 465.
[44] Enea Silvio Piccolomini, *Commentari rerum memorabilium* (Frankfurt, 1614), p. 50; *Angelo Polizianos Tagebuch*, ed. Wesselski, p. 79.
[45] See Salutati, *Il trattato "De tyranno."*
[46] Marzi, p. 152, "il nostro ser Coluccio, per giungere a un fine, non si

His devotion to the Republic went neither unobserved nor unrewarded. He was granted Florentine citizenship *pleno iure;* he enjoyed, untaxed, the fruits of his office; and his sons were shown material preferment both in and outside Florence.[47]

In January 1399 the instructions of the Florentine ambassador to Padua included the following assignment: "Make a special plea for Ser Coluccio [Salutati's] son, Messer Lionardo, the canon of Padua. His canonry is the one previously held by the Cardinal of St. Peter. Lionardo, however, has been unable to obtain the warrant of tenure for it. Use every means at your disposal to get the lord of Padua to back the man who has both the law and the title on his side and who therefore ought to have the warrant. Say that this would be most pleasing to our chancellor, who is truly his friend and who would thus have good reasons for praising his rule. Moreover, he and his large family would always be warmly disposed toward his lordship . . . and press this matter on him as much as you can."[48]

In February 1407, some nine months after the humanist's death, the Signoria returned to the subject of his sons' preferential treatment. A directive to the Florentine ambassadors at the papal court stated: "There is another item to which you must give your special care and immediate attention: using the warmest terms you can muster, recommend Salutato and Messer Lionardo (rector of Montecatino), sons of the late Messer Coluccio, our dearly-remembered chancellor. You know how much affection the people of Florence attach to his memory, owing to his great virtues and the honor he brought to this city. Consequently,

---

curasse troppo dei mezzi, e tutto, anzi fosse disposto ad ammettere, a concedere, pur di compiacere ai suoi Signori e fare ad ogni costo, *per fas,* o *per nefas,* come suol dirsi, l'interesse dello Stato."

[47] On his sons see above Ch. IV, i.

[48] *ASF, Leg. Comm.,* 1, f. 134v, "Fa che in singularita tu parldi (sic) al signore de fatti di messer Lionardo figluolo di Ser Coluccio, el quale e calonaco (sic) di Padova e mai non a potuto avere la tenuta, et proprio quello calonacato avea el cardinale di Sancto Pietro quando vivea. E pero fa che tu el prieghi strettissimamente et con ogni efficacia per nostra parte che gli piaccia volere che costui poi ch'a el titolo el la ragione egli abbi anchora la tenuta, mostrandogli questo ci sia cosa gratissima al nostro cancellieri, el quale e veramente suo servidore ara materia di lodarsi della sua signoria et essere sempre suo egli e la sua famiglia che non e picchola. . . . e di questo el grava e strigni quanto t'e possibile." The ambassador was Biliotto di Sandro Biliotti. A letter of 5 March 1399 returned to the subject, *Ibid.,* f. 135r.

do everything in your power to help his sons. This is obviously
something you can urge at great length. The Florentines would
be very satisfied indeed if his holiness could favor your recommendations or do something else to advance their careers."[49]

As the quotations show, Coluccio Salutati evidently had cut
an impressive figure in Florence, and the honor he earned for
the Republic was in fact the part he contributed to any flattering
image of Florence entertained abroad. The very same motive,
the honor of the state, caused Rinaldo degli Albizzi to insist on
the Count of Urbino's being paid his rightful income on certain
Florentine securities;[50] and it made Cosimo de' Medici demand
more servants and horses for a certain embassy.[51] Here, therefore, as in the passages cited above, *honor* denoted a political ingredient because it was plainly defined in terms of the Republic's reputation abroad.

The tradition of appointing humanist chancellors began with
Salutati. By the middle of the fifteenth century the practice had
become a venerable custom. Thus, in the 1450's the Florentine
who made addenda to Gregorio Dati's *History of Florence* noted
that the chancellor of the Signoria was always a man "of great
esteem, learning, and renown."[52]

When Lionardo Bruni took over the chancellery at the end of
1427, he was already a celebrated figure, respected in literary,
ecclesiastical, and political circles. During his first year as chancellor Bruni composed his *Oratio in funere Nannis Strozae equitis*

[49] *Leg. Comm.*, 4, f. 11r, "fra l'altre racomandigie che a fare avete e dove
vogliamo che abbiate bene l'ochio sic: e che instantissimamente e tanto
caldamente quanto possible v'e sie che racomandiate Messer Lionardo
piovano di Montecatino e Salutato, figliuoli che furono della buona memoria
di Messer Coluccio pello adrieto nostro cancelliere. Sapete quanta affectione
a tutto questo popolo alla memoria del decto Messer Coluccio per le sue
laudabili virtu e perche sapete quanto honore questa nostra citta (sic);
istendendovi in questo quanto v'e possibile, peroche e materia diche larga-
mente potete parlare; e che la sua santita degni nelle cose lequali pe decti
figliuoli di Messer Coluccio si procurassono avergli favorevolmente raco-
mandati, pero che promovedegli ad alcuna cosa sarebbe consolatione non
pichola a tutto questo popolo."

[50] *Lib. Fab.*, 51, f. 33r, where we find Rinaldo backing the Count's
petition "quia comunis honor hoc exigit."

[51] Gutkind, p. 51, note 1.

[52] *L'Istoria*, p. 148, "di grande scienza e riputazione e fama."

florentini,[53] a declamatory work which used the occasion of Giovanni Strozzi's death to praise the Republic's history, civic institutions, territorial expansion, and humanistic achievements. Confirming Bruni as the city's foremost publicist, this work made him the leading advocate of the ideal of civic virtue. But simply having him in the chancellery was already distinctive enough, especially as the office required him to be the official intermediary between the Signoria and foreign legates in Florence. He summoned ambassadors; he conferred with them; he relayed executive messages; and he gave them appointments to appear before the Signoria. In short, he was well-known in all the major Italian courts and city-states. This explains why, in June 1429, the Sienese ambassador to Florence found it important and fitting to inform his government that Bruni "is very warmly disposed towards your lordships."[54]

At the beginning of 1434 Bruni sought and obtained membership in the wool guild. The matriculation fee was waived and he was taken in free of charge. According to the deliberations of the guild consuls, he was "the very famous and highly eloquent man, Messer Lionardo di Francesco Bruni, honorable Florentine citizen and currently chancellor of the illustrious people and Commune of Florence."[55] Nine years later he was matriculated in the Por Santa Maria guild, here too because of his reputation.

In February 1439 the legislative councils renewed and extended Bruni's extraordinary tax privilege, first conferred on him in 1416. The measure contained a frank recognition of, and reward for, his services to Florence. His *Historiarum florentini populi libri xii,* nine books of which he had already "composed in an elegant style," were especially singled out for praise. The reason given was that "the skilful representation of history and the light and brightness of learning give eternal fame and glory

---

[53] In Stephanus Baluzius, *Miscellanea,* 4 vols. (Lucae, 1761), IV, 2-7. Dated by Baron, *The Crisis,* II, 430ff.

[54] *Archivio di Stato di Siena, Concistoro,* 1916, f. 30r, "a la S(ignoria) V(ostra) amicissimo."

[55] ASF, *Lana,* 51, f. 32r-v, "domino Leonardi de aretio cancellarii floren. admissio gratis ad matriculam [in margin] . . . vir famosissimus et eloquentissimus dominus Leonardus olim Francisci Bruni, civis honorabilis florentinus, ad presens cancellarius magnifici populi," etc.

to peoples and cities."[56] Later, in September 1442, when the Signoria decided to have Bruni's *Historiarum* translated into Italian, he was allowed to choose the translator, who was to be paid up to 60.0 florins for his work.[57]

We have already seen how Florence reacted to Bruni's death. His native town, Arezzo, responded by contributing 40.0 florins to the funeral costs. He was, the Aretine Signoria declared, "the light, glory, and special fame of this our city of Arezzo."[58] Two years later, "considering what an honor his outstanding qualities were for Arezzo," the Aretines resolved to erect a statue to him.[59]

Turning next to Roberto de' Rossi and Niccolò Niccoli, we shall find it hard to define the impressions they made on their non-humanist contemporaries. The chief difficulty arises from the absence of primary source material. Having accepted few appointments to civil office, they could not easily catch the public eye, as did Salutati and Bruni; nevertheless, they enjoyed some celebrity in the city.

For years, for example, Roberto de' Rossi gave private lessons in Latin and Greek.[60] His students were a select group of young men from the ruling families: Domenico Buoninsegni (the chronicler), Cosimo de' Medici, Luca di Messer Maso degli Albizzi, Alessandro degli Alessandri, Bartolo de' Tedaldi, and "many other men of parts."[61] In an age when private teachers were sometimes considered the servants of the families they tutored, it might appear that Roberto held a subordinate social position. But this was not true in his case, as has already been shown. He was himself very highly connected socially, and families like the Albizzi, Corsini, Medici, and Strozzi were almost par-

[56] This *provvisione* was published by Santini, *Leonardo Bruni Aretino*, p. 139, "Quantam perpetuitatem fame et glorie populis ac civitatibus afferat historiarum perita descriptio ac litterarum splendor et lumen considerantes magnifici et potentes domini domini priores artium et vexillifer iustitie populi et comunis florentini et actendentes ad praeclara opera peritissimi et egregii viri domini Leonardi Francisci Bruni," etc.

[57] ASF, *Signori e Collegi, Deliberazioni*, 58, f. 36v.

[58] The document cited is in Mancini, "Aggiunte e correzioni," in L. Bruni, *Historiarum florentini populi*, I, 41.

[59] *Ibid.*, I, 42.

[60] Vespasiano, p. 405.

[61] *Ibid.*, pp. 405, 530.

venus by comparison with the Rossi, who were older by a century or more.

Roberto came to his Hellenic studies as a man of leisure. He was in his forties when he began to study Greek under Chrysoloras. Vespasiano gives this picture of his later years: "Since Roberto was unmarried, his pupils generally came to his house for their tutoring. When he went into the streets, he was often accompanied by them—young men who were much esteemed in the city because of their polite breeding and learning. He often entertained them at table."[62] That the urbane Roberto was well-known and much respected is suggested by the fact that he was sometimes invited to counsel the Signoria. He was not asked to do this on the basis of his record in office, for it was undistinguished; therefore, he must have been summoned because of his fame as a man of letters. His counsels reveal the humanist, as when he told the Signoria that men of learning had ever been opposed to war as a method of settling international disputes.[63]

Niccolò di Bartolommeo Niccoli seems to have been arrogant and socially difficult, according to all fifteenth-century accounts. He had a marked sense of his own superior social origins, probably intensified by the fact that his family were very heavy taxpayers. During a period of about half a century, he and his brothers paid some 40,000 florins in taxes of various kinds.[64] For this reason, he cannot have been very warmly disposed towards the oligarchy, but neither had he any sympathy for the humbler social orders. Guarino observed that he was always railing against Florentine statesmen and Florentine foreign policy.[65] Lorenzo di Marco Benvenuti, scion of a political family of medium rank, noted that Niccolò was fond of heaping abuse on the Republic's

[62] *Ibid.*, pp. 405-406, "Roberto non ebbe donna e istavano il più del tempo in casa sua; e quando egli andava fuori, il più delle volte v'erano con lui i più di questi cittadini, che erano avuti in grandissima riputazione, non meno per i buoni costumi che per le lettere. E più volte nell'anno Roberto dava mangiare a questi sua scolari alla filosofia."

[63] *ASF, Consulte*, 42, f. 121r.

[64] See n. 2, pp. 170-172 of Lorenzo Benvenuti, *L'Invettiva contro Niccolò Niccoli*, pp. 166-186.

[65] Guarino Veronese, *Epistolario*, ed. R. Sabbadini, 3 vols. (Venezia, 1915-1919), I, 39.

middle classes, purely on a class basis.[66] And Lionardo Bruni reported that Niccolò condemned Dante's barbarous Latin, as it made the poet fit to be read only by lowly wool workers and bakers.[67]

But no one would have taken the least interest in Niccolò, and certainly no one would have taken the trouble to pen diatribes against him, had he been an obscure man or a citizen of lowly status. The interest he provoked goes to show that he enjoyed a notable standing in the community. His closest friends, after all, were prominent Florentines—Cosimo and Lorenzo de' Medici, Guglielmo Tanagli, Agnolo Acciaiuoli, Antonio Corbinelli, and the General of the Camaldolese Order, Ambrogio Traversari. He was one of the first modern Europeans to exhibit a strong and lasting passion for collecting antique statuary, vases, Roman bronze and silver medals, marble epitaphs, paintings, and cameos.[68] Understandably enough, therefore, "no distinguished man came to Florence without visiting Niccolò," whose house "was always full of outstanding men and youths from the city's first families."[69]

The Florentine attitude towards Poggio Bracciolini is revealed by the executive debates of November and December 1456.[70] It appears that the chancellery had not been functioning smoothly and that the chancellor, Poggio, counting on his name and reputation, had neglected the office's lesser duties. Consequently, the question of reforming the office was brought up for discussion in the *Consulte e Pratiche*. The men invited to take part in the deliberations included some of the city's most prominent political figures.

All the speakers agreed that the chancellery needed to be reformed, but that Poggio's occupancy of the office was an honor for

[66] Benvenuti, *L'Invettiva*, pp. 166-186.

[67] L. Bruni, *Oratio in nebulonem maledicum*, in Zippel, *Niccolò Niccoli*, p. 77; also Bruni, *Ad Petrum Paulum Histrum Dialogus*, in Garin, *Prosatori latini del quattrocento*, p. 70.

[68] Vespasiano, pp. 438, 443.

[69] *Ibid.*, pp. 436, 438, "In Firenze non veniva uomo di condizione che non visitasse Nicolao"; "Aveva Nicolao sempre piena la casa sua d'uomini singulari, e de' primi giovani della città."

[70] Printed in Walser, pp. 404-406.

Florence. Alessandro degli Alessandri declared that Poggio "is a highly cultivated man who reflects honor on our Republic."[71] Carlo Pandolfini said that Poggio "is an excellent chancellor," but that the office had to be re-organized or "another celebrated man assigned to the post."[72] The lawyer and diplomat, Otto Niccolini, stated that "The chancellery is honored by the renowned Messer Poggio," but that younger men should be summoned to help him.[73] Bernardo di Lorenzo asserted that "We can have no better man than Messer Poggio" in the chancellery, but that Ser Bartolo, a highly-skilled notary, should carry out the heavy work of reform.[74] This view was repeated by Dietisalvi Neroni, Ugolino Martelli and Matteo Palmieri. The final report on the question was delivered on 27 December 1456. It was drawn up by Niccolini, Palmieri, and Neroni. They found that Florence "must have an esteemed and very famous chancellor for the sake of the city's honor and to serve as a good example to any worthy man who may hereafter be summoned from afar to come and serve our Signoria, as Messer Poggio was."[75] Poggio was thereupon reconfirmed in his dignity.

Carlo Marsuppini came to public notice for the first time in the autumn of 1431, when he was appointed to teach poetry, rhetoric, philosophy, Greek, and ethics at the University of Florence. Of the twenty lecturers listed in the *Studio* documents, he was to draw the second highest salary: 140 florins for the year.[76] This appointment gained him a sudden celebrity, for he was immediately considered the principal teaching competitor of the redoubtable Francesco Filelfo. Filelfo had recently lectured at the University and now anxiously sought to obtain a reappointment. The rivalry between them came to a head in 1433,

---

[71] *Ibid.*, p. 404, "et est homo doctissimus et ornatissimus pro republica nostra."

[72] *Ibid.*, p. 404, "vetus cancellarius optimus est, et deberet reformari, et si fieri non posset, provideatur de uno alio famosissimo."

[73] *Ibid.*, p. 405, "Cancelleria ornata est de domino Poggio famosissimo."

[74] *Ibid.*, p. 405, "Non possimus habere meliorem domino Poggio."

[75] *Ibid.*, pp. 405-406, "e necessario avere uno cancelliere riputato et famosissimo per honore della città et per buono exemplo di qualunche fusse electo per lo advenire e chiamato da lunga d'amamento degno come fu messer Poggio per venire a servire la nostra Signoria."

[76] Gherardi, *Statuti*, p. 414. The highest-paid lecturer, Antonio Roselli, taught medicine. He received 220 florins for the year.

when the Medici supported Carlo and an opposed faction threw its weight behind Filelfo.[77]

After the victory of the Medici, Carlo was appointed an honorary papal secretary by Eugene IV, and the appointment was renewed under Nicholas V.[78] When Bruni died in 1444, Carlo was given the chancellorship by unanimous consent. The duties of the office had been divided in 1437 and put under two separate departments, one of which, the section on foreign affairs, Bruni managed;[79] the other, which dealt with domestic affairs, was headed by Giovanni Riccio. But the two departments were reunited under Carlo, whose salary was then nearly doubled.

Although Carlo was not a prolific translator, he did produce Latin versions of two books of the *Iliad* and other bits of Greek verse. He wrote epigrams and Latin poetry, including some verses on the idea of nobility, and he composed a funeral oration for Cosimo de' Medici's mother.[80] Despite the scantiness of his output, he enjoyed a remarkable literary reputation, as indicated by his honorary appointments as papal secretary. Even Francesco Sforza invited him to honor the Milanese court by residence there, not because the Duke had the least interest in the civilization of the ancient world, but because one aspect of the competition between Italian courts was the recruitment of outstanding humanists. Carlo was also brought to the attention of the Emperor-elect, Frederick III, who passed through Florence at the beginning of 1452. The Emperor was disposed to confer a distinction on him, such as knighthood, the crown of the poet laureate, or a palatine countship with the power to create imperial notaries. But Carlo refused these honors, specifically declaring "the dignity of knighthood to be inconsistent with our customs."[81]

[77] Carlo de' Rosmini, *Vita di Francesco Filelfo*, I, 35ff.; Zippel, *Il Filelfo a Firenze*, pp. 17ff. At the height of the rivalry a hired assassin tried to kill Filelfo, who accused Marsuppini of having arranged the crime.

[78] R. Sabbadini, "Bricciole umanistiche," in *Gior. stor. d. lett. ital.*, vol. XVII (1891), p. 218; see also Vespasiano, p. 316.

[79] Luiso, "Riforma della cancelleria fiorentina," pp. 132-142.

[80] Vespasiano, p. 317; *Biblioteca Laurenziana di Firenze, Mss. Laur.*, LIII, 20; Ricci, "Una consolatoria."

[81] Sabbadini, *ibid.*, "Respondi honorem equestrem a nostro instituto esse alienum."

Attitude toward the Humanists

The Florentine esteem for Giannozzo Manetti and Matteo Palmieri is revealed by the nature of their political offices and embassies. Both were highly-gifted speakers in an age when, as we have said, eloquence was a political asset of the first order.

Manetti first came to the attention of eminent Florentines in the 1430's, when he began to take part in the discussions of the literary set. The set included Bruni, Niccoli, Marsuppini, Palmieri, Ser Filippo di Ser Ugolino, Pandolfo Pandolfini, Franco Sacchetti, occasionally L. B. Alberti, and others. They met near the stationers'· shops, opposite the Palace of the Podestà, or under the *Tetto de' Pisani* in the main government square, a meeting place which was then "the customary rendezvous of the Florentine ruling class."[82] But it was only after 1437, when Giannozzo negotiated his first embassy, that his reputation as an orator began to grow, and ten years later there was scarcely a man in Florence who excelled him in public speaking. As an ambassador in the late 1440's, his speeches to the Doge Foscari and five hundred Venetian noblemen made him the talk of Venice; in Naples he so impressed King Alfonso that he was begged to remain at the Neapolitan court; in Rome he was one of the great favorites of Nicholas V, who honored him with a secretarial post, a large pension, and the dignity of knighthood; and in Florence he surpassed all, even Carlo Marsuppini, in extemporaneous Latin oratory. In short, everything that contributed to Giannozzo's celebrity combined to make him a leading political figure, which is the reason that his enemies, powerful in their own right, resolved to ruin him.

Although Matteo Palmieri's family could boast of having had more experience in public life than Giannozzo's, the Manetti claimed one of the city's greatest commercial fortunes. Still, once Matteo and Giannozzo began their political careers, each had to give proof of his individual abilities. Like Giannozzo, Matteo first distinguished himself in one of the debating circles of the upper class[83]—it was there he cultivated a superior and forceful

[82] Della Torre, *Accademia*, p. 219.
[83] His book, *Della vita civile*, is dedicated to the prominent Alessandro degli Alessandri. The participants in this dialogue are Agnolo Pandolfini, Franco Sacchetti, Luigi Guicciardini, and Matteo Palmieri.

public manner, the mainstay of his subsequent activity in politics. But eloquence was not his only virtue: eventually his celebrity was based not only on his grace and vigor in oratory, but also on his rectitude in public office.[84]

[84] See the funeral oration in Alamanno Rinuccini, *Lettere ed orazioni*, pp. 78-85.

CHAPTER SEVEN

THE RELATION BETWEEN HUMANISM
AND FLORENTINE SOCIETY: AN ESSAY

1. NOTE

*E*SSAY in the title here is intended to denote attempt or trial. I use the word in order to distinguish this chapter from the others, where the method of analysis is, I hope, somewhat positivistic. In parts of the present chapter, however, I propose to range more freely and speculatively, in an effort to draw together the major themes of this inquiry, but above all to dwell on some of its implications, chiefly in connection with the ideas of the humanists.

2. A RETROSPECTIVE SUMMARY

Having described the social situation of Florence's early humanists and having examined their reputation in the Florentine community, we may do well to begin this section by reviewing the themes of the previous chapters.

In economic terms, the humanists we have studied belonged to the upper and upper-middle classes, into the first of which entered two men of humble origins, Bruni and Poggio. These classes constituted the first 10 or 12 per cent of all Florentine families, and the limits are so fixed because this social sector was identical, more or less, with the effective political class. We may remember that Salutati, one of the Republic's highest-paid functionaries, put his earnings into country estates, a precious collection of manuscripts, and government securities. Roberto de' Rossi, who also possessed a valuable manuscript collection, was the poorest of the humanists: he owned a large urban house, lived on the income from a farm of medium size, and entertained liberally. Cino Rinuccini, landowner, merchant, and big investor in the Monte, was one of the ten richest men in Florence. Niccolò Niccoli inherited a very large fortune; a good deal of it was absorbed by taxation, but some he squandered on dress and amusements, part he may have lost in business investments, and the rest he put into manuscripts, *objets d'art,* and beautiful household furnishings. Lionardo Bruni seems to have been heir only to his family's house in Arezzo; but he gradually amassed a fortune and in the last twenty years of his life was one of Florence's wealthiest citizens. Giannozzo Manetti and Carlo Marsuppini inherited enormous fortunes, chiefly involving finance capital and government securities. Poggio Bracciolini, on the other hand, who came into an insignificant inheritance, acquired his own wealth, and in the 1450's headed one of the city's first 140 families. Matteo Palmieri, the son of a well-to-do confectioner and druggist, lived as a *rentier* most of his life: his chief sources of income were farmlands and investments in the Monte. Leon Battista Alberti grew up accustomed to wealth, but in his early manhood two uncles fraudulently deprived him of a fortune. Later, he took a degree in canon law and had no trouble obtaining ecclesiastical sinecures.

In political terms, our group of humanists belonged to the governing class, the sector from which the Republic drew its statesmen, governors, and administrators. We saw, for example, that Salutati's prestige enabled him to bring great authority to his secretarial post and to get three of his sons into the middle ranks of government. Roberto de' Rossi held only seven offices during his lifetime; hence his formal career in public life was relatively insignificant, though he was sometimes invited to counsel the Signoria. Cino Rinuccini's record in office was not examined, owing to the fact that his family suffered from political vendetta in the 1380's and were excluded from all major offices for nearly half a century. Cino himself, who was appointed a guild consul on four or five occasions, made only several appearances in the legislative councils. Niccolò Niccoli, like his father and brothers, exhibited no calling for public affairs, although he accepted a few minor offices and a half-dozen turns of duty in the legislative councils. Lionardo Bruni directed the Florentine chancellery for nearly seventeen years. He also solicited and obtained more than a dozen other appointments to magistracies such as the Signoria, the Twelve Good Men, the semi-dictatorial Ten of War, and the powerful Eight on Security. Giannozzo Manetti was one of Florence's foremost statesmen in the 1440's and early 1450's:

his range of dignities included governorships, embassies, the Signoria, and highly-coveted administrative posts. Matteo Palmieri, who attained the supreme magistracy (Standard-bearer of Justice), appeared and reappeared in the Signoria, the Ten of War, the Eight on Security, embassies, and important governorships. Carlo Marsuppini directed the Florentine chancellery for nearly ten years, and he was long active in the consulate of the lawyers' guild, but not in other departments of government. Poggio Bracciolini, who also headed the chancellery and often served his guild consulate, obtained a term of office in the Signoria. As for Leon Battista Alberti, who spent most of his life away from Florence, he was in orders and consequently not in a position to pursue a career in public life.

Turning next to family traditions, we found that the experience of the humanists was not uniform. They were descended from both old and new stock. The Alberti, Manetti, Palmieri, Rossi, and Rinuccini were families whose residence in Florence pre-dated 1280. With one or two exceptions, their money went back for generations. Politically, their traditions were uneven. For example, the political heydey of the Rossi was the thirteenth century, but in the fourteenth century they were prominent *magnati* in the critically influential *Parte Guelfa*. By contrast, the Manetti of the same period appeared only in minor administrative offices, though their political connections were always good owing to selective marriage alliances. The Alberti and Rinuccini were important political families in the fourteenth century, though not of the same magnitude. In the 1380's and 1390's they were driven out of office, and it was not until the 1430's that they returned to public life in full force. Niccolò Niccoli's family amassed a considerable fortune before the middle of the fourteenth century; but unlike some of the great houses that came later (e.g., the Martelli, Pucci, and Cocchi-Donati), the Niccoli failed to realize the political promise inherent in their wealth. Only one member of the family, Messer Jacopo, became something of a public figure.

Four humanists could not lay claim to Florentine traditions: Coluccio Salutati, Lionardo Bruni, Poggio Bracciolini, and Carlo Marsuppini. The Salutati and Marsuppini were old county families, native to Stignano and Arezzo. On their arrival in Florence, they already possessed armorial bearings. Coluccio was the founder of the Florentine branch of his house. The Marsuppini were established in Florence by Carlo's father, a wealthy doctor of law, but Carlo himself was the first member of his house to attain distinction in Florentine political society. In like manner, Lionardo Bruni and Poggio Bracciolini were the first of their families to obtain Florentine citizenship. Unlike the other humanists, however, their social point of departure was not the upper or upper-middle class in Florence or elsewhere, but the *petite bourgeoisie* of Arezzo and Terranuova. They abandoned these towns in their youth to study law in Florence, where they joined the company of men born into the city's ruling families. Thenceforth, neither Bruni nor Poggio ever turned from, or fell below, that sector of society.

In marriage, finally, the humanists gave additional testament of their place in society. Only five marriages were examined, each involving either a powerful political family (the Castellani, Corsini, and Serragli) or an illustrious old house (the Buondelmonti and Tebalducci). Greater breadth could have been given to this part of our study by including a brief analysis of related marriages, but no essential change would have been wrought in the conclusions, for the unexamined marriages also involved socially prominent families. Thus, Cino Rinuccini married into ancient feudal nobility, the Adimari. The Niccoli were allied by marriage with the Brancacci and Del Toso, influential political families. Giannozzo Manetti's twice-married brother, Filippo, associated the Manetti with two outstanding families of the oligarchy, the Capponi and Strozzi. Finally, Carlo Marsuppini's brothers contracted marriages with the illustrious Peruzzi and Altoviti and with a rich new family often found in leading public offices, the Carducci.

3. THE SOCIAL BASIS OF HUMANISM: APPENDIX I

A ruling class in historical parlance is one which runs the political affairs of the community. It is made up of men who have wealth and political skill, or who may alone enjoy the privilege of political power and the habit of command. Very often, of course, the men who rule communities can lay claim to all these factors. A ruling class also determines or limits and draws support from the dominant values of the community, values which the members of the class itself esteem or consider vital and necessary. Appropriately enough, such values—whatever else they may do—go to vindicate or secure the place of the ruling class in the community, and not in a random fashion. For economic power and political hegemony tend to go together: the interests of wealth and of those who govern tend to coincide. Where the two are divided, we are apt to get a malfunctioning of institutions. Imbalances arise, discontent becomes public, and in the long run a political or social transformation may well ensue.

The point of this section will be to show that nearly all the men associated with the humanist movement in Florence, not merely the leading humanists, belonged to the ranks of the ruling class. We shall use the profiles in Appendix I to establish this.

The forty-five profiles may be divided according to three classifications: occupation, social tradition, and political stature. I select these classifications because they are, as we shall see, the most meaningful in the context of this chapter.

Taking up first the question of their occupational commitments, we find that about seventeen men out of the forty-five were actively involved in commerce and banking. Since there was occupational overlapping, a few may be taken from or added to this category. Next, eight or more of the forty-five were gentlemen of leisure: namely, men who tended to live entirely off their landed estates, business investments, or government securities. And some eighteen or twenty were professional men. The professional men fall on the whole into two groups: clerics and men in the legal profession (lawyers and notaries). Traversari, Tornaquinci, Marsigli, Dati, Agli, and Buondelmonti were all in holy orders. Pietro di Ser Mino eventually became a cleric. The lawyers were Buonaccorso da Montemagno, Giuliano Davanzati, Guglielmo Tanagli, Giovanni di Gherardo, and Benedetto Accolti. Also in the legal profession were the notaries Domenico da Prato, Antonio di Mario, Giovanni di Messer Nello, and Pietro di Ser Mino before his taking holy vows. Jacopo da Scarperia was

a "professional" humanist and papal secretary, Giovanni Malpaghini a lecturer and university professor, Giovanni Aretino an
expert copyist, Lapo da Castiglionchio a university professor and
papal secretary, and Antonio Rossi a private tutor who may in
later years have got a place in the papal curia. The doctor of
medicine, Paolo Toscanelli, could be ranked with the men of
leisure, for his friend Vespasiano informs us that he was nearly
always occupied with his studies. Occasionally, however, "he
went out to medicate one of his friends, although he did not
practice his profession much" (Vespasiano). About eight of the
forty-five, as we have said, seem to have followed neither trade
nor profession: Antonio Corbinelli, Franco Sacchetti, Agnolo
Acciaiuoli, Niccolò della Luna, Andrea Alamanni, Donato Acciaiuoli, Piero de' Pazzi, and Alamanno Rinuccini. Several of
these men had some business experience and we should bear this
fact in mind. Piero de' Pazzi, for example, was at one point engaged in banking and Corbinelli knew the wool trade from
youthful experience.

Seventeen others have not been mentioned by name. These
were the men actively engaged in business enterprise. But we
must be careful not to conceal the ambiguities here. For it is
difficult to see how statesmen like Alessandro degli Alessandri
and Agnolo Pandolfini, two of the seventeen, could have given
much time to their business interests, considering their many-
sided political activity. Moreover, their lands and businesses were
evidently managed in such a fashion as to release them even for
long hours of study and literary conversation. Palla Strozzi,
Lorenzo Benvenuti, Cosimo de' Medici, Niccolà de' Medici, and
some of the others also astonish us by the amount of time they
seem to have devoted to these pursuits.

If next we consider the forty-five men in the light of their
appropriate traditions or social strata, we find that at least thirty-
three were *grands bourgeois* and noblemen. Three others—Parenti, Ceffi, and Benvenuti—were descended from families which
achieved social place relatively late, the fourteenth century, but
they were all men of rank and wealth. Another three were born
into substantial middle-class families from the Florentine dominion: Giovanni Gherardi (Prato), Domenico del Maestro Andrea

(Prato), and Giovanni di Messer Nello (S. Gimignano). The remaining six had diverse backgrounds. Toscanelli and Pietro di Ser Mino were descended from solid middle-class families whose Florentine connections went back for a century or more, but which had not quite the standing of the Parenti or Ceffi. Toscanelli's father and grandfather were physicians, while Pietro's forebears had been notaries for at least three generations. Finally, we can say virtually nothing concerning the social traditions of four men: Giovanni Malpaghini, Antonio di Mario, Giovanni Aretino, and Antonio Rossi. I suspect that the four were descended from solid professional or merchant families and give reasons for my suspicion in Appendix I, but as yet I can provide no documentary proof.

The fact that I attribute a distinguished social position to the lawyers—all those I have mentioned were doctors of law—will not surprise the experienced student. For the lawyer was usually allied to the powerful burgher class or to the nobility by family ties, political and guild traditions, social custom, marriage, dignity of occupation, or more than likely all of these. Upstart families sometimes tried to secure or enhance their newly-won social position by sending one of their sons to law school. This was done by the three most powerful upstart houses of fifteenth century Florence: the Martelli, Pucci, and Cocchi-Donati. All produced one doctor of law who became very active in political affairs.

The moment we start to assess the forty-five men in political terms, their homogeneity as a group is clearer. Most of them, more than thirty, came from well-known political families, even if in some cases (e.g., Cristoforo Buondelmonti and Jacopo Tornaquinci) they were not themselves active in politics. Six or eight were born into the city's most celebrated political houses, and a few made their own way in public life—Pietro di Ser Mino, Buonaccorso da Montemagno, and Benedetto Accolti. Even Jacopo da Scarperia was descended from a family, the Sostegni, with a good record of experience in the administrative cadres of government. According to Uzielli, Paolo Toscanelli was born into a family which held no offices in the Republic. This detachment from public life he shared with four others treated in

Humanism and Florentine Society

Appendix I: Domenico del Maestro Andrea, Giovanni di Messer Nello, Giovanni Aretino, and Antonio Rossi, who seem to have had no political connections, although Giovanni di Messer Nello's father was a prominent diplomat and counsellor to the Signoria around 1420. As for the copyist and producer of elegant Latin manuscripts, Ser Antonio di Mario, even he held down a few of the government posts especially open to notaries. The professor of rhetoric and lecturer on Dante, Giovanni Malpaghini of Ravenna, appears to have been the only other one of the forty-five who did not appear in official circles as a public servant. Moving to Florence as an older man, he came under the protection of influential Florentine friends, but did not become a citizen nor involve himself in political affairs. On the other hand, even some of the clerics of the group became political personages, for their ecclesiastical dignities not infrequently required them to exercise their authority in public matters: such were Traversari, Dati, and Agli. Finally, in the case of Luigi Marsigli, friend to the Alberti and the counts of Poppi, the Republic did not hesitate to charge him with political missions or to consult him on questions of papal politics.

When the biographical sketches of Appendix I are combined with those of the eleven figures discussed in the main body of the text,[1] we have a body of more than fifty men, all connected in one way or another with the fortunes of humanism in Florence. The main conclusion to be drawn from the review of their backgrounds seems evident: with some exceptions, the men attracted to humanism were drawn from the ruling sectors of society—the great merchants and bankers, the administrative class, the professional class. Even the exceptions involved men most of whom swiftly found their way into these circles.

The nature of its social recruitment indicates why humanism came to dominate the literary culture of Florence in the fifteenth century. In part, in large part, the force of humanism in the Florentine community was the disguised force of the ruling class itself. Associated with noblemen, famous chancellors, and *grands bourgeois*, how could it fail to share their social luster? How could it fail to develop into an influential social force? The

---

[1] Included in the eleven is Filippo de Ser Ugolino Pieruzzi, treated in Ch. II, pp. 69-70.

culture of educated statesmen and rich merchants, of lawyers and *rentiers*, and of great men of the cloth, humanism was bound to be admired and coveted. It was identified with place, power and good breeding. The *studia humanitatis* must therefore have struck contemporaries as difficult and expensive to cultivate, and perhaps best suited to the happy few. This is one of the main reasons for the high advantages enjoyed by humanist tutors, even of humble social origin. Taken into the great houses in their youth or early manhood, such men (e.g., Tommaso of Sarzana and Ludovico Pontano) were treated as friends, as men of respected rank, not as servants. Antonio Rossi and Giovanni di Messer Nello were men of this type; they are indeed the only ones we have found so far among the figures who may be properly associated with Florentine humanism.

Let us turn for a moment to a matter of strategy. On first glance it appears that the link between an intellectual movement and social groups can be established in either of two ways: by a social study of the men associated with the movement, or by scrutinizing the social and political viewpoints in the major ideas of the movement and examining these in their historical context, particularly in relation to the distribution of political and economic power. But it is illusory to suppose that the second of these approaches can be separated from the first. For half the data of the second approach—the investigation of viewpoints in relation to social contexts—must come from a prior study of the men connected with the movement, a study with reference to classes, institutions, and the power of place, office, family, wealth, and social custom.

I chose to make this inquiry a study of men. The time has come, however, to discuss a few of the key topics in the program of humanism, in order to trace the connections between the groups which exercised power in the Florentine community and the ideas and interests of the humanists.

4. THE GENESIS OF CIVIC HUMANISM

Between 1397 and 1406 new accents and ideas are rapidly introduced into the content of Florentine humanism, particularly as reflected in the writings of Lionardo Bruni and Coluccio

Salutati.[2] A kindred note is struck in works by Cino Rinuccini and Goro Dati,[3] although Rinuccini held an intellectual place at the edges of the humanist group, while Dati—a silk merchant much taken up with his own business affairs—was perhaps not directly in touch with the humanists at all. The changes in the make-up of humanism around 1400 involve a more sustained and pressing concern with Florence's traditions as an independent political community, a fervent interest in the city's Roman-republican origins, preoccupation with its role as the leader of republican liberty in Italy, and belief in its great importance as the chief stronghold against the spread of despotic rule in the central regions of the peninsula. The virtues of an active life in worldly affairs are held up to the highest praise. Personified by Cicero, republican and patriot, the citizen moved by a deep sense of public spirit becomes in Florence the new urgent ideal. Prominence is given in humanistic literature to the *uomini-illustri* theme —historical personages who contributed to the honor, achievements, or fame of their native lands. And closely connected with this intellectual trend is the reading fashionable in cultivated Florentine circles, Plutarch's biographies of celebrated public figures in the new Latin translations started by Lionardo Bruni and Jacopo da Scarperia in the second quinquennium of the fifteenth century.

Bringing textual and historical criticism into striking combination with analysis of political and diplomatic events, Hans Baron has demonstrated that this genesis of new ideas, the birth of civic humanism, was to a large extent a function of the Florentine experience with Giangaleazzo Visconti and his policy of aggrandizement in northern and central Italy.[4] In the course of the 1390's, through the skillful deployment of Milanese armies and agents, Giangaleazzo managed to isolate Florence. His aim was to take the city, first cutting off all allies and military buffers. In 1402 Milanese troops finally entered Bologna. The noose was

---

[2] I am not thinking here of Salutati's *De Tyranno* (*ca.* 1400), which raises some exceedingly difficult problems. Cf. Baron, *The Crisis*, I, 121-139.

[3] Rinuccini, *Risponsiva alla invettiva di Messer Antonio Lusco*, in Salutati, *Invectiva in Antonium Luschum*; Dati, *L'Istoria*.

[4] See especially "A Struggle for Liberty in the Renaissance," pp. 265-289, 544-570; *The Crisis of the Early Italian Renaissance*; and *Humanistic and Political Literature. . . .*

complete: Siena, Pisa, Lucca, Perugia, Cortona, and other key towns of Umbria and Tuscany had all been taken. Florence was surrounded and would have fallen, had not the Duke of Milan suddenly died. During these years the Republic underwent an acute *crise de conscience politique*, and from this critical experience, according to Baron, were born the ideas and new accents concerning the city's republican origins and traditions, the crucial place of her free existence in the system of independent Italian states, and the realignment in the intellectual controversy between exponents of the active political life and those who extolled the merits of the apolitical contemplative existence, a life of pure study and thought.

Baron's conception of events and ideas in Florence around 1400 has both amplitude and very particular virtues.[5] It permits a more accurate dating of some of the period's most important humanist sources, and it points clearly and persuasively to the organic link between humanism and the outstanding political question of the day. Consequently Baron's approach to ideas does not become an academic exercise in pure intellectual history, but turns rather on the analysis of a specific set of ideas in a concrete political and historical setting. Still another virtue of his account is that while dealing with the new stresses and ideas of around 1400, he isolates the factors that acted as a catalyst on some of the vague notions already current in the 1370's and 1380's— a catalyst which swiftly produced a full-blown ideology, a specific program of political and cultural orientation. This change was to leave its permanent mark on subsequent Florentine thought, especially with regard to those themes that culminated in the political and social science of men like Machiavelli, Guicciardini, and Giannotti.

In the discussion that follows, I should like to offer an analysis intended to complement Hans Baron's new perspective and insights, and centered around the social and political situation in Florence proper. Baron himself has observed that the Florentine

---

[5] See Claudio Varese's review of Baron's *The Crisis* in *La Rassegna della letteratura italiana*, vii, 1 (Jan.-March, 1957), 106-108; Giulio Cervani, "Il rinascimento italiano nella interpretazione di Hans Baron," *Nuova rivista storica*, xxxix, 3 (1955), 429-503; and the more critical review-discussion by Gennaro Sasso, " 'Florentina libertas' e rinascimento italiano nell' opera di Hans Baron," *Rivista storica italiana*, lxix, 2 (1957), 250-276.

Humanism and Florentine Society

struggle against "the progress of tyranny"—waged essentially outside the city—was not "the only one among the political, or social, or economic factors which may have acted upon the period of transition around 1400."[6] And since writing this, he has published a commentary on two scholarly papers, where he goes into some of the Republic's internal political and social features, adopting an *impostazione* or formulation similar in approach to that of the succeeding pages.[7]

Let us begin with a question which goes, I believe, to the heart of things. Why did Florence stubbornly oppose the relentless advance of Giangaleazzo Visconti, his armies and agents, when all other cities in his path surrendered or collapsed, usually because of defectors and malcontents within? When we answer this question, we shall know something about conditions inside the city, the social and economic conditions which enabled Florentines to develop an ideology against the Duke of Milan at the very moment when writers and humanists nearly everywhere else in central Italy were flocking to the Milanese camp, "ready to celebrate the Viscontean conquests as the long over-due and hoped-for defeat of particularism and unending strife."[8]

In trying to answer this question, one of Baron's perceptions may serve as our point of departure: "From whatever side we approach Florentine conduct in 1402 we are thus led to the conclusion that, in the hour of crisis, moral and ideological forces were at work to help the Florentines to pursue a course different from that of the rest of Italy. In all the other old Italian city-republics *readiness* to obey a unifying 'new Caesar' made citizens and publicists forget their pride in a past of independence and civic freedom."[9]

The word *readiness* here can only refer to the history of internal strife in all the central and north Italian cities, a history which had driven many of them to the final political despair: that of abdicating power by setting up dictatorships which were above all intended to end the strife between factions and classes.

[6] Baron, *The Crisis*, I, viii.
[7] "The Social Background of Political Liberty in the Early Italian Renaissance," *Comparative Studies in Society and History*, II, 4 (July 1960), 440-451.
[8] Baron, *The Crisis*, I, 29.
[9] *Ibid.*, I, 36. Italics mine.

Humanism and Florentine Society

But Florence was an exception: judging by the condition of her political institutions in 1400, the internal conflicts of the Trecento had not gone so far that a despairing solution was necessary or inevitable. The ruling families continued unflinchingly to exhibit faith in their capacity to govern. By a series of *coups* and moves in 1382, 1387, and 1393 they had taken more and more power away from the minor guilds and enemies of the regime, until the lower middle class—and this was as far as the political franchise ever extended in Florence—was left with only one-fourth the seats in the legislative councils and one-fourth to one-fifth the seats in the small but extremely important magistracies. Why should the ruling class doubt its governing abilities?

The discontent of the textile workers and *minori* was not such that it could be manipulated to set up a permanent dictatorship. In September 1378 the feasibility of isolating the workers from all other social groups had been amply demonstrated, since they were cut off then even from the lowliest artisans of the *petite bourgeoisie*, the humble dyers and shirtmakers. Absolutely devoid of political experience, socially isolated and scorned, disorganized—for they were traditionally barred by law from having their own guild—the Florentine textile workers could constitute neither a dependable nor an efficient political force. Furthermore, to look beyond Florence for a moment, they were under the additional handicap of being surrounded by concentric circles of lordships, merchant oligarchies, and principalities. Ultimately, no regime based on the *popolo minuto* could prevail against these.

Much more effective, experienced, and dangerous, the lower middle classes had in recent decades controlled up to one-half the places in government. The *coups* of 1387 and 1393, however, reduced their quota to one-fourth and one-fifth, depending on the council or magistracy. The leaders of the oligarchy, men like Maso degli Albizzi and Niccolò da Uzzano, displayed so much vigor and skill in the two decades or so after 1393, and despite the occasional plot their class backing was so dependable, that the men of the *arti minori* were compelled to content themselves with a lesser place in government. Nevertheless, we must not underestimate the significance of this place. Although the families of the greater guilds maintained the substance of power, and majorities of two-thirds were required to carry legislation or produce executive action, at the same time the minor guilds-man's sense of his own participation in government apparently sufficed to siphon off some discontent and lend stability to the regime. We must remember, moreover, that the shopkeepers and craftsmen also had their men of prominence and substance who tended to monopolize the important places in government al-lotted to the *arti minori*.[10] Judging by their meekness in the executive councils of around 1400,[11] however, and by the acqui-escence suggested in their manner of voting, these men must sometimes have thrown their weight against the more unpleasant forms of discontent within the minor guilds, thus serving also as agents of political stability.

During much of the fourteenth century, particularly the middle decades, there was an influx of new men into government.[12] Although this created tension and hostility in the dominant social strata, it prevented graver tensions of another type and tempo-rarily widened the base of the regime. By 1400, however, the influx of new men had been reduced to a trickle, and the ones who had attained office were now part of the ruling class, at any rate as junior members.

Turning next to the regime's largest and most important group, the representatives of the older or by now traditional ruling class (i.e., the *scioperati, magnati,* and above all the men of the *arti maggiori*), we find that their large numbers would appear to justify our claim that Florentine government was based on a moderately large sector of the more substantial classes: the medium and upper ranks of the bourgeoisie, the nobility in smaller proportions, and a nominal part of the artisan and small-shopkeeping class. Yet we must not be taken in, as in their propaganda (not in their more detached moments) the human-

10 For the early fifteenth century compare, for example, the careers of Banco di Sandro ("coltriciaio") and Piero di Lorenzo di Angiolino ("pe-zarius"), ASF, *Tratte,* 79, 80, under such offices as the "Octo custodiae," "Regulatores," and catasto officials.
11 Note, for example, their infrequent recommendations in ASF, *Consulte,* 35-40.
12 On this whole question see especially Brucker, *Political Conflict in the Florentine Commune: 1343-1378;* cf. also now his *Florentine Politics and Society,* Ch. I.

ists sometimes were. We must not confuse appearance with reality. For propaganda purposes, for reasons of political expedience, and for the humanists in their idealization of the Florentine constitution, Florence might indeed seem a representative democracy of twenty-one guilds, founded on the equality of its citizens.[13] But as Schevill observed, speaking with particular reference to the Albizzi period, "it was in reality a government conducted by, and in the interest of, a small class of the well-to-do. In actual practice, however, even a class government is not run by all its members but rather by a few capable and ambitious individuals."[14] If Schevill meant that Florentine government at the top level was conducted exclusively by the well-to-do, he was wrong. But he was right to speak of it as government in the interests of the well-to-do and right to emphasize the leadership of an oligarchy.

The economic situation, finally, also served to buoy up the confidence of the groups whose power in the city was decisive. The prestanze registers offer some support here. For the numerous entries these record, the high proportion of heavy imposts, and the continuing record of payments made on time, all crudely indicate that the Florentine economy was going through one of its better periods, at least until the movement of commercial traffic was temporarily disrupted by the Viscontean wars. After 1402, however, business picked up again for a generation or more, owing in part to the Florentine acquisitions of Pisa and Livorno.

This analysis provides us, I believe, with the range of pressures and factors that composed the social and political background both of humanism and of the Republic's *readiness* to oppose the Duke of Milan with great determination. First, there was the powerful desire of a still vigorous class, the *grande bourgeoisie*, to govern itself, and hence a belief in its own capacity to rule the city. This belief was reinforced by the successful *coups* of 1382, 1387, and 1393, which also virtually brought to an end the

---

[13] See Lionardo Bruni's remarks in his epistolary description (1413) of the Florentine constitution. The letter is printed in full in Baron, *Humanistic and Political Literature*, pp. 181-184. On a similar set of idealistic representations see Poggio's letter (1438) to Filippo Maria Visconti, in his *Epistolae*, 3 vols., ed. T. de Tonellis (Florence, 1832), II, 183-186.

[14] *History of Florence*, pp. 340-341.

influx of newcomers into government. Then there was the fact that all political sectors of the populace drew loyally around the ruling group during the most critical years (1397-1402) of the Viscontean menace, thus further buttressing the oligarchy's political confidence.[15] This was followed by the conquest of Pisa (1406), the successful resistance during the years 1409-1414 to the ambitions of King Ladislaus, and the purchase of Livorno (1421), all of which served, in the eyes of the populace, to cast a halo of success and durability over the regime. But the most important matter turned on the fact that although the oligarchy always held on to the substance of power, there remained the illusion that power was truly distributed according to constitutional forms. The oligarchy derived two advantages from this: government in Florence was invested with the appearance of being more representative than in fact it was, and it enjoyed a support in the community which went far beyond the real social base of the *reggimento*.

In the optimistic climate of these years (the 1380's and after), the ruling class produced a group of men profoundly interested in the study of antiquity and its literature. Owing to their place in Florentine society, it was *their* social point of view, rather than another, which naturally prevailed in the new program of study. The names which have come down to us are Roberto de' Rossi, Jacopo da Scarperia, Palla Strozzi, Antonio and Angelo Corbinelli, Bartolommeo Valori, Jacopo Corbizzi, and Niccolò Niccoli. Coluccio Salutati, of course, was in his way a preceptor to all. Deeply involved as he was in politics, like the families of most of these men, his civic outlook was one to which they were accustomed. Ugolino Pieruzzi and Pietro di Ser Mino, men with rich experience in public affairs, were also associated with the new intellectual movement. On the edges of this humanist group, though very much their social peers, were Cino Rinuccini, Filippo Villani, and Gregorio Dati. The next generation of such men, to name only a few, included Domenico Buoninsegni, Alessandro degli Alessandri, Lorenzo Benvenuti, Cosimo and Lorenzo de' Medici, Buonaccorso da Montemagno, Franco Sacchetti, Matteo

---

[15] There were of course occasional minor conspiracies. Caggese, *Firenze*, ii, 325-327.

Attitude toward the Humanists

Humanism and Florentine Society

Humanism and Florentine Society

Appendix I: Profiles

4. *Ambrogio di Bencivenni Traversari: 1386-1439.* Ambrogio's place in the history of Christian humanism is so well known that its recitation here would be superfluous. But it may be well to recall that he seems to have enjoyed a humanistic reputation among contemporaries almost as great as Lionardo Bruni's. Yet he had not like Bruni been favored with the opportunity to study with Chrysoloras, and while he may have had some help from Niccolò Niccoli in the study of Greek (although Niccoli's Greek was rudimentary at best), he seems to have been an auto-didact in Hebrew. Ambrogio made some manuscript discoveries (e.g., the letters of Cyprian and thirty-nine homilies of Origen) and did Latin translations of works, or parts thereof, by Diogenes Laertius, Chrysostom, Basilius, Dionysius the Areopagite, Gregorius Nyssenus, and various others. He often dictated his translations to Niccoli, "who was a very swift writer indeed, though he could not keep up with that which friar Ambrogio translated into a polished style ('ornatissimo istile'), requiring no further changes" (Vespasiano). His letters, like those of Bruni, Guarino, and others, were in great demand and he left a fascinating diary-report (the *Hodoeporicon*) of his visits to Camaldolese convents in the early 1430's.

Vespasiano declared that he came of poor country stock. Scholarship (Tiraboschi, Dini-Traversari) has since corrected this to show that he was descended from the ancient and powerful Traversari house of Ravenna. Just after 1300 the friar's branch of the family moved to Portico in the Romagna, a castle at the foot of the Tuscan Apennines. There too Ambrogio's forebears seem to have had large estates. His father, Bencivenni, was a prominent figure in Portico. Through the humanist's relations in Florence, his sister Agostina—who must have had a substantial dowry—was married into an honorable old Florentine family, the Morelli, important men in the S. Croce quarter.

Ambrogio arrived in Florence in 1400 to enter the Camaldolese convent of Santa Maria degli Angeli. The convent became a famous meeting place, frequented by humanists, statesmen, prelates, and visiting literati. It is there Ambrogio established strong and lasting friendships with men like Niccolò Niccoli, Cosimo and Lorenzo de' Medici, Carlo Marsuppini, Agnolo Acciaiuoli,

Giannozzo Manetti, Paolo Toscanelli, Filippo di Ser Ugolino, and many others both from Florence and elsewhere. In Venice, for example, his closest friends were two humanist-patricians: Leonardo Giustiniani and Francesco Barbaro.

Ambrogio was made General of the Camaldolese Order in 1431. This undoubtedly added to his stature, though he was already greatly respected by powerful statesmen like Bartolommeo Valori, Palla di Nofri Strozzi, and Rinaldo degli Albizzi. When in 1433 a palace revolution in Florence brought about the arrest of Cosimo de' Medici, Ambrogio, then in Bologna, rushed back to Florence and went before the Signoria to implore or negotiate his release. He also confronted his many friends— enemies of the Medici in some cases—hoping to influence them in Cosimo's favor; and he records (in the *Hodoeporicon*) a fascinating interview with Rinaldo degli Albizzi, the details of which are such that we cannot doubt Ambrogio's authority. This authority was to be felt once again in his activities at the Council of Ferrara–Florence.

Sources: Mehus, Traversari, *Epistolae et orationes*; Vespasiano, *Vite*, pp. 243-248; Tiraboschi, *Storia della letteratura italiana*, VI, ii, 788-791; Alessandro Dini-Traversari, *Ambrogio Traversari e i suoi tempi* (Florence, 1912), appended to which is the *Hodoeporicon*; and P. Ricci, "Ambrogio Traversari," in *Rinascita*, II (1939), 578-612.

5. *Giovanni Gherardi da Prato: 1367-ca. 1444.* Author of the famous *Paradiso degli Alberti*, a participant therefore in some of the learned conversations held at the Villa Paradiso in the late fourteenth century, Giovanni in his early manhood sought the company of men like Salutati, Marsigli, and Cino Rinuccini. Hans Baron has emphasized Giovanni's attachment to the Volgare tradition in Florentine literary development. But apart from the fact that he "adapted himself to the achievements of Humanism," even if in a superficial fashion, his zeal for vernacular culture was vindicated "when cultivation of the Volgare was at last included in the program of the Florentine humanists." From this standpoint Giovanni's *Paradiso* "remains an important document for the history of Florentine civic Humanism" (Baron).

He was born in Prato, the son of a used-clothes merchant
("rigattiere") and grandson of a notary. The trade of the
rigattiere was more or less honorable at the time—depending on
the social station of the person considering it—and could certainly
give a comfortable life. The family, evidently on the make, sent
Giovanni to study at the University of Padua, and he took a doctorate in law sometime before 1394. Settling in Florence, where
he developed a name as a poet, he was a legal counselor for a
time, lectured on Dante at the Studio Fiorentino, and—interest-
ingly—served the city as an architectural consultant.

As he was not active in the *Arte dei Giudici e Notai* at any
point in the fifteenth century, he seems to have given up practicing law rather early. His catasto reports of 1427 and 1430 show
a man of small means: he owned a house in Prato and some farmland outside the town. He added nothing to his patrimony, for
he had inherited these properties, and his report of 1442 indicates
that for a man of his background he died in great poverty.

Sources: Giovanni da Prato, *Il Paradiso degli Alberti, ritrovi e
ragionamenti del 1389*, ed. A. Wesselofsky (Bologna, 1867),
series "Scelta di curiosità letterarie," vols. 86^i-86^{ii}; C. Guasti,
Un disegno di Giovanni di Gherardi da Prato, in Guasti's *Opere*,
vol. IV (Prato, 1897); Fr. Novati, "Giovanni Gherardi da Prato,"
Miscellanea fiorentina di erudizione e storia I, 11 (November,
1886), 161-171; Baron, *The Crisis of the Early Italian Renaissance*, I, 297ff.; Baron, *Humanistic and Political Literature in
Florence and Venice*, pp. 13-37.

6. *Agnolo Pandolfini: 1360-1446.* Alberti considered him a "most
learned man." Vespasiano praises his Latin erudition and especially stresses his learning in moral and natural philosophy. Agnolo enjoyed the friendship of nearly all the learned Florentines
of the first half of the Quattrocento, but he was particularly close
to Lionardo Bruni, who "released nothing for publication which
he [Bruni] had translated or composed, if he had not first obtained Agnolo Pandolfini's opinion of it" (Vespasiano). The
measure of Agnolo's reputation among leading humanists is perhaps indicated by the fact that he appears as the chief inter-

locutor in two well-known dialogues of the period: Palmieri's *Della vita civile* and Alberti's *Della tranquillità dell' animo.*

The Pandolfini moved from Signa to Florence in the early fourteenth century or before. They were very likely an old county family. The first one about whom we have specific information is Agnolo's grandfather, Ser Giovanni, a notary who lived in the early Trecento. In the next generation Agnolo's father, Filippo, was matriculated in the Por Santa Maria guild and became a prominent and rich merchant, probably in silk and spices. The first of the family to break into the Signoria (1382), Filippo then attained the chief dignity, Gonfalonier of Justice, in 1393 and 1400. He also held many other key offices.

Agnolo himself was one of the most powerful Florentine statesmen of the first forty years or so of the fifteenth century. Enormously wealthy, landlord, merchant, and exemplar of good manners, he held every major Florentine office: e.g., he was thrice Gonfalonier of Justice, twice a member of the *Decem Baliae.* The records show that he was invited to participate in the executive councils (the *Consulte e Pratiche*) hardly less often than statesmen like Maso degli Albizzi, Niccolò da Uzzano, and Neri Capponi. The Pandolfini were related by marriage to more than a score of leading families. They resided in the Chiave gonfalon of S. Giovanni.

Sources: Vespasiano, *Vite*, pp. 458-473; *BNF, Mss. Passerini,* 46; *ASF, Mariani*, v, f. 1071r; *Manoscritti*, 266, f. 27; *Catasto*, 80, see index under name "Agnolo di Filippo di Ser Giovanni"; *Consulte*, e.g., 41 (years: 1411-1413), passim; *Tratte*, 79, 80, passim. Always useful on a figure like Agnolo is Ammirato, *Istorie fiorentine*, vols. IV-V.

7. *Domenico del Maestro Andrea da Prato: ca. 1370-ca. 1433.* Chiefly remembered now as a writer of imitative love sonnets, Domenico in the 1420's also wrote a long patriotic poem concerning Florentine military and diplomatic resistance to Filippo Maria Visconti. His immediate relation to the humanists is based on a diatribe directed against them around 1420, specifically— it is thought—against Niccoli and Bruni. The diatribe is essentially a defense of Trecento vernacular literature and of the

Italian language against those humanists who would tolerate nothing other than Latin and Greek in literary matters. "Surely," he exclaimed, "the vernacular used by Dante is more genuine and praiseworthy than their Latin and Greek."

While showing that Domenico was ignorant of Bruni's real attitude towards the vernacular writers of the Trecento, Hans Baron has also observed that he must have tried at one point to keep up with the doings of the humanists, for he exhibited a familiarity with Bruni's prefaces and letters. Although opposed to the study of Greek, Domenico—a notary—was himself a Latin scholar. The interest he took in the activities of the humanists and his going so far as to make them the object of polemic both suggest that their devotions on occasion were such as to irritate or anger the more traditional-minded citizens who had a fair Latin preparation.

Casella says that Domenico probably frequented the Studio Fiorentino in the 1390's and that he may even have studied under Giovanni Malpaghini. His father was perhaps a physician or schoolmaster, but nothing definite has yet been discovered on his family background. Baron notes that he "was one of the many newcomers from the Florentine territory who entered the intellectual middle-class of the metropolis by way of the notarial profession" (*The Crisis*, ɪ, 253). Domenico's notarial protocols span the period 1415-1432. His home base was Florence, where he owned a house on the Via Larga, but his notarial work constantly took him into the Florentine dominion.

Sources: Domenico's polemic is in Gherardi's *Il Paradiso degli Alberti. Ritrovi e ragionamenti del 1389*, ed. A. Wesselofsky (Bologna, 1867), in "Scelta di curiosità letterarie," vol. 86[ii], 321-330; Mario Casella, "Ser Domenico del Maestro Andrea da Prato Rimatore del Secolo xv," *Rivista delle Biblioteche e degli Archivi*, xxvɪɪ, n. 1-5 (Jan.-May, 1916), 1-40; Baron, *The Crisis of the Early Italian Renaissance*, ɪ, 253ff., 335f., ɪɪ, 548f.

8. *Pietro di Ser Mino: fl. 1390-1424.* Pietro and his forebears were given the surname *Sermini* by later writers. The family originated in a town not far from Florence, Montevarchi, at the beginning of the fourteenth century. His father, grandfather,

great-grandfather, and Pietro himself were all notaries: i.e., men in the legal profession. The Sermini settled in the Bue section of S. Croce, where in Pietro's time they ranked financially among the first 150 families.

Pietro's grandfather, Domenico, was put up for Florentine office as early as 1354. Ser Mino held various specialized offices. In the 1390's Pietro entered the circuit of the city's important notarial posts. When Salutati died in 1406, the young man was appointed chancellor of the Republic, an office which gave him the opportunity to exercise considerable political influence. This observation is prompted in part by his correspondence with Rinaldo degli Albizzi. But he withdrew from public life in 1410, retired to a monastery just outside Florence, and subsequently became a famous preacher.

He studied rhetoric at the Studio under Giovanni Malpaghini. During the years 1400-1402, he belonged to the circle around Salutati, Rossi, Niccoli, and Bruni, who included the young notary in his *Ad Petrum Paulum Histrum Dialogus* (II), where he is described as an "adoloscens impiger atque facundus in primis." On very close terms with Salutati, who encouraged him to study, Pietro sometimes borrowed books from the old chancellor: e.g., his *De fato, fortuna et casu* in 1400 and part of his *De nobilitate legum et medicinae* in 1401. It seems fitting to add that Pietro persisted in his humanistic studies after his father had opposed this interest, preferring that the young man devote himself to more lucrative pursuits. There was a certain social stamp in this advice, the advice of a still-struggling parvenu; for as Carlo Marsuppini's father once observed, the *studia humanitatis* "are meant for honor, not gain."

Sources: ASF, Prestanze, 1995, under Ser Mino di Ser Domenico di Ser Mino da Montevarchi; Salutati, *Epistolario,* III, 422, 523, 528, 556; Bruni, *Ad Petrum Paulum Histrum Dialogus,* ed. Garin, in *Prosatori latini;* C. Guasti, ed., *Commissioni di Rinaldo degli Albizzi,* I, 123, 167, 173, 178; Marzi, *La cancelleria della repubblica fiorentina,* pp. 156-159.

9. *Palla di Nofri Strozzi: 1372-1462.* The story of the Strozzi is inseparable from the history of Florence during a large part

of the fourteenth and fifteenth centuries. They produced dozens of men who distinguished themselves in political life and in the Church, and between 1300 and 1400 no other house was represented in the Signoria so frequently. Their identity—like that of the Albizzi, Medici, and Corsini—emerges clearly for the first time in the second half of the thirteenth century. In their best days (ca. 1325-1434, and again after 1460) they were great landowners, wool merchants, and bankers on an international scale, although some Strozzi took up the profession of arms in the fifteenth century.

Palla was one of the key political figures in Florence during the 1420's and early 1430's. According to government sources, he was the city's richest man in the third decade of the century. His catasto inventory of 1427 runs to thirty-three folio pages and lists some fifty-four farms, nearly 200 separate parcels of land, upwards of thirty houses, approximately 94,000 florins in real Monte holdings, and a banking firm (assigned to the debit column on his balance sheets) with a capital of more than 45,000 florins.

When Chrysoloras arrived in Florence to teach Greek (1397), Palla, one of his first and most brilliant students, was the one who "procured the books needed for that instruction from Constantinople and Greece. He employed the best scribes of the age in Greek and Latin, and at one point entertained the idea of establishing a public library, for which he would have constructed a suitable wing at S. Trinità. Banished to Padua [in 1434], he took his misfortunes like a true stoic and never permitted anyone in his presence to speak less than honorably about his native land. He read Aristotle and the Greek fathers, or had these read to him by Andronicus Callistus and John Argyropulos, two Greeks whom he took into his house at a good salary. He himself translated various works of Greek philosophy and rhetoric into Latin, and gradually built up a beautiful collection of manuscripts, which he left to the monastery of S. Giustina" (V. Rossi). His classmate under Chrysoloras, Lionardo Bruni, seems to have been one of his closest friends in Florence.

Sources: ASF, Catasto, 76, ff. 169v-202v; Carte Strozz., 4a ser., 341; Tratte, 66, 67, 78, 79, 80, passim; Mariani, i, ff. 94r-97r; Mano-

scritti, 266, ff. 259v-261r; Palla Strozzi, "Diario," *A.S.I.*, ser. 4, xi (1883), 20-48, 145-152, 293-309; xii (1883-1884), 3-14; xiii (1884), 153-170; xiv (1885), 3-18; Guasti, ed., *Commissioni di Rinaldo degli Albizzi*, 3 vols., passim; Vespasiano, *Vite*, pp. 385-403; A. Fabroni, *Pallantis Stroctii Vita* (Parma, 1802); L. Strozzi, *Vite degli Strozzi*, ed. Stromboli (Firenze, 1892); Litta, *Famiglie celebri italiane*, v; Rossi, *Il Quattrocento* (Fr. Vallardi, Milano, 1956), pp. 34-35. The reader is advised that these references are a minimum beginning for the study of the Strozzi family in general and Palla in particular. Archives and libraries in Florence contain an enormous quantity of unpublished material on the Strozzi, especially on Palla, who has yet to find a modern biographer.

10. *Angelo di Tommaso Corbinelli: ca. 1373-1419.* Salutati engaged in a minor polemic with the Camaldolese friar, Giovanni da San Miniato, who had tried by various means to dissuade Angelo from devoting himself to humanistic study and particularly from reading the pagan poets. In this venture, however, the young man had the warm support of the celebrated chancellor, who—as Voigt observed—was almost a father to him. Like his brother Antonio, Angelo may well have been a student of Chrysoloras, but if so, he did not then learn very much Greek. In 1410-1414 he frequented Guarino's lectures at the University of Florence, and thereafter carried on a correspondence with him. We gather from one of Guarino's letters to Angelo that the latter's grasp of Greek, in 1411 at any rate, was not thorough enough to enable him to read Plutarch, but he promises Plutarch's *On Education* in Latin, a translation of which he had just completed and was dedicating to Angelo. Blum has noted that from 1415 on Antonio meant to will the use of his rich library to Angelo, but the would-be heir died first.

Angelo's most active years in Florentine public life spanned the years 1404-1419. He held consulships in the Lana guild on two occasions and a place in the Signoria once (1412), but most of his other offices were dignities of medium rank. The lion's share of the family office-quota went to two elder brothers,

Bartolommeo and Giovanni. Angelo married into a famous and powerful S. Spirito family, the Gualterotti-Bardi.

Sources: Epistolario di Guarino Veronese, ed. R. Sabbadini, 3 vols. (Venezia, 1915-1919), ɪ, 15-16, 168-169; *ASF, Notarile antecosimiano*, G 209, f. 49v. For additional information on the family and on Angelo see the material and bibliographical items in the following profile.

11. *Antonio di Tommaso Corbinelli: ca. 1377-1425.* Like Malpaghini and Niccoli, Antonio left no literary legacy. He studied under Malpaghini, Chrysoloras, and Guarino, the last of whom lived in Antonio's house during part of his residence in Florence. Guarino referred to him as "my companion of study," observed that he was well trained in Greek, that he commanded excellent Latin, and deeply mourned his death. Antonio, on his side, had been most influential in obtaining a professorship for Guarino at the Studio Fiorentino. Traversari, Niccoli, Bruni, Aurispa, and Francesco Barbaro all corresponded with Antonio or were on very amicable terms with him.

He had one of the best collections of classical manuscripts in Europe. In 1426, for example, the Visconti library contained nearly 1000 Latin manuscripts, only some 125 of which involved works by classical authors (Blum). Antonio's library, on the other hand, had only 273 titles, but at least 79 of these were Greek works. Furthermore, 105 of the Latin and 65 of the Greek manuscripts were from the classical syllabus. Some Greek authors in his library were Herodotus, Thucydides, Polybius, Plato, Aristotle, Euclid, Aeschylus, Euripides, Sophocles, Aristophanes, Demosthenes, Aeschines, Theocritus, Plutarch, Homer, and Pindar.

Resident in the S. Spirito section of Florence, the Corbinelli ranked with the most respected, powerful, and richest families in the city. Engaged in the manufacture of wool cloth during the fourteenth and fifteenth centuries, they also lent money on interest and were great landowners. They regularly served in the consulate of the Lana guild.

The Corbinelli first entered the Signoria in 1286, when the office of prior was held by Messer Albizzo Corbinelli, a doctor of law. Thereafter they continually appeared in offices at the top level of government. Between 1390 and 1440 Antonio and four of his brothers served in so many offices with such frequency as to suggest that few other Florentine families could have equalled them in this respect. Antonio was not as active in public life as his brothers, but he constantly served in the legislative councils and held nine other offices of medium to first-grade rank, including lieutenant governorships, a term of duty in the Signoria (1416), the Twelve Good Men (1418), and the powerful *Octo Custodiae* (1422), a sort of political or security police. He willed his library to the Badía Fiorentina and died at Rome in the house of a Florentine nobleman, Matteo de' Bardi, also from the S. Spirito quarter.

Sources: Rudolf Blum, *La biblioteca della Badía Fiorentina e i codici di Antonio Corbinelli* (Vatican, 1951); L. Martines, "Addenda to the Life of Antonio Corbinelli," *Rinascimento*, VIII, 1 (June 1957), 3-19.

12. *Jacopo di Niccolò Corbizzi: fl. 1415.* He corresponded with Guarino, on occasion sought out Traversari, and was a very close friend both to Antonio Corbinelli and Ser Filippo Pieruzzi. Jacopo may have been a student of Chrysoloras, as were Antonio and Ser Filippo. He certainly studied Latin rhetoric and Greek under Guarino at the Studio Fiorentino (1410-1414). His great friendship with the studious and modest Antonio Corbinelli is attested to by several facts. In 1417 the two traveled together to Camerino to escape the plague. Furthermore, he was one of the two executors of Antonio's will and on occasion, in the latter's absence from Florence, his proctor or business agent. An admirer and student of the Greek and Latin classics, Jacopo seems to have borrowed books from Antonio with great freedom. Antonio's last will and testament, bequeathing his precious library to the Badía Fiorentina, stipulates that Jacopo is to have full use of the codices, the Greek and Latin ones alike, for as long as he (Jacopo) lives. In Jacopo's own *testamento*, drawn up in 1417, we find Antonio named as one of his executors and also another interesting fact—that Jacopo had his own collection of codices (alas, they are not inventoried), since a clause is provided for their disposal.

Appendix I: Profiles

The Corbizzi were an ancient Florentine family, descended of nobles from Fiesole (Ricordano Malespini). Jacopo's branch of the house resided in S. Spirito, the other in the Chiave gonfalon of S. Giovanni. In the fourteenth and fifteenth centuries they were active in the wool trade, and in Jacopo's time at least one member of the house was moderately wealthy (see App. II, Table VI, no. 72). In public life the Corbizzi ranked with the families of the ruling class, where they occupied a political position of medium importance. Jacopo himself was in the circuit of lesser offices. He may not have been very active in trade, but his will reveals that he had some business investments, government securities, land, and cash. He stipulates, for example, that his heirs are to repay a debt of 400 florins to Messer Antonio Contarini of Venice.

Sources: ASF, Mariani, II, f. 260r; *Carte Pucci,* v, 8; *Arte di Calimala,* 13, f. 48r; *Monte Comune,* 139, f. 66r; *Notarile antecosimiano,* P 428 (Ser Filippo Pieruzzi's notarial papers for the period 1406-1423), ff. 54-55; Guarino, *Epistolario,* letters to Angelo Corbinelli. See also the items by Blum and Martines in the profile on Antonio Corbinelli.

13. *Domenico di Lionardo Buoninsegni: 1385-1467.* All the attributes that conferred social distinction in Florence the Buoninsegni enjoyed: wealth, antiquity, a tradition of public service, and strategic marriage alliances.

Possibly a fashionable cloth retailer in his youth, Domenico in his middle age was a wealthy silk merchant. In 1427 he ranked as the twelfth highest taxpayer in the S. Maria Novella quarter, with reported net assets of more than 11,500 florins. But his commercial preoccupations kept him neither from public affairs nor learning. For in the period from about 1415 to 1458 he was one of the city's principal office holders. He had four terms in the Signoria (1417, 1435, 1441, 1451), three of them as Gonfalonier of Justice; four terms in the Eight on Political and Military Security (1433, 1443, 1449, 1456); two in the famous war commission, the *Decem Baliae* (1437, 1451); three in the mint commission (1433, 1438, 1451), various terms in the colleges, the treasury, and so on for a score of other offices.

Appendix I: Profiles

A good Latinist and devotee of humanistic learning, Domenico studied "for a long time" (Vespasiano) under the tutelage of one of the city's most accomplished humanists, Roberto de' Rossi, who was especially fond of the young merchant and willed part of his library to him, though Domenico already had an excellent one. In the years when Guarino Guarini held a chair in Florence, Rossi's disciple may well have frequented the visitor's lectures at the Studio, for the two definitely struck up an acquaintance then and thereafter carried on a correspondence. Domenico was one of the period's outstanding students of Ptolemy's *Geography*. In the belief that Bruni's Latin history of Florence sufficed the literati, he wrote a well-known Florentine chronicle in the *volgare*.

Sources: ASF, Catasto, 77, f. 378r; *Mariani*, v, f. 1232r; *Tratte*, 39, f. 90v; *Carte Ancisa*, AA, ff. 370, 503; GG, ff. 248-250; *Manoscritti*, 266, under Buoninsegni; *Tratte*, 80, e.g., ff. 13v, 16v, 18v, 30r, 44r, 172r, 172v, 454r; Vespasiano, *Vite*, pp. 530-532; D. Buoninsegni, *Storia della città di Firenze, 1410-1460*; Guarino, *Epistolario*, ı, 169-170.

14. *Cristoforo Buondelmonti: fl. 1422.* A well-known family of great antiquity, the descendants of feudal lords, the Buondelmonti were in and out of public life in the course of their long and unsteady history. During the fourteenth century they were prominent in the ultra-conservative *Parte Guelfa* and often figured among the most intransigeant proponents of extreme oligarchy. In Cristoforo's period, magistracies open to the *magnati* were regularly occupied by members of this family. The reader is referred to a sketch of the family in Chapter v, 2 of this book.

Cristoforo was a priest who traveled widely in the Aegean Islands. A Latin work on his travels reflects the interests of an amateur archaeologist and antiquarian. Attaching a letter of dedication to it, he sent his *Liber insularum archipelagi* to Cardinal Giordano Orsini from Rhodes in 1422. Cristoforo was a "passionate collector of Greek codices" (Weiss).

Sources: Christoph. Buondelmontii Florentini Librum Insularum Archipelagi, ed. G. L. R. De Sinner (Leipzig and Berlin, 1824); Roberto Weiss, "Lineamenti per una storia degli studi

antiquari in Italia," *Rinascimento,* IX, 2 (1958), 179-180. For
sources on the family itself see the notes to Ch. v, 2.

15. *Niccolà di Messer Vieri de' Medici: 1385-1455.* His erudition
won him a reputation among contemporaries. Flavio Biondo
observed that he was a student of "the Aretine," meaning either
Marsuppini or Bruni, perhaps the former, since Bruni does not
seem to have done any teaching. It is more likely, however, that
Niccolà studied either under Giovanni Malpaghini or Guarino,
or both, for in 1407 he already belonged to the circle of Florentines who cultivated the classics. The letters of Poggio and Traversari, above all their letters to Niccoli, show that this banker
was not only an ardent admirer of the Latin classics, but also
that he possessed a valuable collection of manuscripts and
that he lent these freely, often to be copied, to his various
humanist friends—Poggio, Niccoli, Bruni, Traversari, and perhaps
Marsuppini. Judging by the opening lines of Alberti's *Della tranquillità dell' animo,* we must conclude that Niccolà and Alberti
had a very close friendship. Often, in fact, when taking walks
together, they "used to discuss, as was our custom, pleasant sub-
jects pertaining to the doctrine of worthy and unusual matters"
(sic). Like Tanagli, Marsuppini, Toscanelli, Bruni, and others,
Niccolà was one of the executors of Niccolò Niccoli's famous will.
In 1421 Bruni dedicated to him his Latin translation of some
orations by Demosthenes.

Since nothing is actually said about the history of the Medici
family in the profiles on Cosimo and Lorenzo, it may be useful
to offer a summary statement here.

Cosimo and Niccolà de' Medici were fourth cousins: their
kinship went back five generations to a common grandfather,
Filippo, who flourished around 1280. The Medici sprang from
landowners native to the Mugello. They seem to have moved
to Florence in the later twelfth century, but it was not until the
last decades of the thirteenth century that they first attained
public prominence, along with families like the Albizzi, Strozzi,
Capponi, and Corsini. In the course of the thirteenth century
they became money-lenders and merchants, while always keeping
up their landed connections in the Mugello. This pattern, com-

bining land, finance, and trade, was maintained by the Medici throughout the fourteenth century, although sometimes one type of investment prevailed and sometimes another—land chiefly in the later part of the century. Meanwhile, the family captured numerous seats in the Signoria (thirty-one between 1326 and 1400) and won their way into all the state's leading dignities. In 1400 all but two of the Medici houses were excluded from public office for twenty years. The two which escaped this ban included Niccolà and his brothers, and Cosimo's father and uncle. Niccolà held office during a large part of his life, but the principal honors went to Cosimo's branch of the family and to Cosimo's first cousin, Averardo. Niccolà's catasto reports show that he and his brother Cambio were wealthy bankers, landlords, and owners of a great deal of urban real estate.

Sources: The classic study on the early Medici is now Gene A. Brucker, "The Medici in the Fourteenth Century" (see the profile on Cosimo). On Niccolà himself see the following items: Poggio, *Epistolae*, e.g., ɪ, 10, 31, 73, 169, 187; Traversari, *Epistolae*, ɪɪ, viii, letters to Niccoli; Alberti, *Della tranquillità dell' animo;* Bruni, preface to his *Orationes Demosthenes*, in Baron, *L. B. Aretino, Humanistisch-Philosophische Schriften*, p. 129; Voigt, *Risorgimento dell' antichità classica*, ɪ, 308; Flamini, *Lirica toscana*, p. 287; *ASF, Archivio delle Balie*, 17, f. 153r-v; *Catasto*, 78, f. 481; 497, ff. 232-236, 552-556; *Tratte*, e.g., 67, ff. 9v, 40r; 79, ff. 22r, 50v; 80, ff. 48r, 84r.

16. *Lorenzo di Marco Benvenuti: ca. 1383-1423.* In the decade or so before his death, Lorenzo frequented men like Bruni, Traversari, Niccoli, and Poggio when the latter came to Florence. We can only speculate about who his masters were. Was Roberto de' Rossi one? Did he study grammar with Domenico di Bandino, rhetoric and poetry with Giovanni da Ravenna and Guarino, or Greek with Chrysoloras? Surely he could not have been a pupil of all, for the counting house took its toll. And yet these were the opportunities open to him in his lifetime.

He is best remembered now for his Latin diatribe against Niccolò Niccoli, written about 1420. Apart from charging Niccoli with having wrought the financial ruin of his own brothers,

Lorenzo accuses him of class snobbery, intellectual vanity, hypocrisy, anti-civic sentiments, and lack of patriotism. Hans Baron associates Lorenzo with "Bruni's school of civic Humanism" and calls him "the prototype of the kind of citizen-humanist that was later represented by Matteo Palmieri."

The Benvenuti were a new family from the S. Croce quarter. They entered the circuit of major political offices for the first time early in the second half of the fourteenth century. A merchant family, they were successful first as *saponai*, then as wool manufacturers and money-changers. The family evidently enjoyed strong support within the oligarchy, for once the elder Benvenuti attained office—he was honored with two terms as *Gonfaloniere* of Justice—they continued to have political good fortune. Lorenzo's older brother, Niccolò, was a frequent officeholder during the period 1394-1417. And Lorenzo himself, who began to appear in office after 1409, attained the dignity of prior in 1423. In 1427 his heirs reported the possession of nine farms, various land parcels, some houses, and a building "atta a saponaio."

Sources: ASF, *Mariani*, IV, f. 883; *Catasto*, 69, ff. 281v-285r; *Manoscritti*, 265, f. 99; see notes to Zippel's edition of Lorenzo's *Oratio* against Niccoli, *Gior. stor. d. lett. ital.*, XXIV (1894), 166-186; Baron, *The Crisis of the Early Italian Renaissance*, II, 409-415.

17. *Giovanni Aretino: fl. 1415.* We know literally nothing as yet about this man's social background. He was apparently from Arezzo, but in the second decade of the fifteenth century he figures as one of the best and most active manuscript copyists in Florence. B. L. Ullman has shown that Giovanni copied books for members of the Medici, Portinari, Orsini, and Ricci families. He used three types of script: the Gothic *bastarda*, Poggio's formal humanist hand, and a humanistic cursive. Since we know from Poggio, Bruni, and others that first-rate scribes were exceedingly difficult to find, Giovanni—one of the two or three outstanding copyists of the period—must have been remarkably well trained. "One noteworthy point is that Giovanni knew enough Greek to copy it himself and did not leave space for

another to enter it, as Poggio and Niccoli did. Altogether, he was a man we should like to know more about" (Ullman). But like Niccoli and Poggio, he can only have acquired his elegant hand and expertise through much experience; hence he evidently had an excellent basic education, and I should not be surprised to learn that he had studied to be a notary.

Sources: B. L. Ullman, *The Origin and Development of Humanistic Script*, series *Edizioni di storia e letteratura*, no. 79 (Roma, 1960).

18. *Cosimo de' Medici: 1389-1464*. Problems of interpretation aside, Cosimo's importance in the political and business history of the fifteenth century is so universally acknowledged that it would be superfluous to devote more than a few lines to him here, and these chiefly to underline his contact with humanism.

Like other young Florentines of rank and wealth, Cosimo studied under the nobleman, Roberto de' Rossi, and hence had one of the leading humanists of the age as a sort of master of studies. In about 1410, or perhaps a little before, Cosimo began to collect classical manuscripts and by 1430 had one of the richest private collections in Europe. He was particularly fond of Aristotle's *Nicomachean Ethics*, but he also enjoyed conversing about other books in the classical syllabus and especially delighted in listening to the discussions of men more learned than he. In the 1420's he was a prominent member of the discussion group which met at the Camaldolese convent of Santa Maria degli Angeli, where Traversari entertained his lay visitors. Niccolò Niccoli and Carlo Marsuppini were probably Cosimo's closest Florentine friends, but he also won the friendship of men like Lionardo Bruni, Poggio Bracciolini, and Paolo Toscanelli. Indeed, because of the part he played in the lives of Niccoli, Marsuppini, and Traversari, one has difficulty thinking of Florentine humanism in the 1420's and 1430's without also conjuring up the image of Cosimo.

Sources: The best treatment of the Trecento Medici is Gene A. Brucker, "The Medici in the Fourteenth Century," *Speculum*, xxxii, 1 (January 1957), 1-26; on Cosimo's contacts with humanism see especially the letters of Traversari, Poggio, and Aurispa; also G. Zippel, *Niccolò Niccoli* (Firenze, 1890); Zippel, *Carlo Marsup-*

pini (Trento, 1897); P. G. Ricci, "Una consolatoria inedita del Marsuppini," *Rinascita*, III (1940), 363-433; Vespasiano, *Vite*; A. Fabroni, *Vita Magni Cosmi Medicei* (Pisa, 1789); K. D. Ewart, *Cosimo de' Medici* (London, 1889); F. Pellegrini, *Sulla repubblica fiorentina a tempo di Cosimo il Vecchio* (Pisa, 1889); C. Gutkind, *Cosimo de' Medici* (Oxford, 1938).

19. *Antonio di Mario di Francesco di Nino: fl. 1417-1461.* This important Florentine scribe was one of the most active copyists of classical manuscripts in the first half of the fifteenth century. He turned out work for Cosimo and Piero de' Medici, Benedetto Strozzi, Cardinal Albergati, the Bishop of Ely (Wm. Gray), and almost certainly others. B. L. Ullman has tracked down forty-one signed manuscripts from his hand, executed in the period 1417-1456, and asserts that "there are no doubt others" still to be discovered. Antonio used the new humanistic script introduced by Poggio. He learned the script either from Niccolò Niccoli or Giovanni Aretino, or possibly by copying some of Cosimo's manuscripts written in Poggio's hand. At all events, Niccoli sometimes helped him to get transcription jobs.

We gather from several of Antonio's colophons (printed by Ullman, pp. 100-104) that he was an ardent republican, in the tradition apparently of civic humanism, and that he had a sort of reverence for Lionardo Bruni and Giannozzo Manetti. Undoubtedly he enjoyed the friendship of these men, and that of Poggio, Marsuppini, and Benedetto Accolti. For he was a notary, matriculated—like four of the men just named—in the guild of judges and notaries. In the 1430's and 1440's Bruni, Poggio, and Marsuppini were all active office holders in the guild, where they sat among the judges in the consulate. Antonio was twice notary of the Signoria (1436, 1446) and on occasion served the Republic as a notary in the Florentine dominion (e.g., at Montecarlo in 1461). Hence he must have served his guild in a consular and advisory capacity, as did most notaries and lawyers of the period.

A first-rate scribe could earn more than 30.0 florins per year, plus maintenance, and Antonio was perhaps the city's best in his time. Nevertheless, he combined this art with an active notarial practice and with his occasional duties as a public official.

Sources: B. L. Ullman, *The Origin and Development of Humanistic Script* (Roma, 1960), pp. 98-109; cf. judgment and references in Baron, *The Crisis of the Early Italian Renaissance*, I, 351-352; II, 610, 614, 619; on the earnings of scribes see Voigt, *Risorgimento dell' antichità classica*, I, 393f; on the guild offices of the humanists see *ASF, Arte dei Giudici e Notai*, 26, ff. 71r, 76v, 81r.

20. *Giuliano di Niccolaio Davanzati: 1390-1446.* Two of his letters (1431) to Matteo di Simone Strozzi survive. They are one of the several sources—Vespasiano is another—which reveal Matteo's love of learning and give evidence of his large library. The letters show that the two men were very close friends, that Matteo sometimes lent his books to Giuliano, and that Giuliano was an ardent student of classical literature, for we see him eagerly begging to borrow Cicero's *Philippics* and Servius on Virgil. Matteo urged the importance of these studies, and Giuliano declares in his second letter: "Pluribus iam exactis diebus tuas accepi literas, quibus ego quanto amore mihi afficiaris magis magisque cognovi. Persuadebant plurimum illae in divinas ciceronis orationes philippicas diu nocteque lectitare, quam rem et ipse aveo."

Who was this Giuliano? He studied at the University of Bologna, where he took his doctorate in civil law and lectured from 1415 to 1417. Returning then to his native Florence, he entered politics almost at once, for in 1418 we already find him speaking for one of the oligarchy's measures in the Council of the Commune. Subsequently he appeared in all the principal magistracies and became one of the Republic's most powerful political figures of the 1420's and 1430's. With the possible exception of Lorenzo Ridolfi, no lawyer was more prominent than Giuliano in the councils and embassies of those years. He was knighted by Pope Eugene IV in 1435.

Possibly a branch of the old Bostichi family, the Davanzati first entered the Signoria in 1320 and continued to serve in it down to 1523. Bankers and money-lenders in Giuliano's time, they lived in the S. Maria Novella quarter, where their houses were flanked by those of the Strozzi. They possessed farms and houses at S. Martino al Monte, "S. Giusto a Campi," and elsewhere outside Florence.

Sources: *ASF, Catasto,* 75, ff. 146v-150; *Mariani,* III, f. 554; *Manoscritti,* 266, f. 15; *Consulte,* 50, passim (dates: 1432-1436); *Libri Fabarum* 51, ff. 219v-221v; *Otto di Guardia,* 2723 bis, ff. 42r, 44r; Umberto Dallari, *I Rotuli dei lettori legisti e artisti dello studio bolognese dal 1384 al 1799,* vol. IV (Bologna, 1924), 35, 37. The two letters to Matteo Strozzi are in *ASF, Carte Strozz.,* *3a ser.,* 112, ff. 78r, 79r. They are quoted by Della Torre, *Accademia,* in the notes on pp. 290-291. On Giuliano's stature in the 1430's, see the incident reported by a contemporary, Giovanni Cavalcanti, *Istorie fiorentine,* II, 177ff.

21. *Alessandro di Ugo degli Alessandri: 1391-1460.* Alessandro was one of Roberto de' Rossi's best students—an honor he shared with Luca di Maso degli Albizzi, Bartolo de' Tedaldi, and Domenico Buoninsegni. Palmieri dedicated his *Della vita civile* (1439) to him. In the *proemio* he tells Alessandro that the work is inscribed to him partly because of his noble birth, good customs, and the fact that he was reared in the study of the liberal arts.

A branch of the Albizzi, the Alessandri split from them in 1372. In the fifteenth century they continuously figure among the two- or three-score families at the core of the oligarchy. Alessandro and his two brothers, Niccolaio and Bartolommeo, were thus in the major circuit of public office. Alessandro, for example, served three terms in the Signoria (1431, 1441, 1448), Bartolommeo two terms (1443, 1457), and Niccolaio two terms (1435, 1459). Gonfalonier of Justice on two occasions, Alessandro was a shrewd statesman, a prominent ambassador, and a prominent speaker in the executive councils. He was knighted by the Emperor in 1452. His political portrait comes down to us in Giovanni Cavalcanti's chronicle.

Like other leading Florentine families, the Alessandri threw their nets widely in the economic sphere. They were matriculated in the Calimala, Lana, and Por Santa Maria guilds. In 1427 Ales-

sandro and his brothers had various wool shops and wool-processing establishments, two family *palazzi*, at least seven other houses,
nearly twenty-five farms, six stone quarries, some 3500 florins in
Monte securities, and more than 2500 florins in other business
investments.

Sources: Vespasiano, *Vite*, p. 530f.; Palmieri, *Della vita civile*;
Cavalcanti, *Istorie fiorentine*, ii, 524; Passerini, *Alessandri gía
Albizzi di Firenze*. On archival sources: ASF, *Catasto*, 80, f. 73v;
Tratte, 67, 80, passim; *Tratte*, 39, f. 122v; *Medici e Speziali*, 245,
f. 19v.

22. *Buonaccorso da Montemagno: ca. 1392-1429*. A Pistoian by
birth, he took his doctorate in civil law at Bologna around 1415.
In 1417 he was called to Pistoia to help reform the constitution,
but probably he was already residing with his father in Florence,
because in 1418 he married into an illustrious old Florentine
family, the Mannelli. Going to Bologna for six months in 1421, he
served as a judge and aide to his friend, Antonio degli Alessandri,
a Florentine who was then Podestà of Bologna. From 1422 on
Buonaccorso was professor of law at the Studio Fiorentino and
in 1428, the year before his death, he negotiated two embassy
assignments for the Florentine Republic.

We know next to nothing about who Buonaccorso's humanist
preceptors were, but it is clear that in Florence he frequented
the humanists Palla Strozzi and Lionardo Bruni. No evidence
has been found to show that he was one of Traversari's visitors
at the convent of S. Maria degli Angeli. His literary remains indicate, nevertheless, that he was an ardent civic humanist. In his
dialogue, *De nobilitate*, the civic virtue of the self-made good
man is given great prominence. He also wrote an oration for
Catiline against Cicero and a series of timely orations for the
anti-papal republican and rebel, Stefano Porcari, on the occasion
of the latter's assuming the office of Podestà of Florence. In
Zaccagnini's opinion, Buonaccorso was also one of the period's
best poets in the Petrarchan tradition.

He was descended from "one of the oldest and most illustrious
houses of Pistoia, the Montemagni. This family went back to
about 1200 and undoubtedly came from the neighboring castle

of Montemagno, halfway between Prato and Pistoia, where for a long time they held on to their ancestral estates" (Zaccagnini). Bred to the profession of law and arms ever since the early *Duecento,* they stood out in Pistoian public affairs throughout the thirteenth and fourteenth centuries. Between about 1340 and 1380, for example, Buonaccorso's grandfather (another Buonaccorso) held the city's highest offices. Our man's father, also a doctor of law, was himself a leading public official in Pistoia between 1376 and 1406.

Buonaccorso's catasto report of 1427 shows that he had some farmland in the Florentine and Pistoian countrysides and a number of large debtors, including his father and the Republic of Florence, which owed him 75.0 florins in back salary for his Studio lectures. But he did not enter all his assets in this catasto report, for he is listed as paying taxes in Pistoia, where in fact he also enjoyed a fiscal privilege because of his position as municipal lawyer (see his father's catasto declaration).

Sources: ASF, Catasto, 80, f. 282; 81, f. 422; *Prose del giovine Buonaccorso da Montemagno,* ed. G. B. Giuliari (Bologna, Romagnoli, 1874), in *Scelta,* Disp. cxlv; *De nobilitate,* in *Prosatori latini del Quattrocento,* ed. E. Garin, pp. 141-165; but see especially Guido Zaccagnini, "Bonaccorso da Montemagno il giovine," *Studi di letteratura italiana,* i, ii (Naples, 1899), 339-387; also G. Zaccagnini, "Nuove notizie intorno alla vita di Bonaccorso da Montemagno," *Bullettino storico pistoiese,* xxxi, 1 (1929), 1-5.

23. *Guglielmo di Francesco Tanagli: 1391-1460.* This man's association with the humanist movement came through his long and close contact with Niccolò Niccoli, who named him one of the sixteen executors of his will, especially charged with the task of effecting the transfer of Niccoli's library to the convent of S. Marco. Guglielmo had been a friend and protégé of Niccoli since before 1410, the date of a Eusebius' Chronicle (Jerome's translation) in Guglielmo's hand, complete with signature, and considered by Ullman "the best example"—next to Poggio's work—"of humanist writing during the first decade of the fifteenth century." Speculating about where the young man learned

the new script, Ullman fixes on Niccoli as the man who encouraged Guglielmo to write in the new style.

A lawyer who took his doctorate in civil and canon law at Padua in the early 1420's, Guglielmo came from a Florentine family of some antiquity, particularly if the Tanagli really were a branch (as Mariani suspected) of the old Rinaldi. The Tanagli themselves broke into the executive sector of government for the first time in 1338 with a seat in the *Dodici Buonomini*. In the fifteenth century, under Guglielmo's brilliant leadership, the family took a much more aggressive part in public life. Guglielmo became one of the city's most respected and widely-employed statesmen: he sat in the Signoria, the *Octo Custodiae*, the *Canservatores legum*, and practically every other important commission. He was a prominent speaker in the executive councils, a strong supporter of close oligarchy, and one of the diplomats most counted on to carry out major embassy assignments. He was knighted in 1451.

The catasto inventories reveal that he lived off his landed income, government securities, and professional earnings.

Sources: The archival sources on Guglielmo are so extensive that I will list only enough to provide a bare outline. *ASF, Mariani*, vi, f. 1417; *Catasto*, 499, ff. 371-373 (year: 1433); *Manoscritti*, 266, f. 64; *Libri Fabarum*, 62, f. 121r; *Tratte*, 80, passim; Medici e Speziali, 245, f. 9r; *Giudici e Notai*, 670, f. 170; *Consulte e Pratiche*, 51, passim. In printed matter see especially Ammirato, *Istorie fiorentine*, ed. L. Scarabelli (Torino, 1853), vol. v.

24. *Lorenzo di Giovanni de' Medici: 1394-1440.* Owing to the celebrity of his brother Cosimo, Lorenzo has always been relegated to an obscure place by historians. He certainly lacked Cosimo's appeal, energy, and political genius. But Traversari's correspondence clearly shows that the younger brother was deeply interested in humanistic literature, that he devoted a good deal of time to it, and became a relatively accomplished scholar. The last of these observations should not surprise us, for Lorenzo was constantly encouraged and helped in his studies by Niccoli, Traversari, and Marsuppini, particularly by the latter, who was almost a daily guest in the Medici household. Indeed,

Lorenzo and this fastidious Aretine gentleman were the closest of friends. Between about 1430 and 1432, for example, Lorenzo was on very amicable terms with Filelfo, who was then lecturing at the Studio Fiorentino. But when the humanist-professor fell out with Marsuppini and Niccoli, Lorenzo swiftly withdrew his friendship and began turning his back to him in the streets, as Filelfo himself complained in a letter (1433) to Traversari.

Marsuppini's consolatory Latin work for Cosimo and Lorenzo on the occasion of their mother's death indicates something about the flavor of their humanistic environment and level of their preparation. When Lionardo Bruni was working on his translation of Plato's *Phaedrus* (1423), he sent part of the translation to Lorenzo, from whom he apparently expected an informed judgment. Traversari had enough faith in the younger Medici's sense of a good Latin style to quote with approval what he said about the Bruni translation. Lorenzo had found it "rough, harsh, and rude."

Like his brother, though a good deal less often, Lorenzo appeared in leading public offices, but he was not a man who relished an all-absorbing involvement in politics.

Sources: Traversari, *Epistolae et orationes*. See also the sources listed in the profile on Cosimo.

25. *Paolo dal Pozzo Toscanelli: 1397-1482*. A physician trained at the University of Padua, he was a close friend to many of the most learned men of the age—Niccoli, Traversari, Alberti, Filippo Pieruzzi, Leonardo Dati, Landino, and the celebrated Nicholas of Cusa, whom he first met when the two were students at Padua. Paolo was especially renowned for his knowledge of astronomy, mathematics, and geography. His biographer (Uzielli) has shown that he possessed an excellent scientific library, which on his death included sixteen valuable Greek manuscripts. He left a fascinating collection of observations on astronomical phenomena and a long work (now lost) on agriculture. His highly developed ideas on a western route to the Indies are presumed to have been decisive in Columbus' development as an explorer.

The Toscanelli were a family of physicians from S. Spirito. Paolo, his brother Piero, and their father and grandfather were all medical men. For some reason they were not in the circuit of public office—a mystifying lack or indifference in view of the times and place, but one which Uzielli did not bother to explain. The tax returns of 1427 show that Paolo's father, Domenico, was a wealthy man: he employed twelve servants, had various houses in Florence, and a large number of landed possessions in the Florentine contado. Paolo himself was a successful estate manager and investor, for we find that in the middle decades of the fifteenth century and up to the time of his death he had two huge farms in the Val d'Elsa and large investments in some iron and copper mines. His partners in the copper venture were members of prominent oligarchical families: Tommaso Soderini, Luigi Guicciardini, Gino Capponi, and Michele Migliorelli. Owing in part to Paolo's reputation as a scientist and man of learning, his nephews (and heirs) were able to marry with distinction and demand very respectable dowries (800 and 1000 florins). One of them married into the powerful Canigiani family of S. Spirito.

According to Vespasiano, Paolo spent most of his time in study and practiced medicine very little. He evidently lived on the return from his various investments, which also included a large interest in a wholesale spice business operated by his nephews. All told Paolo left the nephews a patrimony of around 9000 florins.

Sources: Vespasiano, *Vite*, pp. 355-356; Tiraboschi, *Storia della letteratura italiana*, vi, i, 406-408; Gustavo Uzielli, *La vita e i tempi di Paolo dal Pozzo Toscanelli, ricerche e studi* (Roma, 1894); E. Garin, "Ritratto di Paolo dal Pozzo Toscanelli," *Belfagor*, xii (1957), 253.

26. *Matteo di Simone Strozzi: 1397-1436.* On the Strozzi family see the summary under Palla above.

Matteo was in the circuit of offices of medium rank (there were more Strozzi than decorum permitted in the chief magistracies). His house, in the Red Lion section of S. Maria Novella, was flanked by the houses of two other members of the clan. He reported net assets in 1427 of nearly 4400 florins and was actively engaged in the wool trade. His business partner was another Strozzi, Lionardo di Filippo.

Appendix I: Profiles

Our man enjoyed a reputation for his learning in Latin and philosophy. An ardent collector of manuscripts, he was on very friendly terms with Filelfo and seems to have been much loved and esteemed by Bruni and (oddly) Marsuppini, one of Filelfo's arch enemies. Together with three other young men of the ruling class—Antonio Barbadori, Benedetto Strozzi, and Alessandro Arrighi—Matteo studied Aristotle's *Ethics* under the tutelage of Giannozzo Manetti.

Sources: ASF, *Catasto*, 76, ff. 137v-140; Vespasiano, *Vite*, pp. 403-404; Strozzi, *Lettere*, and the invaluable notes of Guasti's edition; Della Torre, *Accademia*, pp. 287-291. See also the references under Palla above.

27. *Agnolo di Jacopo Acciaiuoli: 1397-ca. 1468.* The testimony of contemporaries (e.g., Traversari, Bruni, and Vespasiano) goes to support the judgment of Vespasiano's most recent editors that Agnolo "was a highly cultivated man" (D'Ancona and Aeschlimann). We learn from Traversari's correspondence that he liked to visit the friar, who in turn urged Agnolo to the study of classical letters. Francesco Barbaro was visited in Venice by Agnolo and the Venetian admired him. Vespasiano tells us that Agnolo's mastery of Latin was very good, that he frequented the company of learned men and studied Aristotle's *Ethics* under the guidance of his brother-in-law Giannozzo Manetti. In the early 1430's, if not before, Acciaiuoli and Lionardo Bruni met through working together in posts at the head of Florentine government, and in 1440 and 1441 they served two terms together in the powerful Ten of War. Hence there is some connection between their careers in public life and Bruni's dedication to Agnolo of his *Commentarius rerum Graecarum* (1439). The humanist-chancellor observes in the preface that he composed the work for Agnolo, who was expected to see in it the passage from fortune to adversity of powerful city-states. He clearly meant the lessons of ancient history to be an education for Agnolo.

Originally from Brescia, the Acciaiuoli rose to prominence in Florence at the end of the twelfth century. Merchants on a large scale, they passed next to international banking. They were also great landowners and in the fourteenth century had powerful feudal connections in Sicily. During the period 1326-1400 they appeared in the Signoria on an average of once every three years. Agnolo therefore began his career in public life with the advantage of an illustrious family tradition. Dubbed a knight by the King of Naples in 1416, Messer Agnolo went into politics in the mid 1420's, was exiled in 1434 for sympathizing with the Medici, but in that year returned to Florence with Cosimo and soon became one of his half-dozen most important backers. From the 1440's on he seems to have had less and less time for his humanistic studies. Apart from serving in all the chief magistracies, he was a prominent speaker in the councils, one of the city's leading ambassadors, and a powerful member of the oligarchy's inner core. In the course of the 1450's he turned gradually against Cosimo and began, in an expert and quiet fashion, to foster resistance within the oligarchy to Cosimo's leadership. But it was only in 1466 that he joined Luca Pitti, Niccolò Soderini, and Dietisalvi Neroni in a plot against the Medici house. The plot was foiled, and Piero di Cosimo, who had inherited his father's place in 1464, emerged from the affair stronger than ever. With the exception of Luca Pitti, all the conspirators were banished from Florence.

Agnolo lived mainly on his investments. In 1427 he reported several houses, ten large farms, and various cash investments in banking and business houses.

Sources: ASF, *Catasto*, 74, ff. 43-45; *Mariani*, I, ff. 26r-28r; *Tratte*, 80, e.g., ff. 14v, 16v, 17v, 26v, 30r, 32r, 441r, 441v, 454r, 454v; *Leg. Comm.*, 11-13, passim; Vespasiano, *Vite*, pp. 486-499; Palmieri, *La vita di Niccolà Acciaiuoli*; Bruni, preface to his *Commentaria rerum Graecarum*, in Baron, *L. B. Aretino, Humanistisch-Philosophische Schriften*, p. 146; Ammirato, *Istorie fiorentine*, vol. v.

28. *Franco di Niccolò Sacchetti: 1400-1473.* An "ancient and noble family," the Sacchetti were already a distinguished clan in the twelfth century. They were landowners, their *palazzi* were in the S. Croce quarter, and they were very active in public life.

Franco himself began to appear in office in the late 1420's and eventually held all the Republic's leading dignities, that of

Gonfaloniere of Justice on two occasions, in 1450 and 1461. The Signoria sent him on numerous embassies—to Venice a number of times, to the papal curia, to Naples, and elsewhere. His reports to the catasto commission show that he possessed farms, livestock, a country villa, and a town house. A staff of three (one a female slave, Agnesa) helped him to run these properties. Vespasiano asserts that he had neither trade nor profession and lived entirely on his landed income—a claim, like so much in Vespasiano, fully borne out by archival documents.

Deemed by his contemporaries very learned in philosophy, Latin, and Greek, Franco seems to have studied under Filelfo and Marsuppini. He was a great friend and protector of Argyropulos. Niccoli appointed him one of the executors of his (Niccoli's) will. And he appears to have been much loved by Traversari, Bruni, Marsuppini, Manetti, Alamanno Rinuccini, Marco Parenti, and the Medici brothers, Cosimo and Lorenzo. In the 1450's and 1460's he was in the habit of inviting the learned men of Florence to his villa.

Sources: ASF, Catasto, 491, f. 176; 662, ff. 683-686; 697, ff. 44-47; 800, ff. 645-647; *Tratte,* 80, e.g., ff. 3v, 17v, 18v, 20v, 26r, 39v, 49r, 54r, 61r, etc.; *Mariani,* iii, f. 596; Vespasiano, *Vite,* pp. 431-434; Della Torre, *Accademia,* pp. 399-400.

29. *Antonio di Bellincione degli Agli: 1400-1477.* The Agli were a family of great antiquity, the descendants of feudal lords. Their political record was not outstanding in the century before Antonio was born, for they were *magnati* and therefore limited to a restricted number of offices, not often the most authoritative. Members of the Agli family were sometimes called on to sit in the powerful *Decem Baliae,* for example in the period around 1400, when a certain Cipolla was shown preferment. Bonds of marriage associated them with a number of leading houses.

A cathedral canon for many years, Antonio was made Archbishop of Ragusa in 1465, Bishop of Fiesole in 1467, of Volterra in 1470. Where he studied in his youth is unknown, but he had an excellent command of Greek and Latin and during Eugene IV's long stay in Florence, he served as preceptor to the future Paul II. This friend of Ficino's wrote verse, left some theological writings, and composed a book—apparently in elegant Latin—on the lives of the saints.

Sources: Vespasiano, *Vite*, pp. 157-158; Flamini, *Lirica toscana*, pp. 25, 41-45, 471-472; Della Torre, *Accademia*, pp. 775-776, 814. On the family itself see *ASF, Mariani*, ɪ, f. 130; *Carte Pucci*, ɪ, 15.

30. *Lorenzo di Palla Strozzi: 1404-1451*. The pertinent social profile is provided above under Palla, Lorenzo's father.

In 1427 Lorenzo already headed a firm with a large corporate capital, though whether in banking or the wool trade is not clear. If his upbringing followed traditional lines, he was in a counting house as an apprentice by 1415. But he also developed a certain knightly interest, for he was a leading combatant in a Florentine tournament of 1428.

Lorenzo was the eldest son. He and his brothers were tutored by three prominent humanists, none of whom was a Florentine: Giovanni Lamola, Tommaso Parentucelli (later Pope Nicholas V), and Sozomeno of Pistoia. But there is reason to believe that they may have frequented Filelfo's lectures at the *Studio*. Lorenzo was deemed "litteratissimo" by Niccolò della Luna and Vespasiano.

Sources: Vespasiano, *Vite*, pp. 385-403; Della Torre, *Accademia*, pp. 292-295. See also the references under Palla above.

31. *Jacopo Tornaquinci: fl. 1425*. We know virtually nothing about this man, save that he studied Greek under Ambrogio Traversari and acquired a reputation as his most outstanding pupil. Taking holy vows, he became a Camaldolese friar and entered Traversari's convent of Santa Maria degli Angeli, where he must have sat in on the convent's celebrated discussions. If he went into the Church after 1427, he may have been the Jacopo da Urbano Tornaquinci, listed in the catasto inventories of that year—a youth then twenty years old who with his mother lived on the income from eight land parcels, a farm, and two houses.

The Tornaquinci were an illustrious old family once prominent in the wool trade. They were Guelf noblemen in the thirteenth, *magnati* in the fourteenth century. According to the chronicler Malespini, they first emerged around 1200, along with families like the Cavalcanti, Bardi, Frescobaldi, Rossi, and Cerchi. But an anonymous fifteenth-century source takes the Tornaquinci back to the year 1100 and gives details of their various early *palazzi* and rights on the river Arno. Their town houses were in the S. Maria Novella quarter.

Sources: ASF, *Catasto*, 76, f. 333v; BRF, Codex 1885, *Memorie della famiglia Tornaquinci*, ff. 1-6; *Historia antica di Ricordano Malespini* (Florence, 1568), p. 75; Vespasiano, *Vite*, pp. 243-248.

32. *Lapo da Castiglionchio: 1405-1438.* Lapo's forebears were feudal lords from the Valdisieve. In the twelfth century they still had the castle or fortress of Cuona, some ten miles outside Florence. At the time of their wars with the Commune, the family split into two branches: one, the Volognano, remained ardent Ghibellines; the other, our family, moved into Florence, where they joined the Guelf nobility and eventually went into banking, international commerce, and law. Becoming prominent in political affairs, they married into the Cavalcanti, Baroncelli, and other old merchant families. Lapo's grandfather, the elder Lapo, was a doctor of law and one of the most influential statesmen in Florence during the third quarter of the fourteenth century.

In his time at the Studio in Florence, Lapo figured among Filelfo's best pupils. A one-time professor at the University of Bologna (1437), he finally moved on from there and took a post as secretary to Pope Eugene IV. Bruni and Manetti were among his good friends. During the four or five years before his death, he completed a number of elegant Latin translations of works by Plutarch, Demosthenes, Lucian, Theophrastus, Isocrates, and Xenophanes. Vespasiano reports that "Lapo was a man of modest means ('tenui sustanze') and this is why there are many books in Latin and Greek written in his hand."

Sources: Lapo da Castiglionchio (the Elder), *Epistola*, ed. Mehus; Vespasiano, *Vite*, p. 310; Lapo da Castiglionchio, Jr., *Dialogus de Curiae Commodis*, in Garin, *Prosatori Latini*, pp. 170-211; and F. P. Luiso, "Studi sull' epistolario e le traduzioni di Lapo da Castiglionchio juniore," *Studi italiani di Filologia classica*, VII (1899), 205-299.

33. *Giovanni di Messer Nello Martini: 1406-ca. 1483.* An interesting figure, he taught Latin at Prato, S. Gimignano, perhaps Florence, and almost certainly elsewhere in Tuscany. Flamini observed that he preferred teaching to the drafting of legal papers—he was a notary—though he also wrote verse and at least one book on Latin grammar. A letter of his to Piero di Cosimo de' Medici (1448) suggests that he knew Carlo Marsuppini and Donato di Lionardo Bruni. The letter, soliciting the post of Latin master at Arezzo, reveals that Giovanni was rather proud of his learning. Whether or not he could be deemed a humanist is an open question. I include him here only because he seems to typify a man with the sort of interests that might easily lead to "professional" humanism.

The Martini came from S. Gimignano, though Giovanni was probably born in Florence. Nello, his father, was a doctor of law, accorded his first dignity in the lawyers' guild at Florence in 1408. From this time on Nello was active in Florentine political affairs: he entered the circuit of office (by means of a special legislative act) and was commissioned to negotiate a number of extremely important diplomatic assignments. Like his father, Giovanni's older brother, Giuliano, was also a doctor of law. The catasto of 1427 shows that the family enjoyed comfortable means: for we must add to Nello's professional earnings a huge farm at Maiano (valued at 961 florins), two houses with adjacent land parcels, and a capital in 110 law books estimated at a value of 1000 florins.

Sources: ASF, Giudici e Notai, 26, f. 62r; *Catasto,* 81, ff. 481v-482; *Legazioni e Commissarie,* 4, f. 100v; 5, ff. 92v-95r; 6, ff. 46r, 74r/v, 84r; 7, ff. 10r-12v, 30v-33r, 47r, 53v, 59v; *Libri Fabarum,* 52, f. 136v; Flamini, *Lirica toscana,* pp. 291-292, 602-603, where Giovanni's letter to Piero di Cosimo de' Medici is printed in full.

34. *Leonardo di Piero Dati: 1408-1473.* The Dati were a merchant family of medium rank, regularly in the circuit of important public offices, and domiciled in the S. Spirito section of the city. An older cousin, the historian and silk merchant, Gregorio, held many key offices in the 1420's and 1430's. Leonardo's mother, Zenobia, was a Soderini—a wealthy and powerful family of mer-

chants, prominent in the oligarchy and also resident in S. Spirito.

A disciple and protégé of Ambrogio Traversari, he achieved an elegant Latin style, composed a *De bello etrusco*, wrote Latin verse and epigrams. His career is noteworthy: he was a doctor of law, became a secretary to leading princes of the Church (popes and cardinals), was afterwards made Bishop of Massa and cardinal in 1467. On at least one occasion Florentine ambassadors were commissioned to solicit favors for him at the papal curia. In Florence he counted the following men among his friends: Traversari, Bruni, Manetti, Palmieri, Niccolò della Luna, Matteo Strozzi, and the Medici brothers, Cosimo and Lorenzo.

Sources: ASF, *Mariani*, v, f. 1045; *Carte Pucci*, v, 15; *Manoscritti*, 265, f. 84v; Vespasiano, *Vite*, pp. 159-160; L. Dati, *Canonici florentini epistolae XXXIII*, ed. by Lorenzo Mehus (Florence, 1743); Francesco Flamini, "Leonardo di Piero Dati: poeta latino del sec. xv," in *Giornale storico della letteratura italiana*, xvi (1890), 1-107.

35. *Andrea di Francesco Quaratesi: b. 1409*. An old and noble family from Quarata near Galluzzo, the Quaratesi turned to trade in Florence and were remarkably successful. Their many houses —they were a large clan—were located in the S. Spirito quarter, where they shared political power with families like the Bardi, Uzzano, Ridolfi, Soderini, Rossi, Capponi, and Corbinelli. Between 1317 and 1400 they appeared in the Signoria twenty-three times, on six occasions as *Gonfalonieri* of Justice. Andrea's father, a *signore* in 1417 and 1425, held the sixteenth place in the S. Spirito catasto of 1427, with net assets of some 15,000 florins.

Andrea—the information on him is thin indeed—joined Niccolò della Luna in studying under Filelfo. He was a member of that circle of literati which included Leonardo Dati, Ceffi, Alamanni, and Palmieri.

Sources: ASF, *Catasto*, 64, ff. 110r-114v; 393, ff. 33r-35v; *Mariani*, ii, ff. 470r-471v; Della Torre, *Accademia*, pp. 294, 303, 314, 318.

36. *Niccolò di Francesco della Luna: 1410-ca. 1451*. The early history of the Della Luna house is obscure, but very probably

they were descended from an old county family. In the second
half of the fourteenth century they were matriculated in the
guild of doctors and druggists and appear to have been enormously successful spice merchants. But they soon branched out
into silk, wool, finance, and banking. Their wealth in the first
decades of the fifteenth century was on a scale with that of the
richest Medici, Strozzi, and Alberti. Niccolò was himself a Strozzi
on his mother's side, and like them, the Della Luna lived in the
S. Maria Novella quarter.

An important man in public life, Niccolò's father attained the
highest executive office in 1418, Gonfalonier of Justice. But the
political stature of the family did not survive beyond the first
third of the century, owing in part to their close association with
the Strozzi house and hence their estrangement from the ruling
group affiliated with the Medici.

Niccolò's preceptors at the Studio Fiorentino were the humanists Filelfo and Marsuppini, and not surprisingly, therefore, his
learning in Latin and Greek earned him a reputation. Filelfo
dedicated one of his satires to Niccolò, and Alberti considered
him "one of Tuscany's chief men of letters." His letters, still unpublished, show a passionate interest in humanistic literature and
education. In Florence his intellectual companions were six young
humanists from "senatorial" families: Luigi Guicciardini, Matteo
Palmieri, Tommaso Ceffi, Andrea Quaratesi, and later on Alamanno Rinuccini and Andrea Alamanni. Quaratesi's sister, Caterina, was married to one of Niccolò's brothers.

Sources: ASF, Catasto, 77, ff. 161v-166v; *Mariani,* iv, f. 931;
Tratte, 39, f. 109r; 78, ff. 31r, 229v; 79, ff. 21r, 68r; 80, ff. 35r, 61r,
109r; *Manoscritti,* 266, f. 42; *BNF, Mss. Passerini,* 189; Vespasiano, *Vite,* pp. 518-519; Della Torre, *Accademia,* Ch. ii, ii.

37. *Piero di Messer Andrea de' Pazzi: 1416-1464.* Like the
Ricasoli and Buondelmonti, the Pazzi were among the oldest and
most illustrious of all Florentine families. Feudal nobility bred
to the profession of arms and the habit of command in government, they probably scorned trade in the twelfth and early thirteenth centuries. And it may well be, for example, that the Ricasoli did not engage in trade much before about 1400.

Appendix I: Profiles

The Pazzi were in and out of government during their long and irregular history. But they were usually a force to be reckoned with, owing to their traditions, stature, and wealth. In the fifteenth century Piero's branch of the family appeared on the lists of those eligible to hold leading public offices. His father entered the Signoria in 1440, Piero himself in 1447, his brother Antonio in 1450, and Jacopo (another brother) became *Gonfaloniere* of Justice in 1469. In the 1450's and early 1460's Piero appeared in most of the Republic's chief magistracies, both in and outside the city, and he was often used in the negotiation of important embassies.

On the occasion of the first catasto, Piero's father reported a net capital of 31,000 florins, much of it in landed estates. This was the sixth highest tally in the largest and most densely populated quarter of the city, S. Giovanni, where the Pazzi were domiciled.

Urged to study Latin literature by Niccoli, Piero hired Lodovico Pontano as a tutor for 100 florins yearly, took him into his house and, according to Vespasiano, assigned a servant to him. Pontano turned out a man very skilled in Latin and with some knowledge of Greek. Like Corbinelli, Niccoli, Palla Strozzi, and others, Piero spent a patrimony building up an excellent library. He is said to have memorized all of the *Aeneid* and a number of orations. His way of life, his interest in letters, and the pleasure he took in playing literary host, suggest that he frequented the Argyropulos circle in the mid 1450's, along with Sacchetti, Rinuccini, Donato Acciaiuoli, and others.

Piero de' Pazzi—shall we call him a gentleman, a humanist, a humanist-gentleman? Decide what we will, it cannot be denied that he had a humanistic education.

Sources: Vespasiano, *Vite*, pp. 500-506; Ammirato, *Istorie fiorentine*, vi, 5ff.; *BNF, Mss. Passerini*, 8, ff. 186r-187v; *ASF, Mariani*, i, f. 185; *Carte Pucci*, viii, 50; *Tratte*, 443 bis, f. 215r; *Catasto*, 80, f. 593r; 499, ff. 80r-93v.

38. *Benedetto di Messer Michele Accolti: 1415-1464.* This old and honored Aretine family, prominent in legal circles, had close contacts with Florence as early at least as 1333, when two mem-

bers of the house, one of them a physician, were already settled in Florence.

Benedetto's father was a doctor of law; his mother, Margherita Roselli, also came from a well-known family of Aretine lawyers; his brother Francesco became a famous jurist; and Benedetto himself studied at Bologna, where he took his doctorate in civil and canon law. He married Laura di Carlo Federighi, the daughter of a Florentine lawyer who occupied the Republic's principal offices and distinguished himself in the executive councils (the *Consulte e Pratiche*). This constellation of lawyers, created by marriage alliances, may strike the modern observer as somewhat strange, but such alliances were a commonplace of late medieval and Renaissance Italy.

Before his appointment as chancellor of the Republic (1458-1464), Benedetto was a professor of law at Bologna, Volterra, and Florence, where in the 1440's he also set up as a practicing lawyer. In 1461, when it was found that he had earned more money practicing law than serving Florence as chancellor, his salary was raised from 450 to 600 florins per year, a sum which enabled him to live in the style of a very wealthy landlord or international banker.

A fervent student of classical literature, art, and philosophy, Benedetto produced two full-scale works: *Dialogus de praestantia virorum sui aevi*, which reflects a typical humanist interest, and a history of the Crusades in four books, *De bello sacro*. He developed an elegant Latin style, composed Latin and *volgare* verse, and wrote impromptu Latin orations. Understandably, he enjoyed the close friendship of Poggio and Marsuppini.

Sources: Vespasiano, *Vite*, pp. 317-319; Tiraboschi, *Storia della letteratura italiana*, vi, ii, 756-757; Marzi, *La Cancelleria della repubblica fiorentina*, pp. 229-231; Flamini, *Lirica toscana*, pp. 266-270.

39. *Antonio Rossi: fl. 1420-1460.* In a letter to Piero di Cosimo de' Medici (1455), Matteo Palmieri observes that "Antonio de Rosso is one of our young citizens, born of honorable people and a man of breeding. Moreover, he is very learned in Greek and Latin, and this is something to which I can testify, since he was

practically reared with me. Franco Sacchetti would be able to tell you the same things about him." This is the extent of our knowledge concerning Antonio's background. He is given the surname *Rossi* in scholarship, but whether or not he was connected with the illustrious Rossi clan is uncertain.

Antonio was a member of that circle of learned men who met at Alamanno Rinuccini's house in 1454 and 1455. The others, apart from Alamanno, were Andrea Alamanni, Marco Parenti, and Donato Acciaiuoli. Unlike these men, however, Antonio suffered material hardship (Palmieri called him "poverissimo") and was forced to hold classes in his house, where he took in the sons of the great families. He was probably a more accomplished humanist than Donato Acciaiuoli, who at first looked up to him. Failing in 1455 to obtain the post in rhetoric and poetry at the Studio Fiorentino (Argyropulos was appointed), Antonio soon moved to Rome, where he seems to have frequented the Roman Academy of Pomponius Laetus.

Sources: A. Rinuccini, *Lettere ed orazioni*, pp. 48-50; A. Messeri, "Matteo Palmieri," pp. 334-335, where the letter to Piero is printed in full; Della Torre, *Accademia*, pp. 375-383.

40. *Andrea Alamanni: 1422-ca. 1485.* A family of considerable antiquity, noble stock, and irregular fortunes, the Alamanni were prominent in public life. Andrea served in the Signoria twice, in the *Sedici*, in the strong Eight on Political and Military Security, the Ten on Liberty, and a variety of other offices. He also held a number of first-class rectorships—at Pisa, Pistoia, Livorno, and Castelfiorentino.

A collector of Greek and Latin manuscripts, Andrea sometimes put his library at the disposal of Niccolò della Luna and others. Filelfo and Della Luna conducted a correspondence with him and some of these letters survive. Those of the latter show that Andrea was a fervent devotee of humanistic studies, particularly in the later 1440's. We learn from Filelfo's letters that despite Andrea's civic commitments, especially after 1450, he always maintained a close contact with literary circles in Florence.

Sources: BNF, Mss. Passerini, 8, f. 7r; *ASF, Mariani*, IV, f. 793; *Carte Pucci*, XV, 2; *Tratte*, 39, f. 1r; U. Verino, *Carmina illustrium*

Appendix I: Profiles

poetarum italorum, vol. x (Florentiae, 1721), p. 400; Filelfo, *Epistolarum familiarum libri xxxvii* (Venezia, 1502); Della Torre, *Accademia*, pp. 294, 310, 368, 382.

41. *Marco di Parente di Giovanni Parenti: 1421-1497.* The Parenti were *gente nuova* (newcomers) of medium rank. Marco's grandfather, a "corazzarius," made his fortune in the manufacture and sale of armor and was the first member of his house to enter the top level of government, with six terms in the Signoria and appointments to the *Dodici Buonomini* (1356) and *Sedici Gonfalonieri* (1360). In 1435 and 1448 Marco's father sat among the *Dodici* and in those years also saw service in a variety of other offices of moderate importance.

Marco, who held some lesser offices, was himself a silk merchant, though not on a grand scale. His catasto of 1458 shows that he owned farms, houses, and government securities with a real market value of close to 2700 florins. Caterina di Matteo Strozzi, his wife, was the daughter of a humanist-statesman (see profile no. 26 above). Her mother somewhat regretted the fact that she could not give the girl a larger dowry, for Caterina could then have been married into an older, more illustrious, and more "gentle" family.

Nothing is known about the identity of Marco's teachers. Della Torre believed that he was to some extent an auto-didact. He was, at all events, exceptionally well-trained in Latin and philosophy. Proof of his learning appears in the testimony of humanist contemporaries like Filelfo, Alberti, Donato Acciaiuoli, Landino, and Benedetto Colucci of Pistoia. At one point Marco was Alberti's business agent in Florence. He was also on very close terms with Niccolò della Luna, Alamanno Rinuccini, and Donato Acciaiuoli. In the 1450's, like other prominent intellectuals, he frequented Franco Sacchetti's villa.

Sources: ASF, Carte Strozz., 2a ser., 17 bis (Marco's household diary of the 1450's and later); *Catasto,* 825, ff. 492r-494v; *Manoscritti;* 266, f. 44r-v; *Tratte,* 80, e.g., ff. 5v, 39v, 61r, 158r, 178r, 300r, 392v; Vespasiano, *Vite,* p. 432; Strozzi, *Lettere;* Della Torre, *Accademia,* pp. 320-321; Brucker, *Florentine Politics and Society, 1343-1378,* p. 69.

Appendix I: Profiles

42. *Alamanno Rinuccini: 1426-1499.* He perfected his command of the Greek language under John Argyropulos, who held the chair in Greek philosophy at Florence for fifteen years (1456-1471). Alamanno's literary legacy—letters, orations, dialogues, and a variety of Latin translations from the Greek—exhibits a thorough preparation in the humanistic vein, with a particular bent for history, oratory, and moral philosophy. He translated Plutarch on the virtues of women, five of his *Lives*, Philostratus' life of Apollonius, one of Isocrates' political discourses, and two homilies of St. Basil. In his youth he frequented the premises of a famous *libraio*, Vespasiano, where he became acquainted with Bruni, Marsuppini, and Manetti. It was in Alamanno's house in the middle 1450's that a group of young men—Rossi, Parenti, Alamanni, and Donato Acciaiuoli—were accustomed to meet in order to study and discuss classical authors. He had definite views on politics and on the republican nature of the Florentine constitution, but seems to have gone along with the leadership of the Medici until about the time of the Pazzi conspiracy (1478).

Alamanno was descended from an old noble family, one whose nobility was acknowledged even by the haughty and intolerant Giovanni Cavalcanti, the political memorialist. In the fourteenth and fifteenth centuries the Rinuccini were often engaged in international trade on a grand scale, but they also possessed a great deal of urban real estate, large tracts of arable land, and enormous investments in the Monte.

During the third quarter of the fourteenth century, Alamanno's grandfather, Messer Francesco, was one of the most prominent Florentine statesmen of the day. But the family ran into trouble with the oligarchy in the middle 1380's and were excluded from all major offices for about fifty years. Fossi tells us (p. 22) that Alamanno was very dear to Cosimo, Piero, and Lorenzo de' Medici. He certainly enjoyed their friendship and dedicated his translation of Plutarch's portraits of Nicias and Crassus to Piero, and in Cosimo's time he sat in the Signoria (1460) and the Twelve Good Men (1462). Lorenzo's cohorts seem to have kept Alamanno out of most major offices, though even then he held several governorships in the dominion and carried out a number of important ambassadorial assignments. He married into the Capponi family.

Sources: See Aiazzi's history of the family in his edition of the family chronicle, *Ricordi storici di Francesco di Cino Rinuccini dal 1282 al 1460* (Firenze, 1840); on Alamanno see Fossi, *Monumenta ad A. Rinuccini vitam* (Florentiae, 1791); A. Rinuccini, *Lettere ed orazioni*, ed. V. Giustiniani (Firenze, 1953); A. Rinuccini, *Dialogus de libertate*, ed. Fr. Adorno; L. Martines, "Nuovi documenti su Cino Rinuccini e una nota sulle finanze della famiglia Rinuccini," *Archivio storico italiano*, cxix, 1 (1961), 77-90; Della Torre, *Accademia*, p. 355f.

43. *Donato di Neri di Messer Donato Acciaiuoli: 1429-1478.* Older than the Strozzi or Medici, and until the fifteenth century more illustrious, the Acciaiuoli first emerged as an important Florentine family around 1200. They held office during the consular period. In the fourteenth century they were international bankers who sometimes took up the profession of arms, but like most such families they were always great landowners. Between 1326 and 1400 the Acciaiuoli won twenty-four places in the Signoria, the Medici thirty-one. Donato's grandfather was one of the most influential Florentine statesmen of the 1380's and early 1390's.

From the early 1460's to the end of his life Donato was deeply engaged in public affairs. He held nearly every major office in the city, became one of the Republic's principal ambassadors, and in 1474 was invested with the chief dignity, Gonfalonier of Justice.

Paolo Toscanelli taught him logic. Carlo Marsuppini and John Argyropulos were his professors of Greek. He translated Bruni's *Historiarum florentini populi libri XII* into Italian, Plutarch's portraits of Alcibiades and Demetrius into Latin. In the early 1450's he belonged to that study group made up almost exclusively of young humanists from the ruling families: Pandolfo Pandolfini, Alamanno Rinuccini, Marco Parenti, Andrea Alamanni, and Antonio Rossi. Garin and others have called attention to the fact that Donato left a fascinating Latin *epistolario*, still unpublished, which demonstrates his humanistic learning and close contact with humanists both from Florence and elsewhere.

Sources: ASF, Catasto, 74, ff. 213v-216r, being a report of his father's seventeen farms, seven houses, and a list of debts amounting to half the value of his government securities. See also *ASF, Mariani,* ɪ, ff. 26r-28v; Vespasiano, *Vite,* pp. 329-348; Palmieri, *La vita di Niccolà Acciaiuoli;* Litta, *Famiglie celebri italiane,* vol. vɪɪɪ; A. Segni, *Vita di Donato Acciaiuoli,* ed. T. Tonelli (Firenze, 1841); Della Torre, *Accademia,* pp. 322-425; E. Garin, "La giovinezza di Donato Acciaiuoli," *Rinascimento,* ɪ (1950), 43-70; E. Fiumi, "Fioritura e decadenza dell' economia fiorentina," *A.S.I.,* ɪv (1957), 406.

44. *Veri di Giovanni di Messer Forese Salviati: 1411-1474.* "He was learned in Greek and Latin, and very diligent in these languages. Carlo Marsuppini and Francesco Filelfo were his masters. He was especially interested in moral philosophy, and studied Aristotle's *Politics* with Messer Carlo [Marsuppini], the *Ethics* with Battista da Fabriano. . . . So far as we can tell from his letters and some translations, he had quite a good Latin style" (Vespasiano).

The Salviati were a large old merchant family from the S. Croce quarter, where they ranked with the Baroncelli, Peruzzi, Castellani, and Alberti. They were particularly fond of acquiring the dignity of knighthood. Were they an old military family? Whatever their derivation, in Veri's time they were wealthy, very prominent in office, powerful in the oligarchy, and connected by ties of marriage with other families of equal distinction. They appeared and reappeared in the chief magistracies: potent commissions, the Signoria, the colleges, rectorships and embassies.

Sources: ASF, Catasto, 73, f. 90v; *Tratte,* 39, f. 79v; *Mariani,* ɪɪ, f. 603r; *Medici e Speziali,* 247, f. 199r; *BNF, Mss. Passerini,* 8, ff. 35r-37v; Vespasiano, *Vite,* p. 519.

45. *Tommaso di Lorenzo Ceffi: 1418-1479.* A merchant family of minor to medium rank, the Ceffi in politics were of the type often found in the legislative councils and in administrative offices of moderate importance. They lived in the Ruote and Bue sections of S. Croce.

Tommaso himself became much involved in public affairs after 1443 and eventually saw service in numerous offices, including the colleges and the powerful Eight on Political and Military Security.

There is reason to believe that he studied under Filelfo. A prominent member of the Della Luna circle, he must have been greatly esteemed by Leon Battista Alberti, who in 1443 sent him a copy of *Della famiglia*, requesting his views on it and those of Leonardo Dati.

Sources: ASF, Catasto, 402, f. 233v; *Mariani*, vi, f. 1308; *Manoscritti*, 265, f. 77v; Della Torre, *Accademia*, pp. 294, 306, 318.

APPENDIX II

EIGHT TABLES ON WEALTH
IN FLORENCE

*T*HE following tables list the leading Florentine taxpayers of 1403 and 1427. Altogether the tables include 1200 names, 600 under each of the dates given. These names constitute nearly the whole of the city's effective political class, certainly its most active part. But since wealth was by no means uniformly distributed, distinguished Florentine families sometimes included branches which failed to figure among the leading taxpayers. In the first half of the fifteenth century many of the great families reveal this inequality: for example, the Medici, Albizzi, Strozzi, Capponi, Pitti, and Rucellai. Nevertheless, the tables record the names of all the important families of the earlier Quattrocento and list nearly every single household which gave Florence an important administrator or statesman during that period.

Tables I-IV list the principal 600 taxpayers of the prestanze collected in 1403. Specifically, they enumerate the first 150 *prestanziati* in each of the city's four quarters: S. Croce, S. Giovanni, S. Maria Novella, and S. Spirito.

Tables V-VIII, by the same method, list the leading taxpayers of the catasto for 1427.

One of the more interesting facts revealed by the tables is that the quarter century between 1403 and 1427 saw some notable changes in the distribution of wealth among the principal families. Fluctuation of this type seems to have been a permanent feature of republican Florence: we find it throughout the fourteenth and fifteenth centuries. Examined with other kinds of evidence, the high incidence of rapid and continuing changes in upper-class fortunes may be used to reach various conclusions, here summarily stated: commerce and banking were always dangerous, or at best risky, enterprises; even landed wealth had to be carefully and skillfully managed; political vendetta and fiscal discrimination were the ruin of many wealthy families. But, by the same token, political favor could serve as a commercial asset of the first order, and so it was also possible to amass enormous fortunes in relatively short periods of time.

The material presented in the tables was culled from the following sources: *ASF, Prestanze,* 1968-2020; *ASF, Catasto,* 64-69, 72-81, 84. Only the prestanza registers 1990-2020 record the imposts of the year 1403 and these alone served as the basis for the figures presented in Tables I-IV. The other prestanza registers, 1968-1989, dating from 1402, were used purely for the sake of obtaining greater accuracy in names and spelling. Catasto register 84, drafted soon after the first catasto, is a summary of net assets and imposts in the S. Giovanni quarter. I consulted it only to help supplement material taken from the S. Giovanni catasto registers 78-81, where various tax reports were either damaged or missing, so that the use of an additional source seemed necessary.

All the above-mentioned catasto registers, with the single exception of 84, are *campioni del catasto*: that is, official transcripts made from the individual tax returns submitted by each household head. Slight changes in these *campioni* were made as late as 1428, so that my figures in Tables V-VIII really reflect conditions *around* 1427, rather than the immediate circumstances of every man listed in the tables at the time he actually drew up the first report of his finances for the catasto officials.

With some exceptions, I have recorded the taxpayer's trade or profession only in cases where it was given immediately after the name in the source used. In any single entry rarely do I include the names of more than two individuals of the household. Where taxpayers were assessed identical amounts, I list them in alphabetical order by Christian name. Since the Italian word *nipote* can mean either nephew or grandson, I use it and preserve the ambiguity, just as in the sources I consulted.

The few citizens who in 1427 enjoyed a tax privilege of one kind or another are indicated by the asterisk entered alongside their net capitals. At two points in this appendix (VI, no. 65 and VIII, no. 16) net capitals are given in approximate amounts because the final balance sheets of the *campioni* were lost in these cases. It should be noted, finally, that eccentricities of spelling reflect the orthography of my sources.

Appendix II: Tables on Wealth

TABLE I

Prestanze of 1403: S. Croce Quarter

No.	Prestanza in florins/soldi	Name of taxpayer	No.	Prestanza in florins/soldi	Name of taxpayer
1.	199.00	Messer Giovanni di Ser Ristoro [Serristori] (and nipoti)	22.	24.00	Zanobi di Pagolo di Mugnaio di Reccho
2.	120.00	Cino di Messer Francesco Rinuccini	23.	23.00	Jacopo di Bino "cartolaio"
3.	89.00	Ser Cristofano di Ser Bartolo Renaldini	24.	22.00	Andrea di Tommaso Lamberteschi
4.	85.00	Niccolaio di Messer Niccolaio degli Alberti	25.	20.00	Giovanni di Messer Amerigo Cavalcanti
5.	80.00	Calcidonio di Messer Niccolaio degli Alberti	26.	20.00	Rosello di Tommaso Soldani
6.	70.00	Diamante di Messer Niccolaio degli Alberti	27.	19.00	Cherubino di Albertaccio di Bartolommeo degli Alberti
7.	52.00	Marco Benvenuti "lanaiuolo"	28.	19.00	Heirs of Jacopo di Sandro Covoni
8.	50.00	Altobiancho di Messer Niccolaio degli Alberti	29.	18.10	Francesco di Agnolo Malatesti
9.	50.00	Romigi di Niccolò del Ricco [Bucelli] (and brothers)	30.	18.00	Francesco di Messer Giovanni Zati (and brothers)
10.	45.00	Carlo and Otto di Messer Mainardo Cavalcanti	31.	18.00	Maestro Francesco di Ridolfo "medico"
11.	41.00	Messer Tommaso di Messer Jacopo Sacchetti	32.	18.00	Pagnino di Giovanni Pagnini "lanaiuolo"
12.	40.00	Benedetto di Bernardo di Messer Benedetto degli Alberti	33.	18.00	Piero di Jacopo Baroncelli
13.	37.00	Bucello di Francesco del Ricco Bucelli (and brothers)	34.	17.00	Alberto di Zanobi di Alberto
14.	36.00	Heirs of Salamone di Torello [del Maestro Dino]	35.	17.00	Giovanni di Filippo di Simone "ritagliatore" (and brothers)
15.	35.00	Amideo and Pagolo di Santi del Ricco	36.	16.00	Jacopo di Latino Pigli
16.	35.00	Nofri del Buono Busini	37.	16.00	Luca and Giovachino di Jacopo di Ser Grifo
17.	34.00	Bernardo di Lamberto Lamberteschi	38.	16.00	Niccolò del Buono Busini
18.	34.00	Giovanni di Rinieri di Luigi Peruzzi (and brothers)	39.	15.5	Michele di Salvestro Nardi (and brothers)
19.	30.00	Messer Lotto di Vanni Castellani	40.	15.00	Antonio di Lorenzo Spinelli (and brothers)
20.	25.10	Bartolommeo and Guelfo di Cambio Cambi	41.	15.00	Domenico di Domenico Giugni
21.	25.00	Messer Forese di Giovanni Salviati	42.	15.00	Giovanni and Maffeo di Maffeo da Barberino
			43.	15.00	Jacopo di Messer Francesco Rinuccini
			44.	15.00	Lapo di Francesco Corsi

No.	Prestanza in florins/soldi	Name of taxpayer	No.	Prestanza in florins/soldi	Name of taxpayer
45.	15.00	Messer Vanni di Michele Castellani	68.	10.00	Heirs of Lionardo dell' Antella
46.	14.10	Buonaccorso and Andrea di Francesco Cei (and nipoti)	69.	10.00	Lorenzo di Messer Benedetto degli Alberti
47.	14.00	Giovanni di Ser Ugo Orlandi	70.	10.00	Piero di Bernardo "speziale" (and brothers)
48.	14.00	Jacopo and Ludovico di Piero Bonaventura	71.	10.00	Rosso di Piero di Rosso "galigaio"
49.	13.10	Alamanno di Andrea Ghetti	72.	9.2	Piero di Buonaccorso "orafo"
50.	13.10	Giovanni di Michele Castellani	73.	9.00	Averardo di Messer Lapo da Castiglionchio
51.	13.00	Antonia widow of Niccolò di Luigi degli Alberti	74.	9.00	Berto di Bonifazio Peruzzi (and brothers)
52.	13.00	Barone di Filippo di Barone Capelli	75.	9.00	Buonaccorso and Filippozzo di Niccolò Soldani
53.	13.00	Francesco and Giovanni di Zanobi di Cambio Orlandi	76.	9.00	Feo di Giovanni di Feo
54.	12.10	Niccolò di Michele Castellani	77.	9.00	Francesco di Nuto "barbiere"
55.	12.10	Sandro and Bartolo di Lorenzo Talani	78.	9.00	Giovanni di Piero Baroncelli
56.	12.00	Domenico di Francesco Corsi "setaiuolo"	79.	9.00	Heirs of Giovencho Bastari
57.	12.00	Giannozzo di Tommaso di Caroccio degli Alberti	80.	9.00	Inglese and Giovanni di Simone Baroncelli
58.	12.00	Jacopo di Ruffolo Ciafferi	81.	9.00	Lapo di Giovanni Niccolini
59.	12.00	Matteo di Michele di Vanni Castellani	82.	9.00	Lorenzo di Messer Filippo Giamori [Baroncelli]
60.	12.00	Nera widow of Azzo del Antella	83.	9.00	Luigi di Lottino Gherardini
61.	12.00	Salvestro di Ludovico Ceffini (and brothers)	84.	9.00	Nastagio di Benincasa Manetti
62.	11.00	Marco di Jacopo and Lionardo di Giovanni Jacopi	85.	8.10	Lionardo di Berto "speziale"
63.	11.00	Michele di Bartolo del Ciece	86.	8.00	Cavalcante di Cavalcante Cavalcanti
64.	10.10	Bernardo di Ser Ludovico Doffi (and brothers)	87.	8.00	Giovanni and Paolo di Messer Tommaso Falconi
65.	10.5	Ser Ludovico di Francesco di Vanni	88.	8.00	Piero di Cacciatino Gherardini
66.	10.00	Antonio and Giuliano di Pierozzo di Ser Donato	89.	8.00	Piero di Ser Cristofano Benucci
67.	10.00	Antonio di Ser Lando da Pescia	90.	8.00	Tommaso di Nofri dell' Antella (and brothers and nipoti)
			91.	7.15	Salvadore di Tommaso di Bondi del Caccia
			92.	7.10	Antonio di Andrea del Panocchia

No.	Prestanza in florins/soldi	Name of taxpayer	No.	Prestanza in florins/soldi	Name of taxpayer
93.	7.10	Antonio di Pagolo Covoni	118.	5.10	Francesco di Bartolo Sangiugni
94.	7.00	Albertaccio and Pandolfo di Messer Antonio Ricasoli	119.	5.10	Francesco and Giovanni di Niccolaio Niccolini
95.	7.00	Antonio and Fronte di Piero di Fronte	120.	5.10	Giovanni di Biagio Roffi (sic) (and brothers)
96.	7.00	Antonio and Stefano di Vanni Ricoveri	121.	5.10	Giovanni di Renzo Salterelli
97.	7.00	Heirs of Doffo di Bernardino del Guante	122.	5.10	Jacopo di Alamanno Salviati
98.	7.00	Messer Filippo di Filippo Magalotti	123.	5.10	Heirs of Nofri di Filippone "tintore"
99.	7.00	Filippo di Guido Fagni (and brothers)	124.	5.5	Niccolò and Filippo di Franco Sacchetti
100.	7.00	Mariotto di Simone Orlandini	125.	5.00	Agnolo di Francesco Baroncelli
101.	7.00	Niccolò di Giovanni del Bellaccio (and brothers)	126.	5.00	Alberto di Bernardo degli Alberti
102.	6.10	Niccolò di Rinieri Peruzzi	127.	5.00	Alesso and Adovardo di Alberto degli Alberti
103.	6.00	Attaviano di Cacciatino Gherardini	128.	5.00	Ser Coluccio di Piero [Salutati] "cancelliere"
104.	6.00	Bettino di Messer Bindaccio Ricasoli	129.	5.00	Filippo and Andrea di Niccolò Giugni
105.	6.00	Bindaccio and Carlo di Granello [Ricasoli]	130.	5.00	Francesco and Nofri di Duccio Melini
106.	6.00	Ser Bonaventura di Ser Zello (and nipote)	131.	5.00	Gherardino di Ghozzo Gherardini
107.	6.00	Francesco di Andrea di Jacopo Tomasi	132.	5.00	Giovanni di Corbizzino Fracassini
108.	6.00	Gentile del Maestro Tommaso del Garbo	133.	5.00	Gualberto and Giovanni di Bartolommeo Morelli
109.	6.00	Giusto di Barone di Francesco	134.	5.00	Jacopo di Orlando Orlandi
110.	6.00	Heirs of Nerozzo di Bernardo degli Alberti	135.	5.00	Jacopo di Verano Peruzzi
111.	6.00	Niccolò di Messer Alessandro dell' Antella	136.	5.00	Lionardo di Rinieri Rustichi
112.	6.00	Niccolò di Napoleone Franzesi	137.	5.00	Michele Coni
113.	6.00	Niccolò di Riccardo Fagni	138.	5.00	Niccolaio di Messer Bello Mancini
114.	6.00	Simone del Maestro Dino	139.	5.00	Raffaello and Giovanni di Matteo di Maggio
115.	6.00	Zanobi di Zanobi da Limano	140.	5.00	Simone di Ser Piero della Fioraia
116.	5.15	Jacopo di Sandro Covoni	141.	4.15	Buonaccolto di Filippo Buonaccolti
117.	5.10	Betto di Jacopo Betti (and brothers)	142.	4.10	Antonio di Attaviano di Rosellino Gherardini
			143.	4.10	Ceffo di Masino Ceffi "tintore"

Appendix II: Tables on Wealth

No.	Prestanza in florins/soldi	Name of taxpayer	No.	Prestanza in florins/soldi	Name of taxpayer
144.	4.10	Matteo del Paffiere da Gringnano	147.	4.00	Cambio di Orlando Orlandi
145.	4.10	Ser Mino di Ser Domenico di Ser Mino da Montevarchi	148.	4.00	Cionaccio di Francesco Baroncelli
146.	4.00	Amerigo di Bartolo Zati	149.	4.00	Donato di Messer Filippo dell' Antella
			150.	4.00	Giovanni di Rinieri di Tommaso Peruzzi

TABLE II

Prestanze of 1403: S. Giovanni Quarter

No.	Prestanza in florins/soldi	Name of taxpayer	No.	Prestanza in florins/soldi	Name of taxpayer
1.	600.00	Messer Bartolommeo di Bandino de' Panciatichi	16.	42.00	Heirs of Zanobi di Taddeo Gaddi
2.	190.00	Ghucciozzo di Ardingo de' Ricci	17.	41.00	Roberto di Jacopo di Francesco Arrighi (and brothers)
3.	187.00	Niccolà and Cambio di Messer Vieri de' Medici	18.	40.00	Cresci di Lorenzo di Cresci
4.	90.00	Francesco di Marco [Datini] da Prato	19.	40.00	Maestro Francesco di Messer Niccolò da Collegrana
5.	84.00	Francesco and Filippo di Antonio Tanaglia	20.	38.00	Paliano di Falco "tavoliere"
6.	80.00	Filippo di Michele Arrighi	21.	37.10	Giovanni di Bicci de' Medici
7.	74.00	Nofri di Giovanni Bischeri	22.	35.15	Michele di Gino Rondinelli
8.	66.00	Zanobi di Ser Gino "ritagliatore"	23.	35.10	Maso and Ugo di Bartolommeo degli Alessandri
9.	60.00	Filippo di Niccolò Macigni (and brothers)	24.	35.00	Heirs of Lionardo di Bellincione
10.	52.00	Bernardo di Giovanni Portinari	25.	34.00	Piero di Cresci "lanaiuolo"
11.	52.00	Giovanni di Jacopo Orlandini	26.	33.00	Francesco di Bicci de' Medici
12.	48.10	Agnolo and Giovanni di Filippo di Ser Giovanni [Pandolfini]	27.	30.6	Albizzo del Toso da Fortuna
13.	45.00	Nofri and Niccolò di Andrea di Neri di Lippo [del Palagio] (and nipoti)	28.	30.00	Heirs of Barone Balducci da Montecatini
14.	42.8	Ridolfo and Giuliano di Ser Benedetto "merciai"	29.	30.00	Luca di Ser Filippo Carnesecchi
15.	42.00	Michele di Ser Parente "setaiuolo"	30.	29.00	Bernardo and Vieri di Vieri Guadagni
			31.	27.8	Giovanni di Niccolò di Goro (and brothers)

No.	Prestanza in florins/soldi	Name of taxpayer	No.	Prestanza in florins/soldi	Name of taxpayer
32.	27.00	Jacopo di Martino dal Borgo S. Lorenzo (and sons)	59.	16.10	Francesco di Lencio da San Miniato "sarto"
33.	25.00	Antonio and Niccolà di Francesco Giraldi	60.	16.00	Giovanni and Rinieri di Niccolò della Tosa
34.	25.00	Antonio di Santi "mercatante"	61.	15.10	Maestro Niccolò di Francesco "medico" (and sons)
35.	25.00	Matteo di Bartolommeo Tanaglia	62.	15.00	Agnolo di Ghezzo della Casa (and brothers)
36.	25.00	Heirs of Ser Paolo Richoldi	63.	15.00	Andrea di Messer Ugo della Stufa
37.	24.00	Gherardozzo di Bartolo Filippi	64.	15.00	Antonio di Africhello de' Medici
38.	23.00	Luca di Gieri Gieri	65.	15.00	Bartolommeo di Luca Banchelli
39.	22.10	Tedaldo and Bartolo di Bartolo Tedaldi	66.	15.00	Gherardo di Zanobi Cortigiani
40.	22.8	Jacopo di Ser Francesco Ciai "ritagliatore"	67.	15.00	Maso di Mariano degli Albizzi
41.	22.00	Salvi di Giovanni Lippi da Cierreto	68.	15.00	Niccoloso and Jacopo di Francesco Cambi
42.	21.00	Filippo di Salvi di Filippo (and brothers)	69.	15.00	Niccoluccio di Filippo da Prato
43.	21.00	Luca di Piero Rinieri	70.	14.10	Filippo di Piero Rinieri
44.	20.00	Antonio and Giovanni di Tedice degli Albizzi	71.	14.00	Carlo di Zanobi Macigni (and brother and nipote)
45.	20.00	Bernardo di Messer Biagio Guasconi	72.	14.00	Giovanni di Adovardo Portinari (and brothers)
46.	20.00	Gilio di Lapo Gili	73.	13.00	Chimento di Stefano "ritagliatore"
47.	20.00	Spina and Piero di Azzolino da Cignano	74.	13.00	Giraldo di Lorenzo Giraldi
48.	19.5	Jacopo and Tommaso di Vannuccio Arrighi	75.	12.10	Ser Benedetto di Ser Lando Fortini (and brothers)
49.	18.00	Antonio di Alessandro degli Alessandri	76.	12.00	Francesco di Matteo di Luca Mezanghini (sic)
50.	18.00	Antonio di Schiatta di Macci	77.	12.00	Giorgio di Andrea di Tello
51.	18.00	Francesco di Neri Fioravanti	78.	12.00	Michele and Francesco di Jacopo Lottieri
52.	18.00	Guelfo di Giovanni "prestatore"	79.	12.00	Piero di Francesco Brocchardi
53.	18.00	Ser Lorenzo di Ser Tano da Lutiano	80.	12.00	Heirs of Poldo Pazzi
54.	17.10	Messer Maso di Luca degli Albizzi	81.	12.00	Heir of Soldo di Messer Matteo di Federigo
55.	17.00	Giesa and Berna del Bene	82.	11.00	Alamanno di Messer Salvestro de' Medici
56.	17.00	Nello di Ser Bartolommeo di Ser Nello Ghetti (and brothers)	83.	11.00	Dingo di Guerriante Marignolli
57.	16.10	Andrea di Maso "lanaiuolo"			
58.	16.10	Deo di Deo del Bechuto			

No.	Prestanza in florins/soldi	Name of taxpayer	No.	Prestanza in florins/soldi	Name of taxpayer
84.	11.00	Domenico, Piero, and Bartolommeo di Matteo "merciai"	109.	8.00	Bartolommeo di Michelozzo del Bimbo
85.	11.00	Matteo and Castellano di Messer Donato Adimari	110.	8.00	Bianco and Antonio di Salvestro del Maestro Benvenuto
86.	11.00	Matteo di Giovanni Villani	111.	8.00	Bonifazio di Messer Ormanno Cortigiani
87.	10.00	Alderotto di Bernardo Brunelleschi	112.	8.00	Francesco di Niccolò Ferrantini
88.	10.00	Bartolommeo di Filippo Vinaccesi da Quarata	113.	8.00	Ser Manno di Domenico da Villano
89.	10.00	Bindo di Lapo Gili	114.	8.00	Matteo di Bartolo Boni (and brothers) "setaiuoli"
90.	10.00	Giovanni di Domenico Ciampelli	115.	8.00	Nigi and Lottieri di Nerone di Nigi
91.	10.00	Heirs of Giovanni di Jacopo Giani "tavoliere"	116.	8.00	Piero di Currado da Gagliano (and sons)
92.	10.00	Lorenzo di Tommaso Baronci	117.	8.00	Rinieri di Jacopo Bonafè
93.	10.00	Ser Marchione di Bertino Donati	118.	8.00	Stefano di Ser Piero "setaiuolo"
94.	10.00	Neri di Chiarissimo Falconieri	119.	7.10	Antonio di Francesco di Ser Gino
95.	10.00	Niccoloso di Francesco Bettini (and brothers)	120.	7.10	Baldassare di Messer Francesco degli Albizzi
96.	10.00	Piero di Bartolo Macinghi	121.	7.10	Bertoldo di Zarino di Messer Jacopo Zarini
97.	10.00	Piero di Jacopo Martini	122.	7.10	Giorgio di Aldobrandino del Nero
98.	9.00	Heirs of Benino di Guccio	123.	7.10	Jacopo di Francesco Guasconi
99.	9.00	Heirs of Giovanni and Guido d'Andrea de' Ricci	124.	7.10	Zanobi di Bardo da Spicchio
100.	9.00	Madalena di Carlo Strozzi	125.	7.00	Ardingo di Corso de' Ricci
101.	9.00	Marco di Jacopo Bartoli "lanaiuolo"	126.	7.00	Bartolommeo di Messer Giovanni Tedaldini
102.	9.00	Neri di Francesco della Trita	127.	7.00	Bartolommeo di Ser Santi Bruni
103.	9.00	Niccolò di Ugolino Martelli	128.	7.00	Bogio di Roberto Franzesi
104.	9.00	Nofri di Maffeo Tedaldi (and brothers)	129.	7.00	Heirs of Domenico di Lapo Gili
105.	8.15	Giuliano di Francesco di Ser Gino	130.	7.00	Heir of Francesco di Ser Santi [Bruni]
106.	8.10	Michele and Luca di Baldo di Ser Michele "speziali"	131.	7.00	Francesco di Talduccio Talducci (and sons)
107.	8.00	Andrea di Pacchio Adimari	132.	7.00	Giovanni di Bartolo Burci dello Stecutto
108.	8.00	Antonio di Ser Niccolò di Ser Ventura (and brothers)	133.	7.00	Giovanni di Tura da Cignano "speziale"

No.	Prestanza in florins/soldi	Name of taxpayer	No.	Prestanza in florins/soldi	Name of taxpayer
134.	7.00	Jacopo di Francesco di Metto	142.	6.00	Alessandro di Mone de' Ricci
135.	7.00	Manno di Messer Manno Donati	143.	6.00	Antonio di Bartolommeo Guidalorchi
136.	7.00	Pagolo di Berto Carnesecchi	144.	6.00	Messer Baldo di Simone della Tosa
137.	7.00	Villano di Giovanni Villani	145.	6.00	Bartolommeo del Buono "ritagliatore"
138.	6.10	Maestro Antonio del Maestro Guccio	146.	6.00	Benvenuto di Francesco di Ser Gino
139.	6.10	Donato and Antonio di Bernardo di Duccio Portinari	147.	6.00	Dati di Filippo "cambiatore"
140.	6.10	Nepo and Michele di Messer Gieri de' Pazzi	148.	6.00	Luigi di Aghinolfo di Chirico Pazzi
141.	6.10	Ugolino and Amerigo di Niccolò di Ugolino Adimari	149.	6.00	Mainardo and Jacopo di Filippo Adimari
			150.	6.00	Matteo di Jacopo Arrighi

TABLE III

Prestanze of 1403: S. Maria Novella Quarter

No.	Prestanza in florins/soldi	Name of taxpayer	No.	Prestanza in florins/soldi	Name of taxpayer
1.	121.00	Nofri di Palla Strozzi	13.	31.00	Giovanni di Gherardo Davizzi (and brothers)
2.	100.00	Filippo di Messer Simone Tornabuoni	14.	28.00	Ambrogio di Meo Boni
3.	70.00	Giovanni di Bartolommeo di Ser Spinello	15.	26.00	Simone di Gieri Gondi
			16.	26.00	Zanobi and Francesco di Ser Benozzo
4.	58.00	Tommaso and Jacopo di Giacomino di Goggio [Tebalducci]	17.	25.00	Jacopo di Ubaldino Ardinghelli
5.	51.00	Tommaso di Messer Roberto Gianfigliazzi	18.	24.15	Andrea di Messer Lorenzo da Montebuoni
6.	41.00	Francesco di Francesco di Pierozzo della Luna	19.	24.00	Jacopo di Ubertino Strozzi
7.	40.00	Manetto di Giovanni Davanzati	20.	23.00	Agnolo di Luigi Spini
8.	38.00	Domenico di Antonio Allegri	21.	22.00	Morello and Giovanni di Pagolo Morelli
9.	38.00	Francesco di Neri Ardinghelli	22.	21.00	Antonio di Lapaccio Robertini
10.	36.00	Marco di Tommaso Bartoli (and brothers)	23.	20.00	Jacopo di Messer Francesco Spini
11.	33.10	Zanobi di Francesco degli Agolanti	24.	19.00	Messer Cristofano di Anfrione Spini
12.	31.00	Filippo di Messer Lionardo Strozzi	25.	18.00	Benedetto di Ser Michele di Ser Tegna
			26.	18.00	Heirs of Matteo di Ser Michele di Ser Tegna

Appendix II: Tables on Wealth

No.	Prestanza in florins/soldi	Name of taxpayer
27.	18.00	Dino and Attaviano di Messer Guccio di Dino Gucci (and nipoti)
28.	18.00	Ser Viviano di Neri [Viviani]
29.	17.10	Bartolo di Bartolo di Ser Giovanni da Empoli
30.	17.00	Jacopo di Giannotto d'Artimino
31.	17.00	Niccolò and Palla di Guida della Foresta
32.	16.00	Buonaccorso Berardi "setaiuolo"
33.	16.00	Piero and Jacopo di Tommaso Lana
34.	16.00	Scolaio and Doffo di Neppo Spini
35.	15.00	Agnolo di Bindo Vernaccia
36.	15.00	Heir of Giovanni di Gualterotto da Castiglione
37.	15.00	Matteo di Piero Fastelli "tavoliere"
38.	15.00	Ser Nigi di Ser Giovanni (and son)
39.	15.00	Tommaso di Bartolo di Ser Tino
40.	14.2	Marco di Uberto Strozzi
41.	14.00	Gherardo di Piero di Degho Spini (and brothers)
42.	14.00	Lionardo di Domenico [Buoninsegni]
43.	14.00	Niccolò di Domenico Pollina
44.	14.00	Nofri and Matteo di Azzo "lanaiuoli"
45.	14.00	Rosso di Messer Scolaio Cavalcanti
46.	13.5	Taddeo di Pagolo di Tommaso "setaiuolo"
47.	13.00	Antonio di Jacopo Bonbeni
48.	13.00	Antonio di Jacopo da Lugnano
49.	13.00	Benedetto di Lapaccino del Toso
50.	13.00	Feo di Dino "galigaio"
51.	13.00	Ghisello di Bindo Ghiselli
52.	13.00	Matteo di Niccolò Strozzi
53.	12.10	Piero di Giovanni Tornaquinci
54.	12.00	Giovanni di Amerigho del Bene
55.	12.00	Heirs of Giovanni di Bartolo Rucellai
56.	12.00	Giovanni di Filippo Carducci (and sons)
57.	12.00	Heir of Guccio di Brogiotto da Empoli
58.	12.00	Heir of Jacopo di Messer Donato Acciaiuoli
59.	12.00	Ludovico di Jacopo Giandonati
60.	12.00	Matteo del Tegghia "lanaiuolo"
61.	12.00	Pagolo di Messer Pagolo Rucellai
62.	12.00	Heirs of Simone di Bartolo Rucellai
63.	11.10	Lisa widow of Ser Filippo (and sisters)
64.	11.5	Simone di Stefano Stefani
65.	11.00	Heir of Bartolommeo di Piero Cederni
66.	11.00	Guglielmo di Piero "speziale"
67.	11.00	Piero di Messer Guido Bonciani
68.	10.15	Pierozzo di Biagio Strozzi
69.	10.10	Luca di Bartolo Riccardi
70.	10.10	Tommaso di Ubertino Strozzi
71.	10.4	Bernardo di Bruno Ardinghelli
72.	10.00	Maestro Ludovico di Bartolo "medico"
73.	10.00	Benedetto di Andrea da Sommaia
74.	10.00	Cante di Giovanni Compagni
75.	10.00	Gerozzo di Niccolò da Castiglione
76.	10.00	Giovanni di Simone di Messer Bardo [Bindo?] Altoviti
77.	10.00	Niccolò di Francesco di Agnolo "pezaio"

No.	Prestanza in florins/soldi	Name of taxpayer	No.	Prestanza in florins/soldi	Name of taxpayer
78.	10.00	Stoldo di Lorenzo "fondachaio"	103.	7.10	Antonio di Ceccho di Antonio (and brothers)
79.	10.00	Vieri di Francesco del Bene	104.	7.10	Bindo di Nastagio Altoviti
80.	9.10	Domenico di Cambio (and brother) "setaiuoli"	105.	7.10	Francesco di Pasquino "ferravecchio"
81.	9.10	Francesco di Giovanni di Ser Lapo d' Artimino	106.	7.10	Monte di Pugio "ferravecchio"
82.	9.10	Jacopo and Giovanni di Giovanni Gianfigliazzi	107.	7.10	Messer Rinaldo di Giannozzo Gianfigliazzi
83.	9.10	Matteo di Agnolo Malatesti	108.	7.10	Zanobi di Lapaccino del Toso
84.	9.00	Antonio di Antonio di Giovanni "galigaio"	109.	7.5	Piero di Carlo Strozzi
85.	9.00	Antonio di Giovanni di Roberto di Gino	110.	7.00	Alessandro di Jacopo Suponi
86.	9.00	Filippo di Messer Andrea Falconi	111.	7.00	Antonio di Rinieri Squarcialupi
87.	9.00	Giovanni di Messer Palmieri Altoviti (and brothers)	112.	7.00	Antonio di Tano "orafo" (and brothers)
88.	9.00	Giovanni di Simone di Messer Tommaso Altoviti	113.	7.00	Benedetto di Piero di Benedetto Strozzi
89.	9.00	Simone di Lapaccino del Toso	114.	7.00	Bonifazio di Arnaldo Raspi
90.	9.00	Ugo di Ser Teghiaio (?) Altoviti	115.	7.00	Heir of Filippo and Agnolo di Baglione Cavalcanti
91.	8.10	Agnesa widow of Niccolò di Marco Strozzi	116.	7.00	Jacopo di Lorenzo di Matteo Pertini
92.	8.10	Benedetto di Como Federighi	117.	7.00	Piero di Mari [Adimari?] Gianfigliazzi
93.	8.10	Carlo di Gieri di Michele (and brothers)	118.	7.00	Pino di Annibaldo degli Strozzi
94.	8.10	Cecco di Domenico di Cecco Fei	119.	7.00	Tommaso di Neglio Fagiuoli
95.	8.10	Giovanni di Francesco di Jacopo del Bene	120.	6.15	Bartolommeo di Lionardo Bartolini
96.	8.5	Ser Giovanni Bencini	121.	6.10	Andrea di Como Federighi
97.	8.00	Bernardo and Tommaso di Tommaso di Soldo Strozzi	122.	6.10	Barzelone di Spedaliere da Prato
98.	8.00	Gherardino di Salvestro Cavalcanti	123.	6.10	Cristofano di Piero "rigattiere"
99.	8.00	Guido di Michele Guiducci	124.	6.10	Giovanni di Bernardo di Bartolommeo Albertini
100.	8.00	Latino di Primerano Pigli (and brothers)	125.	6.10	Jacopo di Francesco Ventura
101.	8.00	Messer Ricciardo di Francesco del Bene [a lawyer]	126.	6.10	Jacopo di Messer Giovanni Rucellai
102.	8.00	Simone di Domenico called Biagio "lanaiolo"	127.	6.10	Lione di Zanobi Acciaiuoli
			128.	6.10	Niccolò and Federigho di Boccaccio di Messer Arduno

No.	Prestanza in florins/soldi	Name of taxpayer	No.	Prestanza in florins/soldi	Name of taxpayer
129.	6.00	Bartolommea di Bartolommeo di Zanobi Baldesi	140.	5.10	Guido di Giuntino "lanaiuolo"
130.	6.00	Bernardo di Dante da Castiglione	141.	5.10	Roberto and Carlo di Gagliardo Bonciani
131.	6.00	Filippo di Messer Uberto Aldobrandini (and brothers)	142.	5.10	Sandro di Gentile Altoviti
132.	6.00	Francesco di Messer Giovanni Melanesi	143.	5.5	Giovanni di Domenico Manovelli (and brothers)
133.	6.00	Francesco di Messer Palla Strozzi	144.	5.5	Niccolò di Maso Scarlattini
134.	6.00	Giovanni di Ugo Vecchietti	145.	5.00	Andrea di Bonaventura "fondachaio"
135.	6.00	Niccolò di Andrea Buondelmonti	146.	5.00	Andrea di Messer Francesco Rucellai
136.	6.00	Niccolaio di Roberto Davanzati	147.	5.00	Antonio di Davanzato Davanzati
137.	6.00	Pagolo di Gianni Doni (and brothers)	148.	5.00	Berto di Pagolo di Messer Niccolà Lapi (and brothers)
138.	5.14	Vieri di Guido "pollaiuolo"	149.	5.00	Giovanna widow of Giovanni di Marco Strozzi
139.	5.10	Gentile and Niccolò di Baldassare Boni	150.	5.00	Giovanni di Vieri Altoviti (and brothers)

TABLE IV

Prestanze of 1403: S. Spirito Quarter

No.	Prestanza in florins/soldi	Name of taxpayer	No.	Prestanza in florins/soldi	Name of taxpayer
1.	240.00	Messer Luigi di Messer Piero Guicciardini	11.	33.00	Bindo and Tommaso di Gherardo Piaciti
2.	164.00	Giuliano di Bartolo Gini ["prestatore"]	12.	32.15	Filippo di Giovanni Ciari
3.	72.00	Barduccio di Cherichino "tavoliere"	13.	30.00	Tommaso di Francesco di Giovanni
4.	66.00	Messer Tommaso di Guccio Soderini	14.	28.00	Bartolommeo di Tommaso Corbinelli
5.	41.15	Piero di Castello da Quarata [Quaratesi]	15.	28.00	Bernardo di Ugolino Bonsi
6.	40.00	Piero di Bindo Dini	16.	26.10	Cione di Stefano "lanaiuolo"
7.	38.12	Cione di Giorgio Quaratesi	17.	26.00	Gherardo di Francesco di Ser Mino
8.	35.2	Giovanni di Tommaso di Salvestro	18.	25.15	Bernardo di Castello da Quarata [Quaratesi]
9.	35.00	Heir of Francesco di Domenico Sapiti	19.	25.00	Niccolò di Luca di Feo
10.	34.00	Bartolo di Schiatta Ridolfi	20.	25.00	Paperino di Filippo di Jacopo Guidetti

Appendix II: Tables on Wealth

No.	Prestanza in florins/soldi	Name of taxpayer
21.	23.10	Niccolò and Domenico di Gherardo Piaciti
22.	23.00	Lionardo di Stoldo Frescobaldi
23.	22.6	Giovanni di Andrea di Filippozzo de' Bardi
24.	22.6	Niccolaio di Giovanni [di Sinibaldo de' Bardi]
25.	21.00	Agnolo di Ser Pino "mercatante"
26.	21.00	Francesco di Buonaccorso Alderotti
27.	21.00	Giusto di Coverello "ritagliatore"
28.	21.00	Miniato di Piero di Ser Chiaro (and brothers)
29.	20.05	Niccolò di Jacopo Guasconi
30.	20.00	Niccolò and Agnolo di Giovanni da Uzzano
31.	19.00	Bernaba di Giovanni degli Agli "mercatante"
32.	19.00	Giovanni di Boccio Bonbarocci (and "nipoti")
33.	17.17	Francesco di Filippo di Neri di Cambi
34.	17.17	Luca di Ghirighoro di Fetto Ubertini
35.	17.00	Donato di Ugolino Bonsi
36.	17.00	Giorgio Niccoli Bonaventura
37.	17.00	Maffio di Jacopo Corbinelli
38.	16.00	Francesco and Niccolaio di Giovanni di Ser Segna
39.	16.00	Giovanni di Tano Fei
40.	16.00	Heirs of Jacopo di Messer Agnolo de' Bardi
41.	16.00	Piero di Messer Donato Velluti
42.	16.00	Salvestro di Niccolò Alamanni
43.	14.14	Messer Filippo di Messer Tommaso Corsini [a lawyer]
44.	14.00	Giovanni di Giorgio Quaratesi
45.	13.12	Lorenzo di Duccio Montanini
46.	13.5	Bernardo di Giorgio de' Bardi
47.	13.00	Matteo dello Scelto Tinghi
48.	12.00	Filippo di Messer Castellano da Montecastelli
49.	11.11	Cristofano di Francesco Biliotti
50.	11.5	Nofri and Agnolo del Bonecca Rossi
51.	11.00	Lorenzo di Totto de' Bardi
52.	10.10	Baldo di Niccolò Ridolfi
53.	10.10	Zanobi di Messer Andrea de' Bardi
54.	10.8	Bartolommeo di Tuccio di Grezia
55.	10.00	Bartolommeo di Andrea del Benino
56.	10.00	Donato di Michele Velluti (and brothers)
57.	10.00	Francesco di Niccolò Manelli
58.	10.00	Giovanni di Bartolommeo Capponi (and brothers)
59.	10.00	Heir of Lapo di Francesco del Fontana
60.	10.00	Lorenzo di Filippo Machiavelli
61.	10.00	Piero di Bartolommeo Niccoli
62.	9.10	Agnolo di Tommaso Corbinelli
63.	9.10	Antonio di Tommaso Corbinelli
64.	9.10	Parigi di Tommaso Corbinelli
65.	9.9	Jacopo di Piero Bini
66.	9.00	Bernardo di Bartolommeo Niccoli
67.	9.00	Bernardo di Giannozzo Manetti
68.	9.00	Franco and Francesco di Messer Arnaldo Manelli
69.	9.00	Ser Matteo di Ser Meo Lioncini
70.	9.00	Niccolò di Messer Donato Barbadori
71.	9.00	Piero Cesini "setaiuolo"
72.	9.00	Piero di Guido Colombi

Appendix II: Tables on Wealth

No.	Prestanza in florins/soldi	Name of taxpayer
73.	9.00	Ridolfo and Piero di Pagolo Lotti
74.	8.16	Simone di Andrea "orafo"
75.	8.00	Antonio di Giovanni di Tano [del Bianco]
76.	8.00	Antonio di Segna Fei ["setaiuolo"]
77.	8.00	Cesare di Giramonte Bardi
78.	8.00	Chino di Piero di Chino Lippi
79.	8.00	Filippo di Tommaso di Mone Guidetti
80.	8.00	Francesco di Jacopo Manelli
81.	8.00	Giovanni di Cecco (and nipote)
82.	8.00	Heirs of Tommaso di Messer Castellano
83.	8.00	Michele di Banco di Ser Bartolo
84.	8.00	Nofri di Miniato del Bria "ritagliatore"
85.	8.00	Tommaso di Francesco Antinori
86.	7.12	Francesco di Messer Alessandro de' Bardi
87.	7.10	Francesco di Domenico di Andrea Dante
88.	7.10	Giovanni di Notto di Messer Piero de' Bardi (and brothers)
89.	7.10	Niccolò di Andrea del Benino
90.	7.10	Pietro di Ghirighoro di Andrea del Benino
91.	7.10	Tommaso di Francesco Amidei
92.	7.7	Ser Giovanni di Ghino Cecchi
93.	7.6	Giovanni di Tommaso Corbinelli
94.	7.5	Arrigo di Ser Piero Mucini
95.	7.2	Amerigo di Bernardo di Niccolò da Verazzano
96.	7.00	Guido di Giramonte Frescobaldi
97.	7.00	Lorenzo di Messer Barna Rossi
98.	7.00	Pietro di Gherardo Boverelli
99.	6.10	Jacopo di Gherardino di Francesco
100.	6.10	Heirs of Piero di Messer Jacopo Marchi
101.	6.10	Roberto del Sozzo de' Bardi
102.	6.5	Piero di Agostino Martini
103.	6.00	Benedetto di Lipaccio de' Bardi
104.	6.00	Cappone and Gino di Neri Capponi
105.	6.00	Corsino di Jacopo Corsini (and brothers)
106.	6.00	Domenico and Piero di Cenni Bardelli
107.	6.00	Domenico di Stefano Soderini
108.	6.00	Filippo di Messer Andrea de' Bardi
109.	6.00	Francesco di Antonio di Ser Niccolò Serragli (and brothers)
110.	6.00	Giovanni di Messer Donato Barbadori
111.	6.00	Giovanni di Niccolò Soderini
112.	6.00	Giuliano di Tommaso Brancacci
113.	6.00	Nozzo di Vanni Manetti
114.	6.00	Piero di Cambino Cambini
115.	6.00	Rinieri di Lapo Ricasoli
116.	6.00	Stefano di Vanni (and sons)
117.	6.00	Tommaso di Jacopo del Accerito
118.	6.00	Zanobi and Tacino di Bizino "albergatori"
119.	5.15	Filippo di Zanobi di Messer Piero de' Bardi
120.	5.15	Gianbonello di Ambrogio Gianbonelli
121.	5.10	Forte di Piero da Vico
122.	5.10	Niccolò di Giovanni Nelli "speziale"
123.	5.10	Niccolò di Jacopo Manelli
124.	5.10	Maestro Nuto di Bandino "medico"

Appendix II: Tables on Wealth

No.	Prestanza in florins/soldi	Name of taxpayer	No.	Prestanza in florins/soldi	Name of taxpayer
125.	5.10	Paolo di Paolo Ramaglianti	138.	5.00	Bartolommeo di Salvestro Brancacci
126.	5.10	Piero di Antonio da Uzzano (and brothers)	139.	5.00	Bernardo di Simone Quercetanni
127.	5.10	Salvestro di Salvestro Belfredelli	140.	5.00	Filippo di Francesco del Pugliese
128.	5.10	Tieri and Niccolaio di Lorenzo di Niccolaio di Tieri	141.	5.00	Giovanni di Cecco di Moni da Gambassi
129.	5.10	Tommaso di Giovanni da Petrognano	142.	5.00	Giovanni di Guerrieri Benci
130.	5.6	Gierozzo and Andrea di Francesco de' Bardi	143.	5.00	Guido di Jacopo Manelli
131.	5.5	Heirs of Bartolommeo di Giovanni "ferraiuolo"	144.	5.00	Jacopo and Guccio di Piero di Zucheri Soderini
132.	5.5	Giovanni di Pazzino Cicciaporci	145.	5.00	Jacopo di Vannozzo de' Bardi
133.	5.00	Agnolo di Ser Belcharo Serragli	146.	5.00	Manetto Dati della Malvaggia
134.	5.00	Heirs of Andrea and Antonio di Banco di Conte	147.	5.00	Matteo di Tommaso di Guido "lanaiuolo"
135.	5.00	Ser Antonio di Ser Chello	148.	5.00	Orso di Rinieri del Pace
136.	5.00	Antonio di Ser Francesco di Ser Rosso	149.	5.00	Piero and Filippo di Aghinolfo de' Bardi
137.	5.00	Antonio and Jacopo di Filippo da Ruota	150.	5.00	Pierozzo di Domenico Bonaventura

TABLE V

Catasto of 1427: S. Croce Quarter

No.	Net capital in florins	Name of taxpayer	No.	Net capital in florins	Name of taxpayer
1.	41,727	Bernardo di Lamberto Lamberteschi			Messer Francesco Rinuccini
2.	28,239	Antonio di Salvestro di Ser Ristoro [Serristori]	9.	14,180	Francesco di Cino Rinuccini
3.	25,000	Filippo di Tommaso degli Alberti	10.	13,842	Filippo di Cino Rinuccini
4.	23,144	Domenico di Nofri Busini	11.	13,234	Messer Matteo di Michele di Vanni Castellani
5.	20,807	Giovanni di Domenico Giugni (and brothers)	12.	12,431	Giannozzo and Antonio di Tommaso degli Alberti
6.	20,542	Ridolfo di Bonifazio Peruzzi			
7.	17,883	Jacopo di Piero di Jacopo Baroncelli	13.	12,300*	Bartolommea di Gherardo da Bologna ("fu col signore Braccio")
8.	15,816	Jacopo di Cino di			

Appendix II: Tables on Wealth

No.	Net capital in florins	Name of taxpayer
14.	11,818	Uberto di Amerigo Zati (and brothers)
15.	11,000*	Messer Lionardo di Francesco Bruni
16.	10,752	Francesco di Altobianco degli Alberti
17.	9,521	Bernardo di Bindaccio di Bonifazio Peruzzi
18.	9,503	Bernardo di Ambrogio di Meo
19.	8,364	Niccolò and Giovanni di Giovanni del Bellaccio Belacci
20.	7,979	Lionardo di Tommaso di Ser Ristoro [Serristori]
21.	7,958	Simone and Salvadore di Jacopo di Bino
22.	7,956	Ginevra di Messer Giovanni di Ser Ristoro [Serristori]
23.	7,558	Giovanni di Pagolo Morelli
24.	7,454	Niccolò di Conte di Rinieri Peruzzi (and brothers)
25.	7,404	Giovanni di Piero di Jacopo Baroncelli
26.	7,127	Paolo di Piero di Jacopo Baroncelli
27.	6,846	Pierozzo di Giuliano di Pierozzo di Ser Donato
28.	6,838	Tommaso di Messer Tommaso Sacchetti
29.	6,705	Bernardo di Tommaso di Ser Ristoro [Serristori]
30.	6,633	Giovanni di Jacopo Pigli (and brothers)
31.	6,576	Tommaso di Niccolò del Buono Busini
32.	6,434	Lapo di Giovanni Niccolini
33.	6,421	Giovanni di Bartolommeo Morelli
34.	5,918	Francesco di Giachinotto Boscholi
35.	5,837	Smeraldo and Giovanni di Alberto di Zanobi degli Alberti
36.	5,796	Jacopo di Tommaso di Ser Ristoro [Serristori]
37.	5,583	Lorenzo di Antonio Spinelli
38.	5,378	Heir of Antonio di Piero di Fronte
39.	5,360	Buono di Niccolò del Buono Busini
40.	5,179	Mainardo and Donato di Messer Carlo Cavalcanti
41.	4,967	Francesco di Andrea Arnoldi "setaiuolo"
42.	4,955	Vanni di Niccolò di Ser Vanni
43.	4,436	Zanobi di Jacopo di Belcaro [Belcari]
44.	4,283	Donato di Bonifazio Peruzzi
45.	4,148	Jacopo di Jacopo di Zaccheria
46.	4,067	Cristofano Bagnesi
47.	4,006	Jacopo di Giovanni Villani
48.	3,997	Lapo di Pacino da Castelfiorentino "setaiuolo"
49.	3,949	Betta widow of Banco di Fruosino da Verazzano
50.	3,874	Francesco di Ser Ludovico di Vanni
51.	3,769	Simone di Salamone di Torello [del Garbo]
52.	3,757	Piero di Bartolo degli Alberti (and sons)
53.	3,675	Andrea di Zanobi Borgognoni
54.	3,673	Berto di Bonifazio Peruzzi
55.	3,638	Antonio di Pierozzo di Ser Donato
56.	3,627	Antonio di Niccolò del Buono Busini
57.	3,603	Giovanni di Francesco di Spina
58.	3,542	Giovanni di Niccolò Riccalbani (and son)
59.	3,500	Inglese di Simone Baroncelli
60.	3,417	Niccolaio di Messer Torello Torelli (and brothers)
61.	3,380	Bindaccio di Granello di Fibindaccio Ricasoli
62.	3,363	Filippo di Giovanni da Diacceto

No.	Net capital in florins	Name of taxpayer	No.	Net capital in florins	Name of taxpayer
63.	3,246	Giovanni di Jacopo "merciaio"	87.	2,489	Niccolò di Amelio Buonaguisi
64.	3,242	Niccolò di Bellacino di Niccolò Bellaci (and brothers)	88.	2,435	Alamanno di Messer Jacopo Salviati
65.	3,149	Romigi di Ricco di Niccolò Bucelli (and brothers)	89.	2,405	Bartolo di Domenico Corsi
66.	3,148	Giovanni di Zaccheria di Jacopo	90.	2,383	Taddeo di Salamone di Torello [del Garbo]
67.	3,112	Bernardo di Messer Jacopo Salviati	91.	2,377	Francesco di Domenico Corsi
68.	3,108	Luigi and Galeotto di Francesco di Biagio Lioni	92.	2,353	Giovanni di Lionardo Jacopi
69.	3,084	Jacopo di Messer Francesco Rinuccini	93.	2,353	Tommaso di Scolaio Ciacchi
70.	2,965	Bernardo di Bartolommeo Gherardi	94.	2,334	Paolo di Santi di Ricco Bucelli
71.	2,955	Bastiano di Matteo di Antonio Martini	95.	2,310	Niccolò di Doffo di Bernardino
72.	2,949	Bernardo and Francesco del Maestro Francesco di Ridolfo	96.	2,298	Filippo di Guido Fagni
73.	2,915	Messer Bartolommeo di Baldassare Foraboschi [a lawyer] (and brothers)	97.	2,250	Francesco di Piero di Niccolò di Forese
74.	2,909	Guaspare di Francesco da Diacceto	98.	2,194	Giovanni di Michele di Vanni Castellani
75.	2,899	Filippo di Giovanni Niccolini	99.	2,176	Domenico di Francesco Spinelli (and sons)
76.	2,888	Ludovico and Giuliano di Salvestro Ceffini	100.	2,173	Orsino di Zucherino da Cignano (and sons)
77.	2,840	Piero di Niccolaio di Manetto Filicaia	101.	2,172	Andrea di Niccolò Giugni
78.	2,838	Betto di Jacopo di Betto Berlinghieri (and cousins)	102.	2,172	Galeotto di Bettino di Fibindaccio [Ricasoli]
79.	2,826	Michele di Giovanni Galilei "ritagliatore"	103.	2,161	Duccio di Taddeo di Duccio Mancini
80.	2,782	Giovanni di Messer Forese Salviati	104.	2,150	Francesco di Cionaccio di Francesco Baroncelli (and brothers)
81.	2,645	Maestro Galileo di Giovanni Galilei "medico"	105.	2,114	Ardingo di Bartolino Talani (and brothers)
82.	2,601	Paolo di Giovanni di Ludovico Ceffini	106.	2,113	Francesco di Giovanni dello Sciocco
83.	2,598	Aldighieri di Francesco Biliotti	107.	2,100	Francesco and Giovanni di Bernardo Galluzzi
84.	2,556	Niccolò di Nastagio Bucelli	108.	2,098	Stefano di Naldo "merciaio"
85.	2,540	Piero di Messer Vanni Castellani	109.	2,093	Amerigo di Giovanni di Messer Amerigo Cavalcanti (and brothers)
86.	2,517	Tommaso di Domenico Borghini	110.	2,092	Giuliano di Nastagio di Benincasa Manetti
			111.	2,023	Francesco and Lio-

No.	Net capital in florins	Name of taxpayer
		nardo di Ser Viviano di Neri [Viviani]
112.	2,008	Rinaldo di Rinieri Peruzzi
113.	2,003	Bonifazio di Donato "speziale"
114.	1,993	Cederno di Bartolommeo Cederni
115.	1,948	Vieri di Filippo di Bancozzo (and brothers)
116.	1,940	Carlo di Granello Ricasoli
117.	1,930	Niccolò di Cocco di Donato [Cocchi-Donati]
118.	1,928	Matteo di Domenico Corsi
119.	1,887	Riccardo di Niccolò Fagni
120.	1,865	Niccolaio del Chiaro di Niccolaio
121.	1,845	Domenico di Gherardino Rutini
122.	1,832	Bartolommeo di Verano Peruzzi
123.	1,824	Tommaso di Zanobi Guidacci
124.	1,800	Stefano di Vanni Ricoveri
125.	1,785	Caterina di Albertaccio degli Alberti
126.	1,779	Heirs of Amideo di Santi di Ricco [Bucelli]
127.	1,744	Giovanni di Bardo Corsi
128.	1,724	Filippo di Franco Sacchetti
129.	1,723	Bartolommea widow of Messer Michele di Messer Vanni Castellani
130.	1,697	Francesco di Filippo Cei
131.	1,685	Giovanni and Piero di Antonio di Guido Monaldi

No.	Net capital in florins	Name of taxpayer
132.	1,661	Paolo di Bernardo di Piero da Gangalandi
133.	1,635	Donato del Maestro Tommaso del Maestro Donato
134.	1,625	Andrea di Jacopo di Martino
135.	1,604	Piero di Domenico Corsi
136.	1,592	Giachetto di Zanobi Bartoli
137.	1,571	Filippo di Giovanni di Ser Vico
138.	1,570	Calvano di Messer Jacopo Salviati
139.	1,564	Bartolommeo di Gianno Morelli (and brothers)
140.	1,560	Dego and Renzo di Bernardo di Jacopo degli Alberti
141.	1,546	Lisa widow of Giovanni di Feo
142.	1,537	Betta widow of Cino Rinuccini
143.	1,530	Michele del Maestro Guerrieri da Pescia
144.	1,518	Giovanni di Renzo Salterelli
145.	1,517	Agnesa widow of Filippo de' Ricci
146.	1,501	Giuliano di Filippo di Simone da Carmignano "ritagliatore"
147.	1,492	Niccolò di Filippo di Bancozzo
148.	1,486	Francesco di Cambio Orlandi
149.	1,467	Giovanni di Matteo di Mangio "tintore"
150.	1,456	Francesco di Giovanni di Martino Bandi

Appendix II: Tables on Wealth

TABLE VI

Catasto of 1427: S. Giovanni Quarter

No.	Net capital in florins	Name of taxpayer	No.	Net capital in florins	Name of taxpayer
1.	79,472	Giovanni di Bicci de' Medici	22.	11,811	Messer Rinaldo di Messer Maso degli Albizzi
2.	78,166	Gabbriello di Messer Bartolommeo Panciatichi	23.	11,510	Antonio and Giovanni di Matteo di Ugucciozzo de' Ricci
3.	55,815*	Alessandro di Ser Filippo Borromei (and sons)	24.	10,585	Michele di Salvestro "brigliaio"
4.	48,820	Giovanni di Messer Bartolommeo Panciatichi	25.	10,082	Jacopo di Ser Francesco Ciai
5.	31,245	Giovanni di Nofri Bischeri	26.	9,760	Carlo di Niccolò Macinghi
6.	31,000	Andrea di Guglielmo de' Pazzi	27.	9,537	Antonio di Lorenzo and Michele di Galeotto Baronci
7.	27,706	Agnolo and Giovanni di Filippo di Ser Giovanni [Pandolfini]	28.	9,646	Heir of Bartolommeo di Niccolò di Taldo Valori
8.	23,171	Bartolommeo and Giovanni di Antonio di Ser Bartolommeo di Ser Nello [Ghetti]	29.	9,445	Stefano di Ser Bartolommeo Nello (and brothers)
9.	19,874	Ser Paolo and Andrea di Ser Lando Fortini (and nipote)	30.	8,735	Lionardo di Salvestro "brigliaio"
10.	18,663	Luca di Piero Rinieri (and sons)	31.	8,133	Alamanno and Gieri di Poldo de' Pazzi
11.	18,174	Bernardo di Giovanni Portinari	32.	8,102	Antonio di Schiatta Macci
12.	16,914	Giovacchino di Niccolò Macinghi	33.	8,012	Simione di Paolo di Berto Carnesecchi (and brothers)
13.	16,874	Heirs of Jacopo di Anichino di Riccardo [Riccardi]	34.	8,010	Luca di Luca di Ser Filippo Carnesecchi
14.	15,097	Averardo di Francesco de' Medici	35.	7,977	Luca di Messer Maso degli Albizzi
15.	14,868	Baldassare di Luigi Melanesi	36.	7,898	Tommaso di Zanobi di Ser Gino [Ginori]
16.	14,727	Niccolaio and Alessandro di Ugo degli Alessandri (and brothers)	37.	7,655	Andrea di Niccolò Macinghi
17.	14,292	Giovanni di Michele di Ser Parente	38.	7,634	Niccolò di Zanobi di Ser Gino [Ginori]
18.	13,448	Parente di Michele di Ser Parente	39.	7,593	Maestro Giovanni del Maestro Antonio da San Miniato
19.	13,133	Bartolo di Nofri Bischeri	40.	7,403	Filippo di Bernaba Filippeschi
20.	12,282	Giuliano di Giovanni Torrigiani	41.	7,265	Guglielmo di Giunta Bindi
21.	11,818	Ghezzo di Agnolo di Ghezzo (and brothers)	42.	7,265	Zanobi di Filippo Macinghi

No.	Net capital in florins	Name of taxpayer	No.	Net capital in florins	Name of taxpayer
43.	7,137	Taddeo di Zanobi Gaddi	67.	5,142	Bartolo di Bartolo Tedaldi
44.	6,946	Deo di Deo Becchuti	68.	5,100	Tora di Piero de' Pazzi (in Avignon)
45.	6,762	Giovanni di Andrea di Bonanno	69.	5,000	Toso di Albizzo del Toso da Fortuna
46.	6,684	Bartolommeo and Roberto del Mancino Sostegni	70.	4,931	Giovanni di Lando "vinattiere"
47.	6,679	Agnolo di Zanobi di Taddeo Gaddi	71.	4,881	Ser Nofri di Niccolò di Dante Ughi
48.	6,524	Taddeo di Filippo di Taddeo [Donati?] "lanaiuolo"	72.	4,794	Giovanni di Filippo Corbizzi
49.	6,448	Migliore di Tommaso Guidotti	73.	4,706	Bernardo and Giovanni di Andrea di Maso
50.	6,413	Federico di Niccolò Goro (and nephew)	74.	4,677	Giovanni di Jacopo Bonafè
51.	6,387	Filippo di Messer Biagio Guasconi	75.	4,610	Antonio di Ghezzo della Casa
52.	6,344	Banco and Stagio di Berardo "calzaiuoli"	76.	4,589	Piero di Francesco di Ser Gino
53.	6,294	Giovanni di Domenico Ciampelli	77.	4,293	Bartolommeo di Tommaso Baldovini
54.	6,245	Niccolà and Cambio di Messer Vieri de' Medici	78.	4,019	Antonio di Tedice degli Albizzi
55.	6,241	Bernardo di Cristofano Carnesecchi	79.	4,017	Maestro Giovanni di Ser Bartolo da Radda
56.	6,235	Mariotto and Lorenzo di Giovanni dello Stecutto	80.	4,000	Michele di Messer Gieri de' Pazzi (in Avignon)
57.	5,949	Giuliano di Francesco di Ser Gino [Ginori]	81.	3,880	Stagio di Matteo di Francesco Buonaguisi (and brothers)
58.	5,943	Simone di Francesco di Ser Gino [Ginori]	82.	3,847	Domenico di Antonio di Bartolommeo di Ser Santi
59.	5,868	Heir of Giovanni di Ghezzo della Casa	83.	3,821	Daniello di Zanobi di Francesco "speziale"
60.	5,834	Ser Giovanni Buonaiuti "lanaiuolo"	84.	3,816	Salvi di Salvi Lotti
61.	5,774	Niccolò di Francesco Giraldi	85.	3,780	Antonio di Bernardo di Ligi
62.	5,720	Bernardo di Bindo Gili	86.	3,752	Panuzio di Zanobi di Nofri del Bria
63.	5,615	Giovanni and Francesco di Albizzo del Toso da Fortuna	87.	3,739	Stefano di Giovanni di Piero Parenti (and nipote)
64.	5,352	Francesco and Migliore di Vieri Guadagni (and brothers)	88.	3,717	Giovanni di Tedice degli Albizzi
65.	ca.5,200	Brunaccio di Guido Brunaccio	89.	3,715	Pagolo di Ser Giovanni Mini "speziale" (and nipote)
66.	5,183	Jacopo di Bartolo "bottaio" (and sons) "setaiuoli"	90.	3,695	Bartolommeo di Matteo Tanagli

No.	Net capital in florins	Name of taxpayer	No.	Net capital in florins	Name of taxpayer
91.	3,657	Fabrino and Niccolò di Stefano di Ser Piero	115.	3,142	Antonio di Filippo di Piero Rinieri (and brothers)
92.	3,643	Beni ("possessions") of Sandro di Jacopo di Francesco Cambi	116.	3,114	Piera widow of Messer Matteo Scolari
93.	3,641	Antonio di Modeo Scollaio	117.	3,094	Heirs of Messer Filippo and Messer Matteo Scolari
94.	3,584	Taddeo di Bartolommeo di Lorino	118.	3,036	Marco di Antonio Palmieri
95.	3,559	Berto di Zanobi Carnesecchi	119.	3,034	Tita widow of Antonio di Alessandro degli Alessandri
96.	3,546	Jacopo di Geppo da Monte Rinaldi	120.	2,991	Ser Martino di Luca Martini (and brothers)
97.	3,529	Giovanni di Ser Benedetto Tempi	121.	2,977	Giuliano di Ser Benedetto Ciai
98.	3,527	Bartolommeo di Taldo "linaiuolo"	122.	2,965	Simone di Salvi di Filippo Salvi
99.	3,523	Francesco di Antonio Palmieri	123.	2,960	Niccolò and Bernardo di Messer Baldo della Tosa
100.	3,511	Neri di Francesco Fioravanti (and sons)	124.	2,912	Ser Piero di Ser Lorenzo della Volpaia
101.	3,502	Luca di Giovanni di Guido "sensale"	125.	2,840	Antonio di Rinieri Squarcialupi
102.	3,500*	Antonio di Roberto di Messer Tommaso degli Albizzi	126.	2,775	Bernardo di Vieri Guadagni
103.	3,493	Matteo di Benedetto "scodellaio"	127.	2,760	Francesco di Giovanni di Salvi
104.	3,474	Maestro Antonio di Maestro Guccio della Scarperia	128.	2,708	Dioneo di Matteo di Messer Donato Adimari (and brothers)
105.	3,436	Manno di Manno Donati	129.	2,690	Francesco di Antonio Giraldi (and brothers)
106.	3,404	Heirs of Lionardo di Zanobi "fu speziale"	130.	2,684	Cristofano di Bartolommeo di Ser Santi
107.	3,389	Messer Bartolommeo di Giovanni da Monteghonzi	131.	2,680	Alessandro di Antonio di Pagolo Covoni
108.	3,389	Salvi di Filippo di Salvi (and brothers)	132.	2,654	Alesso di Donato "lanaiuolo"
109.	3,381	Lotteringo di Andrea di Messer Ugo della Stufa	133.	2,588	Francesco and Tommaso di Tommaso Pecori
110.	3,318	Jacopo di Tommaso Tani	134.	2,583	Niccolò and Giovanni di Jacopo di Messer Niccolò Baldovini
111.	3,311	Nofri and Piero di Maffeo Tedaldi	135.	2,543	Boccaccio di Salvestro di Messer Filippo Adimari
112.	3,310	Bartolommeo di Filippo Vinaccesi	136.	2,530	Piero di Francesco Ferrantini (and brothers)
113.	3,268	Jacopo di Ser Benedetto Tempi	137.	2,446	Giovanni di Bartolommeo di Ser Santi
114.	3,265	Stefano di Salvi di Filippo [Salvi]			

No.	Net capital in florins	Name of taxpayer	No.	Net capital in florins	Name of taxpayer
138.	2,412	Lorenzo di Andrea di Messer Ugo della Stufa	145.	2,324	Niccolò di Lotto Liberali
139.	2,387	Niccolò di Maso di Strinato	146.	2,320	Piera widow of Filippo di Bartolommeo Gori
140.	2,381	Niccolò di Gentile degli Albizzi	147.	2,319	Lorenzo di Buonaccorso Baldinacci (and brothers)
141.	2,351	Bernardo di Arrigo Falconieri	148.	2,314	Manetto di Zanobi Carnesecchi
142.	2,347	Niccolò and Pierozzo di Talento Tedaldi	149.	2,295	Matteo di Piero "fabro"
143.	2,326	Orlando di Guccio de' Medici	150.	2,286	Piero di Jacopo Martini
144.	2,325	Giusafa di Mariano degli Albizzi			

TABLE VII

Catasto of 1427: S. Maria Novella Quarter

No.	Net capital in florins	Name of taxpayer	No.	Net capital in florins	Name of taxpayer
1.	101,422	Messer Palla di Nofri Strozzi	13.	10,940	Lorenzo di Piero di Lenzo Lenzi
2.	46,320	Francesco and Niccolò di Messer Simone Tornabuoni (and nipoti)	14.	10,921	Matteo di Azzo "lanaiuolo"
3.	34,987	Francesco di Francesco di Pierozzo della Luna	15.	10,907	Domenico di Antonio di Francesco Allegri
4.	29,965	Piero di Neri Ardinghelli	16.	10,358	Piero di Jacopo Ardinghelli
5.	21,366	Tommaso di Giacomino di Goggio [Tebalducci]	17.	9,720*	Madalena di Carlo Strozzi [widow of Luchino Visconti]
6.	20,090	Francesco di Ser Benozzo (and nipote)	18.	9,618	Francesco and Zanobi di Benedetto di Caroccio Strozzi
7.	14,971	Daniello di Nofri di Azzo "lanaiuolo"	19.	8,736	Giovanni di Jacopo di Piero dal Borgo [S. Lorenzo]
8.	14,425	Giovanni di Bartolommeo di Ser Spinello	20.	8,669	Giovanni di Domenico Bartoli
9.	12,610	Michele del Bene di Spinello (and nipote)	21.	8,534	Giuliano and Alessandro di Piero Borromei
10.	12,407	Giannozzo di Stoldo Gianfigliazzi	22.	7,957	Giovanni di Gherardo Davizzi
11.	11,837	Cante di Giovanni Compagni	23.	7,601	Heirs of Tommaso Fini
12.	11,627	Domenico di Lionardo di Domenico [Buoninsegni]	24.	7,538	Carlo di Tommaso Bartoli
			25.	7,074*	Giovanni di Messer Piero Gaetani

No.	Net capital in florins	Name of taxpayer
26.	6,618	Bernardo and Giovanni di Giovanni Strozzi
27.	6,495	Lionardo and Giovanni di Giacomino [Tebalducci]
28.	6,279	Simone di Salvestro di Simone Gondi
29.	6,164	Antonio di Giovanni di Messer Giovanni Rucellai (and brothers)
30.	5,935	Lapaccino di Benedetto di Lapaccino del Toso (and brothers)
31.	5,798*	Benedetto di Messer Piero Gaetani
32.	5,777	Giovanni di Andrea Minerbetti
33.	5,763	Bartolommeo di Giovanni Carducci
34.	5,621	Agnolo di Bindo Vernaccia
35.	5,374	Giovanni di Francesco di Bartolo (and brothers)
36.	5,109	Paolo di Niccolò di Ciuto
37.	4,999	Tommaso and Alessandro di Marco di Tommaso Bartoli
38.	4,983	Francesco di Jacopo di Francesco Venturi
39.	4,972	Giovanni di Simone di Messer Tommaso Altoviti (and sons)
40.	4,912	Calvano di Attaviano di Messer Guccio de' Nobili
41.	4,654	Filippo di Giovanni Carduccci
42.	4,618	Giovanni di Paolo di Messer Paolo Rucellai (and brothers)
43.	4,539	Giuliano di Lapo Vespucci
44.	4,459	Matteo di Marco Bartoli (and brothers)
45.	4,426	Neridonato and Antonio di Franco di Messer Donato Acciaiuoli
46.	4,396	Matteo di Simone Strozzi
47.	4,349	Giovanni di Salvestro Carradori
48.	4,325	Gierozzo di Niccolò da Castiglione
49.	4,320	Benedetto di Marco Strozzi
50.	4,096	Dego di Piero di Dego Spini
51.	4,071	Niccolà di Filippo Bonciani
52.	3,931	Giovanni di Niccolò del Maestro Francesco da Empoli (and brothers)
53.	3,878	Neri di Messer Donato Acciaiuoli
54.	3,873	Giovanni di Messer Rinaldo Gianfigliazzi (and brothers)
55.	3,750*	Luca del Sera [resident elsewhere]
56.	3,653	Biagio di Simone di Domenico Perini
57.	3,599	Andrea di Domenico Davizzi
58.	3,517	Antonio di Piero di Dego Spini
59.	3,494	Andrea and Lionardo di Tommaso di Bartolo di Ser Tino
60.	3,419	Luigi di Ramondino Vecchietti
61.	3,314	Michele di Benedetto di Ser Michele
62.	3,307	Nanna widow of Bartolommeo Bartolini
63.	3,283	Tommaso di Andrea Minerbetti
64.	3,214	Jacopo di Antonio di Lapaccio
65.	3,118	Maestro Lorenzo di Agnolo Sassoli da Prato
66.	3,108	Giovanni di Bartolommeo Cederni
67.	3,066	Guido di Giovanni di Guido Guiducci (and brothers)
68.	2,910	Nepo and Bartolommeo di Bartolommeo Spini
69.	2,859	Jacopo di Monte di Pugio
70.	2,816	Cristofano di Matteo del Tegghia
71.	2,807	Tommaso di Domenico Fagiuoli

No.	Net capital in florins	Name of taxpayer
72.	2,770	Domenico di Tano Petrucci "coltriciaio"
73.	2,673	Guccio di Andrea da Sommaia
74.	2,671	Cardinale Rucellai (and sons)
75.	2,659	Bruno di Bernardo Ardinghelli
76.	2,654	Filippo di Simone di Lippo Bondi
77.	2,612	Antonio di Messer Ricciardo del Bene
78.	2,606	Urbano di Jacopo Bartoli
79.	2,567	Piero del Maestro Bartolommeo del Maestro Ludovico
80.	2,556	Bellozzo di Lorenzo Bartoli
81.	2,536	Niccolosa widow of Messer Rinaldo Gianfigliazzi
82.	2,532	Heir of Ludovico di Michele di Ghieri Saluzzi
83.	2,492	Pinaccio di Filippo di Messer Lionardo Strozzi
84.	2,486	Barzelone di Spedaliere da Prato
85.	2,439	Lionardo di Guccio Brogiotti
86.	2,437	Taddeo di Cristofano di Piero Giusti
87.	2,434	Bartolommeo di Tommaso di Bartolo di Ser Tino
88.	2,423	Jacopo and Schiatta di Filippo Cavalcanti
89.	2,409	Michele di Jacopo "fabro"
90.	2,397	Berto di Guido Trinciavelli
91.	2,368	Salvestro di Tommaso Popoleschi
92.	2,262	Lionardo di Marco di Tommaso Bartoli
93.	2,243	Ghostanza widow of Rosso di Messer Scolaio Cavalcanti
94.	2,229	Ser Ugolino Pieruzzi
95.	2,193	Dino di Messer Guccio [de' Nobili]
96.	2,189	Filippo di Filippo Melanesi (and brothers)

No.	Net capital in florins	Name of taxpayer
97.	2,187	Niccolò di Domenico Pollini
98.	2,186	Ludovico di Ser Viviano di Neri Franchi [Viviani]
99.	2,182	Cipriano and Giovanni di Jacopo Rucellai
100.	2,162	Spinetta widow of Niccolò di Giovanni Carducci
101.	2,144	Messer Agnolo di Jacopo Acciaiuoli
102.	2,135	Oddo del Buono "lanaiuolo"
103.	2,134	Bernardo di Francesco Malatesti (and brothers)
104.	2,094	Giovanni di Salvi di Giovanni Borgherini (and brothers)
105.	2,068	Strozza and Smeraldo Strozzi
106.	2,064	Antonio di Andrea Borghi "linaiuolo"
107.	2,063	Gherardo di Piero di Dego Spini
108.	2,062	Carlo di Marco Strozzi
109.	2,047	Andrea and Alessandro di Guido di Giuntino "lanaiuoli"
110.	2,045	Filippo di Antonio del Buono
111.	2,037	Adovardo di Cipriano Giachinotti
112.	2,007	Piero del Maestro Ugolino da Montecatini
113.	1,965	Jacopo di Agnolo di Franco "setaiuolo"
114.	1,960	Guidetto di Francesco Monaldi (and brothers)
115.	1,942	Guido di Francesco di Messer Niccolò Baldovinetti (and brothers)
116.	1,938	Niccolò di Piero Tornaquinci
117.	1,868	Cantino di Matteo Cavalcanti
118.	1,814	Luca di Bartolo Riccardi
119.	1,799	Francesco di Marco di Tommaso Bartoli
120.	1,763	Niccolò di Andrea Carducci "ritagliatore"

No.	Net capital in florins	Name of taxpayer	No.	Net capital in florins	Name of taxpayer
121.	1,750	Palla and Carlo di Francesco di Messer Palla Strozzi	135.	1,493	Luigi di Zanobi di Lapaccino del Toso
122.	1,705	Alessandro di Manetto Davanzati	136.	1,489	Altobianco di Ludovico Giandonati
123.	1,700	Caterina widow of Paolo di Messer Paolo Rucellai	137.	1,482	Nofri di Jacopo Cardinali
124.	1,698	Bruno di Cristofano di Piero del Gioppante	138.	1,469	Nanna di Paolo di Guglielmo "speziale"
125.	1,661	Pasquino di Francesco Pasquini	139.	1,458	Carlo and Lancelotto di Bartolommeo di Bardo [Bindo?] Altoviti
126.	1,622	Ser Cristofano di Andrea da Laterina	140.	1,430	Piero di Filippo di Messer Lionardo Strozzi
127.	1,566	Lionardo di Messer Guccio de' Nobili (and brothers)	141.	1,428	Francesco di Zanobi di Lapaccino del Toso
128.	1,560	Villana widow of Stoldo di Lorenzo da Prato	142.	1,427	Arnoldo di Adimari Spini
129.	1,558	Benvenuto di Ugolino Michi	143.	1,425	Ser Tommaso di Ser Luca Franceschi
130.	1,548	Rosso di Rosso di Messer Scolaio Cavalcanti	144.	1,404	Tommaso di Rinieri Popolani
131.	1,520	Lodovico di Tommaso del Gheldola (sic)	145.	1,388	Giulio di Vieri di Guido (and brothers) "setaiuoli"
132.	1,517	Salimbene di Lionardo Bartolini	146.	1,367	Matteo di Filippo di Giovanni Ciari
133.	1,501	Piero di Messer Guido Bonciani	147.	1,366	Gherardo di Guido Pesce
134.	1,498	Isabetta widow of Ser Lionardo di Ser Giovanni Andrea	148.	1,360	Niccolò di Agnolo Bonciani
			149.	1,352	Francesco di Guardi di Gherardo Guardi
			150.	1,346	Giovanni di Bencino Baldesi

TABLE VIII

Catasto of 1427: S. Spirito Quarter

No.	Net capital in florins	Name of taxpayer	No.	Net capital in florins	Name of taxpayer
1.	46,402	Niccolò di Giovanni da Uzzano	5.	24,438	Niccolò di Messer Donato Barbadori
2.	31,480	Bernardo di Giannozzo Manetti	6.	24,117	Bardo di Francesco de' Bardi
3.	27,601	Benedetto di Giuliano di Bartolo Gini	7.	21,053	Castello di Piero Quaratesi
4.	26,140*	Francesco Nerli (in Avignon)	8.	20,508	Jacopo di Filippo Guidetti

	Net capital			Net capital	
No.	in florins	Name of taxpayer	No.	in florins	Name of taxpayer
9.	19,940	Giovanni di Barduccio di Cherichino	34.	7,909	Simone and Antonio di Niccolaio del Lapeggia de' Bardi
10.	19,287	Giovanni di Messer Donato Barbadori	35.	7,895	Bindo di Gherardo Piaciti
11.	19,182	Donato di Ugolino Bonsi	36.	7,665	Bernardo di Uguccione di Francesco Lippi
12.	18,891	Francesco di Tommaso di Francesco Giovanni (and brothers)	37.	7,566	Domenico di Bernaba Filippeschi
13.	18,595	Messer Giovanni di Messer Luigi Guicciardini	38.	7,524	Giovanni and Uguccione di Mico Capponi
14.	17,577	Lippaccio and Francesco di Benedetto de' Bardi	39.	7,441	Andrea di Francesco di Banco
15.	16,684	Vannozzo di Giovanni Serragli	40.	7,422	Filippo di Benedetto Nerli
16.	ca.15,000	Francesco di Andrea Quaratesi	41.	7,329	Mariotto di Francesco di Giovanni di Ser Segna (and brothers)
17.	14,853	Larione di Lippaccio de' Bardi	42.	7,175	Giovanni di Tommaso Corbinelli
18.	13,241	Jacopo di Piero di Jacopo Bini	43.	7,136	Maestro Domenico di Piero [Toscanelli] "medico"
19.	13,175	Isau di Agnolo Martellini	44.	6,785	Bernardo di Bartolommeo di Andrea del Benino "setaiuolo"
20.	12,268	Bernardo di Ugolino Bonsi			
21.	11,863	Luigi di Giovanni di Luigi Quaratesi (and brothers)	45.	6,722	Luca di Ghirigoro di Fetto Ubertini
22.	11,045	Batista di Niccolò Guicciardini	46.	6,624	Donato di Bartolommeo Barbadori
23.	10,936	Parigi di Tommaso Corbinelli	47.	6,243	Niccolà di Piero di Bartolommeo Capponi (and brothers)
24.	10,927	Francesco di Messer Tommaso Soderini	48.	6,163	Bartolommeo and Ubertino di Andrea di Bartolommeo de' Bardi
25.	10,574	Schiatta di Uberto Ridolfi	49.	6,019	Antonio di Antonio di Giovanni "galigaio"
26.	10,450	Bernardo di Agnolo Corbinelli (and brothers)	50.	5,972	Bernardo and Vieri di Bartolo di Messer Bindo de' Bardi
27.	10,450	Giovanni di Niccolò Guicciardini			
28.	10,444	Chino di Piero di Chino Lippi	51.	5,585	Luttozzo di Jacopo di Luttozzo Nasi
29.	10,068	Andrea di Lippaccio de' Bardi	52.	5,517	Antonio di Jacopo Canigiani
30.	9,350	Bernardo di Antonio Uzzano	53.	5,249	Messer Lorenzo di Antonio Ridolfi [a lawyer]
31.	8,852	Luti di Michele di Luti "mercatante"	54.	5,218	Bamba widow of Agnolo di Giovanni Uzzano
32.	8,647	Jacopo di Bernaba Filippeschi	55.	5,166	Jacopo and Buonaccorso di Filippo del Pugliese
33.	8,077	Giovanni di Guccio "mercatante" (and nipote)			

No.	Net capital in florins	Name of taxpayer
56.	5,016	Jacopo di Vannozzo de' Bardi
57.	5,002	Gherardo di Bartolommeo Barbadori
58.	4,942	Maestro Lionardo del Maestro Agnolo "medico"
59.	4,841	Stoldo and Giovanni di Matteo de' Bardi
60.	4,720	Neri di Gino Capponi
61.	4,580	Guido and Agnolo di Niccolò di Guido della Foresta
62.	4,425	Francesco di Filippo Cambi
63.	4,409	Agostino di Gino Capponi
64.	4,394	Jacopo di Filippo da Ruota (and nipoti)
65.	4,377	Bartolommeo di Tommaso Corbinelli
66.	4,342	Antonio di Piero Benizzi (and brothers)
67.	4,201	Ser Giovanni Ghini "lanaiuolo"
68.	4,184	Paolo di Giannozzo Vettori
69.	4,000*	Venanzio di Pierozzo Pieruzzi da Camerino
70.	3,996	Tommaso di Francesco Antinori (and sons)
71.	3,993	Andrea di Giusto di Coverello "ritagliatore"
72.	3,984	Giovanni di Jacopo di Piero Bini
73.	3,748	Piero di Messer Luigi Guicciardini
74.	3,568	Donato di Michele Velluti
75.	3,411	Bernardo di Francesco Sapiti
76.	3,405	Piero di Ser Lapo "setaiuolo"
77.	3,377	Pietro di Ghirigoro di Andrea del Benino "setaiuolo"
78.	3,375	Domenico del Maestro Jacopo da San Gimignano
79.	3,269	Messer Niccolò di Giovanni di Niccolò Soderini (and brothers)
80.	3,202	Carlo and Giuliano di Primerano Girolami

No.	Net capital in florins	Name of taxpayer
81.	3,177	Guccio di Piero di Zucherini Soderini
82.	3,160	Giovanni di Jacopo di Luttozzo Nasi
83.	3,106	Lipaccio and Giovanni di Bartolommeo Brancacci
84.	3,013	Andrea and Giovanni di Bartolommeo Serragli
85.	2,970	Antonio di Jacopo Pucci "lanaiuolo"
86.	2,903	Giovanni di Pazzino Cicciaporci (and sons) "lanaiuoli"
87.	2,808	Simone and Bartolommeo del Nero "rigattieri"
88.	2,788	Andrea di Michele Velluti "lanaiuolo"
89.	2,709	Bartolo di Noffo Ridolfi
90.	2,707	Gualterotto di Lorenzo Gualterotti
91.	2,693	Jacopo di Paolo di Bartolo di Schiatta Ridolfi
92.	2,676	Andrea di Giovanni de' Bardi
93.	2,664	Caterina di Jacopo di Francesco de' Bardi
94.	2,664	Lorenzo di Gino Capponi
95.	2,654	Cesare di Giramonte de' Bardi
96.	2,641	Domenico di Francesco Sapiti
97.	2,597	Piero di Paolo Lotti
98.	2,568	Bartolommeo di Lorenzo di Totto Gualterotti
99.	2,519	Malatesta and Dante di Bernardo da Castiglione
100.	2,494	Antonio di Tommaso Amidei
101.	2,492	Agnolo di Jacopo Mori
102.	2,457	Lorenzo di Giovanni Amadori
103.	2,444	Salvestro and Piero di Lionardo di Puccio "vinattieri"
104.	2,429	Piero di Cambino di Bartolo Cambini
105.	2,385	Filippo di Tommaso Piaciti
106.	2,382	Agnolo di Francesco di Agnolo "speziale"

No.	Net capital in florins	Name of taxpayer
107.	2,349	Raimondo di Amaretto Manelli
108.	2,338	Niccolò di Bartolommeo Corbinelli
109.	2,302	Antonio di Bernardo Ridolfi
110.	2,283	Giovanni di Cenni Ugolini
111.	2,281	Felice di Michele Brancacci
112.	2,251	Lorenzo di Sandro Mazzetti
113.	2,196	Jacopo di Giovanni di Jacopo di Moccio (and brothers)
114.	2,194	Lionardo di Piero di Ser Antonio di Ser Chello (and brothers)
115.	2,193	Francesco and Niccolò di Bartolommeo Cambioni
116.	2,139	Lionardo di Bartolommeo dei Bardi
117.	2,077	Tommaso di Piero di Messer Ridolfo dei Bardi
118.	2,057	Jacopo di Bardo "lanaiuolo"
119.	2,044	Agnola widow of Forte da Vico
120.	1,999	Piero and Bartolommeo di Paolo Serragli
121.	1,994	Stoldo and Lamberto di Lionardo Frescobaldi
122.	1,922	Orso di Orso di Rinieri [del Pace]
123.	1,856	Antonio di Bartolommeo Ridolfi
124.	1,824	Giovanni del Maestro Agnolo "lanaiuolo"
125.	1,819	Guido and Taddeo di Tommaso Deti
126.	1,772	Gherardo di Lionardo Frescobaldi
127.	1,730	Totto di Buoninsegna Machiavelli
128.	1,725	Orsino di Lanfredino Lanfredini
129.	1,722	Gherardo di Messer Filippo Corsini

No.	Net capital in florins	Name of taxpayer
130.	1,722	Niccolò di Naccio da Gambassi
131.	1,718	Niccolò and Tommaso di Lorenzo di Messer Tommaso Soderini
132.	1,717	Lorenzo di Donato Bellotti "lanaiuolo"
133.	1,687	Gherardo di Buoninsegna Machiavelli
134.	1,682	Piero di Salamone di Torello [del Garbo]
135.	1,664	Niccolò di Lapo Falconi
136.	1,621	Ser Filippo di Cristofano di Lionardo
137.	1,603	Stagio di Lionardo di Giovanni Niccolà "setaiuolo"
138.	1,573	Francesco and Giovanni di Jacopo del Pugliese
139.	1,559	Giovanni di Buoninsegna Machiavelli
140.	1,538	Guido di Piero Velluti (and brothers)
141.	1,506	Lena widow of Cambio di Bartolo
142.	1,497	Ser Guido di Piero da San Miniato (and sons)
143.	1,486	Antonio di Scarlatto
144.	1,465	Rinieri di Piero di Bernardo di Chiarino Davanzati
145.	1,451	Niccolò di Feduccio Falconi
146.	1,441	Margherita widow of Lorenzo di Messer Filippo Portinari
147.	1,432	Fia widow of Nofri di Andrea di Neri di Lippo
148.	1,431	Bartolommeo di Bertoldo di Messer Filippo Corsini (and brothers)
149.	1,423	Pagnozzo di Bartolommeo Ridolfi
150.	1,420	Bernardo di Jacopo della Leccia

BIBLIOGRAPHY

SELECT BIBLIOGRAPHY

I. MANUSCRIPT SOURCES

1. State Archives of Florence
   Acquisti e Doni
   Archivio delle Arti
   Archivio Notarile Antecosimiano
   Archivio di Parte Guelfa
   Camera del Comune
   Carte dell'Ancisa
   Carte Pucci
   Carte Strozziane
   Inventario Peruzzi-Medici
   Manoscritti
   Notaio della Camera del Comune
   Priorista Mariani
   Registri del Catasto
   Registri delle Consulte detti anche Libri Fabarum
   Registri delle Consulte e Pratiche
   Registri delle Deliberazioni dei Signori e Collegi
   Registri e filze dell' Estimo
   Registri del Monte Comune
   Registri delle Prestanze
   Registri delle Provvisioni
   Registri dei Signori: Legazioni e Commissarie
   Registri, volumi, e filze delle Tratte
2. State Archives of Siena
   Archivio del Concistoro
3. National Library of Florence
   Fondo Magliabechiano
   Fondo Panciatichiano
   Manoscritti Nazionale
   Manoscritti Palatini
   Manoscritti Passerini
4. Laurenziana Library of Florence
   Codici Laurenziani
5. Riccardiana Library of Florence
   Manoscritti

6. Library of the Galleria degli Uffizi
   Neri di Bicci, *Ricordanze*

II. SOURCES IN PRINT

Alberti, L. B., *Dialogo de republica*, Venezia, 1543.

————, *I primi tre libri della famiglia*, ed. F. C. Pellegrini and
E. R. Spongano, Firenze, 1946.

————, *Opere volgari*, ed. A. Bonucci, 5 vols., Firenze, 1842-
1849.

————, *Momus seu de principe*, ed. G. Martini, Bologna, 1942.

————, "Il testamento di L. B. Alberti," ed. G. Mancini,
Archivio storico italiano, LXXII, 2 (1914), 20-52.

Accolti, B., *Dialogus de praestantia virorum sui aevi*, in F. Villani,
Liber de civitatis Florentiae famosis civibus, ed. G. C. Galletti, Florentiae, 1847.

Arlotto, Piovano, *Facezie*, ed. Giuseppe Baccini, Firenze, 1884.

Aurispa, Giovanni, *Carteggio di G. A.*, ed. R. Sabbadini (Roma,
1931).

Baluzius, Stephanus, ed., *Miscellanea*, 4 vols., Lucae, 1761.

Bandini, A. M., *Specimen literaturae florentinae saeculi xv*, 2 vols.,
Florentiae, 1749-1751.

Benvenuti, Lorenzo, *L'invettiva contro Niccolò Niccoli*, ed. G.
Zippel, *Giornale storico della letteratura italiana*, XXIV (1894).

Bisticci, Vespasiano da, *Vite di uomini illustri del secolo xv*, ed.
P. D'Ancona and E. Aeschlimann, Milano, 1951.

Bracciolini, Poggio, *Istoria dall origine di Firenze al 1454*, Firenze,
1598.

————, *Opera*, Basileae, 1538.

————, *Oratio funebris in obitu Leonardo Arretini*, in Lionardo Bruni, *Epistolarum libri viii*, 2 vols., ed. L. Mehus.

Bruni, Lionardo, *Epistolarum libri viii*, 2 vols., ed. Laurentio
Mehus, Florentiae, 1741.

————, *Historiarum florentini populi*, 3 vols., eds. G. Mancini,
P. Leoni, and Fr. Tonietti, Florentiae, 1855-1860.

————, *Leonardo Bruni Aretino: Humanistisch-Philosophische
Schriften*, ed. with an introduction by Hans Baron, Leipzig-
Berlin, 1928.

Bibliography

————, *De Militia*, ed. C. C. Bayley, *War and Society in Renaissance Florence*, Toronto, 1961.

————, *Oratio in nebulonem maledicum*, in G. Zippel, *Niccolò Niccoli*, Firenze, 1890.

————, *Ad Petrum Paulum Histrum Dialogus*, ed. E. Garin, in *Prosatori latini del Quattrocento*, Milano-Napoli, 1952

————, *Rerum suo tempore in Italia gestarum commentarius*, Lugduni, 1539.

————, *De studiis et litteris liber*, in H. Baron, ed., *Leonardo Bruni Aretino: Humanistisch-Philosophische Schriften.*

Buondelmonti, C., *Florentini librum insularum archipelagi*, ed. G. L. R. De Sinner, Leipzig and Berlin, 1824.

Buoninsegni, Domenico, *Storia della città di Firenze dall' anno 1410 al 1460*, Firenze, 1637.

Cambi, Giovanni, *Istorie*, in *Delizie degli eruditi toscani*, vol. XX.

Capponi, Gino, *Commentari dell'acquisto di Pisa*, in *Cronichette antiche*, ed. D. M. Manni, Firenze, 1733.

Castiglionchio, Lapo da, *Epistola*, ed. L. Mehus, Bologna, 1753.

Cavalcanti, Giovanni, *Della carcere, del ingiusto esilio e del trionfal ritorno di Cosimo, padre della patria*, ed. Domenico Moreni, Firenze, 1821.

————, *Istorie fiorentine*, 2 vols., Firenze, 1838-1839.

Certaldo, Paolo da, *Libro di buoni costumi*, ed. A. Schiaffini, Firenze, 1945.

Cicero, *De Officiis*, London, 1928.

Compagni, Dino, *Cronica fiorentina*, Livorno, 1830.

Corti, Gino, ed., "Consigli sulla mercatura di un anonimo trecentista," *Archivio storico italiano*, CX (1952), 114-119.

Dallari, U., ed., *I rotuli dei lettori legisti e artisti dello studio bolognese dal 1384 al 1799*, IV, Bologna, 1924.

Dati, G., *L'Istoria di Firenze dal 1380 al 1405*, ed. L. Pratesi, Norcia, 1904.

————, *Il libro segreto di G. D.*, ed. Carlo Gargiolli, Bologna, 1869.

Dati, L., *Canonici florentini epistolae xxxiii*, ed. L. Mehus, Florentiae, 1743.

Del Corazza, Bartolommeo di Michele, *Diario fiorentino* (1405-1438), in *Archivio storico italiano*, ser. 5, XIV (1894).

Bibliography

Delizie degli eruditi toscani, ed. Fr. Ildefonso di San Luigi, 24 vols., Firenze, 1770-1789.

Ficino, M., *Oration on the Dignity of Man*, tr. E. L. Forbes, in *The Renaissance Philosophy of Man*, eds. Cassirer, Kristeller, Randall.

Filelfo, F., *Epistolarum familiarum libri xxxvii*, Venezia, 1502.

———, *Commentationes florentinae de exilio*, ed. C. Errera, *Archivio storico italiano*, ser. 5, v (1890), 193-227.

Fossi, *Monumenta ad A. Rinuccini vitam contexendam ex manuscriptis codicibus plerumque eruta*, Florentiae, 1791.

Garin, Eugenio, ed., *Filosofi italiani del Quattrocento*, Firenze, 1942.

———, ed., *Prosatori latini del Quattrocento*, Milano-Napoli, 1952.

Gelli, A., ed., "L'esilio di Cosimo de' Medici: Documenti," *Archivio storico italiano*, ser. 4, x (1882), 53ff.

Gherardi, Alessandro, ed., *Le consulte della repubblica fiorentina*, 2 vols., Firenze, 1896.

———, ed., *Statuti della Università e Studio fiorentino*, Firenze, 1881.

Giannotti, Donato, *Della repubblica fiorentina*, Venezia, 1721.

Giovanni Rucellai ed il suo Zibaldone, ed. A. Perosa, London, 1960.

Guarino, *see* Veronese, Guarino.

Guasti, Cesare, ed., *Commissioni di Rinaldo degli Albizzi*, 3 vols., Firenze, 1867-1873.

Guicciardini, Francesco, *Dialogo e discorsi del reggimento di Firenze*, ed. Roberto Palmarocchi, Bari, 1932.

———, *Storie fiorentine*, ed. R. Palmarocchi, Bari, 1931.

Landino, C., *Disputationes Camaldulenses*, ed. E. Garin, *Prosatori latini del Quattrocento*, pp. 716-791.

Landucci, Luca, *A Florentine Diary*, tr. A. Jervis, London, 1927.

Machiavelli, Niccolò, *Istorie fiorentine*, ed. *Nuova Biblioteca Popolare*, Torino, 1853.

Malespini, Ricordano, *Storia fiorentina*, 2 vols., Livorno, 1830.

———, *Historia antica di Ricordano Malespini*, Fiorenza, 1568.

Bibliography

Manetti, Antonio, *Vita di Filippo di Ser Brunellesco*, ed. Elena Toesca, Firenze, 1927.

Manetti, Giannozzo, *Oratio funebris*, in L. Bruni, *Epistolarum*.

Marsuppini, C., "Una consolatoria inedita del Marsuppini," ed. P. G. Ricci, *Rinascita*, III (1940), 363-433.

Mazzei, Lapo, *Lettere di un notaro a un mercante*, ed. C. Guasti, 2 vols., Firenze, 1880.

Monaldi, Guido, *Diario dal 1340 al 1381*, in *Istorie pistolesi, o sia Istoria delle cose avvenute in Toscana dal 1300 al 1348*, ed. Ant. M. Biscioni, Firenze, 1733.

Montemagno, Buonaccorso da, *Prose del giovine B. da M.*, ed. G. B. Giuliari, Bologna, 1874, in *Scelta*, Disp. CXLV.

————, *De nobilitate*, ed. E. Garin, *Prosatori latini del Quattrocento*.

Morelli, Giovanni, *Ricordi*, ed. V. Branca, Firenze, 1956.

Morelli, Lionardo, *Cronaca*, in *Delizie degli eruditi toscani*, vol. XIX.

Naldi, Naldo, *Vita di Giannozzo Manetti*, in Filippo Villani, *Liber de civitatis florentiae famosis civibus*, Firenze, 1847.

Nerli, Filippo de', *Commentari*, —, 1728.

"Nuovi documenti intorno al catasto fiorentino," ed. P. Berti, *Giornale storico degli archivi toscani*, IV (1860), 40-59.

Palmieri, Matteo, *De captivitate pisarum liber*, ed. G. Scaramella, Città di Castello, 1906.

————, *Della vita civile*, ed. F. Battaglia, Bologna, 1944.

————, *La vita di Niccolà Acciaioli*, in G. B. Ubaldini, *Istoria della casa degli Ubaldini*, Firenze, 1588.

Petrarca, Francesco, *De viris illustribus vitae*, Bologna, 1874.

Piccolomini, Enea Silvio, *Commentari rerum memorabilium*, Frankfurt, 1614.

Pitti, Buonaccorso, *Cronica*, ed. A. B. della Lega, Bologna, 1905.

Poggio, *see* Bracciolini, Poggio.

Poliziano, *Angelo Polizianos Tagebuch: 1477-1479*, ed. A. Wesselski, Jena, 1929.

Rinuccini, Alamanno, *Dialogus de libertate*, ed. Fr. Adorno, *Atti e memorie dell' accademia toscana "La Colombaria,"* XXII, n.s. viii (1957), 265-303.

————, *Lettere ed orazioni*, ed. V. Giustiniani, Firenze, 1953.

Bibliography

Rinuccini, Cino, *Risponsiva alla invettiva di messer Antonio Lusco*, in Salutati, *Invectiva in Antonium Luschum*, ed. D. Moreni, Florentiae, 1826.

————, *Invettiva contro a cierti caluniatori di Dante e di messer Francesco Petrarca e di messer Giovanni Boccacci*, in Giovanni da Prato, *Il Paradiso degli Alberti*, ed. A. Wesselofsky, i, ii, Bologna, 1867.

Rinuccini, Filippo di Cino, *Ricordi Storici*, ed. G. Aiazzi, Firenze, 1840.

Sabbadini, R., "Bricciole umanistiche," *Giornale storico della letteratura italiana*, xvii (1891), 218ff.

Salutati, Coluccio, *L'Epistolario di Coluccio Salutati*, ed. Francesco Novati, 4 vols., Rome, 1891-1911.

————, *Il trattato "De Tyranno" e lettere scelte*, ed. F. Ercole, Bologna, 1942.

Santini, P., ed., *Documenti dell'antica costituzione del comune di Firenze*, 1895.

Statuta Populi et Communis Florentiae, 3 vols., Friburgi, 1778-1783.

Statuti della repubblica fiorentina, ed. R. Caggese, 2 vols., Firenze, 1910, 1921.

Strozzi, Alessandra, *Lettere di una gentildonna fiorentina del secolo xv ai figliuoli esuli*, ed. C. Guasti, Firenze, 1877.

Strozzi, Palla, "Diario," *Archivio storico italiano*, ser. 4, xi (1883), 20-48, 145-152, 293-309; xii (1883-84), 3-14; xiii (1884), 153-170; xiv (1884), 3-18.

Traversari, Ambrogio, *Latinae epistolae a Petro Canneto in libros xxv tributae*, ed. L. Mehus, 2 vols., Florentiae, 1759.

————, *Hodoeporicon*, appended to A. Dini-Traversari, *Ambrogio Traversari e i suoi tempi*.

Velluti, Donato, *Cronica domestica*, eds. I. del Lungo and G. Volpi, Firenze, 1914.

Verino, U., *Carmina illustrium poetarum italorum*, vol. x, Florentiae, 1721.

Veronese, Guarino, *Epistolario*, ed. R. Sabbadini, 3 vols., Venezia, 1915-1919.

"Versi fatti da Niccolò da Uzzano predicendo la mutazione dello stato," ed. G. Canestrini, *Archivio storico italiano*, ser. 1, IV (1843), 297-300.

Vespasiano, *see* Bisticci, Vespasiano da.

Villani, Filippo, *Liber de civitatis florentiae famosis civibus*, ed. Gustavo Galletti, Florentiae, 1847.

Villani, Giovanni, *Cronica*, ed. F. G. Dragomanni, 4 vols., Firenze, 1844-1845.

Villani, Matteo, *Cronica*, ed. F. G. Dragomanni, 2 vols., Firenze, 1846.

III. SECONDARY WORKS

Adorno, Fr., "La crisi dell' umanesimo civile fiorentino da Alamanno Rinuccini al Machiavelli," *Rivista critica di storia della filosofia*, VII (January-February 1952), 19-40.

Albertini, R. von, *Das florentinische Staatsbewusstsein im Übergang von der Republik zum Prinzipat*, Bern, 1955.

Ammirato, Scipione, *Istorie fiorentine*, ed. L. Scarabelli, 7 vols., Torino, 1853.

Antonelli, Giovanni, "La magistratura degli Otto di Guardia a Firenze," *Archivio storico italiano*, 402, I (1954).

Anzilotti, A., *La crisi costituzionale della repubblica fiorentina*, Firenze, 1912.

Barfucci, Enrico, *Lorenzo de' Medici e la società artistica del suo tempo*, Firenze, 1945.

Baron, Hans, *The Crisis of the Early Italian Renaissance*, 2 vols., Princeton, 1955.

―――――, *Humanistic and Political Literature in Florence and Venice*, Cambridge, Mass., 1955.

―――――, ed. with an introduction, *Leonardo Bruni Aretino: Humanistisch-Philosophische Schriften*, Leipzig and Berlin, 1928.

―――――, "A Struggle for Liberty in the Renaissance: Florence, Venice, and Milan in the Early Quattrocento," *American Historical Review*, LVIII (1953), 265-289, 544-570.

―――――, "The Social Background of Political Liberty in the Early Italian Renaissance," *Comparative Studies in Society and History*, II (July 1960), 440-451.

―――――, "Secularization of Wisdom and Political Humanism in

the Renaissance," *Journal of the History of Ideas*, xxi (*Jan.-March 1960*), 131-150.

————, "A Sociological Interpretation of the Early Renaissance in Florence," *South Atlantic Quarterly*, xxxviii (1939), 427ff.

————, "The Historical Background of the Florentine Renaissance," *History*, n.s. xxii (1938), 315ff.

————, "Cicero and the Roman Civic Spirit in the Middle Ages and the Early Renaissance," *Bulletin of the John Rylands Library*, xxii (April 1938), 3-28.

————, "Franciscan Poverty and Civic Wealth as Factors in the Rise of Humanistic Thought," *Speculum*, xiii (January 1938), 1-37.

————, "Das Erwachen des Historischen Denkens im Humanismus des Quattrocento," *Historische Zeitschrift*, cxlvii (1932), 5-20.

Bayley C. C., *War and Society in Renaissance Florence: The De Militia of Leonardo Bruni*, Torento, 1961.

Beck, Franz, *Studien zu Leonardo Bruni*, Berlin-Leipzig, 1912.

Becker, Marvin B., "The Republican City State in Florence: An Inquiry into its Origin and Survival (1280-1434)," *Speculum*, xxxv, 1 (January 1960), 39-50.

————, "Some Aspects of Oligarchical, Dictatorial and Popular Signorie in Florence, 1282-1382," *Comparative Studies in Society and History*, ii, 4 (July 1960), 421-439.

————, "Some Economic Implications of the Conflict between Church and State in 'Trecento' Florence," *Mediaeval Studies*, xxi (1959), 1-16.

————, "Florentine Politics and the Diffusion of Heresy in the Trecento: A Socio-Economic Inquiry," *Speculum*, xxxiv, 1 (January 1959), 60-75.

————, "Three Cases Concerning the Restitution of Usury in Florence," *Journal of Economic History*, xvii (September 1957), 445-450.

Becker, M. B. and Brucker, G. A., "The *Arti Minori* in Florentine Politics, 1342-1378," *Mediaeval Studies*, xviii (1956), 93-104.

Bencini, I., "Neri Capponi," *Rivista delle biblioteche e degli archivi*, xvi (1905), 91-100, 138-154, 158-174.

Bibliography

————, "Note e appunti tratti da documenti sulla vita politica di Neri Capponi," *Rivista delle biblioteche e degli archivi*, xx (1909), 15-31, 33-56.

Benvenuti, G. B., *Quadri storici fiorentini*, Firenze, 1889.

Blum, Rudolf, *La biblioteca della Badía fiorentina e i codici di Antonio Corbinelli*, Città del Vaticano, 1951.

Bombe, Walter, *Nachlass-Inventare des Angelo da Uzzano und des Ludovico di Gino Capponi*, Leipzig-Berlin, 1928.

Bonolis, Guido, *La giurisdizione della Mercanzia in Firenze nel secolo xiv*, Firenze, 1901.

Brosch, M., *Albizzi und Medici*, Leipzig, 1908.

Brucker, Gene A., *Florentine Politics and Society, 1343-1378*, Princeton, 1962.

————, "The Ghibelline Trial of Matteo Villani (1362)," *Medievalia et Humanistica*, xiii (1960), 48-55.

————, "Un documento fiorentino sulla guerra, sulla finanza e sulla aministrazione pubblica (1375)," *Archivio storico italiano*, cxv, 2 (1957), 165-176.

————, "The Medici in the Fourteenth Century," *Speculum*, xxxii, 1 (January 1957), 1-26.

————, *Political Conflict in the Florentine Commune: 1343-1378*, unpublished doctoral dissertation, Princeton University, 1954.

Burckhardt, Jacob, *The Civilization of the Renaissance in Italy*, tr. S. G. C. Middlemore, London, 1951. Also Harper Torch books, 2 vols., New York, 1958.

Caggese, Romolo, *Firenze dalla decadenza di Roma al Risorgimento d'Italia*, 3 vols., Firenze, 1912-1921.

Cambridge Economic History of Europe, vol. ii, eds. M. Postan and E. E. Rich, Cambridge, 1952.

Camugliano, G. Niccolini di, *The Chronicles of a Florentine Family, 1200-1470*, London, 1933.

Canestrini, G., *La scienza e l'arte di stato, desunta degli atti ufficiali della repubblica fiorentina e dei Medici*, Firenze, 1862.

Cantimori, D., "Rhetoric and Politics in Italian Humanism," *Journal of the Warburg and Courtauld Institutes*, i (1937-1938).

Bibliography

Capponi, Gino, *Storia della Repubblica di Firenze*, 2 vols., Firenze, 1888.

Caprin, Giulio, "Il libraio fiorentino degli umanisti, Vespasiano da Bisticci," in *Il Quattrocento*, published under the auspices of the "Libera cattedra di storia della civiltà fiorentina," Firenze, 1954.

Casari, Cornelia, *Notizie intorno a Luigi Marsili*, Lovere, 1900.

Casella, Mario, "Ser Domenico del Maestro Andrea da Prato: Rimatore del Secolo xv," *Rivista delle biblioteche e degli archivi*, xxvii (January-May 1916), 1-40.

Cassirer, E., *Individuum und Kosmos in der Philosophie der Renaissance*, Leipzig, 1927.

Catalano, Franco, "La crisi italiana alla fine del secolo xv," *Belfagor*, xi, 4-5 (July-September 1956), 393-414, 505-527.

Cervani, Giulio, "Il rinascimento italiano nella interpretazione di Hans Baron," *Nuova rivista storica*, xxxix, 3 (1955), 429-503.

Cognasso, Francesco (and others), *Il ducato visconteo e la repubblica ambrosiana*, Milano, 1955, vol. vi of the collective work, *Storia di Milano*, ed. Giuseppe Martini.

Dami, Brunetto, *Giovanni Bicci dei Medici*, Firenze, 1899.

Danielli, A., "Niccolò da Uzzano nella vita politica dei suoi tempi," *Archivio storico italiano*, ser. 7, xvii (1932), 35-86, 186-216.

Davidsohn, Robert, *Geschichte von Florenz*, 4 vols., Berlin, 1896-1927.

————, *Storia di Firenze*, tr. G. B. Klein, Firenze, 1956.

————, *Forschungen zur Geschichte von Florenz*, 4 vols., Berlin, 1896-1908.

Del Badia, Iodoco, *Miscellanea fiorentina di erudizione e storia*, 2 vols., Firenze, 1902.

Del Secolo, F., *Un teologo dell'ultimo Trecento: Luigi Marsili*, Trani, 1898.

Della Torre, Arnaldo, *Storia dell'Accademia platonica di Firenze*, Firenze, 1902. Also edition of 1960, by "riproduzione anastatica," Torino.

Dini-Traversari, A., *Ambrogio Traversari e i suoi tempi*, Firenze, 1912.

Bibliography

Doren, Alfred, *Le arti fiorentine*, tr. G. B. Klein, 2 vols., Firenze, 1940.

Edler, Florence, *Glossary of Medieval Terms of Business*, Cambridge, Mass., 1934.

Engel-Janosi, Friedrich, *Soziale Probleme der Renaissance*, Stuttgart, 1924.

Ewart, K. D., *Cosimo de' Medici*, London, 1889.

Fabroni, Angelo, *Laurentii Medicis Magnifici Vita*, 2 vols., Pisa, 1784.

————, *Vita Magni Cosmi Medicei*, Pisa, 1789.

————, *Pallantis Stroctii Vita*, Parma, 1802.

Ferguson, W. K., *The Renaissance in Historical Thought: Five Centuries of Interpretation*, Cambridge, Mass., 1948.

Filippi, Giovanni, *L'arte dei mercanti di calimala in Firenze*, Torino, 1889.

Fiumi, E., "Fioritura e decadenza dell' economia fiorentina," *Archivio storico italiano*, cxv (1957), 385-439; cxvi (1958), 443-510; cxvii (1959), 427-502.

Flamini, Fr., *La lirica toscana del Rinascimento anteriore ai tempi di Lorenzo il Magnifico*, Pisa, 1891.

Foresti, A., *Aneddoti della vita di Francesco Petrarca*, Brescia, 1928.

Fossi, *Monumenta ad A. Rinuccini vitam contexendam ex manuscriptis codicibus plerumque eruta*, Florentiae, 1791.

Garin, Eugenio, *L'Educazione in Europa (1400-1600)*, Bari, 1957.

————, *Medioevo e Rinascimento: studi e ricerche*, Bari, 1954.

————, *L'Umanesimo italiano: filosofia e vita civile nel rinascimento*, Bari, 1952.

————, *Il Rinascimento italiano*, Milano, Ispi, 1941.

————, "I cancellieri umanisti della repubblica fiorentina da Coluccio Salutati a Bartolomeo Scala," *Rivista storica italiana*, lxxi, ii (1959), 185-208.

————, "L'Ambiente del Poliziano," *Il Poliziano e suo tempo*, atti del iv convegno internazionale di studi sul rinascimento, Firenze, 1957.

————, "Ritratto di Paolo dal Pozzo Toscanelli," *Belfagor*, xii (1957), 253.

Bibliography

Garin, Eugenio, "Ritratto di Marsilio Ficino," *Il Quattrocento*, published under the auspices of the "Libera cattedra di storia della civiltà fiorentina," Firenze, 1954.

Gaspary, A., *Storia della letteratura italiana*, tr. V. Rossi, 2 vols., Torino, 1899-1901.

Gilbert, Felix, "Florentine Political Assumptions in the Period of Savonarola and Soderini," *Journal of the Warburg and Courtauld Institutes*, xx (1957), 187-214.

Guasti, C., "Un disegno di Giovanni di Gherardi da Prato," *Opere*, iv, Prato, 1897.

Gutkind, Curt S., *Cosimo de' Medici*, Oxford, 1938.

Hauser, A., *The Social History of Art*, Vintage ed., 3 vols., New York, 1960.

Hay, Denys, *The Italian Renaissance in its Historical Background*, Cambridge, 1961.

Jacob, E. F., ed., *Italian Renaissance Studies: A Tribute to the late Cecilia M. Ady*, New York, 1960.

Jones, Philip, "Florentine families and Florentine diaries in the fourteenth century," in *Papers of the British School at Rome*, xxiv (1956), 183-205.

Karmin, Otto, *La legge del catasto fiorentino*, Firenze, 1906.

Kristeller, P. O., *Studies in Renaissance Thought and Letters*, Roma, 1956.

———, *The Classics and Renaissance Thought*, Cambridge, Mass., 1955.

Litta, Pompeo, *Famiglie celebri italiane*, Torino and Milano, 1819-1888.

———, *Buondelmonti di Firenze*, 6 tavole, Milano, 1850.

Lopez, R. S., "Hard Times and Investment in Culture," in *The Renaissance, a Symposium*, New York, 1952.

———, "The Trade of Medieval Europe: The South," Chap. v of *The Cambridge Economic History of Europe*, ii, eds. M. Postan and E. E. Rich, Cambridge, 1952.

Luiso, F. P., "Riforma della cancelleria fiorentina," *Archivio storico italiano*, ser. 5, xxi (1898), 132-142.

———, "Studi sull' epistolario e le traduzioni di Lapo da Castiglionchio juniore," *Studi italiani di filologia classica*, vii (1899), 205-299.

Bibliography

Mancini, Gustavo, "Aggiunte e correzioni alla vita di Leonardo Bruni," in Bruni, *Historiarum florentini populi*, 3 vols., Florentiae, 1855-1860.

Mancini, Girolamo, *Vita di Leon Battista Alberti*, Firenze, 1911.

Manetti, Aldo, "Roberto de' Rossi," *Rinascimento*, ii (1951), 33-56.

Marcotti, G., *Un mercatante fiorentino e la sua famiglia*, Firenze, 1881.

Mariani, M., "Gino Capponi nella vita politica fiorentina dal 1393 al 1421," *Archivio storico italiano*, cxv, 4 (1957).

Marks, L. F., "La crisi finanziaria a Firenze dal 1494 al 1502," *Archivio storico italiano*, cxii (1954), 40-72.

————, "The Financial Oligarchy in Florence under Lorenzo," in *Italian Renaissance Studies: A Tribute to the late Cecilia M. Ady*, ed. E. F. Jacob, New York, 1960.

Martin, A. von, "Der Humanismus als soziologisches Phänomen," *Archiv für Sozialwissenschaft und Sozialpolitik*, lxv (1931), 441-474.

————, *Sociology of the Renaissance*, Oxford, 1944.

Martines, L., "Nuovi documenti su Cino Rinuccini e una nota sulle finanze della famiglia Rinuccini," *Archivio storico italiano*, cxix (1961), 77-90.

————, "The Career and Library of a 15th-Century Lawyer," *Annali di storia del diritto: rassegna internazionale*, iii-iv (1959-60), 323-332.

————, "La famiglia Martelli e un documento sulla vigilia del ritorno dall' esilio di Cosimo de' Medici (1434)," *Archivio storico italiano*, cxvii (1959), 29-43.

————, "Addenda to the Life of Antonio Corbinelli," *Rinascimento*, viii (1957), 3-19.

Marzi, Demetrio, *La cancelleria della repubblica fiorentina*, Rocca S. Casciano, 1910.

Masi, Gino, *La struttura sociale delle fazioni politiche fiorentine ai tempi di Dante*, Firenze, 1930.

Mecatti, G. B., *Storia cronologica della città di Firenze*, 2 vols., Napoli, 1755.

Messeri, A., "Matteo Palmieri cittadino di Firenze del secolo xv," *Archivio storico italiano*, xiii, 2 (1894), 257-340.

Bibliography

Monnier, Ph., *Le Quattrocento: Essai sur l'histoire littéraire du XVe siècle italien*, 2 vols., Paris, 1931.

Monzani, C., "Di Leonardo Bruni Aretino Discorso," *Archivio storico italiano*, v, i (1857), 29-59; v, ii (1857), 3-34.

Olschki, Leonardo, *The Genius of Italy*, New York, 1949. Also Ithaca, N.Y., 1954.

————, *L'Italia e il suo genio*, Ital. tr. Laurana Palombi and Marisa Bulgheroni, Milano-Verona, 1953.

Origo, Iris, *The Merchant of Prato, Francesco di Marco Datini*, New York, 1957.

Ottokar, Nicola, *Il Comune di Firenze alla fine del dugento*, Firenze, 1926.

Pagnini, G. F., *Della decima e di varie altre gravezze imposte dal comune di Firenze*, 4 vols., Lisbona and Lucca, 1765-1766.

Partner, Peter, "Camera Papae: Problems of Papal Finance in the later Middle Ages," *The Journal of Ecclesiastical History*, iv, 1 (1953), 55-68.

————, *The Papal State Under Martin V*, Rome-London, 1958.

Passerini, Luigi, *Gli Alberti di Firenze*, 2 vols., Firenze, 1869.

————, *Albizzi di Firenze*, Torino, 1876, in Litta, *Famiglie celebri italiane*.

————, *Alessandri già Albizzi di Firenze*, Torino, 1879, in Litta, *Famiglie celebri italiane*.

————, *Genealogia e storia della famiglia Corsini*, Firenze, 1858.

————, *Genealogia e storia della famiglia Panciatichi*, Firenze, 1858.

————, *Pucci di Firenze*, Milano, 1869, in Litta, *Famiglie celebri italiane*.

————, *Genealogia e storia della famiglia Ricasoli*, Firenze, 1861.

————, *Genealogia e storia della famiglia Rucellai*, Firenze, 1861.

————, *Soderini di Firenze*, Milano, 1861, in Litta, *Famiglie celebri italiane*.

Pellegrini, Francesco C., *Sulla repubblica fiorentina a tempo di Cosimo il Vecchio*, Pisa, 1880.

Bibliography

Perrens, F. T., *Histoire de Florence*, 6 vols., Paris, 1877-1883.

————, *Histoire de Florence depuis la domination des Médicis jusqu' à la chute de la république (1434-1531)*, 3 vols., Paris, 1889-1890.

Pieri, P., *Il Rinascimento e la crisi militare italiana*, Torino, 1952.

Polidori-Calamandrei, E., *Le vesti delle donne fiorentine nel Quattrocento*, Firenze, 1924.

Rado, A., *Maso degli Albizzi e il partito oligarchico in Firenze dal 1382 al 1393*, Firenze, 1927.

Renouard, Yves, *Les Hommes d'Affaires Italiens du Moyen Âge*, Paris, 1949.

Repetti, Emanuele, *Dizionario geografico, fisico, storico della Toscana*, 6 vols., Firenze, 1833-1846.

Rezasco, Giulio, *Dizionario del linguaggio italiano storico ed amministrativo*, Firenze, 1881.

Ricchioni, Vincenzo, *La costituzione politica di Firenze ai tempi di Lorenzo il Magnifico*, Siena, 1913.

Ricci, P. G., "Ambrogio Traversari," *Rinascita*, ii (1939), 578-612.

————, "Una consolatoria inedita del Marsuppini," *Rinascita*, iii (1940), 363ff.

Rodolico, Niccolò, *La democrazia fiorentina nel suo tramonto*, Bologna, 1905.

Rondini, G., "Ordinamenti e vicende principali dell'antico studio fiorentino," *Archivio storico italiano*, xiv, 4 (1884), 41-64.

Roover, Raymond de, *The Medici Bank: Its Organization, Management, Operations and Decline*, New York and London, 1948.

————, "I libri segreti del Banco de' Medici," in *Archivio storico italiano*, ii (1949), 236-240.

————, "Il trattato di fra Santi Rucellai sul cambio, il monte comune e il monte delle doti," in *Archivio storico italiano*, i (1953), 3-41.

————, "Lorenzo il Magnifico e il tramonto del Banco de' Medici," in *Archivio storico italiano*, ii (1949), 172-185.

————, "New Interpretations of the History of Banking," in *Cahiers d'Histoire Mondiale*, ii (1954), 38-76.

Roscoe, William, *Vita di Lorenzo de' Medici*, 6 vols., Pisa, 1816.

Rosmini, Carlo de', *Vita di Francesco Filelfo*, 3 vols., Milano, 1808.

Rossi, Luigi, "Firenze e Venezia dopo la battaglia di Caravaggio," *Archivio storico italiano*, ser. 5, xxxiv (1904).

Rossi, Vittorio, *Il Quattrocento*, ed. A. Vallone, Milano, 1956.

Sabbadini, R., *Giovanni da Ravenna*, Como, 1924.

————, *Il metodo degli umanisti*, Firenze, 1922.

————, *Le scoperte dei codici latini e greci ne' secoli xiv e xv*, 2 vols., Firenze, 1905, 1914.

Saitta, G., *L'Umanesimo: il pensiero italiano nell' umanesimo e nel rinascimento*, 3 vols., Bologna, 1949-1951.

Salvemini, Gaetano, *La dignità cavalleresca*, Firenze, 1896.

————, *Magnati e popolani a Firenze dal 1280 al 1295*, Firenze, 1899.

Salvini, Salvino, *Catalogo cronologico dei canonici della chiesa metropolitana fiorentina*, Firenze, 1782.

Sanctis, Francesco de, *The History of Italian Literature*, tr. Joan Redfern, 2 vols., New York, 1959.

Sandys, J. E., *A History of Classical Scholarship*, 3 vols., Cambridge, 1903-1921.

Santini, Emilio, *Firenze e i suoi oratori nel Quattrocento*, Milano, 1922.

————, *Leonardo Bruni Aretino*, in *Annali della R. Scuola Normale Superiore di Pisa*, xxii, 1910.

————, "La *protestatio de iustitia* nella Firenze medicea del sec. xv," *Rinascimento*, x (1959), 33-106.

Sapori, Armando, *Una compagnia di calimala ai primi del Trecento*, Firenze, 1932.

————, *Studi di storia economica medievale*, Firenze, 1946.

Sasso, Gennaro, "Florentina Libertas e rinascimento italiano nell' opera di Hans Baron," *Rivista storica italiana*, ii (1957), 250-276.

Schevill, Ferdinand, *History of Florence*, New York, 1936.

Schiaparelli, A., *La casa fiorentina e i suoi arredi nei secoli xiv e xv*, Firenze, 1904.

Segni, A., *Vita di Donato Acciaiuoli*, ed. T. Tonelli, Firenze, 1841.

Sheedy, Anna T., *Bartolus on Social Conditions in the Fourteenth Century*, New York, 1942.

Shepherd, William, *The Life of Poggio Bracciolini*, Liverpool, 1837.

Bibliography

Strozzi, L., *Vite degli Strozzi*, ed. Stromboli, Firenze, 1892.

Tamassia, Nino, *La famiglia italiana nei secoli decimoquinto e decimosesto*, Milano, 1910.

Tiraboschi, G., *Storia della letteratura italiana*, 26 vols., Venezia, 1822-1827.

Trinkaus, Charles E., *Adversity's Noblemen: The Italian Humanists on Happiness*, New York, 1940.

Ullman, B. L., *The Origin and Development of Humanistic Script*, Rome, 1960.

————, "Leonardo Bruni and Humanistic Historiography," *Medievalia et Humanistica*, IV (1946), 45-61.

Uzielli, G., *La vita e i tempi di Paolo dal Pozzo Toscanelli, ricerche e studi*, Roma, 1894.

Varese, Claudio, *Storia e politica nella prosa del Quattrocento*, Torino, 1961.

Voigt, G., *Die Wiederbelebung des Classischen Alterthums*, 2 vols., Berlin, 1893.

————, *Il risorgimento dell'antichità classica*, Ital. tr. D. Valbusa, 2 vols., Firenze, 1888-1890.

Wackernagel, M., *Der Lebensraum des Künstlers in der Florentinischen Renaissance*, Leipzig, 1938.

Walser, Ernst, *Poggius Florentinus: Leben und Werke*, Leipzig, 1914.

Weiss, Roberto, "Jacopo Angeli da Scarperia (c. 1360—1410-11)," in *Medioevo e Rinascimento, studi in onore di Bruno Nardi*, II, Firenze, 1955, 803-827.

————, "Lineamenti per una storia degli studi antiquari in Italia," *Rinascimento*, IX, 2 (1958).

————, "Italian Humanism in Western Europe: 1460-1520," in *Italian Renaissance Studies*, ed. E. F. Jacob, New York, 1960.

Zaccagnini, Guido, "Bonaccorso da Montemagno il giovine," *Studi di letteratura italiana*, I, 2 (1899), 339-387.

————, "Nuove notizie intorno alla vita di B. da M.," *Bullettino storico pistoiese*, XXXI (1929), 1-5.

Zippel, Giuseppe, *Carlo Marsuppini*, Trento, 1897.

————, *Il Filelfo a Firenze*, Roma, 1899.

————, *Niccolò Niccoli*, Firenze, 1890.

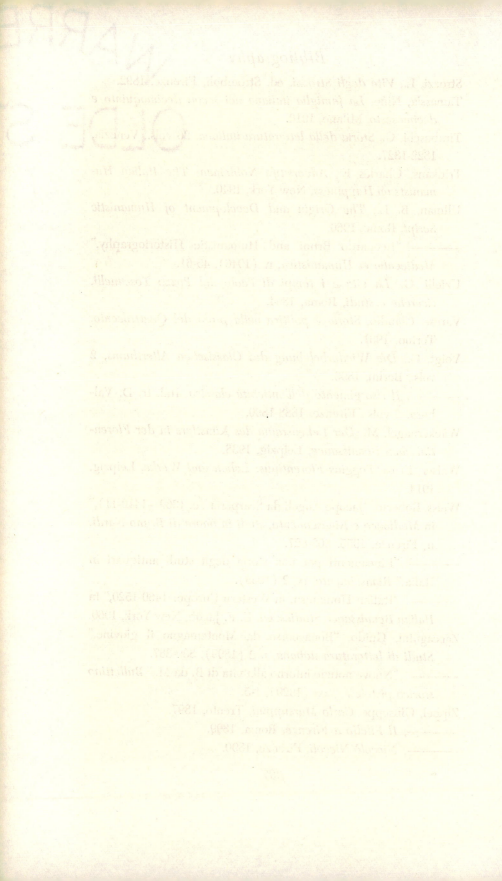

WHERE the same surname is given more than one listing, entirely different families or houses are involved. In cases where surnames were unavailable, entries are determined by Christian names. The four quarters of the city and their districts, *gonfaloni*, are listed only when the text makes a substantive statement about them. Titles of works are entered under authors. The 1,200 names in Appendix II are of course not indexed, unless they are cited elsewhere in the text.

Index

223; houses burnt, 224; marriages, 228-29; Messer Amerigo di Messer Filippo, Archbishop of Florence, 224, 229; Caterina di Gherardo, 221, 222, 223, 224, 226, 227; Gherardo di Messer Filippo, 51n, 226, 229; catasto, 223-24; offices, 227-28; Ghita di Messer Filippo, 229; Giovanni, 25; Neri, family founder, 223; Piero di Messer Filippo, 229

Messer Filippo di Messer Tommaso, lawyer and statesman: 83n, 109, 207n, 227, 250; financial rank, 223; political career, 224-26; in office of Gonfalonier of Justice, 225; public funeral, 226n, 241; as orator, 248

Cortona, 247, 273; Lord of, *see* Casali

Councils of the Republic:

Council of Commune: 50, 64n, 158, 160, 171, 194, 206, 328; powers, 157; Panciatichi in, 64n; *grandi* in, 156; absence fined, 175; resistance in, 207

Council of One Hundred: 7, 49

Council of People: 50, 64n, 66, 171, 193, 194, 206; Panciatichi in, 64n; Cino Rinuccini in, 66; and guild consuls, 161; absence fined, 175; resistance in, 207

Council of Seventy: 7, 50, 146, 291n

Council of Two Hundred: 181, 192, 206; powers, 194; eligibility, 194; absence fined, 175; resistance in, 207

country life, attitude towards, 36-37
courtier, the, 5-6, 294
Covoni, family, 198; Jacopo, 82
Crassus, 347
Cresci, family, 198, 291
Crusades, 344
culture, and ruling class, 5
Cuona, castle, 339
Cusa, Nicholas of, 333
Cyprian, letters, 311

Dagomari, Paolo, physician, 306
Dandolo, Fantino, Venetian humanist, 97
Dante Alighieri, 43, 218, 270, 282, 309, 313, 315
Dati, Gregorio (Goro), chronicler, 4, 109, 160, 180, 182, 254, 272,

278, 291, 340; on international merchant, 32; Leonardo di Piero, humanist and Bishop of Massa, 70, 267, 270, 295, 304, 333, 350; profile, 340-41; his *De bello etrusco,* 341

Davanzati, family, 63, 205; and Bostichi family, 328; Messer Giuliano di Niccolò, lawyer, 51n, 53n, 83n, 164n, 174, 250, 267, 303; profile, 328-29; Mariotto, 294

Dalle Serre, Bernardino, *condottiere,* 213

Datini, Francesco, 76
Dauphine, 237
Della Fioraia, family, 176n
Dello Strinato, family, 75

Decem Baliae (Ten of War), 44, 50, 52, 82, 152, 154, 176, 179, 184, 190, 191, 193, 196, 206n, 207-08, 213, 220, 233, 264, 265, 314, 321, 337; powers, 146, 171-73, 214; and Coluccio Salutati, 148; magnates in, 155, 214; ranked, 172-73; composition, 173n

Decem Libertatis (Ten on Liberty), 49n, 195, 214, 227n, 228, 345; powers, 152, 157; and magnates, 155

Decembrio, Pier Candido, Milanese humanist, 90

decine, 174n

Decio, Filippo, jurist, 97

Defectuum Officiales, 162, 163, 165, 195n; powers, 150, 162

Defenders of the Laws, *see Conservatores Legum*

Del Benino, Francesco, 279
Del Palagio, family, 205; Niccolò di Andrea, 205n
Del Pugliese, family, 235, 236
Del Toso, family, 164, 266; Zanobi di Lapaccino, 164n
Della Luna, family, 61; background, 341-42; Francesco di Francesco, 119, 128-29, 147n, 152, 162, 342; Niccolò di Francesco, humanist, 127, 268, 304, 305, 338, 341, 346, 350; profile, 341-42; and Andrea Alamanni, 345
Della Torre, Arnaldo, 295, 305, 346
Demetrius, 348
Demosthenes, 249, 281, 319, 323, 339
De Sanctis, Francesco, 88, 89, 91

Index

grandi, see magnates; family (*magnati*)

Grascia Officials or Commission (*Grasciae Officiales*), 182; functions, 158, 179

Grassi, Bolognese family, 144; Antonio, lawyer, 144

Gray, William, Bishop of Ely, 327

Greece, 317

Gregory XII, Pope, 82, 118n, 149, 167

Guadagni, family, 54n, 213; Bernardo di Vieri, 207n

Gualterotti-Bardi, family, 319

Guarenti, Guarente di Giovanni, "magister," 73n

Guarini, Guarino, 14, 16-17, 85, 90, 113, 311, 318, 319, 320, 322, 323, 324; on Niccoli, 257

Guasconi, Bindo di Messer Jacopo, 164; Filippo di Messer Biagio, 143n

Guaspare del Maestro Ludovico, *see* Accorambuoni

Guelf society (*Parte Guelfa*), 207, 214, 242, 265, 322; Captains, 173, 174, 176, 193, 195n, 235; papers, 195n; political activity, 211; Guelfism, 58, 59, 66

Gugialferri, family, 217n

Guicciardini, family, 51, 62n, 65, 72, 156, 209, 215; ranked, 73; Francesco, historian, 41n, 145, 146, 273, 302; on *Sei di Mercanzia*, 233; on period 1393-1420, 247; Messer Giovanni, public funeral, 241; Messer Luigi (elder), 113n; Luigi di Piero, 196, 261n, 334, 342; Piero di Messer Luigi, 72; his funeral bill rejected, 241

Guidetti, family, 60, 65, 205; Filippo di Jacopo, 113n

guild structure, 30

guilds, see *arti maggiori; arti minori*

guildsmen, minor, 73n

Hauser, Arnold, 93-94

Henry the Navigator, Prince, 133

Herodotus, 319

historiography, Florentine, lacunae, 146-47, 192n, 206n, 289, 318

Homer, 319

Honestatis Officiales (Commission on Decency), powers, 152

honor, as politics, 254

hostages, diplomatic, 51

house (*palazzo*), the Florentine, 38

humanism, relation to upper classes, 13-15; in Venice, 89, 97-98; lower classes, 238; and grammar, 251; as social force, 270-71; changes in, 271-72; and Roman Republic, 282-83; and republican liberty, 283; and office of historian, 284-85; new history and relation to ruling class, 285-86; *civic humanism*: emergence, 3, 9, 279-80; decline, 4-7, 294ff

humanist, defined, 8; leaders of Florentine movement, 11; "professional" and "amateur," 12-15, 98-99; scholarship, 85ff; alienation question, 94; humanist as problem in scholarship, 95-99; in aristocratic courts, 96-97; his contribution to ideology, 250-52; his civic value, 251-52; social position summarized, 263-66

ideas, in history, 305

Iliad, the, 260

Imola, Giovanni da, 97

Innocent VII, Pope, 167

intellectual movement, social analysis of, 271

Isocrates, 339, 347

Jails, Commission on, 179

John XXIII, Pope, 118, 167

jurists, *see* lawyers

knight, and social protocol, 68

Kristeller, Paul Oskar, 8, 12n, 245

Ladislaus, King of Naples, 278

Laetus, Pomponius, 345

Lamberteschi, family, 35, 112; Bernardo di Lamberto, 203

Lamberti, family, 39, 59

Lamola, Giovanni, 91; and Lorenzo Strozzi, 338

Lana guild, see *arti maggiori*

land, incidence of investment in, 35, 290-91

Landino, Cristoforo, 7, 127, 303, 333, 346; his *Disputationes Camaldulenses*, on action *vs.* contemplation, 297-98

Larga, via, in Florence, 315

lawyers, 68, 83, 97, 169, 242, 344; and social protocol, 68; social types among, 83; tax on law books,

Index

Index

falonier of Justice; *Octo Custodiae*; Signoria; Six on Commerce

oligarchy, 164; contraction of, 4, 49; cohesive forces in, 30; pre-1434 aims and character, 42-43, 287; relations with Panciatichi family, 64-65; composition and resurgence, 172, 246-47, 275-76; some prominent members, 242; post-1434 character, 286-87; internal system of balances, 287. *See also* family (ruling type)

Olschki, Leonardo, 91-92

oratory, *see* eloquence

Ordinances of Justice (1293), 39

Origen, 311

Orlandi, Messer Rosso di Andreozzo, 109n

Orlandini, family, 55

Orleans, Duke of, 248n

Orsini, family, 184, 325; Giordano, Cardinal, 322

Otto di Guardia, see *Octo Custodiae*

Ovid, 307

Padua, 16, 81n, 87, 95, 253, 317, 332; University, 98, 313, 333

Pagnini, G. F., 100

palazzo, see house

Palermo, 95

Palmieri, family, 138; political status, 191; socially assessed, 198; origins, 229; Serragli alliance, 230; Agnolo di Giovanni, 140, 141; Antonio di Giovanni, 141; Antonio di Palmieri, 138n; Francesco di Antonio, 138; offices, 194-96; Giovanni di Francesco, 195-96; Marco di Antonio, 138-39, 197n; offices, 193-94

Matteo di Marco: 6, 9, 11, 12, 44, 57n, 70, 105, 127, 198, 229-30, 238, 242, 278-79, 280, 282, 284, 295, 325, 341, 342; his taxes in twelve-year period, 131; finances, 138-42; personality, 139-40; offices, 192-93; friends, 196; Serragli marriage, 237; public funeral, 243; on Poggio, 259; contemporary reputation, 261-62; on Antonio Rossi, 344-45; his *Della vita civile*, 314; its social viewpoint, 31; on petty trades, 31; on international trade, 32-33; interlocutors in, 261n; dedication to Alessandro degli Alessandri, 329

Panciatichi, family, 24, 55, 63-65, 74, 76, 77, 101, 178, 205, 215; marriages, 64, 67; Antonio, 65n; Messer Bartolommeo di Bandino, 76-77; his prestanze, 63n; Bartolommeo di Gabbriello, 65n; Gabbriello di Messer Bartolommeo, 24, 119; Piero di Messer Bartolommeo, 63n; Piero di Giovanni, 64

Pandolfini, family, 55, 63, 184, 198, 212, 227; background, 314; Agnolo di Filippo, statesman, 8, 21, 33, 36, 180, 196, 239, 261n, 268, 304; profile, 313-14; Messer Carlo, 188; on Poggio, 259; Filippo di Ser Giovanni, 314; Giannozzo, 181; Ser Giovanni, 314; Pandolfo, humanist of Rinuccini circle, 261, 348

Panormita, Antonio Beccadelli, 97

Panzano, family, 78; Antonio di Messer Luca, 161

Paolo di Ser Pace da Certaldo, author of manual on good conduct, 27; on country life, 36; on communal authorities, 47-48; on ambassador, 248n

papacy, conflict with Florence, 4

papal secretary, 118n, 124, 167, 190, 210, 260, 268

Paradiso, Alberti villa, 307, 312

Parente, Parente di Michele, 129

Parenti, family, 269; background, 346; Giovanni, "corazzarius," offices, 346; Marco di Parente, humanist, 44-45, 57n, 60, 142n, 268, 297, 337, 345, 347, 348; profile, 346; Parente di Giovanni, 346; Piero, 57n

Parentucelli, *see* Nicholas V

Paris, 306, 307

Parte Guelfa, see Guelf society

Partner, Peter D., 124n

parvenus, *see gente nuova*

Passerini, L., 77

Passi, Luigi, 144

patronage, 75, 84

Paul II, Pope, 192, 337

Pavia, 95

Pazzi, family, 39, 212, 222, 290; background, 342-43; conspiracy, 347; Messer Andrea, 180, 343; Antonio di Messer Andrea, 343; Guglielmo, 293; Jacopo di Messer Andrea, 122n, 343; Piero di Mes-

Index

Index

110n; ruling families in, 113, 341; some leading taxpayers, 113; prestanze, 109-10, 114n, 223, 231; catasto returns, 223-24

S. Trinità, church, 317

Sandys, J. E., 11, 307

Santini, E., 245, 247

Santini, G., 167n

Sapientes (legal advisors), 161; salary, 148

Sapiti, Francesco di Domenico, 113n

Sarzana, Tommaso da, *see* Nicholas V

Sassetti, family, 217

Sassolini, family, 176n, 193; ranked, 138, 198; old Guelfs, 230; Antonio di Marignano, offices, 197-98; Papera, 213; Tommasa de Antonio, 197

Sassolo of Prato, humanist, 91

Scala, Bartolomeo, 6, 7

Scali, family, 78, 79

Scarperia, Jacopo di Agnolo da, 10, 14, 16, 199, 267-68, 269, 272, 278, 304, 307; profile, 309-10; member of Sostegni family, 310

Schevill, F., on government of Albizzi period, 277

scioperato, defined, 35; his social place, 35

Scipio Aemilianus, 282

Scolari, family, 222; Filippo (Pippo Spano), 282

scribes, wages of, 329. *See also* Ser Antonio di Mario; Aretino, Giovanni

Sea Consuls, *see Consules Maris*

secretary, *see* chancellor; papal secretary

Sedici Gonfalonieri, membership, 67, 81-82, 83, 149, 151, 172, 173, 174, 176, 179, 181, 182, 184, 192, 194, 195, 197, 208, 220, 225, 241, 242, 345, 346; powers, 40, 149-50; magnates excluded, 155

Sei di Mercanzia, see Six on Commerce

Seneca, 307

Ser, meaning, 169n

Sermini, family, notaries, 269, 315-16; Messer Domenico di Ser Mino, lawyer, 83; Ser Domenico, notary, 316; Ser Mino, notary, 316; Ser Pietro di Ser Mino, chancellor, 267, 269, 278; profile, 315-16

Serragli, family, 77, 79n, 113, 132, 140, 184, 209, 266, 287n; social portrait, 230ff; Buonaiuti connection, 230; number in office, 234; traditions, 235; marriages, 235-36; barred from office 237; Agnolo, 231; Ser Belcaro Buonaiuti, family founder, 230; Cosa di Niccolò, 140, 230; Francesco di Vannozzo, 237n; Niccolò di Agnolo, 140n, 237; offices, 230-31, 234-35; finances, 231-33; bankruptcy, 232-33; Vannozzo di Giovanni, fined, 209n; in office of Gonfalonier of Justice, 234

Serristori, family, 112; ranked, 111; Antonio, 128

servants, wages, 117

Servi di Maria, 310

Servius, 328

Serzelli, family, 72, 176n, 198

Seta guild, *see arti maggiori (Por Santa Maria)*

Sforza, family, 91; Francesco, Duke of Milan, 184, 185, 190, 242, 260; and Milanese succession, 185-89

Sicily, 44, 161, 216, 336

Siena, 51n, 67, 82, 186, 188, 190, 207, 223, 230, 273; ambassadors from, 71, 255

Signa, 314

Signoria (Priorate), 64n, 112, 146, 152, 154, 159, 162, 168, 170, 171, 179, 181, 183n, 184, 194, 205, 208, 222, 226, 233, 242, 243, 252, 255, 257, 286, 312; membership in, 44, 54, 67, 174, 176, 177, 192, 196, 197, 206, 218, 220, 227, 235, 264, 265, 307, 308, 314, 317, 318, 319, 320, 321, 328, 329, 332, 336, 345, 346, 347, 349; powers, 147, 150, 162; Acciaiuoli in, 348; Beccanugi, 83; Corsini, 223, 229; Gianfigliazzi, 81; Medici, 236, 324, 348; Panciatichi, 63n; Pazzi, 343; Quaratesi, 219, 341; Salutati, 148, 149; Strozzi, 236; Rucellai, 236; on importance of merchant, 33; established, 40; traditional executive body, 41; observes formalities, 69; vis-à-vis strife in chancellery, 71; favors L. B. Alberti, 143; magnates barred, 155; favors Piero Niccoli, 163; relations with *Decem Baliae*, 172; eligibility question,

Index

172-73; acts in distant commercial litigation, 51, 190-91; certain families in, 201; some family frequencies, 236; favors Salutati house, 253-54

Sindici Potestatis, see Podestà (syndics)

Six on Arezzo and Pistoia, 149; powers, 153

Six on Commerce, 62, 154, 157, 173, 174, 176, 182, 195, 196, 197, 202, 231, 237; powers, 146-47, 160; syndics, 170; pressures on, 178; membership hardens, 233

Sixteen Standard-bearers, see *Sedici Gonfalonieri*

Sixtus IV, Pope, 192

social climbers, 279

social mobility, arrested, 75, 276, 277-78, 291

social place, determining factors, 18, 62; and political prominence, 47

Soderini, family, 51, 54n, 65, 113, 132, 135, 215, 216, 221, 235-36, 341; Francesco di Messer Tommaso, 121, 175-76; Niccolò, 135, 189, 242, 336; Tommaso, 193, 334; Zenobia, Leonardo Dati's mother, 340

sophists, 87

Sophocles, 319

Sostegni, family, 269, 310; Sostegno, vicar general of *Servi di Maria,* 310

Sozomeno of Pistoia, 338

Spain, 32, 131, 177

spending habits, see money

Spinelli, family, 73-74; Bartolommea di Tommaso, 73

Spini, family, 44, 54n, 62n, 72, 78, 79n; ranked, 72-73; Bartolommea di Giovanni, 74; Messer Cristofano, statesman, 72-73, 77, 225; public funeral, 240

Squarcialupi, family, 78, 155

Stefani, Marchionne, chronicler, 46

Stignano, 107, 149, 266

Strozzi, family, 23, 41, 46n, 51, 62n, 65, 69, 77, 80, 84, 87, 177, 198, 203, 205, 211, 212, 213, 222, 223, 229, 235, 256, 287n, 290, 323, 342, 348; frequency in Signoria, 201, 236; background, 316-17; link with Niccolò della Luna, 342; unequal wealth, 351; Alessandra Macinghi, letter writer, 38,

44, 45, 48, 60, 291; Benedetto, 327, 335; Caterina di Matteo, wife of Marco Parenti, 44, 346; Filippo di Matteo, 44, 60; Lionardo di Filippo, 334; Lorenzo di Palla, 119, 128; profile, 338; Madalena di Carlo, 168n; Messer Marcello, lawyer, 109n, 250; Matteo di Simone, 181, 341; friendship with Messer Giuliano Davanzati, 328; profile, 334-35; Nanni or Giovanni (from Ferrara branch of Strozzi), 254-55; Nofri di Palla, 80; Messer Palla di Messer Palla, 175; Salamone di Carlo, 229

Palla di Nofri: 6, 12, 21, 27, 51n, 80, 130, 150n, 162, 166, 167, 175, 239, 268, 278, 304, 309, 310, 312, 330, 343; as translator, 249; profile, 316-18

Studio Fiorentino, 13, 16, 117, 124, 127, 139, 177, 221, 242, 250, 251, 259, 309, 313, 315, 316, 318, 319, 320, 322, 330, 331, 333, 338, 339, 342, 345; salaries, 130; officials or trustees, 162, 179, 182-83

Sulla, Roman general, 282

Tanagli, family, 60; background, 332; Messer Guglielmo, lawyer, 83n, 164, 239, 250, 258, 267, 323; profile, 331-32

Tani, Andrea, 136; Tommaso, 136-37

taxation, 174-75; indulgence, 24, 112n, 114n, 163n; confiscatory, 103, 134-35; privilege, 120, 168n, 171, 255, 352; administration, 147; as key political issue, 171. See *also* catasto; prestanze

Tebalducci, family, 212, 266; social portrait, 214ff; bank branches, 215; origins, 217; marriages, 217-18; political fortunes, 219-20; Alessandra di Tommaso, 214, 218, 219; Alessandro di Giacomino, 128; Bartolommea di Giacomino, 218; Duccio di Messer Chirico, 219n; Giacomino di Goggio, 218, 220; Giacomino di Tommaso, 219; Giovanni di Giacomino, 216; Jacopo di Giacomino, 220; Jacopo di Tommaso, 219; Lionardo di Giacomino, 216n; Saracina di Tommaso, 219; Tommaso di Gia-